READING AND LANGUAGE PROCESSING

Edited by

John M. Henderson
Michigan State University

Murray Singer
University of Manitoba

Fernanda Ferreira
Michigan State University

 LAWRENCE ERLBAUM ASSOCIATES, PUBLISHERS
1995 Mahwah, New Jersey   Hove, UK

Most of the chapters in this book were published as a special issue
of the Canadian Journal of Experimental Psychology by the Canadian
Psychological Association.

Lawrence Erlbaum Associates, Inc., Publishers
10 Industrial Avenue
Mahwah, New Jersey 07430

Library of Congress Cataloging-in-Publication Data

Reading and language processing / edited by John M. Henderson, Murray
  Singer, Fernanda Ferreira.
      p.   cm.
  Most of the chapters were originally published as a special issue
of the Canadian journal of experimental psychology, June 1993.
  Includes bibliographical references and index.
  ISBN 0-8058-1903-7 (pbk. : alk. paper)
  1. Reading, Psychology of. 2. Psycholinguistics. 3. Human
information processing.   I. Henderson, John M. (John Michael).,
  1958- . II. Singer, Murray. III. Ferreira, Fernanda.
BF456.R2R337 1995
401'.9--dc20   95-12525
                                               CIP

Books published by Lawrence Erlbaum Associates are printed
on acid-free paper, and their bindings are chosen
for strength and durability.

Printed in the United States of America

10 9 8 7 6 5 4 3 2 1

Contents

1 Reading and Language Processing: Paradigms, Proposals, and Procedures

MURRAY SINGER *University of Manitoba*
JOHN M. HENDERSON *Michigan State University*
FERNANDA FERREIRA *Michigan State University*

This volume is devoted to reading and language processing, an area that has been central to the study of human cognition since the inception of modern cognitive psychology. For example, in his classic book, *Cognitive Psychology*, Neisser (1967) devoted 4 of 11 chapters to topics in reading and language. These chapters were Words as Visual Patterns, Speech Perception, Active Verbal Memory, and Sentences. In addition, most of the other chapters in Neisser's book included discussions of related topics and presented experiments in which reading and/or language played a major role.

In the 1990s, many of the topics discussed by Neisser continue to draw the attention of researchers, and new ones have been assigned high research priority. The early maturation of this field is characterized both by the evolution of new topic matter and by serious debates concerning the competing paradigms, global proposals, and methods that form the foundation of the enterprise. Our attempt to identify a representative set of contributors who are conducting research on problems that are currently cutting-edge or controversial in reading and language processing has dovetailed with our desire to highlight the latter debates. We will briefly identify these features, and link them to some of the present contributions.

Competition among *paradigms* in the study of language processes has resulted from the emergence of connectionist modeling (Rumelhart & McClelland, 1986) as a serious competitor to the antecedent symbol processing systems in cognition (Newell & Simon, 1972). The tension between these paradigms is evident in the field of language processing, but the advantages of the two approaches may also be fruitfully merged. In the present volume, for example, Just and Carpenter apply their Capacity Constrained READER model to their pupillometric data reflecting the fluctuation of effort during reading. CC READER is a hybrid model consisting of a symbolic production system and an activation-based connectionist model (see Spivey-Knowlton, Trueswell, & Tanenhaus for a purer connectionist approach). Likewise, the construction-integration model of Kintsch (1988; see Moravcsik & Kintsch, this volume) blends the symbolic construction of propositional networks with the settling, according to connectionist principles, of activation in those networks. The interplay between the two paradigms will likely characterize research in this field in the 1990s and perhaps beyond.

These dominant paradigms form a backdrop for the evaluation of *global proposals* which, although general to the study of cognition, also take forms specific to the problems of language processing. Theorists must ask whether language processes are modular or interactionist, serial or parallel, and bottom-up or top-down; and whether or not these processes are executed to completion *immediately* upon the encoding of a spoken or written phrase. The modularity hypothesis of Fodor (1983), for example, suggests that a syntactic module might form an important basis of parsing processes. Clifton concludes that his data favor the existence of a dedicated and informationally-encapsulated syntactic module, whereas Spivey-Knowlton et al. interpret their own data to favor the free interaction of information from syntactic, semantic, and other levels of analysis.

Global proposals such as the modular versus interactionist competitors may be associated with the paradigms discussed earlier. For example, the alternative of unrestricted interaction of information is correlated with the connectionist framework, but this correlation is by no means perfect. Many connectionist models posit different cognitive systems, such as those devoted to lexical, syntactic, and semantic processing. These systems represent a degree of segregation of function, although they are not modules according to Fodor's (1983) definition. As a result, a connectionist model may exhibit elements of both of the ostensively antagonist modular and interactionist processing analyses.

Because the modern study of language processes is barely a quarter of a century old, the logic and value of relevant research *procedures* are still being worked out. This emerges as a prominent theme of this volume. In the use of eye fixations to gain insight about language processing, researchers are still considering subtle but important differences in the value of first pass, second pass, and cumulative fixations; as well as of the significance of fixations upon different text regions (current region, previous region, next region) relative to a critical word or phrase. Eye fixation measures are reported by Daneman and Reingold, Ferreira and Henderson, Henderson and Ferreira, Pollatsek, Raney, Lagasse, and Rayner, and Clifton. New implications of these data were highlighted in the two chapters by Ferreira and Henderson. Another incisive technique, the use of pupillometry to monitor on-line fluctuations of resource demands in reading, was explored by Just and Carpenter. Caveats concerning the use of the "moving window" display technique, in which successive sections of text are revealed in response to a subject's button presses, were offered by Spivey-Knowlton et al.

It would be pointless for language processing researchers to be embarrassed about controversies of method, and unwise for them not to address the controversies. The debates indicate that investigators are conscientiously scrutinizing the alternative methods that are available, and the alternate interpretations of each one.

Paradigms, theories, and methods serve, of course, to expose and organize the subject matter and content of a field. In reading and language processing, a major advance and prevailing analysis recognizes that language comprehension results in numerous levels of representation, including the levels of surface features, lexical properties, linguistic structures, and idea networks (or textbases) underlying a message, as well as the situations to which a message refers. The interplay among these levels is emphasized in the study of Moravcsik and Kintsch. Surface features are particularly highlighted in Levy, Barnes, and Martin's study of the impact of the repetition of words and syntactic structures on reading fluency. Lexical access was scrutinized by Buchanan and Besner and by Daneman and Reingold. Linguistic and parsing processes constituted a primary focus in the investigations of Clifton, of Ferreira and Henderson, Just and Carpenter, and Spivey-Knowlton et al. The construction of a propositional textbase is addressed in the chapters of Masson and of Singer, and both of those studies also bear on the extraction of a causal situation model from the textbase. The situational level was also emphasized in Dixon, Harrison, and Taylor's study of the derivation of action plans from procedural texts.

Many other trends and issues can be discerned in the present chapters. One that promises to be of considerable importance in the near future is the growing evidence that individual differences among readers are associated with qualitative differences in their processing patterns. Reader differences in cognitive resources were examined by Just and Carpenter, and differences in readers' background knowledge were addressed by Moravcsik and Kintsch.

The present chapters may be of most direct concern to experimental psychologists, but we hope that the findings will be of interest to investigators in several of psychology's companion disciplines in cognitive science. Those chapters that inspect parsing processes may bear on linguistic theories of language structure. The computational models explicit or implicit to these investigations are pertinent to studies of natural language processing in computer science. Reading practitioners may detect important clues about basic reading processes in several of the chapters.

The collection of the chapters in this volume was undertaken in order to produce a special issue of the *Canadian Journal of Experimental Psychology*. We thank Gordon Winocur, editor of the *Journal* at the initiation of the project, for inviting us to edit the special issue. With his consultation, we invited the contributors to submit empirical reports of new research on topics central to their overall research programs in reading and language processing. We were very gratified that all of the researchers whom we invited to contribute agreed to do so. The result is 13 articles covering what we think are some of the most important and interesting areas of contemporary cognitive research.

We would like to thank the authors for giving us the honor of presenting their work. Most of the authors also served as reviewers, and we thank them for their time and effort in that regard as well. We would also like to thank Michael Anes, Tom Carr, Vic Ferreira, Albrecht Inhoff, Karen McClure, Paul van den Broek, and one anonymous reviewer for providing insightful comments on the articles. We are grateful to Colin Macleod, current editor of the *Canadian Journal of Experimental Psychology*, who provided us with guidance during the later stages of the journal phase of the project. Finally, thanks are due to Judi Amsel, who helped us transform the special issue into book form.

References

Fodor, J. A. (1983). *The modularity of mind*. Cambridge, MA: The M.I.T. Press.

Kintsch, W. (1988). The role of knowledge in discourse comprehension: A construction-integration model. *Psychological Review*, *95*, 163-182.

Neisser, U. (1967). *Cognitive psychology*. New York: Appleton Century Crofts.

Newell, A., & Simon, H. A. (1972). *Human problem solving*. Englewood Cliffs, NJ: Prentice Hall.

Rumelhart, D. E., McClelland, J. L., and the PDP Research Group. (1986). *Parallel distributed processing: Explorations in the microstructure of cognition* (Vol. I). Cambridge, MA: Bradford Books.

2 Reading Aloud: Evidence for the Use of a Whole Word Nonsemantic Pathway

LORI BUCHANAN and DEREK BESNER
University of Waterloo

Abstract It is widely assumed that the presence of an associative priming effect during the oral reading of orthographies with consistent spelling-sound correspondences signals the use of an orthographic code for lexical access (the addressed routine). Relatedly, the failure to observe such a priming effect has been taken to indicate the use of a routine that relies on subword spelling-sound correspondence knowledge (the assembled routine). This logic depends on the assumptions that (a) only the addressed routine (whole word orthographic knowledge) can produce priming, and (b) that it necessarily does so (i.e., is automatic). The present experiments show that, *taken alone*, neither the presence nor absence of priming effects in oral reading permit an inference as to whether the addressed or assembled routine is used. Converging operations which do permit such an inference are reported. The data support the view that (i) components of the word recognition system operate interactively such that use of the assembled routine yields priming under certain conditions, and (ii) normal readers of a shallow orthography use a nonsemantic, whole word pathway to name words.

Résumé Il est généralement admis que, dans le cas d'orthographes peu profondes (où il y a correspondance systématique entre la graphie et la prononciation), la présence d'un effet d'amorçage associatif durant la lecture orale marque l'utilisation d'un code orthographique pour accéder au lexique (programme adressé). Par ailleurs, on considère que l'absence d'un effet d'amorçage indique l'utilisation d'un programme qui repose sur la connaissance des correspondances entre la graphie et la prononciation à un niveau inférieur à celui du mot (programme assemblé). Cette logique dépend des hypothèses suivantes: a) seul le programme adressé (connaissance orthographique des mots complets) peut produire l'amorçage et b) il le produit nécessairement (c'est-à-dire automatiquement). Les expériences que nous avons menées montrent qu'on ne peut inférer, *uniquement* de la présence d'effets d'amorçage ou de leur absence durant la lecture orale, que le programme adressé ou bien le programme assemblé est utilisé. Les opérations convergentes qui permettent une telle inférence sont exposées dans le rapport. Les données recueillies montrent que i) les composantes du système de reconnaissance des mots fonctionnent en interaction de sorte que l'utilisation du programme assemblé produit un effet d'amorçage dans certaines conditions et ii) les lecteurs normaux qui utilisent une orthographe peu profonde empruntent une voie d'accès non sémantique aux mots complets pour nommer les mots.

Until recently, research on visual word recognition has focussed on questions concerning how words printed in English are read. This analysis has yielded a remarkable consensus concerning some of the underlying processes (e.g., see reviews by Carr & Pollatsek, 1985; Patterson & Coltheart, 1987; see also Paap, Noel & Johansen, 1992) and has resulted in the dual route model[1]. An extension of this work to cross-orthography investigations has resulted in a large body of research. One position was articulated in the strong version of the Orthographic Depth Hypothesis, which held that the consistency of spelling-sound correspondences within an orthography dictates which of the routines of the dual route model are used during reading. Shallow orthographies (i.e., those with consistent spelling-sound correspondences) were argued to be always read aloud prelexically (e.g., Allport, 1979; Bridgeman, 1987; Hung & Tzeng, 1981; Morton & Sasanuma, 1984; Turvey, Feldman, & Lukatela, 1984). This position has since been tempered by the linguistic observation that syllabic stress can not always be derived on the basis of prelexical phonology (e.g., Katz & Frost, 1992). Consequently, some researchers assume that prelexical phonology serves to activate a phonological lexicon which then serves to mediate naming or semantic access (e.g., Carello, Lukatela & Turvey, 1988; Besner & Smith, 1992). Another solution is to assume that, additionally, a whole word orthographic routine which addresses lexical phonology is also functional in shallow orthographies (e.g., Besner, 1987; Besner & Hildebrandt, 1987; Besner & Smith, 1992; Besner, Patterson, Lee & Hildebrandt, 1993; Frost, Katz & Bentin, 1987; Katz & Feldman, 1983; Katz & Frost, 1992; Patterson, 1990; Sebastian-Galles, 1991; Seidenberg, 1985a,b).

While the strong version of the Orthographic Depth Hypothesis can thus be rejected on logical grounds, the methodology that has been used to investigate reading in various orthographies nevertheless bears on some issues which are

1 Not all theorists subscribe to this point of view. In particular, Seidenberg and McClelland (1989; 1990) argue that a single nonsemantic processing routine pronounces all kinds of letter strings be they regular, irregular, or nonwords. It suffices to say that this claim is disputed (e.g., Baluch and Besner, 1991; Besner et al., 1990; Besner, 1993; Monsell et al., 1992; Paap & Noel, 1991). See also Van Orden, Pennington and Stone (1990) and Lukatela and Turvey (1991) for the view that lexical access in English is entirely driven by subword spelling-sound correspondence knowledge. Our view is that it is one thing to produce an existence proof (e.g., a simulation) that one routine can name all kinds of words and nonwords, but quite another to show that this is what humans do.

important in their own right. Several lines of evidence relevant to how different orthographies are read are based on critical but untested assumptions regarding how associative priming effects in naming occur. The results of the present experiments, in concert with other findings, are taken to imply that there are three routines available to normal readers, at least two of which can produce a priming effect under certain conditons. We argue that, *on its own*, the presence or absence of priming effects does not identify which of several possible routines is being used. In aid of these goals we first briefly describe a three route model of word naming. We then discuss several naming experiments in the literature that examine how different orthographies are processed, and report two new experiments that illuminate which of the several available routines are used during the reading of a shallow orthography.

A Three Route Framework

Most researchers agree that reading aloud in English can be accomplished in a number of ways (e.g., see reviews by Carr & Pollatsek, 1985; Patterson & Coltheart, 1987). Figure 1 illustrates this framework.

The orthographic input lexicon contains orthographic descriptions for every word the reader knows, while the phonological input and output lexicons represent knowledge about the sounds of these words. The semantic system represents meaning, and phonemic information is represented in the phonemic buffer. Activation of entries in these lexicons and the semantic system forms the basis of reading for meaning, and reading aloud.

The assembled routine (pathway E) identifies sub-word orthographic segments and converts them into sub-word phonological segments. These segments are ultimately assembled to form a phonological code corresponding to the letter string. This procedure only produces the correct phonological code for letter strings which conform to typical spelling-sound correspondences. English has many of these regular words but it also has a number of exceptions. For example, consider the *ou* in *cougar, bough, rough*, and *ought*. Since there is no way to assign the correct pronunciation to the segment ou without word-specific knowledge, these exception words can not be read aloud correctly by a pathway which relies exclusively on subword spelling-sound knowledge.

In contrast, the addressed routine relies on whole word knowledge. A printed word first activates its representation in the orthographic lexicon. Activation then spreads through two distinct pathways. In pathway D it spreads from the orthographic input lexicon directly to the corresponding lexical entry in the phonological output lexicon. In pathways A/B the activation spreads from the orthographic input lexicon to the phonological output lexicon via the semantic system. Both of these pathways produce the correct pronunciation for all words known to the reader. Pathways A/B, D and E thus reflect three ways in which a word can be read aloud.

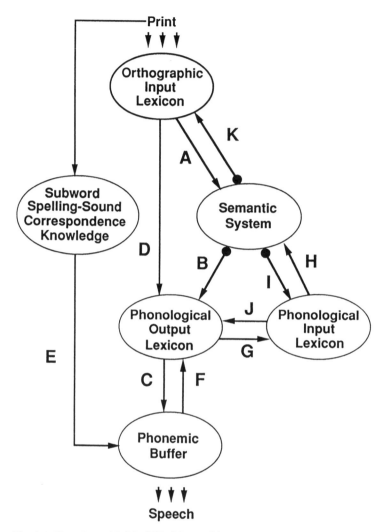

Fig. 1 A Three Route Model of Word Recognition

Evidence from Cognitive Neuropsychology

The distinction between these three pathways is supported by single case studies of patients with an acquired dyslexia who produce distinct patterns of impairment. These patterns are described in the following section.

PATHWAY E

There are a number of patients who correctly read aloud regular words such as *gave, save* and *wave* but who are poor at reading exception words like *have*. Instead, these patients often regularize exception words so that the pronunciation of their bodies rhymes with the bodies of regular words. For example, *pint* is pronounced such that it rhymes with *hint, mint, lint,* and *dint*. This pattern of preserved reading of regular words and impaired reading of exception words is most easily understood as the expression of an intact assembled routine along with impaired access by the addressed routine to, or loss of, lexical entries in the orthographic input lexicon (e.g., Coltheart, Masterson, Byng, Prior, & Riddoch, 1983).

PATHWAYS A/B

A second group of patients' nonword reading is completely abolished, while their word reading is impaired. For example, given *tulip* they may read it aloud as *crocus*. Such semantic errors are often taken to imply that words are read via a functioning but damaged semantic system (pathways A and B). An entire book is devoted to investigations of this dyslexia (Coltheart, Patterson & Marshall, 1980).

PATHWAY D

Finally, there are other dyslexic patients who correctly read some exception words aloud but who are impaired at accessing semantic information about them. Since pathway E cannot correctly pronounce exception words, and since pathway A which accesses semantic information is impaired, the only remaining functional route is pathway D (e.g., Bub, Cancellière, & Kertesz, 1985; Schwartz, Saffran & Marin, 1980; Funnell, 1983).

These oral reading impairments are consistent with the view that the assembled and addressed routines are at least partially independent, and further, that the addressed routine can be subdivided into a semantic pathway (pathway A/B) and a whole word but nonsemantic pathway (pathway D). While this neurological evidence demonstrates that these pathways are used by impaired readers it does not force the conclusion that they are all used by intact readers. Such support comes from experiments on intact college level readers; these data distinguish between the use of the assembled and the addressed routine. In contrast, the separation of the addressed routine into two distinct pathways has received little attention in the literature on intact readers. The next section briefly describes results which support the distinction between the assembled and the addressed routine as well as the pattern of data necessary to distinguish between the use of pathways D and A.

Multiple Pathways Used by Intact Readers

Reading aloud via the assembled routine is arguably successful only when the target word follows conventional spelling-sound correspondences. Since a whole word orthographic representation of the word is not required, even pronounceable nonwords can be read aloud (e.g., *ish, lar,* and *fon*). Reading these nonwords aloud demonstrates that this routine is available to normal readers. It does not, however, constitute evidence that this routine makes a contribution to the oral reading of familiar words. More convincing evidence comes from experiments which show that regular words (i.e., words which can be read via the assembled routine) are less affected by lexical variables such as word frequency than are exception words. Since the assembled routine operates at a sub-word level, it is by definition insensitive to whole word manipulations such as word frequency. In contrast, the addressed routine operates at the whole word level and is therefore sensitive to word frequency; this routine reads high frequency words faster than low frequency words (e.g., Forster & Chambers, 1973). Both the assembled and the addressed routines are available to read regular words, but only the addressed routine can read exception words. Since regular words typically produce a smaller frequency effect than do exception words (e.g., Paap & Noel, 1991; Seidenberg et al., 1984; Waters & Seidenberg, 1985) the interaction between regularity and word frequency implies that the assembled routine (pathway E) plays a role in reading aloud.

Do Normal Readers Use Pathway D?
The involvement of the semantic system via pathway A seems irrefutable given that we typically read words in text for meaning. We may nevertheless read exception words aloud without always first activating the semantic system, as in pathway D. No evidence yet exists for the use of this routine in intact readers of English; such evidence would be provided by a demonstration that exception words are read aloud without any benefit from a preceding related context. An analogous demonstration involving the naming of Japanese Kana is reported here.

We turn now to a consideration of priming experiments in shallow orthographies, along with a discussion of some of the critical assumptions upon which they are predicated.

Priming Effects in Naming: Standard Interpretations
Presentation of a semantically or associatively-related word prior to the target word typically yields a priming effect in a deep orthography like English (see Neely's 1991 review). It is widely assumed that the *presence* of a priming effect in *naming* reflects the use of the addressed routine, since in the dual route model pathway A directly activates the semantic system. It is also widely assumed that a *failure* to find a priming effect in naming is evidence for the use of the assembled routine. For example, in a cross orthography comparison of naming, Katz and Feldman (1983) found that English subjects showed a priming effect when reading English, a deep orthography, but Serbo-Croatian subjects did not when reading Serbo-Croatian, a shallow orthography. Frost, Katz & Bentin (1987) extended this research in a comparison of three orthographies; Hebrew, English and Serbo-Croatian. They

also report an absence of priming for Serbo-Croatian and the presence of priming for both Hebrew, another deep orthography, and English. The results of both these studies are often taken as evidence that the addressed routine was not used to name Serbo-Croatian words. In another cross orthography comparison of priming effects, Tabossi & Laghi (1992) compared the effects of priming in Italian (a shallow orthography) and English. The presence of a priming effect in both orthographies was taken as evidence that the addressed routine was used. Sabastian-Galles (1991) has reported similar findings in Spanish (another shallow orthography) and also concludes that the addressed routine is used to name words. Similar results and conclusions can be found in Seidenberg & Vidanovic (1985) and Besner & Smith (1992). It can thus be seen that the *absence* of a priming effect is standardly taken as evidence for the use of the assembled routine, while the *presence* of a priming effect is standardly taken as evidence for the use of the addressed routine.

Priming Effects in Naming: Alternative Interpretations

The presence of a priming effect in studies of shallow orthographies by Tabossi and Laghi (1992), Sebastian-Galles (1991), Seidenberg and Vidanovic (1985) and Besner and Smith (1992) do not, however, force the conclusion that the addressed routine is involved because there is no reason why the assembled routine could not also produce one (see Carello et al., 1988 for a related argument). If the semantic system operates interactively with the phonological lexicons and the phonemic buffer (i.e., pathways E,F,G,H,B and C, or E,F,G,H,I,J and C) then activation in the phonemic buffer given input from pathway E may lead to activation in the semantic system. This activation in the semantic system may be fed back to the phonemic buffer via the phonological output lexicon prior to pronunciation, thus producing a priming effect[2]. As Carello et al. (1988) suggest, in some scripts this feedback may be required as a check of the pronunciation prior to an utterance. The prior presentation of a related context may activate the semantic system and in turn the phonological output system. This would then result in a priming effect on the basis of a reduction in the time required to "check" the assembled pronunciation. It follows from this that the mere *presence* of a priming effect, *on its own*, does not distinguish between the use of the addressed and assembled routines. Similarly, the *failure* to observe priming effects during naming cannot, *on its own*, be taken as evidence for the use of the assembled routine, since pathway D (which bypasses the semantic system) might be

---

2 It would be more parsimonious to suppose that priming could also be produced by activation from the prime spreading from the semantic system to related entries in the phonological output lexicon prior to the appearance of the target. In this scheme, only the phonological output lexicon and the phonemic buffer need be engaged in interactive activation. However, as seen later, the data require a more elaborate account.

responsible. Indeed, while it is widely assumed that priming is "automatic" (e.g., Posner & Snyder, 1975; Neely, 1977; 1991 among others) there is evidence that even simple changes in context can eliminate priming (e.g., Friedrich et al., 1991; Smith, 1979; Smith, Besner, & Myoshi, 1992; Smith & Besner, 1992; Snow & Neely, 1987). Facilitation of target processing is not an inevitable consequence of the prior presentation of a related context.

Priming via Pathway E

Evidence that the assembled routine activates, or its output is activated by the semantic system prior to pronunciation when reading English can be found in an experiment by Rosson (1983). Rosson reported that naming a nonword like *louch* is facilitated by the prior presentation of a word like *sofa*, which is semantically related to *couch*, an orthographic and phonological neighbour of *louch*. In an extension of this approach, Lukatela & Turvey (1991) report that priming occurs when the prime is a word and the target is a pseudohomophone (e.g., *chare* was pronounced faster when it followed *table* as compared to when it followed an unrelated word). Lukatela and Turvey argue that the presence of this priming effect weakens the position of the dual route model since there is no need for a second, addressed routine if words read via the assembled routine can access lexical/semantic information.

"In light of the evidence presented here and elsewhere for phonological mediation, we are tempted to ask whether there is experimental support for another process separate from phonological mediation". (Lukatela & Turvey, 1991, p. 960)

We believe that this conclusion is too strong, given their data. The critical data in support of this claim would involve a comparison between the priming effect for word-word pairs and word-pseudohomophone pairs. The pseudohomophones must be read by the assembled routine (since such a stimulus has no representation in an orthographic input lexicon) but, following the dual route model, words have both assembled and addressed routines available to them. Lukatela and Turvey's conclusion would be more interesting if they had demonstrated that both types of targets produced similar patterns of priming. This issue is examined in the experiments reported here.

Recapitulation

Following a review of a three route framework of oral reading in a deep orthography, we suggested that these pathways may all play a role when words printed in a shallow orthography are read aloud. Two central and widely accepted assumptions that are nevertheless problematic and require further investigation were described. These assumptions are (a) that only the addressed routine can produce priming, and (b) that when the addressed routine is employed it necessarily produces priming. Both of these assumptions are examined here in the context of reading Japanese Kana, because the characteristics of this shallow orthography make it possible to *force* subjects to read using the assembled routine.

Reading Japanese

Written Japanese consists of three distinct scripts. The logographic *Kanji* represents content words while the syllabic *Kana* scripts consist of *Hiragana* which represents grammatical morphemes and *Katakana* which represents borrowed words such as *television* and *computer*. Both Hiragana and Katakana have very consistent spelling-sound correspondences (i.e., they are shallow scripts). Transcribing a word which normally appears in one Kana script into the other Kana script produces a *pseudohomophone*, a word that is orthographically unfamiliar at the whole word level but retains its original pronunciation. Since readers must rely entirely on the assembled routine to read such character strings aloud, any evidence of priming for these words is evidence that the use of assembled routine can result in priming.

Determining whether the addressed routine is used (especially pathway D) is slightly more complicated. Besner and Hildebrandt (1987) and Besner, Patterson, Lee, and Hildebrandt (1993) found that orthographically familiar Kana words are named faster than Kana words which have been transcribed into an orthographically unfamiliar form. Similar results are expected in the present experiment and, following Besner and his colleagues, will also be taken as evidence that the addressed routine is used to read these familiar words. Our interest here, however, also centers on the issue of whether pathway(s) D and/or A/B are used to read such words. The use of pathway A must produce priming while the use of pathway D need not. If the orthographically familiar words in the present experiment are read faster than the orthographically unfamiliar words, yet fail to produce priming, then the use of a whole word pathway which bypasses semantics (pathway D) is implied. Experiment 1 therefore manipulates both relatedness and orthographic familiarity in the context of a naming task.

Experiment 1

METHOD

Subjects

The 12 subjects were fluent, native Japanese readers residing in the Waterloo region. Ten of the subjects were graduate students in the sciences, two were housewives. Each subject was paid ten dollars for his/her participation.

Apparatus

The stimuli were presented on a Commodore 1084 display driven by an Amiga 2000 computer. Vocal responses triggered a voice activated relay connected to a timing routine in the computer. Each trial was monitored by the experimenter and both errors and spoiled trials were recorded.

Stimulus Materials

The stimulus set consisted of 120 prime-target word combinations. Each combination consisted of: (a) a Kanji prime (one to three characters in length) together with (b) a semantically or associatively related Katakana target word or (c) the Hiragana transcription of that Katakana word. The length of the Kana target words ranged from two to eleven characters. Twenty additional prime-target word combinations were used for the practice trials.

Procedure

Subjects were tested individually; each session lasted approximately twenty minutes and consisted of 120 trials. Each trial consisted of a presentation of a Kanji prime followed by a target printed in either Hiragana or Katakana. The targets were presented in their familiar Katakana form on half of the trials and in their orthographically unfamiliar Hiragana form on the remaining trials. Relatedness was manipulated such that on half of the trials the Kanji prime was related to the target, and unrelated on the remaining trials. The presentation order of conditions was random with the constraint that no condition be repeated on more than three successive trials. Each subject received a different random order of trials and saw each target item only once during the session. Assignment of primes to targets in the unrelated condition was also random and varied across subjects. These manipulations resulted in a subject being exposed to thirty pairs of words for each of the four conditions given by the crossing of relatedness by orthographic familiarity. The targets were rotated through each of the four conditions, thus requiring a set of four subjects to complete the design. Subjects were instructed to pronounce the target word of each pair as quickly and accurately as possible. They were told to read the prime but not to pronounce it. The timing of events was as follows: An asterisk appeared briefly in the center of the screen and was followed by a 750 ms presentation of the Kanji prime. A 250 ms ISI was followed by the onset of the target word which remained on the screen until a response was recorded. The subject then pushed a button to initiate the next trial.

RESULTS

Mean *RTs* and error rates for each of the four conditions are displayed in Table 1. Spoiled trials accounted for no more than one percent of the data in any condition; these are not discussed further. Error data were not formally analyzed as there were too many cells with zero as an entry. One prime-target word set was removed from the analysis because the transcription from Katakana to Hiragana was incorrect. The item analysis was therefore performed on the correct RT data from the remaining 119 prime-target word sets[3].

Following McCann and Besner (1987), interest centers on the item analysis. In order to partial out subject variability, each subjects' mean correct RT to all items was subtracted from their RTs for each item. The effect is similar to a regression analysis which partials out subject variability[4]. The adjusted mean RTs for correct responses to each item in each condition were then submitted to a 2 × 2 analysis of variance (relatedness × familiarity).

The main effect of Orthographic Familiarity was reliable; familiar words were named faster than the orthographically unfamiliar words, $F(1,118) = 89.64$, $MSe = 354325$, $p < .001$. The main effect of Relatedness was marginal, $F(1,118) = 3.67$, $MSe = 22314$, $p < .06$. The interaction between relatedness and familiarity was reliable, $F(1,118) = 5.49$, $MSe = 19341$, $p < .05$. An analysis of the interaction confirms that the priming effect is restricted to the orthographically unfamiliar words, $t(118) = 2.51$, $sd = 115.07$, $p < .05$. The familiar words did not yield a priming effect, $t(118) = .13$, $sd = 77.18$, $p > .50$.

Discussion

Experiment 1 produced a highly reliable effect of orthographic familiarity with the familiar words being named faster than the unfamiliar words[5]. This replicates previous observations (Besner & Hildebrandt, 1987; Besner et al., 1993) and suggests that there are two routines available: the assembled routine for the unfamiliar words and the faster addressed routine for the familiar words.

Converging evidence comes from the interaction between relatedness and

3 Besner and Smith (1992) reported a preliminary analysis of these data in which there was one item that was subsequently removed because it was transcribed incorrectly. The means appearing in this paper are therefore slightly different from those reported in Besner and Smith.

4 This analysis was suggested by P. Jolicoeur.

5 It might be argued that the main effect of Orthographic Familiarity is due to words in Katakana being easier to name than words in Hiragana. This argument can be rejected on the basis of Besner et al.'s (1993) observation that words normally printed in Hiragana are named as fast as words normally printed in Katakana. It might also be argued that the orthographically unfamiliar words named slower in this experiment were unfamiliar at the subword level as well as being unfamiliar at the whole word level (e.g., they might have smaller summed bigram frequency counts). This argument is difficult to address directly since no published bigram frequency count exists for Kana. We note, however, that Besner et al. also report that the Orthographic Familiarity effect is length dependent. It is seen for words with four or more characters; it does not occur for shorter words in their sample. If differences in the summed bigram frequency were to offer a general account of the Orthographic Familiarity effect, they might be expected to also exert an effect on short words. A final point is that if the Orthographic Familiarity effect were simply due to differences in subword orthographic familiarity then all words would have been read by recourse to the assembled route and thus should have shown similar patterns of priming. This was not the case; orthographically familiar words showed no priming effect in Experiment 1.

TABLE 1

Mean RTs and Error Rates as a Function of Orthographic Familiarity and Relatedness in Experiment 1 and Relatedness in Experiment 2

Context	Experiment 1				Experiment 2	
	Familiar		Unfamiliar		Familiar	
	RT	%E	RT	%E	RT	%E
Unrelated	540	(0.02)	609	(0.08)	496	(0.03)
Related	540	(0.00)	583	(0.07)	475	(0.01)
Difference	0	(0.02)	26	(0.01)	21	(0.02)

familiarity. Since the unfamiliar words can only be read via the assembled routine, and only these items produced a priming effect, it must be the case that the assembled routine in this shallow orthography is influenced by semantic information prior to pronunciation. Further, since the familiar words did not produce a priming effect they must be processed by a routine that is sensitive to orthographic familiarity at the whole word level, but need not be influenced by semantic activation. The only routine that could accomplish this is the direct pathway from the orthographic input lexicon to the phonological output lexicon (pathway D). Further discussion regarding this issue follows Experiment 2.

In all previous studies with shallow orthographies, a failure to observe a priming effect in naming is associated with the presence of nonwords in the target set[6]. In contrast, when only words appear in the target set all such experiments have yielded priming (Baluch & Besner, 1991; Besner & Smith, 1992; Seidenberg & Vidanovic, 1985; Tabossi & Laghi, 1992). The results of these experiments thus suggest that priming effects can be quite sensitive to context. Experiment 2 therefore removes the orthographically unfamiliar items in order to determine whether the familiar words would now produce a priming effect.

Experiment 2

METHOD

Subjects

The eight subjects were fluent, native Japanese readers. Four were visiting graduate students and four were housewives. Each subject was paid ten dollars for his/her participation. None of these subjects participated in Experiment 1.

Materials and Procedure

The materials and procedure were identical to that of Experiment 1 with the exception that the stimulus list contained only the 120 orthographically

6 Though note that Carello et al. (1988) and Sebastian-Galles (1991) found a priming effect with nonwords in the stimulus set. This has been discussed by Besner and Smith (1992).

familiar Katakana target words and their Kanji primes. Each subject saw 60 related prime-target pairs and 60 unrelated prime-target pairs. The order of presentation and the assignment of primes to unrelated targets were random-ized across subjects.

RESULTS

Mean *RT*s and error rates are displayed in the bottom half of Table 1. One item had no entries in the unrelated condition and was therefore removed from the data prior to the analysis. The analysis was therefore done on 119 items. As in Experiment 1, only correct responses were analysed. Spoiled trials accounted for no more than one percent of the observations in either condition and are not discussed further. The error data were not formally analysed, as there were too many cells with zero as an entry. Subject variability was again partialled out by subtracting the mean of each subject's correct responses to all items from their *RT*s for individual items. The data are clear; words preceded by a related prime were named faster than the same words preceded by an unrelated prime, $t(118) = 4.14$, $sd = 53.30$, $p < .001$.

Discussion

The priming effect seen in Experiment 1 results from the exclusive use of the assembled routine since only orthographically unfamiliar words (which can only be read via that routine) produce priming. Experiment 2, in which the orthographically unfamiliar words were deleted from the stimulus set, now exhibits priming for the familiar words. There are two reasons for believing that the words in Experiment 2 were read by the addressed rather than the assembled routine. First, the absolute *RT*s are much faster for the unrelated orthographically familiar words in Experiment 2 than for the unrelated orthographically unfamiliar words in Experiment 1. This replicates the within experiment familiarity effect observed in Experiment 1. Secondly, Besner et al. (1993) observed that character length effects are much smaller for orthographically familiar words than for orthographically unfamiliar words, as would be expected if the subword routine is dependent upon a serial assembly process. Therefore, if the words in Experiment 2 are read by the addressed routine, the length effect should be smaller than that seen for the orthographically unfamiliar words in Experiment 1, and should be similar to that observed for the orthographically familiar words in Experiment 1. The data are consistent with this argument (see Table 2). The slopes for *RT* as a function of word length do not differ significantly for the familiar words in Experiments 1 versus 2, $t(116) = .41$, $p > .50$. In contrast, the word length effect for the unfamiliar words in Experiment 1 is significantly larger than the word length effect for familiar words in Experiment 1, $t(116) = 2.36, p < .05$ and Experiment 2, $t(116) = 2.26$, $p < .05$.

TABLE 2
Length effects (ms per character) as a Function of Orthographic
Familiarity for Experiments 1 and 2 Collapsed across Relatedness

Experiment	Condition	Slope
1	Unfamiliar Words	17.2
1	Familiar Words	6.7
2	Familiar Words	8.1

Conclusions

USE OF THE ADDRESSED ROUTINE AS INDEXED BY THE ORTHOGRAPHIC FAMILIARITY EFFECT

Only the assembled routine can be used to read the orthographically unfamiliar words. If all words were read by this routine then orthographic familiarity at the whole word level should not affect performance. Since it did, this suggests the operation of a separate routine (the addressed routine) used to read the orthographically familiar words.

UNDERSTANDING PRIMING EFFECTS

As discussed earlier, the standard assumption is that the presence of priming reflects the use of the addressed routine. However, the interaction of orthographic familiarity and relatedness observed in Experiment 1 demonstrates that this assumption is too strong. Since orthographically unfamiliar words are necessarily read via the assembled routine, the priming effect observed for these words is conclusive evidence that use of the assembled routine can result in priming. Thus, the presence of a priming effect, *on its own*, does not differentiate between use of the addressed routine and the assembled routine. In contrast, priming effects combined with converging operations such as word frequency (e.g., Baluch & Besner, 1991) and orthographic familiarity (as in the present experiment) do permit a conclusion as to which routine is used.

The standard explanation for a *failure* to find priming has been that it signals the use of the assembled routine (e.g., Frost et al., 1987; Katz & Feldman, 1983; Tabossi & Laghi, 1992). The accompanying (albeit implicit) assumption in these papers is that the addressed routine *necessarily* produces priming effects. The problem here is that this interpretation neglects the possibility that pathway D can be used and not produce priming. The orthographically familiar words in Experiment 1 are argued to be read by the addressed routine because they were read faster than the orthographically unfamiliar words which can only be read by the assembled routine. However, relatedness affected only the unfamiliar words. This constitutes evidence that the orthographically familiar words are read via pathway D; a lexical but nonsemantic routine. If they had been read via the semantic pathway (pathway A/B) they should have produced priming.

These data thus support a division of the addressed route into two pathways; one which is driven through semantics (A/B), and one which is not (D). To our knowledge these data are the first to support this distinction in intact readers. They therefore extend and complement the argument for three separate routines based upon data from acquired dyslexia reviewed in the introduction. This evidence for a distinction between a nonsemantic whole word routine and a subword routine is also inconsistent with the assertion that a single routine underlies the oral reading of all types of letter strings (Seidenberg & McClelland, 1989; 1990; Patterson, Seidenberg & McClelland, 1989).

INTERACTIVE PROCESSES

The interaction between orthographic familiarity and relatedness suggests that *some* of the components in the visual word recognition system are engaged in interactive activation (cf. McClelland & Rumelhart, 1981; Rumelhart & McClelland, 1982; McClelland, 1987). The priming effect observed in Experiment 1 was limited to those words which were necessarily read via the assembled routine. If presentation of the prime served merely to activate related targets in the phonological output lexicon via the semantic system, then all words (both familiar and unfamiliar) would yield priming. Since this did not happen it is necessary to assume that while related items in the semantic system are primed, this activation does not spread automatically from the semantic sytem to the orthographic input lexicon and the phonological lexicons (i.e., through pathways K, B, and I). Instead, it may be released or accessed by the assembled routine via the phonemic buffer and the phonological lexicons (i.e., pathways E, F, G, H, B, C, or, E, F, G, H, I, J, C). It is assumed that while an orthographically familiar target word may activate the semantic system via the assembled routine and the phonological lexicons (i.e., pathway E,F,G, and H), directly from the orthographic input lexicon (i.e., pathway A) or from the orthographic input lexicon via the phonological lexicons (i.e., pathways D, G, AND H), previous activation in the semantic system is not released until target processing is in progress. Since pathway D results in the direct activation of a whole word representation in the phonological output lexicon, priming need not result if pathway C is fast relative to feedback from the semantic system (i.e., from pathway B or pathways I, J). The interaction between the phonemic buffer, the phonological output and input lexicons and the semantic system can be seen to yield priming for orthographically unfamiliar words because input via the assembled routine is more spread out over time. In contrast, the priming observed for the orthographically familiar words in Experiment 2 may reflect a change in organization such that spreading activation from the semantic system now feeds back to the orthographic input lexicon and/or forward to the phonological output lexicon or, alternatively, processing is based on the use of pathways

A/B rather than D. If the lexical system and the semantic system are normally engaged in interactive activation, then inhibition of pathways from the semantic system (i.e., K, B, and I as indicated in Figure 1 by the filled circles) will lead to slower naming of orthographically familiar words in the unrelated condition of Experiment 1 relative to Experiment 2. The data are consistent with this claim, as can be seen in Tables 1 and 2.

The central notion here is that inhibition plays a major role in the visual word recognition system. More specifically, activation does not appear to spread throughout the word recognition system as a matter of course. Instead, under some circumstances activation appears to spread to some subsystems, but then require additional input to spread further. The same argument has been advanced and elaborated in order to accommodate the presence/absence of word frequency effects in the oral reading of shallow orthographies as a function of the presence/absence of nonwords in the experiment (see the review by Besner & Smith, 1992). This idea can be contrasted with an interactive activation model in which activation is assumed to automatically spread between levels of representation (cf. McClelland, 1987). The present data, along with the data discussed by Besner and Smith (1992) cannot be accommodated within a framework in which activation *always* spreads to all levels within the visual word recognition system.

A major remaining issue concerns the need for an explanation as to why the word recognition system in shallow orthographies should appear to inhibit the spread of activation under some circumstances (e.g., Experiment 1) but, possibly, not others (Experiment 2). One speculative answer is that activation and its associated processes are resource limited and are not automatic (see also Baluch & Besner, 1991; Paap & Noel, 1991; Smith & Besner, 1993; Smith, Besner, & Myoshi, 1993). Different types of stimuli (words, nonwords) can use different processing paths; the attentional demands of these pathways may differ. Since fifty percent of the targets in Experiment 1 would not benefit from priming in the orthographic input lexicon, an inhibition of the spread of activation to that lexicon may reflect an adaptive sensitivity to context that would be most advantageous to a resource limited system.

Difficult questions remain concerning how goal setting (e.g., read this, pronounce that) and control over activation is accomplished; all the word recognition models in the literature are currently silent on this issue. These questions are among the major issues needing theoretical development if we are ever to have a comprehensive account of visual word recognition.

Summary
Contrary to the received view, (i) priming is not automatic; (ii) neither the presence nor absence of priming, on its own, is sufficient to identify the routine(s) that are being used; (iii) intact readers use a whole word nonsemantic routine to read aloud at least some of the time; (iv) the data are

inconsistent with any model which denies a distinction between a routine which processes at the subword level and one which processes at the whole word nonsemantic level (e.g., Seidenberg & McClelland, 1989, 1990; Lukatela & Turvey, 1991, Van Orden, et al., 1990); and (v) the data are most easily understood in terms of a three route model of visual word recognition where both inhibition and activation play important roles.

This research was supported by NSERC grant A0998 to DB. Correspondence may be directed to either author c/o Psychology Department., University of Waterloo, Waterloo, Ontario, N2L 3G1 or by email: buchanan@watserv1.uwaterloo.ca, besner@watarts.uwaterloo.ca

References

Allport, D.A. (1979). Word recognition in reading: A tutorial review. In P.A. Kolers, H. Bouma, and M. Wrolstad (Eds.). *Processing of visible language* Vol. 1, (pp. 227-257). New York: Plenum Press.

Baluch, B., & Besner, D. (1991). Visual word recognition: Evidence for strategic control of lexical and nonlexical routines in oral reading. *Journal of Experimental Psychology: Learning, Memory and Cognition, 17,* 644-652.

Besner, D. (1987). On the relationship between orthographies and phonologies in visual word recognition. In D.A. Allport, D. McKay, W. Prinz, and E. Sheerer (Eds.). *Language perception and production: Shared mechanisms in listening, speaking, reading and writing.* New York: Academic Press.

Besner, D., Twilley, L., McCann, R.S., & Seergobin, K. (1990). On the association between connectionism and data: Are a few words necessary? *Psychological Review, 97,* 432-446.

Besner, D. (1993). *Barking at print: Some exceptions, regularities and inconsistencies.* Invited paper presented to the Midwestern Psychological Association, Chicago.

Besner, D., & Hildebrandt, N. (1987). Orthographic and phonological codes in the oral reading of Japanese Kana. *Journal of Experimental Psychology: Learning, Memory, and Cognition, 13,* 335-343.

Besner, D., Patterson, K., Lee, L., & Hildebrandt, N. (1993). Two forms of Japanese Kana: Phonologically but NOT orthographically interchangable. *Journal of Experimental Psychology: Learning, Memory, and Cognition.* (in press).

Besner, D. & Smith, M. (1992). Basic processes in reading: Is the orthographic depth hypothesis sinking? In R. Frost and L. Katz (Eds.) *Orthography, phonology, morphology and meaning.* Amsterdam: North Holland Press.

Bridgeman, B. (1987). Is the dual-route theory possible in phonetically regular languages? *Behavioral and Brain Sciences, 10,* 331-332.

Bub, D., Cancellière, A., & Kertesz, A. (1985). Whole-word and analytic translation of spelling to sound in a non-semantic reader. In Patterson, K., Marshall, J.C., & Coltheart, M. (Eds.) *Surface dyslexia: Cognitive and neuropsychological studies of phonological reading.* London: Lawrence Erlbaum Associates.

Carello, C., Lukatela, G., & Turvey, M.T. (1988). Rapid naming is affected by association but not by syntax. *Memory and Cognition, 16,* 187-195.

Carr, T.H., & Pollatsek, A. (1985). Recognizing printed words: A look at current models. In D. Besner, T.G. Waller, & G.E. MacKinnon (Eds). *Reading research: Advances in theory and practice* (Vol. 5). New York: Academic Press.

Coltheart, M., Patterson, K.E., & Marshall, J.C. (1980). *Deep Dyslexia.* London: Routledge and Kegan Paul.

Coltheart, M., Masterson, J., Byng, S., Prior, M., & Riddoch, J. (1983). Surface dyslexia. *Quarterly Journal of Experimental Psychology, 35,* 469-496.

Feldman, L.B., & Turvey, M.T. (1983). Word recognition in Serbo-Croatian is phonologically analytic. *Journal of Experimental Psychology: Human Perception and Performance, 9,* 288-298.

Forster, K.I., & Chambers, S.M. (1973). Lexical access and naming time. *Journal of Verbal Learning and Verbal Behavior, 12,* 672-635.

Frost, R., Katz, L., & Bentin, S. (1987). Strategies for visual word recognition and orthographic depth: A multilingual comparison. *Journal of Experimental Psychology: Human Perception and Performance, 13,* 104-115.

Friedrich, F.J., Henik, A., & Tzelgov, J. (1991). Automatic processes in lexical access and spreading activation. *Journal of Experimental Psychology: Human Perception and Performance, 17,* 792-806.

Funnell, E. (1983). Phonological processes in reading: New evidence from acquired dyslexia. *British Journal of Psychology, 74,* 159-180.

Hung, D.L., & Tzeng, O.J.L. (1981). Orthographic variations and visual information processing. *Psychological Bulletin, 90,* 377-414.

Katz, L., & Feldman, L.B. (1983). Relation between pronunciation and recognition of printed words in deep and shallow orthographies. *Journal of Experimental Psychology: Learning, Memory, and Cognition, 9,* 157-166.

Katz, L., & Frost, R. (1992). The reading process is different for different orthographies: The orthographic depth hypothesis. In R. Frost and L. Katz (Eds.) *Orthography, phonology, morphology and meaning.* North Holland Press.

Lukatela, G., & Turvey, M.T. (1991). Phonological access of the lexicon: Evidence from associative priming with pseudohomophones. *Journal of Experimental Psychology: Learning, Memory, and Cognition, 17,* 951-966.

McCann, R.S., & Besner, D. (1987). Reading pseudohomophones: Implications for models of pronunciation and the locus of the word-frequency effect in word naming. *Journal of Experimental Psychology: Human Perception and Performance, 13,* 13-24.

McClelland, J.L., & Rumelhart, D.E. (1982). An interactive activation model of context effects in letter perception: Part 1. An account of basic findings. *Psychological Review, 88,* 374-407.

McClelland, J.L. (1987). The case for interactionism in language processing. In M. Coltheart (Ed.), *Attention and Performance XII: The Psychology of Reading,* (pp. 1-36). Hillsdale, NJ: Erlbaum.

McCusker, L.X., Hillinger, M.L., & Bias, R.W. (1981). Phonological recoding and reading. *Psychological Bulletin, 89,* 217-245.

Monsell, S., Patterson, K.E. Graham, A., Hughes, A., & Milroy, R. (1992). Lexical and sublexical translation of spelling to sound: Strategic anticipation of lexical status. *Journal of Experimental Psychology: Learning, Memory and Cognition, 18,* 3, 452-467.

Morton, J., & Sasanuma, E. (1984). Lexical access in Japanese. In L. Henderson (Ed.). *Orthographies and reading.* Hillsdale, NJ: Erlbaum.

Neely, J.H. (1977). Semantic priming and retrieval from lexical memory: Roles of inhibitionless spreading activation and limited-capacity attention. *Journal of Experimental Psychology: General, 106,* 226-254.

Neely, J.H. (1991). Semantic priming effects in visual word recognition: A selective review of current findings and theories. In D. Besner & G. Humphreys (Eds.), *Basic processes in reading: Visual word recognition.* Hillsdale, NJ: Erlbaum.

Paap, K., & Noel, R.W. (1991). Dual-route model of print to sound: Still a good horse race. *Psychological Research, 96,* 523-568.

Paap, K., Noel, R.W., & Johansen, L.S. (1992). Dual-route models of print to sound: Red herrings and real horses. In R. Frost and L. Katz (Eds.) *Orthography, phonology, morphology and meaning.* Amsterdam: North Holland Press.

Patterson, K.E. (1990). Basic processes of reading: Do they differ in Japanese and English? *Japanese Journal of Neuropsychology, 6,* 4-14.

Patterson, K. & Coltheart, V. (1987). Phonological processes in reading: A Tutorial review. In M. Coltheart (Ed.) *Attention and Performance XII: The Psychology of Reading.* Hillsdale NJ: Erlbaum.

Patterson, K. Seidenberg, M.S., & McClelland, J.L. (1989). Word recognition and dyslexia: A connectionist approach. In P. Morris (Ed.) *Connectionism: The Oxford Symposium.* Cambridge: Cambridge University Press.

Posner, M.I., & Snyder, C.R. (1975). Attention and Cognitive control. In R.L. Solso (Ed.) *Information processing and cognition: The Loyola Symposium* (pp. 55-83). Hillsdale, NJ: Lawrence Erlbaum Associates.

Rosson, M.B. (1983). From SOFA to LOUCH: Lexical contributions to pseudoword pronunciation. *Memory & Cognition, 11,* 152-160.

Rumelhart, D.E., & McClelland, J. L. (1982). An interactive activation model of context effects in letter perception: Part 2. The contextual enhancement effect and some tests and extensions of the model. *Psychological Review, 89,* 60-94.

Schwartz, M.F., Saffran, E.M., & Marin, E.M. (1980). Fractioning the reading processes in dementia: Evidence for word specific print-to-sound associations. In M. Coltheart, K.E. Patterson, & J.C. Marshall (Eds.) *Deep Dyslexia.* London: Routledge and Kegan Paul.

Sebastain-Galles, N. (1991). Reading by analogy in a shallow orthography. *Journal of Experimental Psychology: Human Perception and Performance, 17,* 471-477.

Seidenberg, M. (1985a). The time course of information activation and utilization in visual word recognition. In D. Besner, T.G. Waller and E. MacKinnon (1985), Reading research: Advances in theory and instruction. Orlando, Florida: Academic Press.

Seidenberg, M. (1985b). Time course of phonological code activation in two writing systems. *Cognition, 19,* 1-30.

Seidenberg, M.S. & Vidanovic, S. (1985). *Word recognition in Serbo-Croatian and English: Do they differ?* Paper presented at the annual meeting of the Psychonomic Society, Boston.

Seidenberg, M.S., & McClelland, J.L. (1989). A distributed, developmental model of of word recognition and naming. *Psychological Review, 96,* 523-568.

Seidenberg, M.S., & McClelland, J.L. (1990). More words but still no lexicon: Reply to Besner et al. (1990). *Psychological Review, 97,* 477-482.

Seidenberg, M.S., Waters, G.S., Barnes, M.A., & Tannehaus, M. (1984). When does irregular spelling or pronunciation influence word recognition? *Journal of Verbal Learning and Verbal Behavior, 23,* 383-404.

Smith, M.C. (1979). Contextual facilitation in a letter search task depends on how the prime is processed. *Journal of Experimental Psychology: Human Perception and Performance, 5,* 239-251.

Smith, M., Besner, D., & Myoshi, H. (1993). New limits to automaticity: Context modulates semantic priming. *Journal of Experimental Psychology: Learning, Memory and Cognition* (in press).

Smith, M., & Besner, D. (1993). *Limitations to semantic activation: Evidence for between level inhibition.* Manuscript submitted for publication.

Tabossi, P., & Laghi, L. (1992). Semantic priming in the pronunciation of words in two writing systems: Italian and English. *Memory & Cognition, 20,* 303-313.

Snow, N., & Neely, J.H. (1987). *Reduction of semantic priming from inclusion of physically or nominally related prime-target pairs.* Paper presented at the annual meeting of the Psychonomic Society, Seattle, WA.

Turvey, M.T., Feldman, L.B., & Lukatela, G. (1984). The Serbo-Croatian orthography constrains the reader to a phonologically analytic strategy. In L. Henderson (Ed.) *Orthographies and reading: Perspectives from cognitive psychology, neuropsychology, and linguistics* (pp. 81-91). London: Erlbaum.

Van Orden, G.C., Pennington, B.F., & Stone, G.O. (1990). Word identification in reading and the promise of subsymbolic psycholinguistics. *Psychological Review, 4,* 488-523.

Waters, G.S., & Seidenberg, M.S. (1985). Spelling-sound effects in reading: Time-course and decision criteria. *Memory and Cognition, 13,* 557-572.

3 What Eye Fixations Tell Us About Phonological Recoding During Reading

MEREDYTH DANEMAN and EYAL REINGOLD
Erindale College, University of Toronto

Abstract Evidence for phonological recoding during reading has depended on paradigms requiring readers to make some response in addition to reading (e.g., proofreading, concurrent speaking). Our subjects simply read text for comprehension, and their eye movements were monitored for spontaneous disruptions when encountering homophonic errors (e.g., *He wore blew jeans.*) versus nonhomophonic errors (e.g., *He wore blow jeans.*). Eye fixation behaviour revealed that readers initially experienced as much difficulty when encountering a homophonic error as a nonhomophonic one; however homophony facilitated the recovery process, at least for homophones that shared the same length as their context correct mates (e.g., *blew/blue* but not *war/wore*). The results support a theory of lexical access in which phonological sources of activation and influence are delayed relative to orthographic sources, rather than a theory in which phonological codes predominate.

Résumé Les éléments de preuve à l'appui de l'enregistrement phonologique durant la lecture reposent sur des paradigmes selon lesquels les lecteurs doivent non seulement lire un texte, mais également fournir une certaine réponse (p. ex. correction d'épreuves, langage simultané). Dans notre expérience, les sujets devaient simplement lire un texte et le comprendre, tandis que leurs mouvements oculaires étaient enregistrés pour y détecter les perturbations spontanées en présence d'erreurs homophoniques (p. ex. *He wore blew jeans*) par opposition à des erreurs non homophoniques (p. ex. *He wore blow jeans*). D'après les fixations oculaires, les lecteurs éprouvaient d'abord autant de difficulté avec les erreurs homophoniques qu'avec les autres erreurs; cependant, l'homophonie facilitait le processus de redressement, du moins dans le cas des homophones de même longueur (p. ex. *blew/blue*, mais non *war/wore*). Plutôt que d'appuyer une théorie de la prédominance des codes phonologiques, les résultats corroborent une théorie de l'accès au lexique, selon laquelle les sources d'activation et l'influence d'ordre phonologique interviennent après les sources orthographiques.

Consider encountering the following passage during the course of reading a short story about a bank holdup:

The teller ducked his head and saw a vein little man only for feet high who paced up and down, stopping at intervals to flex his impressive arm muscles. He wore a tee shirt, suede jacket, and blew jeans. Over his furrowed forehead and apelike brows perched a wig, apparently put on with glue. His nose went straight for a bit, then took a sharp turn to the side. Yet Harry 'Peewee' Farplotz, the world's smallest and most inept bank robber, had style...

Did you notice that there were three spelling errors in the passage? Now consider the following version:

The teller ducked his head and saw a vine little man only fir feet high who paced up and down, stopping at intervals to flex his impressive arm muscles. He wore a tee shirt, suede jacket, and blow jeans. Over his furrowed forehead and apelike brows perched a wig, apparently put on with glue. His nose went straight for a bit, then took a sharp turn to the side. Yet Harry 'Peewee' Farplotz, the world's smallest and most inept bank robber, had style...

Did you find it more difficult to detect the errors *vein*, *for*, and *blew* in the first version than the errors *vine*, *fir*, and *blow* in the second? All six words are semantically inconsistent in the context of the passage. However, *vein*, *for*, and *blew* happen to sound identical to the words *vain*, *four*, and *blue* which are perfectly consistent in that context, whereas *vine*, *fir*, and *blow* do not. If readers are less likely to notice an error that was a homophone of the correct word, this might suggest that they translate orthographic representations to phonological representations when comprehending printed text. By translating the orthographic representation *vein* to its phonological representation /veIn/, the clause ...*and saw a vein little man* would still sound correct and the error may be more likely to go undetected.

Rather than asking their subjects simply to read the passage (as we asked you in the opening paragraph of this article), Daneman and Stainton (1991) had them proofread the text for incorrect words as they read. When deliberately instructed to proofread, readers were less likely to detect homophonic error words than nonhomophonic ones, a finding that Daneman and Stainton (1991) took as evidence for the activation of phonological codes during normal silent reading. Although Daneman and Stainton's (1991) comprehension-sensitive proofreading task[1] approximated real-life reading more than any of the tasks

1 The proofreading task was comprehension-sensitive in the sense that only errors producing legal English words were introduced into the text (e.g., *vain* misspelled as *vein* or *vine*); this meant that an error could only be detected if the reader understood the semantic and syntactic context in which the error word occurred. Indeed, there is some evidence to suggest (e.g., Daneman, 1988) that this kind of proofreading task is more likely to correlate with reading

used in previous studies of homophone confusion effects, there is still the concern that the proofreading requirement changed the nature of the reading process itself. In this study we looked for evidence of phonological recoding in a task that demanded nothing other than normal reading for comprehension. Our readers were not asked to proofread for errors while they read. In fact, they were not required to perform any other secondary task (e.g., concurrent speaking); nor were they required to make any unnatural judgements about what they were reading (e.g., decide on the lexical status of a letter string, or the semantic acceptability of a sentence). They were simply given the goal of reading for comprehension, and we monitored their eye fixation behaviour for evidence of disruptions when encountering homophonic errors (e.g., *a vein little man for feet high*) versus nonhomophonic errors (e.g., *a vine little man fir feet high*). As we will show, not only did the eye fixation data provide evidence for the activation of phonological codes during natural silent reading, but they provided evidence concerning the time course of the activation. We will first describe the kinds of homophone tasks on which previous evidence has been based, paying particular attention to the Daneman and Stainton (1991) task. Then we will describe the unobtrusive technique used here.

Although our review of the literature will be limited to research based on homophone confusions, this is not the only paradigm that has been used to investigate phonological processes during silent reading. Edfelt (1960) used electromyography (EMG) recordings to determine whether there was any muscular activity in the area of the larynx during reading. Numerous other researchers (e.g., Daneman & Newson, 1992; Kleiman, 1975; Levy, 1977, 1978; Slowiaczek & Clifton, 1980; Waters, Caplan, & Hildebrandt, 1987) have used a speech suppression paradigm; in this paradigm, subjects are given a concurrent speaking task while reading a set of sentences or passages; they may be asked to count out loud from 1 to 10 over and over, repeat the same irrelevant word (e.g., *cola, cola*), or listen to and repeat (shadow) a list of spoken words as quickly as possible. Any evidence that the speaking task interferes with reading performance is taken to suggest that concurrent speaking competes for the speech codes and mechanisms normally used during silent reading (although see Waters, Komoda, & Arbuckle, 1985, for an alternative interpretation). Of course, the concurrent speaking paradigm has the same disadvantage as the proofreading paradigm in that it requires some response from the subject in addition to reading.

In the homophone research tradition, much of the evidence for the recoding of print to sound comes from lexical decision tasks in which subjects judge

comprehension ability than is the more typical proofreading task (e.g., Haber & Schindler, 1981; Healy, 1980; Levy, 1983) in which misspellings always produce nonwords (e.g., *vain* misspelled as *voin*) that can be detected simply on the basis of word-nonword discriminations.

whether a given letter string is a word. Subjects typically take more time to reject pseudohomophone foils, such as *brane*, than to reject control foils, such as *brene* (Coltheart, Davelaar, Jonasson, & Besner, 1977; Rubenstein, Lewis, & Rubenstein, 1971). A common explanation for the effect is that a pseudohomophone such as *brane* activates the phonological representation /breIn/, which in turn activates the lexical entry for the word *brain*. The activation of a lexical entry makes *brane* more difficult to classify as a nonword.[2]

There are at least two problems in generalizing from the pseudohomophone effect to normal reading. The first problem is that the effect is observed on *no* trials which are usually slower than *yes* trials. Hence, the nonword's effect in the lexical decision task may occur after the time has elapsed that is typically needed for *word* identification. This means that the pseudohomophone effect may have no relevance with respect to whether phonological processes are involved in real word recognition (Coltheart et al., 1977; McCusker, Hillinger, & Bias, 1981; Van Orden, 1987). And even if the pseudohomophone effect were relevant to word identification, there remains the more pervasive problem of generalizing from word identification in the laboratory-created lexical decision task to word identification in the more natural reading of connected text.

Van Orden's (1987) categorization task avoids the problem of extrapolating from *no* trials. In his task, subjects are presented a category name (e.g., *type of flower*) followed by a target word (e.g., *rows*, *robs*, or *tulip*), and their task is to decide whether or not the target word is a member of the category. The key dependent measure is the number of false *yes* responses to a homophone word foil (e.g., *rows* which sounds like a genuine category member *rose*) as compared with the number of false positives to nonhomophonic control words matched for orthographic similarity (e.g., *robs* which looks but does not sound like a genuine category member). Van Orden (1987) found that homophonic word foils were erroneously categorized as category exemplars in 18.5% of trials as compared with only 3% false positive categorizations for the nonhomophonic control words, a finding that has since been replicated (Van Orden, Johnston, & Hale, 1988) and taken to suggest that the phonological representations of words are activated during word identification. Because the categorization task draws on a homophone effect for *yes* trials, it avoids the problem of making inferences based on the slower *no* latencies. However, like the lexical decision task, it involves an artificial or laboratory-created response to isolated words. Thus, there still remains the need to demonstrate homophone effects in a more normal reading situation.

The sentence decision experiments are somewhat more reading-like in that

---

2 See also Lukatela and Turvey (1991) for a more recent demonstration of pseudohomophone effects in an associative-priming paradigm.

subjects' decisions depend on the comprehension of an entire sentence rather than an isolated word. In these experiments, subjects are required to judge the acceptability of short sentences, with some of the incorrect sentences containing a homophonic word that makes the sentence sound correct, for example, *She has blond hare*. (Treiman, Freyd, & Baron, 1983), *The none says her prayers*. (Coltheart, Avons & Trollope, 1990). These studies have consistently shown that both adults and children make more errors (false-positive decisions) on incorrect sentences that sound correct, for example, *She has blond hare*., than on incorrect sentences that do not sound correct, for example, *She has blond harm*. (Coltheart, Laxon, Rickard, & Elton, 1988; Coltheart et al., 1990; Doctor & Coltheart, 1980; Johnston, Rugg, & Scott, 1987; Treiman, et al., 1983). It is important to note that error rates to sentences with homophones tend to be rather low for adults, in the 10-25% range; thus, when orthographic and phonological codes suggest different decisions, orthography is still more likely to determine the decision (see also Patterson & Coltheart, 1987). Nevertheless, the presence of a small but reliable homophone effect has usually been taken to imply that fluent adult readers access the phonological representations of all words during silent reading, with misleading phonology only sometimes duping them. Daneman and Stainton (1991) argued that the low error rates for homophone sentences and even lower rates for nonhomophone controls (0-6%) are indicative of a reading comprehension task that is altogether much too easy. The stimulus sentences all tend to be short, stereotyped expressions that are very simple to comprehend. In other words, even though the sentence decision paradigm involves reading for meaning, it does not draw on the kinds of complex comprehension processes that are part and parcel of full-blown reading.

Daneman and Stainton (1991) improved upon the ecological validity of the homophone paradigm by having subjects read a fairly lengthy prose passage rather than a list of unrelated words or sentences; and by showing that their proofreading task was not only much more difficult than the sentence decision tasks (overall error detection rates were less than 64%), but that it was significantly and positively correlated with an independent, standardized test of reading comprehension ability. There were two versions of their comprehension-sensitive proofreading task. In one version, readers had to identify the error words; in a second version they had not only to identify the error words but repair them as well. When readers merely had to identify the error words, evidence for phonological recoding came in the form of a homophone interference effect; phonological likeness interfered with the detection of homophonic error words, presumably because the printed word *vein* activated the phonological code /veIn/ which in turn activated the contextually consistent homophone *vain*, making the inconsistency in the phrase *vein little man* go unnoticed. When subjects had to identify *and* repair the inconsistent words, evidence for phonological recoding was in the form of a facilitation effect; phonological likeness facilitated the recovery of correct words, presumably because for those cases in which the reader had successfully detected the inconsistent impostor word *vein*, that same activated phonological code /*veIn*/ could be used as a retrieval route to the correct alternative *vain*. Thus, there was a cost and benefit associated with the availability of lexical phonological codes in Daneman and Stainton's (1991) proofreading tasks; the activation of contextually consistent homophones interfered with the initial detection of semantic inconsistencies, but facilitated the process of recovering the correct word for those inconsistencies that were detected.

Not only did Daneman and Stainton (1991) establish that phonological codes are activated during the silent reading of normal connected prose, but they claimed to provide evidence for the locus and function of these codes. Psychologists have proposed two possible roles for phonological codes. On the one hand, the reader might generate transient phonological representations that are used, in conjunction with the orthographic representations, by the processes involved in word identification and lexical access (Besner, Davies, & Daniels, 1981; Coltheart, 1978; Meyer, Schvaneveldt, & Ruddy, 1974; Rubenstein et al., 1971; Van Orden, 1987; Van Orden, et al., 1988). In this case, observed homophone effects would arise during the process of lexical access itself. However, phonology may have its influence beyond the level of individual word comprehension. During reading, sequences of words must be held in a temporary storage buffer while the comprehension processes integrate them into a meaningful conceptual structure that can be stored in long-term memory (Daneman & Carpenter, 1983; Kintsch & van Dijk, 1978). It has been argued that the most stable and retrievable short-term memory (or working memory) code is a sound based one (see Baddeley, 1986, for an extensive discussion of the properties of working memory and its articulatory loop). By generating phonological representations that are less vulnerable to memory loss, the reader could keep track of exact words rather than rough meanings (Baddeley, 1979; Baddeley, Eldridge, & Lewis, 1981). According to this account, the availability of phonological codes in working memory would be responsible for any observed homophone effects during proofreading. Daneman and Stainton (1991) claimed that their findings supported the former position, that the phonological codes are transient and activated as part of the lexical access process itself. Their claim was based on their finding that a concurrent speaking manipulation did not abolish or even reduce the homophone interference effect. Because previous researchers have argued that concurrent speaking interferes with the reader's ability to maintain phonological codes in working memory (Baddeley, 1979; Baddeley et al., 1981) but not with the reader's ability to generate the kind of phonological code that is used for lexical access (Baddeley, 1986; Besner, 1987; Besner & Davelaar, 1982; Besner, et al., 1981), Daneman and Stainton (1991) took the persistence of a homophone effect to mean that the locus of the effect was at lexical access.

Although Daneman and Stainton (1991) acknowledged that their results were consistent with "any number of models that allow lexical phonology to combine with or dominate orthographic information in guiding the reader to the meaning of a word" (p. 624), they opted for a model in which phonology plays the dominant role. In their model (a context-sensitive adaptation of Van Orden's 1987 model), the phonological code is computed immediately and used exclusively to gain access to a word's meaning representation in memory, with the orthographic code playing a post-activation verification role. For example, when a reader encounters a printed word (e.g., *vein*), its phonological representation (/veIn/) is immediately computed from the orthographic features (see also Perfetti, Bell, & Delaney, 1988), and it is this phonological representation that activates candidate lexical entries (e.g., *vain* meaning "conceited" and *vein* meaning "blood vessel"). However, before an activated lexical entry can be selected, it must pass a verification test or spelling check. The orthographic representation associated with the most active candidate is retrieved from memory and compared with the ortho-graphic representation of the word being read. If a match occurs, the lexical entry is selected; if not, the verification process is repeated on the next most active candidate lexical entry. According to this model, the printed word *vein* might occasionally be mistaken for *vain* if the false candidate *vain* were made available to the verification procedure and the mismatch in spelling slipped by undetected. *Vein* would be even more likely to be mistaken for *vain* if readers had previously been exposed to *The teller ducked and saw a vain little man*; according to the context-sensitive feature of the model, rereading or "expectancy-driven" reading leads to a relaxation of the orthographic verification standards, allowing even more spelling mismatches to slip by undetected.

Based on the findings from our more unobtrusive and naturalistic reading task, we will argue that orthographic information plays a much more dominant role in lexical access than Daneman and Stainton's model allows, and the phonological activation appears to be postlexical rather than prelexical; that is, it appears to be a by-product of lexical access rather than a route to it (see also McCutchen & Perfetti, 1982).

The Experiments

Our experiments looked for evidence of phonological recoding during the most natural or typical of reading situations possible, reading for compre-hension and entertainment. The basic task was as follows. Adult subjects were asked to read the same text used in the Daneman and Stainton (1991) study: an 1,100-word story about the misadventures of a bank teller named Russell Wood. However, two important modifications were introduced. The first was to the Russell Wood text. Daneman and Stainton's (1991) manipulation involved the introduction of 48 errors to homophonic words (e.g., *vain*), half of which produced the homophone mate (e.g., *vein*), and the other half, a nonhomophonic orthographically similar control word (e.g., *vine*). In the present experiments, some of the target words were retained in their original contextually correct form (e.g., *vain*). In Experiment 1, half the target words appeared in their correct form, half as the contextually inconsistent homophone mate. In Experiment 2, one third of the target words appeared in their correct form, one third as homophone errors, and one third as orthographically similar nonhomophone errors. The second modification was to the reading task itself. Daneman and Stainton's (1991) subjects were told that inconsistent words had been introduced into the text and they were given explicit instructions to proofread the text for the inconsistent words as they read; the activation of phonological codes was inferred from the proofreading response rather than from the reading *per se*. In the present experiments, we neither forewarned our subjects about the presence of the errors, nor gave them any instructions to proofread for the errors; rather, we simply had them read for comprehension and we recorded their eye fixations to examine whether phonological involvement is spontaneously revealed in the moment-to-moment computational processes of regular reading. Previous research has shown that readers pause longer on words that are inconsistent with previously read information (Carpenter & Daneman, 1981; Just & Carpenter, 1980) and frequently make regressive fixations as they attempt to resolve the inconsistencies (Carpenter & Daneman, 1981). Thus, any additional time spent fixating an inconsistent phrase (e.g., *vein little man*) relative to the consistent one (e.g., *vain little man*) could be attributed to the processes involved in inconsistency detection and recovery. If the Daneman and Stainton (1991) proofreading tasks reflected what occurs more spontaneously during natural reading and comprehension monitoring, then we might expect to find that readers frequently fail to detect homophone errors, showing no additional processing time when first encountering *vein* relative to processing time spent when first encountering the contextually appropriate *vain*. However, for those homophones that *are* detected, readers should show quicker error recovery than for the nonhomophone errors, with less time spent in regressive fixations after encountering the inconsistency.

The rationale for including an experiment without the nonhomophone control errors was as follows. We were concerned that the potentially easy-to-detect nonhomophone errors might draw attention to the manipulation and somehow interfere with natural reading; by excluding these error types in Experiment 1, we could observe any possible phonological influences uncontaminated by the other errors. For example, strong evidence for phonologically-mediated lexical access would be a null finding in Experiment 1; that is, no difference in the processing of homophone errors relative to their contextually compatible homophone counterparts. It is not that we predicted this finding. Previous homophone research has shown that readers are only sometimes seduced by homophone impostors (see also Patterson & Coltheart, 1987; Van Orden, 1987); consequently, the *mean* processing time for the contextually inconsistent homophones should be greater than for the contextually consistent ones. Nevertheless, we included this experiment to see whether we could replicate the pattern for homophone errors across texts that did and did not contain the nonhomophonic errors.

Not only did we include two kinds of errors (e.g., *vein*; *vine*) in order to examine the effects of homophony independent of orthographic similarity, but we also included two kinds of homophones (e.g., *vein/vain*; *for/four*) in order to examine the effects of orthographic similarity independent of homophony. As in the Daneman and Stainton (1991) study, half our homophone errors shared considerable spelling similarity with their contextually correct homophone mates because they were the same length as them (e.g., *vein* which is the same length as *vain*; *blew* which is the same length as *blue*); the other half were less similarly spelled because they were a different length than their contextually correct homophone mates (e.g., *for* which is shorter than *four*; *none* which is longer than *nun*). Daneman and Stainton (1991) were not able to demonstrate consistent differences in either detection rates or repair rates for the two kinds of homophone errors. However, it is possible that our on-line reading measure might expose processing differences that their proofreading measures were not sensitive enough to do.

METHOD
Subjects
The subjects were 50 University of Toronto undergraduates who were all fluent speakers of English; 20 participated in Experiment 1, and the other 30 participated in Experiment 2. Each subject was tested individually in a session lasting approximately 50 minutes.

Materials and Procedure
The experimental manipulation involved 48 homophonic words that appeared in the Russell Wood story; all 48 original words and their two corresponding error forms are listed in the Appendix. The Russell Wood text was selected by Daneman and Stainton (1991) because it was a fairly complex yet engaging piece of prose and because it contained a large number of homophonic words.[3] Of these, the 48 that were selected for the experimental manipulation met the following criteria: (a) They were distributed across the entire story with no more than 2 occurring in the same sentence; (b) each was

---

3 The Russell Wood text is an extensively edited version of a story entitled "Good Knight, Suite Prints" by Mary Ellen Slate that appeared in an issue of a magazine called *Games* (Chicago: Playboy Enterprises).

spelled with the same initial letter as its homophone mate (e.g., *s*teal-*s*teel but not *n*ight-*k*night); (c) readers were likely to know the meanings and spellings of both homophones in the pair; (d) in half of the cases, the homophone pairs were identical in length (e.g., *vain* and its substitute form *vein*; *bored* and its substitute form *board*); in the other half they were not (e.g., *four* and its substitute *for*; *nun* and its substitute *none*); in the case of the 24 different-length homophone pairs, 12 appeared as the longer of the two in the original story (e.g., *four*, which is one character longer than its mate, *for*), and 12 appeared as the shorter of the two (e.g., *nun*, which is shorter than its mate, *none*); and (e) a nonhomophonic control word could be created such that it shared the same consonant sounds as the correct word and its homophone mate, but differed only in the vowel sound (e.g., *vine* for *vain/vein* and *fir* for *four/for*). This consonant-same manipulation ensured that the homophonic and nonhomophonic error words had equal orthographic similarity to the correct word, and that the nonhomophonic control was as phonologically similar to the homophones as it could be.[4]

In Experiment 1, subjects read a version of the text in which 24 of the homophonic words appeared in their original contextually correct form, and 24 appeared as homophone errors. Counterbalancing of target words across the two word forms (correct word or homophone error) was accomplished by creating two versions of the Russell Wood story; a target word that appeared in its contextually correct form in the one version appeared as its homophone mate in the other. Each subject was randomly assigned to read one of the two error-filled versions.

In Experiment 2, subjects read a version of the text in which 16 of the target words appeared in their correct form, 16 as homophone errors, and 16 as nonhomophone errors matched for orthographic similarity to the correct word. Counterbalancing of target words was accomplished by creating three versions of the text; a target word appeared in a different form (correct word, homophone error, nonhomophone error) in each version. Each subject was randomly assigned to read one of the three error-filled versions.

---

4 To rule out alternative interpretations of a homophone effect, care must be taken in constructing and matching homophonic and nonhomophonic error words (Martin, 1982; Patterson & Coltheart, 1987). For example, most words that sound alike are also spelled alike; hence it is necessary to ensure that homophone errors are not going undetected because of spelling similarity. Recent investigations of the homophone effect in reading have taken great care to ensure that homophone and nonhomophone alternatives have equal orthographic similarity to the words in question (e.g., Coltheart et al., 1988; Treiman et al., 1983). Daneman and Stainton (1991) matched each homophone error with four kinds of nonhomophone control words in an attempt not only to control for orthographic similarity but phonological similarity and semantic similarity too. In this study we use Daneman and Stainton's "consonant-same" controls, the ones most orthographically and phonologically similar to the correct word.

The procedure was identical for both experiments. Subjects were told that they would be presented with a short story on successive screens of a computer monitor. They were instructed to read the story silently at their own pace, making sure that they understood it well enough to answer questions about its content later. The text was displayed on a VGA monochrome monitor in conventional upper and lower case black font with white background. In all, there were 20 screens of text, each containing no more than eight double-spaced lines of text. Subjects controlled the rate of presentation of each screen by pressing a start button to initiate presentation of the screen display and a stop button to remove it.

Subjects viewed the screen with their heads positioned in a chin rest (to minimize head movements). Viewing was binocular but only the position of the right eye was measured and recorded. Subjects' eye fixations were recorded by an Iscan (Model RK-416) pupil-center eye tracking system which calculated the x and y coordinates of the reader's point of regard every 16.7 milliseconds. A 386 IBM-compatible microcomputer was used to record the eye movement data as well as to display the stimulus text on the subject's monitor and on the experimenter's monitor. In addition to the stimulus text, the experimenter's monitor displayed the subject's gaze position in real time via an overlaid circular cursor measuring one degree of visual angle in diameter. This display enabled the experimenter to monitor the quality of the subject's calibration throughout the experiment so that a recalibration could be implemented during the course of the experiment if necessary. Prior to reading, a formal nine-point calibration procedure assured that the tracker was accurate to one-half degree of visual angle to either side of the reader's fixation center (an area subtended by approximately 1.1 characters of print). For an in-depth description of the calibration system and other features of our eye tracker's capabilities, see Stampe (in press).

Because Daneman and Stainton (1991) found a greater homophone interference effect if subjects were exposed to an intact error-free version of the Russell Wood text before proofreading, we included a familiarization manipulation in our experiments too. Before the eye-tracking portion of the experiment, half of the subjects were given an error-free print-out of the Russell Wood story and asked to read it silently for comprehension; the other half were not familiarized on the error-free version first.

After completing the eye-tracking phase, subjects were given two tests, one that tested their comprehension of the Russell Wood story, and a second that tested their knowledge of how the 48 homophone pairs were spelled. Comprehension of the story was tested with ten questions of the following sort: "Who was Harry 'Peewee' Farplotz?" "Why couldn't Russell Wood see him at first?" In Experiment 1, the mean comprehension score was 7.50 out of a possible 10 ($SD = 2.23$); in Experiment 2, the mean comprehension score was 7.77 ($SD = 2.05$); the reasonably high performance on the comprehension check indicated that readers had followed instructions to read for understanding. The purpose of the homophone spelling test was to ensure that any failure to detect a homophone error (e.g., *vein* substituted for *vain*) could not have been be attributed to lack of knowledge about how the two different words were spelled. Subjects were given 48 fill-in-the-blank items of the following sort: (a) The needle entered the _____ (*vain* or *vein*); (b) The _____ corners of the room had cobwebs (*four* or *for*). In each case, their task was to circle which of the two words belonged in the sentence. For half the items, the correct word was the homophone that appeared in the original story; for the other half, the correct word was the homophone substitution. A second version of the spelling test was created by constructing 48 new items, each of which required the opposite solution to its counterpart in the first version: (a) The _____ woman looked at herself in the mirror (*vain* or *vein*); (b) The boy went to look _____ his younger brother (*four* or *for*). Subjects were randomly assigned to complete one of the two versions of the spelling test. In Experiment 1, the mean score on the homophone spelling test was 47.75 out of a possible 48 ($SD = 0.55$); in Experiment 2 it was 47.80 ($SD = 0.48$); the almost perfect performance indicated that any failure to detect homophone errors could not have been attributed to lack of knowledge about how the 48 homophone word pairs were spelled.

Data Analysis

Three dependent measures were used to determine whether an incorrect word was detected and error recovery processes initiated. They were (a) first pass reading time on the target word; (b) total time on the target word; (c) total repair time. An example from three readers' eye fixation protocols will illustrate how the three dependent measures were computed. Figure 1 shows the three readers' eye fixations while reading the phrase *...a vain/vein/vine little man...* In each case, the sequence of fixations is denoted by the successive numbers below the word being fixated, with the duration of each fixation (in milliseconds) indicated in parentheses below the associated fixation.[5] The *first pass reading time on the target word* was simply the time spent fixating the target word when first encountered; for the reader who saw the *vain* version in Figure 1, first pass reading time was 266 msec; for the reader who saw *vein* it was 334 msec; and for the reader who saw *vine* it was 334 msec as well. *Total time on the target word* included the first pass time plus any subsequent time spent in regressive fixations to it; for the reader of *vain*, total time was still 266 msec because *vain* was not refixated; for the reader of *vein* it was 584 msec (the sum of fixations 1 and 3); and for the reader of *vine* it was 1051 msec (the sum of fixations 1, 3, 5, and 7). *Total*

5 The duration of consecutive fixations on a word have been summed together; see Carpenter & Daneman, 1981; Just & Carpenter, 1980.

CORRECT WORD

. . . a vain little man . . .

| 1 | 2 | 3 |
| (266) | (217) | (283) |

HOMOPHONE ERROR

. . . a vein little man . . .

| 1 | 2 |
| (334) | (217) |

| 3 | 4 |
| (250) | (317) |

NONHOMOPHONE ERROR

. . . a vine little man . . .

| 1 | 2 |
| (334) | (384) |

| 3 | 4 |
| (250) | (183) |

| 5 | 6 |
| (217) | (183) |

| 7 | 8 |
| (250) | (367) |

Fig. 1 Three readers' eye fixations while reading the phrase containing the target words vain, *vein*, and *vine*, respectively. In each case, the sequence of fixations is denoted by successive numbers below the fixated word, with the duration of each fixation (in msec) indicated in parentheses below the associated fixation. Note that readers paused longer on the errors *vein* and *vine* than on the contextually consistent *vain*. Note also that the first pass reading time for the same-length homophone error *vein* was no shorter than that for the nonhomophone control error *vine*; however, total repair time for *vein* was much shorter than for *vine*, indicating the typical homophone facilitation effect for same-length homophones.

repair time included all consecutive fixations, forward and regressive, from the first fixation on the target word up to but not including any fixations in advance of the target word once the reader proceeded in a forward direction (that is, did not regress back to the target word or to any word preceding the

---

CORRECT WORD

. . . only four feet high . . .

1	2	3	4
(150)	(150)	(183)	(217)

HOMOPHONE ERROR

. . . only for feet high . . .

1	2	3
(150)	(300)	(150)

4	5
(334)	(183)

6	7	8	9
(350)	(233)	(167)	(217)

NONHOMOPHONE ERROR

. . . only fir feet high . . .

1	2	3
(167)	(300)	(367)

4	5
(183)	(433)

6	7
(267)	(283)

Fig. 2 Three readers' eye fixations while reading the phrase containing the target words *four*, *for*, and *fir*, respectively. Note that readers paused longer on the errors *for* and *fir* than on the contextually correct *four*. Note also that the first pass reading times showed that the different-length homophone error *for* was initially as disruptive as the nonhomophone error *fir*; moreover, the total repair times for *for* and *fir* were equivalent, indicating the typical lack of a homophone facilitation effect for the different-length homophone errors.

target); for the reader of *vain* total repair time included only the 266 msec fixation on the target word because no regressions were initiated; for the reader of *vein*, total repair time was 801 msec (the sum of fixations $1 - 3$); for the reader of *vine*, it was 1801 msec (the sum of fixations $1 - 7$).[6] For

---

6 Note that fixations 2, 4, and 6 were included in the computation of total repair time even

additional illustrations of how the three dependent measures were computed, see Figure 2, which depicts the eye fixation protocols of three subjects reading the continuing phrase *...only four/for/fir feet high...*[7] The individual eye fixation protocols in Figures 1 and 2 also serve as prototypical examples of the results to be presented next; Figure 1 shows the typical pattern for same-length homophones (e.g., *vein/vain*); Figure 2 shows the pattern for different-length homophones (e.g., *for/four*).

Results and Discussion
EXPERIMENT 1
Table 1 demonstrates the effect of same-length and different-length homophone errors on the reader's eye fixation behaviour. The data have been averaged across the two familiarization conditions (familiarized and unfamiliarized) because preliminary analyses showed that familiarization did not influence eye fixation patterns or interact with any of the experimental manipulations (all $Fs < 1$). As seen in Table 1, all three dependent measures showed that readers took more time to process a homophone if it was inconsistent with the context, thereby providing strong evidence for the spontaneous detection of homophone errors during normal reading. The first dependent measure, *first pass time on the target word*, provided evidence that the detection was immediate, that is, that it occurred when the reader first encountered the error, rather than later on, say at the end of a clause or sentence (see also Carpenter & Daneman, 1981; Just & Carpenter, 1980). As seen in Table 1, readers spent on average 347 msec when first encountering a homophone error, as compared to only 299 msec fixating the correct word, a 48 msec difference that was significant across subjects, $F_1(1,19) = 18.13$, $MS_e = 2554$, $p < .001$, and across items, $F_2(1,46) = 8.46$, $MS_e = 6319$, $p < .01$, and presumably reflected the difficulty readers were experiencing integrating the inconsistent word (e.g., *board*) with the prior text (*Alone at his teller's cage, idle and board,...*).[8] There was no difference in the additional processing

though they were fixations in advance of the target word *vine*; this is because regressions to the target word were initiated after them; however, fixation 8 was not included in the calculation because the reader did not initiate a regression back to the target word or to any word(s) preceding it, but resumed reading in a forward direction.

7 For the *four* reader, first pass reading time, total time on the target word, and total repair time were all 150 msec, the duration of fixation 2. For the *for* reader, first pass reading time was 300 msec, the duration of fixation 2; total time on the target word was 716 msec, the sum of fixations 2, 5 and 7; total repair time was 1550 msec, the sum of fixations 2 – 7. For the *fir* reader, first pass reading time was 300 msec, the duration of fixation 2; total time on the target word was 750 msec, the sum of fixations 2, 4, and 6; total repair time was 1550 msec, the sum of fixations 2 – 6.

8 There was already evidence for inconsistency detection on the first fixation. An analysis that

time for homophone errors that were the same length as their homophone mates (e.g., *board* substituted for *bored*; *vein* substituted for *vain*) or a different length than their homophone mates (e.g., *none* substituted for *nun*; *for* substituted for *four*), (subject and item interaction Fs < 1), a finding which suggests that both error types were equally likely to be detected. However, there were differences across the two kinds of homophone errors for the dependent measures that included regressive fixations, a finding which suggests that the more similarly spelled same-length homophone errors may have been easier to repair. As seen in Table 1, *total time spent on the target word* was much greater for incorrect homophones (M = 554 msec) than for correct ones (M = 351 msec), $F_1(1,19)$ = 30.31, MS_e = 27264, $p < .001$, and $F_2(1,46)$ = 65.43, MS_e = 14901, $p < .001$; and *total repair time* was also much greater for incorrect homophones (M = 789 msec) than for correct homophones (M = 449 msec), $F_1(1,19)$ = 25.35, MS_e = 91263, $p < .001$, and $F_2(1,46)$ = 65.56, MS_e = 42435, $p < .001$. However, for both dependent measures the processing cost of an inconsistent word was significantly less for the same-length homophones than for the different-length homophones. As Table 1 shows, readers only spent an additional 148 msec processing a same-length homophone error than its contextually consistent homophone mate; in contrast, they spent an additional 258 msec processing a different-length homophone than its contextually consistent homophone mate, interaction $F_1(1,19)$ = 6.45, MS_e = 9471, $p < .03$, and interaction $F_2(1,46)$ = 4.60, MS_e = 14910, $p < .04$. Similarly, the processing cost associated with an incorrect homophone that was the same length as its correct homophone mate was 236 extra msec in total repair time; the processing cost associated with an incorrect homophone that was a different length than its correct mate was 443 extra msec of repair time, interaction $F_1(1,19)$ = 7.62, MS_e = 28077, $p < .02$, and interaction $F_2(1,46)$ = 5.66, MS_e = 42435, $p < .03$. Although we have no overt measure of whether or not readers successfully repaired the inconsistency, the shorter time spent reading and rereading phrases containing same-length homophone errors strongly suggests that readers could recover from these errors more easily.

Experiment 1 ruled out the possibility, albeit an unlikely one, that readers would fail to detect *all* "sound-okay" errors during normal silent reading for comprehension. Instead, Experiment 1 provided strong evidence that readers are able to detect at least some substantial proportion of the homophonic errors (e.g., *board* in *Alone at his teller's cage, idle and board,...*), a finding

included only the first fixation on the target word showed that readers spent on average 260 msec when first fixating a homophone error, as compared to only 241 msec when first fixating the correct word, a difference that was significant across subjects, $t(19)$ = 2.42, $p < .03$, and across items, $t(47)$ = 2.01, $p < .05$. Of course, the 19 msec difference is smaller than the 48 msec difference found for first pass reading time, presumably because the latter measure would be more likely to capture the later stages of processing (Inhoff, 1984) that are involved in detecting a semantic inconsistency between the target word and the prior text.

TABLE 1

Mean reading times (milliseconds) in Experiment 1

	Correct Word	Homophone Error
First Pass Time on Target Word		
Same Length	310	353
Different Length	288	341
Mean	299	347
Total Time on Target Word		
Same Length	357	505
Different Length	345	603
Mean	351	554
Total Repair Time		
Same Length	442	678
Different Length	456	899
Mean	449	789

which suggests that readers pay attention to orthographic codes in determining the meanings for words. However, phonological processes would still be implicated if homophonic errors (e.g., *board*) went unnoticed more frequently than orthographically matched nonhomophonic errors (e.g., *beard*), or if there was a difference in recovery time for the two kinds of errors. This possibility was tested directly in Experiment 2.

EXPERIMENT 2

Table 2 demonstrates the effect of same-length and different-length homophone and nonhomophone errors on the reader's eye fixation behaviour. As in Experiment 1, the data have been averaged across the two familiarization conditions (familiarized and unfamiliarized) because preliminary analyses showed that familiarization did not affect the eye fixation durations or interact with any of the other experimental manipulations (all $Fs < 1$).

The first point to note is that the homophone error data closely replicated those found in Experiment 1. All three dependent measures showed that readers spent longer processing homophone errors than their contextually correct homophone mates, and only in the case of the two dependent measures that included regressive fixations was there the additional finding that the processing cost of an inconsistent homophone was smaller if the homophone was the same length as its context correct mate. Not only was this pattern of results identical to that for Experiment 1, but the size of each effect was the same too. This was revealed in a series of across-experiment analyses of variance (ANOVAs) that included the data for homophone errors and correct words from all 20 subjects in Experiment 1 as well as all 30 subjects in Experiment 2; for each of the three dependent measures, the ANOVAs revealed no main effect of experiment, and no interactions between experiment and the

TABLE 2
Mean reading times (milliseconds) in Experiment 2

	Correct Word	Homophone Error	Nonhomophone Error
First Pass Time on Target Word			
Same Length	271	318	307
Different Length	284	327	334
Mean	278	323	321
Total Time on Target Word			
Same Length	305	450	554
Different Length	322	534	553
Mean	314	492	554
Total Repair Time			
Same Length	370	677	890
Different Length	399	911	909
Mean	385	794	900

other manipulations (all $ps > .18$). Thus, the mere presence of nonhomophonic errors in the Experiment 2 text did not affect the way readers processed the homophone errors.

When the eye fixation data for all three types of target words in Experiment 2 were considered, an interesting pattern emerged. In a nutshell, the data revealed that readers initially experienced as much difficulty when encountering a homophonic error as a nonhomophonic one; however, homophony facilitated the recovery process, at least for homophones that shared the same length as their context correct mates.

Initial detection: The *first pass reading times* revealed a significant main effect for type of target word, $F_1(2,58) = 7.38$, $MS_e = 5167$, $p < .001$, and $F_2(2,90) = 7.53$, $MS_e = 3611$, $p < .01$. A seen in Table 2, readers spent on average 278 msec when first encountering a contextually consistent word, whereas they spent an additional 45 msec on a homophone error and an additional 43 msec on a nonhomophone error. Pair-wise t-tests showed that the main effect could be attributed to the difference between processing a semantically consistent target word versus a semantically inconsistent one. Readers initially took longer to process a homophone error than its contextually correct homophone mate, a finding that was significant across subjects $t(29) = 3.40$, $p < .01$, and items, $t(47) = 3.47$, $p < .001$; similarly, they took longer to process a nonhomophone error than the contextually correct word, subject $t(29) = 3.77$, $p < .001$, and item $t(47) = 3.69$, $p < .001$. However, there was no difference in initial processing time for homophone versus nonhomophone errors, subject $t(29) = 0.02$, $p > .95$, item $t(47) = 0.07$, $p > .90$, a result which shows that homophonic errors were as disruptive as nonhomophonic errors, and suggests that homophonic errors were detected as easily.[9] The finding was consistent across same-length and different-length homophone errors (subject and item interaction $Fs < 1$), thus suggesting that both types of homophone errors were detected as easily as the nonhomophone errors. In contradistinction to the findings from proofreading responses (Daneman & Stainton, 1991), the results from our on-line reading measure provide no evidence for a homophone interference effect. We take this lack of phonological interference in the early detection of homophonic errors as evidence against those models that assume phonological sources of activation invariably precede word identification (Daneman & Stainton, 1991; Van Orden, 1987).

Error Recovery: When the post-detection error-recovery fixations were included in the analysis, a homophone effect finally emerged. In the interests of brevity, only the results for *total repair time* will be presented in detail because the other measure of recovery time, *total time on the target word*, produced the identical pattern of results. The ANOVA on total repair time revealed a significant main effect of type of target word, $F_1(2,58) = 40.23$, $MS_e = 110444$, $p < .001$, and $F_2(2,90) = 51.21$, $MS_e = 65603$, $p < .001$. In addition, the target word x length-similarity interaction was significant across subjects, $F_1(2,58) = 3.90$, $MS_e = 56947$, $p < .03$, and marginally significant across items, $F_2(2,90) = 2.42$, $MS_e = 65603$, $p < .10$. As was the case for the first pass data, pair-wise t-tests showed that readers took longer to process both kinds of semantically inconsistent target words relative to the semantically consistent ones. Readers took longer in repair time for a homophone error than for its contextually correct homophone mate: 307 msec longer if it was the same length as its mate, subject $t(29) = 5.05$, $p < .001$, item $t(23) = 6.39$, $p < .001$, and 512 msec longer if it was a different length, subject $t(29) = 5.60$, $p < .001$, item $t(23) = 7.38$, $p < .001$. Similarly, readers took longer in repair time for a nonhomophone error than for the contextually correct word: 520 msec for same-length pairs, subject $t(29) = 5.56$, $p < .001$, item $t(23) = 7.24$, $p < .001$, and 510 msec for the different-length pairs, subject $t(29) = 7.57$, $p < .001$, and item $t(23) = 5.86$, $p < .001$. However, unlike the first pass data which showed no difference in initial processing time for homophone versus nonhomophone errors, the repair time data revealed that readers spent significantly less time (213 msec) repairing a homophonic error than a

9 An analysis of the first fixation on the target word produced a similar, albeit smaller effect. There was no difference in first fixation duration for homophone errors ($M = 245$ msec) versus nonhomophone errors ($M = 247$ msec); subject $t(29) = 0.30$, $p > .75$, item $t(47) = 0.10$, $p > .90$. However, for both error types, duration of the first fixation was longer than for the correct target word ($M = 231$ msec); pairwise t-tests showed that the 14 msec difference between homophone errors and correct words was marginally significant, $t(29) = 1.85$, $p < .07$, item $t(47) = 1.88$, $p < .07$, whereas the 16 msec difference between nonhomophone errors and correct words was statistically significant, subject $t(29) = 2.29$, $p < .03$, item $t(47) = 2.32$, $p < .03$.

nonhomophonic one, but only if the homophone error was the same length as its context correct mate, subject $t(29) = 3.06$, $p < .01$, and item $t(23) = 2.69$, $p < .02$. Of course, we have no overt measure of whether our readers successfully resolved the inconsistency by recovering the correct word; however, the shorter time spent reading and rereading phrases containing same-length homophonic errors (e.g., *...idle and board*) relative to phrases containing the orthographically-matched nonhomophonic errors (e.g., *...idle and beard*), strongly implies that readers were able to recover from the "sound-okay" errors more easily. Because the two kinds of errors (e.g., *board, beard*) were equated for their orthographic similarity to the correct word (e.g., *bored*), but only the former (e.g., *board*) shared the same phonological representation as the correct word (e.g., *bored*), we attribute the facilitation effect to the availability of the shared phonology /bɔrd/ and its usefulness in providing readers with a route to recovering the correct alternative. Daneman and Stainton (1991) showed that homophony facilitated error recovery when readers were explicitly asked to repair the errors they encountered while reading. Our replication of this homophone facilitation effect shows that readers initiate error recovery heuristics spontaneously during normal reading for meaning. However, our study also revealed that homophony was not sufficient to facilitate error recovery; orthographic similarity was necessary too. As Table 2 shows, readers were no faster to recover from a different-length homophonic error (e.g., *Russell stopped and wade the situation...*) than they were to recover from the nonhomophonic control error (e.g., *Russell stopped and wide the situation*), subject $t(29) = 0.04$, $p > .95$, item $t(23) = 0.20$, $p > .80$; thus even though the homophonic error (*wade*) shared the same phonological representation (/weId/) as the correct alternative (*weighed*), the orthographic dissimilarity appeared to prevent readers from using the shared phonology to facilitate recovery. Because the present homophone facilitation was limited to the more similarly spelled same-length homophone errors (e.g., *board/bored* not *wade/weighed*), and because homophony did not interfere with the initial detection of either kind of homophonic error (*board* or *wade*), we believe our results call for a more restricted and delayed involvement of phonological processes than Daneman and Stainton (1991) have proposed.

Conclusions

The results from our on-line eye fixation data support a theory of word identification in which phonological sources of activation and influence are delayed relative to orthographic sources (see also, Coltheart, 1978; McCusker, et al., 1981), rather than a theory in which phonological codes play an early and/or dominant role (e.g., Daneman & Stainton, 1991; Pollatsek, Lesch, Morris, & Rayner, 1992; Van Orden, 1987; Van Orden, Pennington & Stone, 1990). Two aspects of our eye fixation data are inconsistent with theories that give phonological codes an early, important role in word identification and lexical access: the eye fixations that reflect the initial detection of homophonic errors, and the eye fixations that reflect subsequent attempts to repair the errors.

Contrary to Daneman and Stainton's (1991) results from their secondary proofreading task, we found no differences in the initial detection of homophonic errors (e.g., *board*) relative to nonhomophonic orthographic controls (e.g., *beard*), whether readers had been previously exposed to an error-free version of the text (e.g., *Alone at his teller's cage, idle and bored...*) or not. The complete lack of a homophone confusion effect is inconsistent with a model that assumes phonologically-mediated lexical access. If phonological sources of activation preceded lexical access, then readers should have had more difficulty detecting inconsistencies arising from homophonic errors (e.g., *board*) than from nonhomophonic ones (e.g., *beard*). The tendency would have been for *board*'s phonological representation, /bɔrd/, to have activated the false lexical entry *bored*, meaning "disinterested"; because *bored*'s meaning is compatible with the semantic and syntactic constraints of the sentence context, *Alone at his teller's cage, idle and...*, the inconsistency would have remained unnoticed. By contrast, the error word *beard*'s phonological representation /bɪrd/ would have activated the lexical entry *beard* whose meaning "facial hair" contradicts the semantic and syntactic constraints of the sentence, making the nonhomophonic inconsistency much easier to detect. By showing that homophony did not interfere with inconsistency detection, the present results strongly suggest that readers bypassed phonology, using the orthographic representations for *board* and *beard* as a direct route to their contextually inconsistent meanings, "plank" and "facial hair."

Whereas our initial detection data did not provide evidence for the early engagement of phonological processes in word identification, our post-detection data provided some evidence for the delayed involvement of phonology in the error recovery processes. Consistent with Daneman and Stainton's (1991) findings from the problem-solving version of their proofreading task, we found evidence for a homophone facilitation effect in the error recovery processes that are initiated after an inconsistency is detected. When explicitly instructed to repair the errors that they identified, Daneman and Stainton's (1991) subjects were better able to repair homophonic errors (e.g., *board*) than nonhomophonic controls (e.g., *beard*), presumably because they could use the shared phonology of homophonic pairs (e.g., /bɔrd/) to recover the correct alternative (e.g., *bored*). Our readers were not explicitly instructed to repair the errors; however, regressive eye fixations initiated spontaneously after detecting an inconsistency revealed that error recovery processes are an integral part of normal reading for understanding, and that readers can exploit shared phonological codes to repair inconsistencies arising from homophonic words. However, whether these phonological codes are activated automatically as a by-product of lexical access (McCutchen & Perfetti, 1982), or whether they are deliberately and consciously computed as part of a reader's repertoire of error-recovery heuristics (Carpenter & Daneman, 1981), we cannot say. All we can conclude from the present data is that the ability to exploit these phonological codes appears to be somewhat limited because the orthographic dissimilarity between our different-length homophone pairs (e.g., *wade/weighed; none/nun*) eliminated the homophone facilitation effect. Thus, even when it comes to post-inconsistency-detection recovery processes, readers appear to pay considerable attention to orthographic sources of information as they attempt to interpret and reinterpret inconsistent words.

This research was supported by grants from the Natural Sciences and Engineering Research Council of Canada to both authors. We thank Monica Davidson, Murray Stainton, and David Weinstock for their help in data collection, and Carrie Hill for her technical assistance. We also thank David Stampe for his indispensable role in developing our eye tracking system. Correspondence concerning this article should be addressed to Meredyth Daneman, Department of Psychology, Erindale College, University of Toronto, Mississauga, Ontario, Canada, L5L 1C6.

References

Baddeley, A.D. (1979). Working memory and reading. In P.A. Kolers, M.E. Wrolstad, & H. Bouma (Eds.) *Processing of visible language* (pp. 355-370). New York: Plenum Press.

Baddeley, A.D. (1986). *Working memory.* Oxford: Clarendon Press.

Baddeley, A.D., Eldridge, M., & Lewis, V. (1981). The role of subvocalization in reading. *Quarterly Journal of Experimental Psychology, 33A,* 439-454.

Besner, D. (1987). Phonology, lexical access in reading, and articulatory suppression: A critical review. *Quarterly Journal of Experimental Psychology, 39A,* 467-478.

Besner, D., & Davelaar, E. (1982). Basic processes in reading: Two phonological codes. *Canadian Journal of Psychology, 36,* 701-711.

Besner, D., Davies, J., & Daniels, S. (1981). Reading for meaning: The effects of concurrent articulation. *Quarterly Journal of Experimental Psychology, 33A,* 415-438.

Carpenter, P.A., & Daneman, M. (1981). Lexical retrieval and error recovery in reading: A model based on eye fixations. *Journal of Verbal Learning and Verbal Behavior, 20,* 137-160.

Coltheart, M. (1978). Lexical access in simple reading tasks. In G. Underwood (Ed.), *Strategies in information processing* (pp. 151-216). London: Academic Press.

Coltheart, M., Davelaar, E., Jonasson, J.T., & Besner, D. (1977). Access to the internal lexicon. In S. Dornic (Ed.), *Attention and Performance VI* (pp. 534-555). New York: Academic Press.

Coltheart, V., Avons, S.E., & Trollope, J. (1990). Articulatory suppression and phonological codes in reading for meaning. *Quarterly Journal of Experimental Psychology, 42A*, 375-399.

Coltheart, V., Laxon, V., Rickard, M., & Elton, C. (1988). Phonological recoding in reading for meaning by adults and children. *Journal of Experimental Psychology: Learning, Memory and Cognition, 14*, 387-397.

Daneman, M. (1988). How reading braille is both like and unlike reading print. *Memory & Cognition, 16*, 497-504.

Daneman, M., & Carpenter, P.A. (1983). Individual differences in integrating information between and within sentences. *Journal of Experimental Psychology: Learning, Memory, and Cognition, 9*, 561-584.

Daneman, M., & Newson, M. (1992). Assessing the importance of subvocalization during normal silent reading. *Reading and Writing: An Interdisciplinary Journal, 4*, 55-77.

Daneman, M., & Stainton, M. (1991). Phonological recoding in silent reading. *Journal of Experimental Psychology: Learning, Memory, and Cognition, 17*, 618-632.

Doctor, E.A., & Coltheart, M. (1980). Children's use of phonological encoding when reading for meaning. *Memory & Cognition, 8*, 195-209.

Edfelt, A.W. (1960). *Silent speech and silent reading.* Chicago: University Press.

Haber, R., & Schindler, R.M. (1981) Errors in proofreading: Evidence of syntactic control of letter processing? *Journal of Experimental Psychology: Human Perception and Performance, 7*, 573-579.

Healy, A.F. (1980). Proofreading errors in the word *the*: New evidence on reading units. *Journal of Experimental Psychology: Human Perception and Performance, 6*, 45-57.

Inhoff, A.W. (1984). Two stages of word processing during eye fixations in the reading of prose. *Journal of Verbal Learning and Verbal Behavior, 23*, 612-624.

Johnston, R.S., Rugg, M.D., & Scott, T. (1987). The influence of phonology on good and poor readers when reading for meaning. *Journal of Memory and Language, 26*, 57-68.

Just, M.A., & Carpenter, P.A. (1980). A theory of reading: From eye fixations to comprehension. *Psychological Review, 87*, 329-354.

Kintsch, W., & van Dijk, T.A. (1978). Toward a model of text comprehension and production. *Psychological Review, 85*, 363-394.

Kleiman, G.M. (1975). Speech recoding in reading. *Journal of Verbal Learning and Verbal Behavior, 14*, 323-329.

Levy, B.A. (1977). Reading: Speech and meaning processes. *Journal of Verbal Learning and Verbal Behavior, 16*, 623-628.

Levy, B.A. (1978). Speech processing during reading. In A.M. Lesgold, S.W. Pellegrino, S.W. Fokkema, & R. Glaser (Eds.), *Cognitive psychology and instruction* (pp. 123-151). New York: Plenum Press.

Levy, B.A. (1983). Proofreading familiar text: Constraints on visual processing. *Memory & Cognition, 11*, 1-12.

Lukatela, G., & Turvey, M.T. (1991). Phonological access of the lexicon: Evidence from associative priming with pseudohomophones. *Journal of Experimental Psychology: Human Perception and Performance, 17*, 951-966.

Martin, R.C. (1982). The pseudohomophone effect: The role of visual similarity in nonword decisions. *Quarterly Journal of Experimental Psychology, 34A*, 395-409.

McCusker, L.X., Hillinger, M.L., & Bias, R.G. (1981). Phonological recoding and reading. *Psychological Bulletin, 89*, 217-245.

McCutchen, D., & Perfetti, C.A. (1982). The visual tongue-twister effect: Phonological activation in silent reading. *Journal of Verbal Learning and Verbal Behavior, 21*, 672-687.

Meyer, D.E., Schvaneveldt, R.W., & Ruddy, M.G. (1974). Functions of graphemic and phonemic codes in visual word recognition. *Memory & Cognition, 2*, 309-321.

Patterson, K., & Coltheart, V. (1987). Phonological processes in reading: A tutorial review. In M. Coltheart (Ed.) *Attention and Performance XII: The psychology of reading* (pp. 421-447). Hove: Erlbaum.

Perfetti, C.A., Bell, L.C., & Delaney, S.M. (1988). Automatic (prelexical) phonetic activation in silent word reading: Evidence from backward masking. *Journal of Memory and Language, 27*, 59-70.

Pollatsek, A., Lesch, M., Morris, R.K., & Rayner, K. (1992). Phonological codes are used in integrating information across saccades in word identification and reading. *Journal of Experimental Psychology: Human Perception and Performance, 18*, 148-162.

Rubenstein, H., Lewis, S.S., & Rubenstein, M.A. (1971). Evidence for phonemic recoding in visual word recognition. *Journal of Verbal Learning and Verbal Behavior, 10*, 645-657.

Slowiaczek, M.L., & Clifton, C. (1980). Subvocalization and reading for meaning. *Journal of Verbal Learning and Verbal Behavior, 19*, 573-582.

Stampe, D. (in press). Heuristic filtering and reliable calibration methods for video-based pupil tracking systems. *Behavior Research Methods, Instruments, & Computers.*

Treiman, R., Freyd, J., & Baron, J. (1983). Phonological recoding and use of spelling-sound rules in reading of sentences. *Journal of Verbal Learning and Verbal Behavior, 22*, 682-700.

Van Orden, G.C. (1987). A ROWS is a ROSE: Spelling, sound and reading. *Memory & Cognition, 15*, 181-198.

Van Orden, G.C., Johnston, J.C., & Hale, B.L. (1988). Word identification in reading proceeds from spelling to sound to meaning. *Journal of Experimental Psychology: Learning, Memory, and Cognition, 14*, 371-386.

Van Orden, G. C., Pennington, B.F., & Stone, G.O. (1990). Word identification in reading and the promise of subsymbolic psycholinguistics. *Psychological Review, 97*, 488-522.

Waters, G. S., Caplan, D., & Hildebrandt, N. (1987). Working memory and written sentence comprehension. In M. Coltheart (Ed.) *Attention and Performance XII: The psychology of reading* (pp. 531-555). Hove: Erlbaum.

Waters, G.S., Komoda, M.K., & Arbuckle, T.Y. (1985). The effects of concurrent tasks on reading: Implications for phonological recoding. *Journal of Memory and Language, 24*, 27-45.

Appendix
TARGET WORDS USED IN EXPERIMENTS 1 AND 2

Correct Word	Homophone Error	Nonhomophone Error
Same Length		
beat	beet	boat
blue	blew	blow
bored	board	beard
break	brake	broke
daze	days	dyes
feat	feet	foot
graze	grays	grows
grown	groan	grain
hair	hare	hire
hear	here	hour
loan	lone	lean
meet	meat	moat
maid	made	mode
pail	pale	peal
piece	peace	pace
real	reel	rule
rode	road	rude
rows	rose	rise
see	sea	sow
soul	sole	seal
steal	steel	stale
tide	tied	toad
weak	week	wake
vain	vein	vine
Different Length		
bolder	boulder	builder
bread	bred	breed
brows	browse	bruise

Appendix (continued)

Correct Word	Homophone Error	Nonhomophone Error
flower	flour	flier
four	for	fir
guessed	guest	gust
guys	guise	goose
heard	herd	hard
hoarse	horse	hearse
mined	mind	mend
nun	none	noon
paws	pause	pews
rays	raise	ruse
sew	so	say
side	sighed	said
sighs	size	sows
sum	some	seem
tact	tacked	tucked
threw	through	throw
too	to	tee
we	wee	woe
weighed	wade	wide
wined	whined	waned
wore	war	wire

4 The Use of Information Below Fixation in Reading and in Visual Search

ALEXANDER POLLATSEK, GARY E. RANEY,
LINDA LAGASSE, and KEITH RAYNER
University of Massachusetts

Abstract   Two experiments examined whether or not readers obtain useful information from below the currently fixated line. In Experiment 1, subjects read passages of text and the availability of visual information below the line fixated was manipulated using a variant of the moving window technique. Reading was no slower when there was no letter information below the fixated line than when there was full information below the fixated line. However, a condition which made the strings of letters below the fixated line less "wordlike" caused reading to be slowed down by about 6% relative to the other conditions. In Experiment 2, subjects searched for a target word through passages of text. Subjects occasionally detected targets below the line they were fixating; however, there was no clear evidence that the availability of information below the line made search more efficient. It thus appears that in reading (or in other tasks where words are being identified and the eyes move horizontally along a line of text), little visual information is extracted below the line of text fixated.

Résumé   À l'aide de deux expériences, nous avons examiné si les lecteurs extraient ou non des renseignements utiles de dessous la ligne qu'ils fixent en lisant. Dans l'expérience 1, les sujets ont lu des passages d'un texte et l'information visuelle disponible dessous la ligne fixée était manipulée au moyen d'une variante de la technique de la fenêtre mobile. Le temps de lecture n'était pas plus long lorsqu'il n'y avait aucune lettre sous la ligne fixée que lorsque toutes les informations y apparaissaient. Cependant, quand les séries de lettres apparaissant sous la ligne fixée ressemblaient moins à des mots, le temps de lecture était ralenti d'environ 6 % par rapport aux autres conditions. Dans l'expérience 2, les sujets devaient repérer un mot cible dans les passages qui leur étaient présentés. Ils repéraient à l'occasion les mots cibles sous la ligne qu'ils fixaient, mais rien ne démontre clairement à l'évidence que les renseignements se trouvant sous la ligne fixée rendaient la recherche plus efficiente. Il semble donc que très peu d'informations visuelles sont extraites de dessous la ligne fixée durant la lecture (ou durant toutes autres tâches où des mots sont identifiés et où le regard est dirigé horizontalement le long d'une ligne de texte).

An important question in reading research is the size and shape of the *perceptual span*: the region on the printed page from which information can be extracted on a single fixation. Perhaps the best tool for studying the perceptual span is the *moving window* technique developed by McConkie and Rayner (1975). In a moving window experiment, text is read from a video display in which a "window" of normal text is presented around the subject's fixation point (see Figure 1). Outside this window, the text is altered in some way (e.g., all the letters outside the window are replaced by xs). Each time the subject moves his or her eyes to another fixation point, a new window of normal text is presented around the new fixation point and the text outside the new window is mutilated.

The logic of the method is as follows. If reading is perfectly normal (i.e., both speed and comprehension are unimpaired) in a given window condition, then one can infer that the reader was extracting no useful information from beyond the window region (see Figure 1a and 1b). For adult readers, a window region extending from 4 letter positions to the left of fixation to about 14 or 15 letter positions to the right of fixation (Figure 1c) is sufficient to ensure both normal reading speed and comprehension. Hence, one can infer that no useful information from a line of text is extracted beyond this region (McConkie & Rayner, 1976; Rayner, Inhoff, Morrison, Slowiaczek & Bertera, 1981; Rayner, Well & Pollatsek, 1980). When the window region is further restricted, reading speed (but not comprehension) is affected. For example, when the window is restricted so that only the fixated word is visible (Figure 1e), reading speed declines to about 60% of what it would be if there was no window present (Rayner, Well, Pollatsek & Bertera, 1982).

A finding relevant to our current concerns is that the perceptual span is asymmetric. As noted above, reading rate is normal (for readers of English) when the window extends from 4 characters to the left of fixation of the window to about 14 characters to the right; in contrast, reading rate is slowed markedly when the window extends from 14 characters to the left of fixation to 4 characters to the right of fixation, as illustrated in Figure 1d (McConkie & Rayner, 1976; Rayner et al., 1980). Several experiments indicate that this rightward asymmetry is almost certainly due to the rightward movement of the eyes across the printed page and to likely shifts of covert attention related to these movements (Wurtz, Goldberg & Robinson, 1982). First, for Hebrew readers (who read from right to left), the perceptual span is asymmetric in the opposite direction, so that a window restricted to four characters to the left of fixation slows down reading whereas a window restricted to four characters to the right of fixation does not (Pollatsek, Bolozky, Well & Rayner, 1981); in contrast, the perceptual span of these same subjects is similar to that of native-speaking English readers when they read English. Second, readers of English obtain information to the left of the fixated word when the order of the words on a line of text is from right to left (Inhoff, Pollatsek, Posner, &

```
A.    much higher than those found in less developed countries


                       *
B.    xxxh higher than those found in xxxx xxxxxxxxx xxxxxxxxx
                       *
      xxxx xxxxxr than those found in less dexxxxxxx xxxxxxxxx
                              *
      xxxx xxxxxr xxxx xxxse found in less developed coxxxxxxx


                              *
C.    xxxx xxxxxx xxxx xxxse found in less dexxxxxxx xxxxxxxxx


                       *
D.    xxxx xxxxxr than those found xx xxxx xxxxxxxxx xxxxxxxxx


                       *
E.    xxxx xxxxxx xxxx xxxxx found xx xxxx xxxxxxxxx xxxxxxxxx
```

Fig. 1 Illustrations of conditions in moving window experiments. The top line (A) represents a line of normal text. The next three lines (B) illustrate what could occur on three successive fixations when there is a window extending 14 characters to the left and 14 characters to the right of fixation (represented by an asterisk above the fixated letter). In these circumstances, reading is perfectly normal (see text). The three lines below illustrate three other possible window conditions when the reader fixates the letter *o* in *found*. In the first (C), the window extends 4 character spaces to the left and 14 character spaces to the right of fixation, while in the second (D), the window extends 14 character spaces to the left and 4 character spaces to the right of fixation. Reading is normal in the former condition while it is slowed down in the latter, illustrating the asymmetry of the perceptual span (see text). The last line (E) indicates a window condition where the window is defined by word boundaries (in this case, only the fixated word is visible). Reading in this condition is slower than normal reading, indicating that readers extract more information than the fixated word.

Rayner, 1989).

The above findings indicate that the reason the perceptual span extends such a small distance to the left of fixation for English readers is because the reader is no longer attending to that portion of the text. In contrast, the right boundary of the perceptual span appears to be due to acuity limitations. Two pieces of evidence support this claim. First, when readers are presented with a foveal mask (the inverse of a window) which covers the central seven letters around fixation, reading is quite difficult; if the mask extends 6 characters on either side of fixation, readers can extract little information about the text (Rayner & Bertera, 1979; Rayner et al., 1981). Second, when a single word (with each character subtending 1/3 of a degree of visual angle horizontally) is presented with its nearest letter 5 degrees from fixation, no information is extracted that is of value in identifying the word when later fixated (Rayner,

McConkie & Ehrlich, 1978). That is, readers do not appear to be extracting information from words further than 15 character spaces or 5 degrees in the horizontal direction even when the information beyond that point is the only useful information in the display and the subject is aware that no other useful information is present[1].

None of these experiments, however, manipulated text other than on the line being read. Hence it is still unknown whether the perceptual span extends vertically beyond the currently fixated line when people read passages of normal text. The above discussion indicates, however, that the vertical limits of the perceptual span in reading are likely to be attentional. First, consider that acuity limitations are not likely to prevent the extraction of a large amount of visual information above or below the line. For example, if pica text is single-spaced, then 15 characters subtend the same angle as 9 lines of text. Even allowing for the fact that acuity falls off somewhat faster in the vertical direction than in the horizontal direction, this indicates that quite a bit of visual information above and below the line currently fixated is potentially available to the reader. However, the asymmetry of the perceptual span in the horizontal direction indicates that information not lying in the direction of the planned eye movement – and possibly the recipient of covert attention – may be irrelevant to the reading process.

We should note that three other studies (Willows & MacKinnon, 1973; Inhoff & Briihl, 1991; Inhoff & Topolski, 1992) probed whether readers extracted information on lines of text other than the one being read by presenting readers with a line of text to be read and a line below the text which was to be ignored. Willows and MacKinnon provided evidence that readers were obtaining semantic information about the line of text that was to be ignored. However, Inhoff and Briihl, in a better controlled study in which eye movements were recorded, concluded that such semantic information was extracted only when subjects moved their eyes to the "unattended" line. In a subsequent study, Inhoff and Topolski examined fixation time on a target word when either a semantically related or unrelated word was directly below the target word. They likewise found no evidence that information below the line of text was used to process semantically related target words. While these studies are interesting, none of them may be relevant to the question of whether readers extract information below the fixated line of text in normal reading, because readers given such selective attention instructions may not be able to suppress a desire to see what is on the forbidden line of text. In

---

1 Most of the experiments described here used three characters per degree, so that a window of 15 characters is equal to 5 degrees of visual angle. However, for reading experiments, character spaces appears to be the better metric as, for example, the size of forward saccades appears to be relatively constant (in terms of character spaces) even when the visual angle is changed by a factor of two (Morrison & Rayner, 1981).

1. Normal

```
  these are beetles.  In fact, there are more species of
* beetles in the world than any other animal.  Beetles live
  throughout most of the world.  Most any type of organic
  matter may serve as food.  Some beetles eat plants, while
```

2. X

```
  these are beetles.  In fact, there are more species of
* beetles in the world than any other animal.  Beetles live
  xxxxxxxxxx xxxx xx xxx xxxxx.  Xxxx xxx xxxx xx xxxxxxx
  xxxxxx xxx xxxxx xx xxxx.  Xxxx xxxxxxx xxx xxxxxx, xxxxx
```

3. Similar Letter

```
  these are beetles.  In fact, there are more species of
* beetles in the world than any other animal.  Beetles live
  fkievykevf neaf et fkc ueihb.  Neaf smj fjqc et eiysmro
  nsffci nsj aciwc sa teeb.  Zenc dccfhca csf qhsmfa, ukrhc
```

4. Dissimilar Letter

```
  these are beetles.  In fact, there are more species of
* beetles in the world than any other animal.  Beetles live
  naqfkhafkn bfln fy nat pfqco.  Sfln ljr nrvt fy fqhljpk
  blnntq blr ltqtt ll yffo.  Mfbt gttnctl tln vcljnl, papct
```

5. Text Change

```
  these are beetles.  In fact, there are more species of
* beetles in the world than any other animal.  Beetles live
  that it was easier to wash clothes at this spot than at
  others.  The combination of fats or tallow and the sodium
```

Fig. 2 Illustrations of the window conditions in Experiment 1. In all cases, the text is what would be seen on lines 3 through 6 of a 15 line passage of text when the subject was reading line 4 (the line of text marked with an asterisk in the illustration).

contrast, the line below the fixated line in normal text will be fixated shortly and may not have the same seductive power.

Experiment 1

The key question addressed in Experiment 1 was whether readers extract useful information from below the line they are reading, and if they do, what kind of information is being extracted. The technique used to determine whether information is extracted was an extension of the moving window paradigm described above in which the availability of information below the line of text being read was manipulated. In some conditions, the window of normal text extended from the top of the passage to the line currently fixated, while in other conditions, the entire passage was visible (see Figure 2). This manipulation is thus a test of whether information below the currently fixated line has any effect on the reading process. We did not test whether subjects used information above the currently fixated line, since the asymmetry of the perceptual span indicated that it was unlikely that the availability of text already read would be relevant.

To address the issue of the kinds of information extracted below the line, we manipulated the type of information available outside the window region, a technique also employed in many of the moving window experiments discussed above (e.g., McConkie & Rayner, 1975; Rayner et al., 1982). In the *normal text condition*, the 15 line passage was continuously visible. In the *x* condition, all letters below the currently fixated line (henceforth *line n*) were replaced by xs. The comparison between this condition and the normal text condition allows us to assess whether readers extract any significant information below line *n*. In two other conditions, each letter below line *n* was replaced by another unique letter. In the *similar letter* condition, each letter was replaced by the letter judged most similar to it, while in the *dissimilar letter* condition, each letter was replaced by the letter judged most dissimilar to it[2]. The comparison of these conditions allowed us to assess whether subjects were extracting letter information from below line *n*, and if so, whether that information was facilitating or inhibiting. (The logic of this comparison will be elaborated later.) In the *text change* condition, the text below line *n* was coherent text from a different passage. The comparison between this condition and the normal text condition allowed us to assess whether subjects were processing the meaning of the text below the line currently fixated.

METHOD

Subjects

Fifteen members of the University of Massachusetts community participated in the experiment. They were all native English speakers and had normal vision. They were paid for their participation.

Stimuli and design

The stimuli were 15 line single-spaced paragraphs of text, presented on a Cathode Ray Tube (CRT) display. Each line was at most 60 character spaces. The 20 paragraphs used in the experment were self-contained passages that were a maximum of 150 words. The passages were moderately difficult to read, containing factual information that was probed by a true/false comprehension question that followed each paragraph.

---

2 The selection of most similar and most dissimilar letters for lower case letters comes from a study by Bouma (1971). As there were no similar norms for upper case letters, we selected the most similar and most dissimilar upper case letters intuitively. Since upper case letters occur rarely in normal text, we felt that the difference we observed between the letters we selected and those obtained after careful norming would be negligible.

As indicated above, there were five window conditions (see Figure 2). In the *normal text* condition, the entire passage was visible throughout the trial. In the other four conditions, the text on the line currently fixated and all text above the line was unchanged; however, all the text below the currently fixated line was altered. In the *X* condition, all the letters were changed to Xs. In the *similar letter* condition, each letter was replaced by the letter judged most visually similar, while in the *dissimilar letter* condition, each letter was replaced by the letter judged most visually dissimilar. In all three of these conditions, the spaces between words were preserved (see Figure 2). In the *text change* condition, the stimulus below the currently fixated line was the text from another of the passages used in the experiment[3]. Thus, for example, when reading line 6 of passage 3, the subject was exposed to lines 1-6 of passage 3 and lines 7-15 of passage 18. Also, as indicated in Figure 2, the spaces between words were generally in different locations in the real text and in the changed text.

Each subject saw all 5 window conditions in a counterbalanced design. The 20 paragraphs were arranged as 10 blocks of 2 paragraphs each. The conditions were presented across the 10 blocks in an ABCDEEDCBA design so that the average serial position of each condition was the same for each subject. In addition, the assignment of blocks to conditions was counterbalanced across subjects, using 5 different orders of conditions. The passages always appeared in the same order. Hence, differences among the passages were completely confounded with the serial order of the passages; however, both these factors were counterbalanced across window conditions.

Apparatus and procedure

The eye movement recording system was a Stanford Research Institute Generation V Dual Purkinje Eyetracker interfaced to a VAX 11-730 computer and a Megatek Whizzard vector-graphics display with a P-31 phosphor. The eye-tracker has a temporal resolution of 1 ms and a spatial resolution of 10 minutes of arc; the output was sampled by the computer every millisecond. Viewing was binocular, but only the position of the right eye was measured.

The subjects viewed the screen with their heads held fixed by means of a bite bar at a distance of 91 cm from the screen. At this distance, individual characters subtended .25 deg visual angle in the horizontal direction and no more than .4 deg visual angle in the vertical direction. For the single-spaced text, the vertical distance between the bottoms of two successive lines was .5 deg. At the beginning of the experiment, the eye tracking system was calibrat-

---

3 When reading passage number X, the altered text was taken from passage number 21-X. As in the example below, the altered text for passage 3 was the text from passage number 18 (and vice versa). For passage number 1, the altered text was passage 20; for passage 2, the altered text was passage 19, etc.

ed for the subject. At the beginning of each trial, a "check calibration" pattern came on with 3 fixed target crosses and a calibration cross that moved in synchrony with the eye. If, while fixating one of the target crosses, there was a discrepancy between the calibration cross and the fixed cross, the subject was recalibrated.

A trial consisted of the following events. First, the "check calibration" pattern came on. If the calibration was deemed to be good, the experimenter instructed the subject to fixate a cross two character positions to the left of where the first word of the paragraph would appear. When the subject fixated that location, the experimenter pushed a button to display the text. The subject then read through the text and pushed a button when he or she was done. A true/false comprehension question then appeared on the screen, which the subject responded to with a manual response.

The goal of the display change algorithm was to change the text each time the subject moved from one line to the next (as in Figure 2) and to accomplish that change during the "return sweep" saccade. The temporal aspects posed no problem, since the plotter accomplished a display change within about 5 ms of a line change being detected, and these large saccades typically take over 50 ms. However, the accuracy of the computation of the vertical coordinate of the screen was not sufficient with single-spaced text to allow the display change to be made contingent on the vertical coordinate. That is, since there was about a 5% error rate in the line being fixated, this would cause the wrong window to be displayed 5% of the time and severely compromise the conclusions of the experiment. One possible solution was to double space the text; however, we wanted the text below the line to be close to the line being read in order to enhance the possibility that such information was used.

The solution adopted was to leave the text single-spaced, but to make display changes contingent on the horizontal position of the eyes (although the vertical position was monitored). The algorithm was as follows. A flag was set when the reader was to the right of the 43rd character on a line. Once the flag was set, a "line change" was detected once the eyes moved to the left of the 14th character on a line. That is, line changes were computed from return sweeps and there was always well over 5 ms between the crossing of the 14th character and the beginning of the first fixation on the next line. There was no provision either for large regressions or large skips forward; once a reader reached line n, the only display change possible was to make line $n+1$ visible. To minimize the chances that line changes would be spuriously detected, and to maximize chances that the window conditions applied to the line actually being read, readers were encouraged to keep reading through the text and not make any large regressions.

Before reading the 20 experimental passages, subjects read 2 practice passages. The first was with no window and the second was with an X window. All 22 passages were read in a single 60 minute session.

RESULTS AND DISCUSSION

The primary dependent variable was mean reading time per line. This was measured from the time that one return sweep was detected until the time that the next line sweep was detected. Time on the fifteenth line of each passage was not included in this calculation because the last line was of variable length and there was no line of text below it. For about 15% of the passages, extra return sweeps were detected by the computer. These were due either to a large regressive eye movement that was not a return sweep, a brief "track loss" by the eye movement recording system, or a return to a prior line. In addition, subjects answered the comprehension question incorrectly about 15% of the time. The percent of "bad" trials – trials on which at least one of these two events occurred – is listed by condition in Table 1. These passages were not included in the data analyses discussed below, although the basic pattern of data was the same when these passages were included.

There was a lower error rate on the comprehension question in the normal text condition than in the other window conditions. This suggests either that readers were extracting useful information below the line or that the unnatural text below the line in the other conditions was distracting. However, this difference was not reliable, $F(4,40) = 1.58$, $MS_e = .45$, $p = .20$. Moreover, the percentage of "bad trials" in the normal text condition was at least as high as in the other conditions. This suggests that (for some reason) subjects in this condition may have traded off errors by making large regressions (contrary to instructions).

As can be seen in the top line of Table 1, there were only modest differences among the five window conditions. To enhance the power of the analyses, the 15 subjects were viewed as being in 5 groups (the 5 different counterbalancing conditions); this allowed us to remove differences in difficulty among the passages from the error term (thus the error term in all of the analyses below has df equal to 10 times the numerator df). In this analysis, the 5 window conditions differed significantly, $F(4,40) = 5.01$, $MS_e = 20,739$, $p < .005$. More important are planned comparisons between some of the conditions. First consider the comparison between the X and normal text conditions. This is probably the simplest comparison, since there was no information about the text below line n in the X condition except for the positions of the spaces between words. In fact, subjects were 62 ms per line faster in the X condition than in the normal text condition, although the difference was far from significant, $t(10) = 1.13$, $p > .20$. This indicates either: (a) that no useful information (other than the position of word boundaries) is extracted from below the line during normal reading; or (b) that both facilitating and interfering information are extracted and the effects of the two are approximately equal.

An examination of the other conditions, however, suggests that the former conclusion is the more likely. First consider the text change condition. The

TABLE 1
Reading Measures as a Function of Window Condition

	Window Condition				
	x	Similar Letters	Dissimilar Letters	Text Change	Normal (No Window)
Reading Measure					
Mean reading time per line	2785	2869	3000	2849	2827
Number of forward fixations per passage	100	102	103	101	102
Mean forward fixation duration	298	298	304	301	299
Mean forward saccade length	9.0	8.8	8.7	8.7	8.9
Number of regressive fixations per passage	13	15	16	14	15
Mean regressive fixation duration	264	267	273	278	261
Mean regressive saccade length	6.2	4.9	5.8	5.5	5.6
Return sweep time per line	91	90	97	84	82
Percent of "bad trials"[a]	23%	37%	28%	28%	37%
Percent errors on comprehension questions	13%	20%	11%	15%	5%

a The "bad trials" include the trials in which errors were made on the comprehension question as well as other trials (see text).

reading times in this condition were only 22 ms per line more than in the normal reading condition. In the text change condition, extraction of word and letter information below the line would be inappropriate and should slow reading down; moreover, since the positions of the spaces are altered, this should also slow reading time if extraction of this space information was functional. Thus, it appears that essentially no useful information is extracted below the line in reading. In the similar letter condition, the shape of both the letters and the words of the text is preserved below the line (as well as the position of letters). If either the position of the spaces between words below the line or partial information about the visual characteristics of the words is of value in normal reading, one would expect reading in the similar letter condition to be faster than in the text change condition. The fact that readers were 20 ms per line slower in the similar letter condition than in the text change condition again indicates that no useful information is extracted below the line.

The data from the above four conditions in fact seem to indicate that the information below the fixated line is completely irrelevant to the reading process. However, readers in the dissimilar letter condition were over 100 ms per line slower than in any of the other four conditions, and all four pairwise contrasts between the dissimilar letter condition and the other conditions were significant ($ps < .01$). This indicates that some information below the line can interfere with the reading process. It is less clear, however, what this information is and how it operates. For example, one reason why the dissimilar letter condition might be slower is that the strings made up of dissimilar letters may be similar to inappropriate words, and the identification of these words slows down the reading process. This is not plausible, however, since the text change condition should produce even more frequent identification of inappropriate words than the dissimilar letter condition.

The most satisfactory explanation seems to be that the altered text with the dissimilar letters was visually anomalous and was, for some reason, distracting to the reader. One corroborating piece of evidence for this hypothesis was that subjects were usually aware that the material below the line was not normal text in the dissimilar letter condition, whereas they were usually unaware that there was anything but normal text on the screen in both the similar letter and text change conditions. Moreover, most of the subjects commented that the information below the line "looked funny" in the dissimilar letter condition. They were also aware that the material below the line was not normal text in the X condition as well. However, since the Xs were uniform, they apparently could be tuned out, while for some reason, the varying shapes of the letter strings in the dissimilar letter condition were distracting[4].

The dissimilar letter condition thus indicates that some visual information is extracted in reading from below the currently fixated line in some circumstances. However, this information is distracting, and the rest of the data indicate that the interference observed in the dissimilar letter condition is probably irrelevant to the normal reading process, since the interference is observed only when the information below the line does not look like normal text.

The lack of an effect can always be due, as indicated earlier, to offsetting facilitating and interfering effects. To test further for this possibility, we examined the eye movement records in more detail (see Table 1). First, consider the measures relating to forward fixations, which account for most of the time spent on the task. The pattern for both number of forward

4 We wondered whether the distraction effect of the dissimilar letters was largely an effect that occurred at the beginning of a passage before the subject was fully engaged in the reading task. In a separate analysis on reading time where position in the passage was made an explicit variable (adjacent pairs of lines were the units), there was a hint of an interaction between window condition and position, $F(24,336) = 1.54$, $p < .10$. However, the pattern was not consistent, and if anything, the difference between the different letter conditions and the others tended to get larger as the subjects progressed through a passage.

fixations and mean forward fixation duration[5] roughly mirror those for reading time, with the dissimilar letter condition being the slowest. However, the differences among conditions for the two measures were quite small and non-significant, $F(4,40) = 2.34, MS_e = 10, p > .10$, and $F(4,40) = 1.48 \, p > .20$, $MS_e = 82$, respectively. The mean saccade length differences were also small and not all reliable, $F < 1$.

The measures from regressions were obviously based on fewer data points. However, the effects were similar to those for forward saccades. Thus, readers in the dissimilar letter condition had the most regressive fixations, $F(4,40) = 2.40$, $MS_e = 6.9$, $p < .10$. The pattern for mean regressive fixation duration (i.e., mean duration of fixations after regressions) was a bit different, with the text change condition being the longest and the dissimilar letter condition being second longest, $F(4,40) = 2.14$, $MS_e = 2.14$, $p < .10$. The pattern was also a bit different for mean regressive saccade length, with the X condition having the longest regressive saccades, $F(4,40) = 2.81, MS_e = 1.9, p < .05$. The differences among return sweep times were not at all reliable, $F < 1$.

The individual measures thus indicate, for the most part, that the modest differences in reading time per line between the different letter condition and the other four conditions were due to a cumulation of effects from many of the other measures rather than to the effect of a single measure. The pattern among the individual measures bounced around a bit, although there was nothing in the pattern that was particularly interpretable. For example, fixations in the text change condition were a bit longer than the remaining three conditions (although only 3 ms longer on average for forward fixations), but this was compensated for by somewhat longer forward saccades and somewhat shorter regressive saccades. Given the marginal significance and small size of most of these effects, and given that much of the variability is accounted for by the different letter conditions being worse than the other four conditions, there is certainly no compelling evidence that the equality in reading rate in the other conditions is the result of cancelling facilitative and inhibitory effects of extracting information below the line of text being fixated.

Finally, since all of the data analyses described above relied on fairly "global" measures, a more "local" analysis was undertaken. In this analysis, we picked four words per passage that were judged to be central to the passage. For example, in a passage about beer production, the four topical words chosen were *beer*, *brewery*, *poured*, and *alcohol*. If one of the topical words occurred more than once in the passage, the first occurrence was used. We then computed the first fixation duration (which is the duration of the

---

5 The mean fixation duration values shown in Table 1 are a bit longer than we often obtain in studies in our lab. We suspect that this is due to individual differences and the fact that subjects were reading fairly carefully since the passages and the display monitor have both been used in other experiments which have yielded shorter average fixation durations.

initial fixation on a word) and gaze duration (which is the sum of all fixations on a word prior to moving off of that word) on those words as a function of experimental condition. Our rationale was that if readers were able to obtain useful information below the fixated line then there may be shorter fixations on these words that were topically related to the passage in the normal condition, compared to the other conditions. However, the data analyses showed no indication that this happened. There was little difference in first fixation durations (mean = 292 ms) as a function of what was below the line, $F < 1$; the pattern in the gaze duration means was identical to the overall mean fixation durations shown in Table 1, but statistically there was no difference among the means, $F(4,56) = 1.12, p > .05$. This local analysis was, therefore, quite consistent with the more global analyses reported above.

To summarize, the overall finding was that there was little effect of information below the line on the reading process. Indeed, since readers were non-significantly faster in the X condition than in the normal text condition, it appears that the material below the line is, if anything, a slight hindrance to the reading process. However, all differences between conditions were small, with the difference between the fastest (X) and slowest (dissimilar letter) conditions representing a difference of about 6% or about 20 words per minute. Excluding the dissimilar letter condition, the differences between the other conditions represent a maximum difference of about 6 words per minute. Thus, it appears that the attentional demands of normal silent reading involve the gating of information from outside the line of text being read. The small differences among our conditions leave open the possibility that this gating may not be perfect and that some information may affect the reading process on some fixations, especially if the stimuli below the line look unusual and non-wordlike.

Experiment 2

Experiment 1 leaves open the question of what task demands of the reading process cause the exclusion of information below the current line of text. Two non-exclusive classes of explanation seem the most plausible. First, reading involves the process of fixating words, identifying them, and then fixating another word to be identified on the same line (except during return sweeps). Perhaps this is sufficient and any process that involves successive rapid identification of words arranged in a horizontal line would cause the information outside the line of words to be ignored. Another possibility is that there is something special about the reading process. That is, reading not only involves the identification of words, but the integration of these meanings into syntactic structures and some sort of coherent discourse structure (Rayner & Pollatsek, 1989). Thus, it could be that the text integration processes cause attention to be fixed on the words that are fixated (or the next word or two to the right) because these integration processes would break down if the sequencing of the input was not clear (e.g., "boy hits girl" vs. "girl hits boy"). It also could be that the global attentional demands of these integration processes cause a tunnelling of visual attention.

To summarize, the virtual nonuse of information below the line in reading observed in Experiment 1 could be a specific feature of the reading process, or it could be a general feature of any task in which the subject is asked to identify words in a horizontal sequence. To test which of these is the case, in Experiment 2 we had subjects perform a visual search task through passages of text with the pattern of eye movements and the sequence of word identification mimicking those of silent reading. Specifically, the subjects' task was to examine the passage of text for a given target word. They were told to go line by line, but that they could respond (indicating that the target word had been identified) at any time, regardless of whether it was on the line being fixated or not.

METHOD
Subjects
The 15 subjects were from the University of Massachusetts community. They were all native English speakers and had normal vision. They were paid for their participation.

Apparatus and procedure
The apparatus was the same as in Experiment 1 and window changes (to be described below) were triggered by the same algorithm. A trial consisted of the following events. First, the target word appeared for several seconds while the computer was calculating the visual displays that would appear. Then, the display appeared that allowed the experimenter to check whether the subject's calibration was accurate. If it was, the experimenter initiated the trial. The subject fixated a cross two character positions to the left of the first line of the passage, and when the experimenter determined that the subject was fixating there, the target word was repeated verbally, and then the passage was presented. The subject scanned the lines of text successively and pressed a switch when the target word was found. There was no target word in 20% of the passages. For those passages, the subject pressed the switch when the end of the passage had been reached. Each subject saw 25 experimental passages and 2 practice passages. They completed the session in about 45 minutes.

Stimuli and design
The stimuli were again 15 line passages of meaningful text, with virtually the same characteristics as in Experiment 1. As in Experiment 1, there were 5 window conditions, but the nature of the window conditions was somewhat different. The primary question in Experiment 2 was how far information about the target could be extracted below the fixated line. Accordingly, the

size of the window of normal text below the fixated line was varied rather than the nature of the material outside the window. One of the five conditions was the normal text condition. In all the other conditions, the material outside the window was Xs with the spaces between words preserved. In the *plus zero* condition (identical to the X condition of Experiment 1) the line fixated and all above it were normal text, but all the words below the line were replaced by Xs. In the *plus one* condition, the line below the fixated line was normal text as well. The *plus two* and *plus three* conditions were defined analogously (see Figure 3).

The conditions in Experiment 2 were counterbalanced somewhat differently than those in Experiment 1. The 25 passages were divided into 5 subsets. Each subset of five passages was constructed so that: (a) all 5 window conditions were represented; and (b) all 5 target locations were represented (target present in the first, second, third or fourth quarter of the passage, or target absent). Moreover, for a given subject, all possible combinations of window condition and target location each appeared once. The identity and location of the target was fixed for each passage and the order of the passages were fixed. However, the window conditions were counterbalanced across all of these variables across subjects.

RESULTS AND DISCUSSION

There are two principal ways to ask the question whether information below the line is influencing visual search. The first is to ask whether a target word can be detected when it is below the line fixated. The second is to ask whether visual search is, in some sense, more efficient when information below the line is available. As we will see, the answer to the first question is clearly "yes" while the answer to the second question is "probably not". As in our analysis of Experiment 1, we grouped the 15 subjects into 5 counterbalancing sequence groups.

First let us examine the probability of finding a target when it was below the line fixated (see Table 2). When no meaningful text information was below the line fixated (condition plus zero), subjects never made a false alarm by "detecting" the target in advance of the word being physically present. In contrast, in the other four conditions, there was an average probability of .065 of detecting the target before fixating the line with the target, $t(10) = 2.72$, $p < .05$. We need to put these detections of targets below the line in some perspective, however; there was a total of only 15 such detections, and these 15 came from only 6 of the 15 subjects. Thus, the data indicate that at least some subjects were able to extract information about the target below the fixated line[6].

6 To make certain that it was not simply the case that when subjects detected the target below the line it was because they moved their eyes below the one that they were supposed to be

1. Normal

flower. This substance must make contact with the egg
* substance located in the pistil. Fertilization of the egg
by the pollen yields seeds and fruit. Pollination can
sometimes occur within the same flower. Some plants produce
pollen that is carried to another flower by the wind. But
many fruits and vegetables require an insect to pick up the

2. Plus Zero

flower. This substance must make contact with the egg
* substance located in the pistil. Fertilization of the egg
xx xxx xxxxxx xxxxxx xxxxx xxx xxxxx. Xxxxxxxxxxx xxx
xxxxxxxxx xxxxx xxxxxx xxx xxxx xxxxxx. Xxxx xxxxxx xxxxxxx
xxxxxx xxxx xx xxxxxxx xx xxxxxxx xxxxxx xx xxx xxxx. Xxx
xxxx xxxxxx xxx xxxxxxxxxx xxxxxxx xx xxxxxx xx xxxx xx xxx

3. Plus One

flower. This substance must make contact with the egg
* substance located in the pistil. Fertilization of the egg
by the pollen yields seeds and fruit. Pollination can
xxxxxxxxx xxxxx xxxxxx xxx xxxx xxxxxx. Xxxx xxxxxx xxxxxxx
xxxxxx xxxx xx xxxxxxx xx xxxxxxx xxxxxx xx xxx xxxx. Xxx
xxxx xxxxxx xxx xxxxxxxxxx xxxxxxx xx xxxxxx xx xxxx xx xxx

4. Plus Two

flower. This substance must make contact with the egg
* substance located in the pistil. Fertilization of the egg
by the pollen yields seeds and fruit. Pollination can
sometimes occur within the same flower. Some plants produce
xxxxxx xxxx xx xxxxxxx xx xxxxxxx xxxxxx xx xxx xxxx. Xxx
xxxx xxxxxx xxx xxxxxxxxxx xxxxxxx xx xxxxxx xx xxxx xx xxx

5. Plus Three

flower. This substance must make contact with the egg
* substance located in the pistil. Fertilization of the egg
by the pollen yields seeds and fruit. Pollination can
sometimes occur within the same flower. Some plants produce
pollen that is carried to another flower by the wind. But
xxxx xxxxxx xxx xxxxxxxxxx xxxxxxx xx xxxxxx xx xxxx xx xxx

Fig. 3 Illustrations of the window conditions in Experiment 2. In all cases, the text is
what would be seen on lines 3 through 8 of a 15 line passage of text when the
subject was reading line 4 (the line of text marked with an asterisk in the illustration).

The target, however, was never detected when it was more than two lines
below fixation. Thus, for these displays, the window of information appears
to extend only two lines below fixation. We further analyzed these 15 trials
on which the target was detected below the line to determine how far the
target was from fixation horizontally when it was detected. This analysis is
provisional, since we don't know for sure when (i.e., on which fixation) the
target was detected; we only know when the response was made. On

fixated on (see Inhoff & Briihl, 1991), we examined the eye movement record for the
presence of vertical saccades in the target location vicinity. There was no indication that
subjects' made vertical saccades on those trials when they located the target below the line.

TABLE 2
Measures of Visual Search as a Function of Window Condition

	Window Condition				
	Plus Zero	Plus One	Plus Two	Plus Three	No Window
Measure of Visual Search					
Prob. of find target below line	.00	.02	.08	.07	.09
One line below	.00	.02	.05	.05	.07
Two lines below	.00	.00	.03	.02	.02
Prob. of missing target	.08	.08	.15	.08	.02
Scan Time per line scanned	1571	1595	1552	1592	1605
Scan Time to target	1571	1593	1532	1575	1580
Time per word to target	185	181	172	184	184
Number of forward fixations per passage	41.1	41.1	42.8	40.5	38.9
Mean forward fixation duration	239	237	236	238	235
Mean forward saccade length	11.8	11.9	11.7	11.7	11.7
Number of regressive fixations per passage	1.3	1.7	1.5	1.7	1.6

examining the eye movement records on the 15 trials there was always a fixation that began within 1100 ms of the button being pushed that was relatively near the target word (most of these fixations began within 500 ms of the button being pushed). "Relatively near" means between 2 characters to the right of the target word and 10 characters to the left of the target word. (These fixations, remember, were also either one or two lines above the target word.) Thus, the horizontal extent of the window for targets below the line seems to be about the same as for words on a line (a few characters to the left of fixation and about 10-14 characters to the right of fixation).

There is also a suggestion that having two or more lines of normal text available makes it easier to detect a target below the fixated line; detection probability was only .02 in the plus one condition, whereas it was an average of .08 in the three conditions that had more than one line of text available below the fixated line, $t(10) = 2.35, p < .05$. Moreover, targets that appear for the first time in the window (on line $n + 1$ in the plus one condition and on line $n + 2$ in the plus two, plus three, and normal conditions) have about a .02 chance of being detected, whereas targets that appear for a second time in the window (those on line plus one in the plus two, plus three and normal conditions) have at least a .05 chance of being detected. The data thus suggest that detection of the targets that appear a second time is enhanced by the first appearance; however the difference between the probability of detecting one line below and two lines below for the three righthand conditions of Table 2 was not significant, $t < 1$.

We next turn to the question of search efficiency. The question is perhaps best framed if one considers two possible simple models of the visual search process. The first is that on all fixations, the perceptual span extends from 4 characters to the left of fixation to about 14 characters to the right of fixation and two lines below fixation (although the region from which information is extracted need not be rectangular). The second is that the perceptual span is normally confined to the line fixated, but that occasionally attention wanders, and at those times, the perceptual span extends below the line fixated, but not very far to the right. If the first model is true, one would expect search to procede more efficiently when there is meaningful information below the fixated line. In contrast, if the second model is true, one might expect that use of information below the line will be at the expense of use of information on the line. Hence, search may not be any more efficient in conditions when meaningful information is below the line than when Xs are below the line and signal that no meaningful information is to be found there.

The data do not clearly adjudicate between these two models; however, there is no clear evidence that search is any more efficient when information is available below the line than when it is not. First, let us consider *scan time per line scanned*: this is the total time spent scanning the lines prior to fixating the line on which the target was detected divided by the number of lines scanned. For example, if the target was on line twelve and was detected when fixating line ten, this measure would use the time spent scanning the first nine lines and divide it by nine. The idea behind this measure was to get a background rate for the efficiency of rejection of non-targets. On trials in which there was no target, we used the time to scan the first fourteen lines divided by fourteen. (For this measure, as for all other measures of search efficiency, trials on which the target was missed were excluded from the analysis)[7]. As can be seen in Table 2, there is no particular evidence that having information below the line makes search any faster, since the normal condition was even a bit slower than the plus zero condition ($t < 1$, however).

---

7 Unlike in Experiment 1, there were no trials counted as "bad trials" because of blinks, track losses or large regressive movements other than return sweeps. There were few trials that caused any reason for suspicion, probably because trials in Experiment 2 were shorter than in Experiment 1 and there were few regressive movements other than return sweeps. Moreover, on trials on which there was a target present, there was no definitive way of knowing how many lines had actually been scanned.

It thus appears that information below the line does not particularly aid in the rejection of non-targets. Perhaps, though, overall detection of the target is faster due to the fact that it can be located below the line. We devised two measures of this. The first is a variant of the measure in the above paragraph, which is called *scan time to target*. This uses the same numerator as the former measure, but then divides it by the target line minus one. In the above example, it would take the time to scan the first nine lines and then divide by eleven. Hence, this measure combines the background scanning time with the probability of finding the target below the line. Using this measure, there was no clear evidence that search was any more efficient with bigger windows, $F(4,40) = 1.314$, $p > .20$.

A significant difference emerges, however, when a second, somewhat more direct measure of scanning efficiency was used: *time per word*, the response time on a trial divided by the ordinal position of the target word in the paragraph (or the total number of words in a paragraph when no target was present). Here the five window conditions differed reliably, $F(4,40) = 3.423$, $MS_e = 115$, $p < .05$. However, the pattern is strange, since virtually the whole effect is captured by the difference between the plus two condition and the other four conditions, $t(10) = 2.97$, $p < .05$. A posteriori, one could rationalize that this should be the most efficient condition because it contains all the information that can be extracted, and no more. In other words, subjects might be less efficient in the plus three and normal conditions because they were trying to extract information where they couldn't, and less efficient in the plus zero and plus one conditions because there was less information to extract. However, while search rate was fastest in this condition, the miss rate was also the highest (see Table 2). Thus, this difference in search rate may merely be a product of a speed-accuracy trade-off, rather than a reflection of greater efficiency in search. (The one "false alarm" – judging a target to be present when it was not – occurred in the plus two condition as well.)

To summarize, subjects were able to detect targets up to two lines below the line fixated when such information was available. On the other hand, there was little evidence that search was substantially more efficient in such circumstances. There was an indication that search was somewhat more rapid in the plus two condition than in the other conditions; however, subjects missed the target most often in this condition, so that there are no data that allow us to reject the null hypothesis that search was equally efficient in all conditions.

There were no surprises when finer measures of performance were examined. As can be seen in Table 2, the mean forward fixation duration, the mean saccade length, and the number of forward and regressive fixations were just about the same for all conditions. (These analyses excluded trials on which the target was missed.) The only F that exceeded one was that for number of forward fixations, $F(4,40) = 1.09$, $MS_e = 27.5$. Thus, the lack of difference observed in the conditions above does not seem to result from a trade-off among the various eye movement measures[8].

General Discussion

The central finding of the present experiments is that information below the fixated line of text has very little influence either on reading or on visual search when subjects scan horizontally across the lines of text. In reading, the only effect observed was inhibitory (dissimilar letters slowed reading), whereas in visual search, the effect was mildly facilitory (targets could be found below the line, although it wasn't clear that search efficiency was enhanced by information below the line). These small effects may merely reflect the fact that the subjects are not always on task and their attention wanders occasionally rather than revealing anything deep about perceptual processes during reading or visual search. That is, the information below the line may be irrelevant on all but a few fixations when the subject consciously or unconsciously attends to information below the line. Indeed, another way of casting the results of Experiment 2 is that nine out of the fifteen subjects never detected a target below the line, even though the target was only a fraction of a degree below fixation when in the two lines below.

Note that we are not claiming that the virtual irrelevance of information outside the currently fixated line we observed is due to "hard-wiring" of the visual system. Instead, the irrelevance of information below the line in these tasks is most parsimoniously explained by the same mechanism that we posited to explain the irrelevance of information to the left of the fixated word when reading English: information that is not in the direction of the eye movements and associated movements of covert attention is not used. Hence we would predict that if the scanning pattern were different for the stimuli we used, the perceptual span almost certainly would be different as well. When Japanese readers read Kanji text arranged vertically, the perceptual span extended roughly the same number of characters as when the text was arranged horizontally (Osaka & Oda, 1991)[9]. Hence, they are extracting useful information from characters below the character being fixated. Also consistent with our hypothesis, Prinz (1984) found that a target letter could often be located a few lines below the fixation point when subjects scaned vertically through arrays of letters for a target letter. Analogously, we have no reason to doubt that if subjects were scanning vertically through our

8 The regressive fixation durations and regressive saccade lengths are not presented in the table because there were so few regressions, with zero observations in many cells.

9 Sun, Morita and Stark (1985) compared Chinese readers when reading vertically arranged text and when reading horizontally arranged text. They found that vertical reading was somewhat more efficient; however, their data also suggest that useful information is obtained below fixation when reading vertical text.

paragraphs for a target word, that their scanning would be faster when allowed a window of information below fixation than when such information was not available.

In summary, our data indicate that when adults read text or scan through text with a pattern of eye movements similar to those in reading, little visual information is extracted outside the line of text; moreover, the information that is extracted in reading, if anything, appears to be interfering. Hence, the hypothesis that the perceptual span in reading extends from 4 characters to the left of fixation to 14 characters to the right of fixation on the line currently fixated appears to be substantially correct.

This research was supported by Grant HD26765 from the National Institute of Health. The research was conducted while the second and third authors held post-doctoral fellowships on Grant MH16745 from the National Institute of Mental Health. We thank John Henderson, Fernanda Ferreira, Murray Singer, and Albrecht Inhoff for their helpful comments on an earlier version of the paper.

Requests for reprints should be addressed to Alexander Pollatsek or Keith Rayner, Department of Psychology, University of Massachusetts, Amherst, MA 01003.

References

Bouma, H. (1971). Visual recognition of isolated lower-case letters. *Vision Research, 11*, 459-471.

Inhoff, A.W. & Briihl, D. (1991). Semantic processing of unattended text during selective reading: How the eyes see it. *Perception and Psychophysics, 49*, 289-294.

Inhoff, A.W., Pollatsek, A., Posner, M.I., & Rayner, K. (1989). Covert attention and eye movements during reading. *Quarterly Journal of Experimental Psychology, 41A*, 63-89.

Inhoff, A.W., & Topolski, R. (1992). Lack of semantic activation from unattended text during passage reading. *Bulletin of the Psychonomic Society, 30*, 365-366.

McConkie, G.W., & Rayner, K. (1975). The span of the effective stimulus during a fixation in reading. *Perception & Psychophysics, 17*, 578-586.

McConkie, G.W., & Rayner, K. (1976). Asymmetry of the perceptual span in reading. *Bulletin of the Psychonomic Society, 8*, 365-368.

Morrison, R.E., & Rayner, K. (1981). Saccade size in reading depends upon character spaces and not visual angle. *Perception & Psychophysics, 30*, 395-396.

Osaka, N., & Oda, K. (1991). Effective visual field size necessary for vertical reading during Japanese text processing. *Bulletin of the Psychonomic Society, 29*, 345-347.

Pollatsek, A., Bolozky, S., Well, A.D., & Rayner K. (1981). Asymmetries in the perceptual span for Israeli readers. *Brain and Language, 14*, 174-180.

Prinz, W. (1984). Attention and sensitivity in visual search. *Psychological Research, 45*, 355-366.

Rayner, K., & Bertera, J.H. (1979). Reading without a fovea. *Science, 206,* 468-469.

Rayner, K., Inhoff, A.W., Morrison, R., Slowiaczek, M.L., & Bertera, J.H. (1981). Masking of foveal and parfoveal vision during eye fixations in reading. *Journal of Experimental Psychology: Human Perception and Performance, 7,* 167-179.

Rayner, K., McConkie, G.W., & Ehrlich, S.F. (1978). Eye movements and integrating information across fixations. *Journal of Experimental Psychology: Human Perception and Performance, 4,* 529-544.

Rayner, K., & Pollatsek, A. (1989). *The psychology of reading.* Englewood Cliffs, NJ: Prentice Hall.

Rayner, K., Well, A.D., & Pollatsek, A. (1980). Asymmetry of the effective visual field in reading. *Perception & Psychophysics, 27,* 537-544.

Rayner, K., Well, A.D., Pollatsek, A. & Bertera, J.H. (1982). The availability of useful information to the right of fixation in reading. *Perception & Psychophysics, 31,* 537-550.

Sun, F., Morita, M., & Stark, L.W. (1985). Comparative patterns of reading eye movements in Chinese and English. *Perception & Psychophysics, 37,* 502-506.

Willows, D.M., & MacKinnon, G.E. (1973). Selective reading: Attention to the "unattended" lines. *Canadian Journal of Psychology, 27,* 292-304.

Wurtz, R.H., Goldberg, M.E., & Robinson, D.L. (1982). Brain mechanisms of visual attention. *Scientific American, 246,* 124-135.

5 Eye Movement Control During Reading: Fixation Measures Reflect Foveal but Not Parafoveal Processing Difficulty

JOHN M. HENDERSON and FERNANDA FERREIRA
University of Alberta

Abstract   The main purpose of this study was to determine whether, during natural reading, the difficulty of the upcoming parafoveal word affects eye movement behaviour on the currently fixated word. A model in which visual attention is allocated in parallel over both the fixated and the upcoming parafoveal word predicts such an effect, while a sequential attention allocation model in which attention is directed first to the fixated word and then to the upcoming parafoveal word, does not. The data reported here show that neither the frequency nor the combined length, frequency and class of the upcoming word affect eye movement behaviour on the current word. These data support the sequential attention – parallel programming model of eye movement control in reading.

Résumé   L'étude que nous avons réalisée avait pour principal objet de déterminer si, durant la lecture naturelle, la difficulté que pose le mot périfovéal suivant influence la fixation oculaire sur le mot fovéal. Un modèle dans lequel l'attention visuelle se porte parallèlement sur le mot fixé et sur le mot périfovéal suivant prédit un tel effet, mais non un modèle de répartition séquentielle dans lequel l'attention est d'abord dirigée vers le mot fixé, puis vers le mot périfovéal suivant. D'après les données recueillies, ni la fréquence ni la combinaison de la longueur, de la fréquence et de la classe du mot suivant n'influencent la fixation sur le mot fovéal. Ces données appuient le modèle de programmation parallèle – attention séquentielle relativement au contrôle des mouvements oculaires durant la lecture.

Recently, studies employing eye movement recording techniques have provided a great deal of insight into the nature of the reading process (for reviews, see Just & Carpenter, 1987; Rayner & Pollatsek, 1989). In an innovative use of eye movement recording, McConkie and Rayner (1975) introduced the "moving window" paradigm, in which the amount of text presented to the reader during any given fixation is directly manipulated by changing the display as a function of eye position. Text within the window region is displayed normally, while text outside of the window is mutilated in some way (e.g., replaced with X's). According to the logic of the paradigm, if information that is typically acquired during a fixation is outside of the window (i.e., mutilated), then reading will be disrupted. On the other hand, if the information outside of the window is not typically acquired, then the mutilation beyond the window should produce no disruption. Using this paradigm, researchers have shown that the *perceptual span* in reading (the region from which useful information is acquired during an eye fixation) is asymmetric, extending from a maximum of about 4 character spaces to the left of the currently fixated character (McConkie & Rayner, 1976; Rayner, Well, & Pollatsek, 1980; Underwood & McConkie, 1985) to a maximum of about 15 character spaces to the right (McConkie & Rayner, 1975; Rayner, Inhoff, Morrison, Slowiaczek, & Bertera, 1981).

One explanation of the asymmetric nature of the perceptual span in reading is that the allocation of visual-spatial attention partially controls the acquisition of information during each eye fixation (Henderson & Ferreira, 1990; McConkie, 1979; Morrison, 1984). In general, it appears that a covert change in the locus of visual-spatial attention precedes an impending saccade to the location about to be fixated (e.g., Bryden, 1961; Crovitz & Daves, 1962; Henderson, 1993; Henderson, Pollatsek, & Rayner, 1989; Rayner, McConkie, & Ehrlich, 1978; Remington, 1980; Shepherd, Findlay, & Hockey, 1986; for a review, see Henderson, 1992). In reading, evidence supporting the hypothesis that the asymmetry of the perceptual span is due to attentional factors is provided by studies showing that the direction of the perceptual span reverses when the text is read from right to left. For example, Pollatsek, Bolozky, Well, and Rayner (1981) found that the perceptual span for readers fluent in both English and Hebrew was asymmetric to the right when they were reading English, but asymmetric to the left when they were reading Hebrew. Because Hebrew is read from right to left, these results indicate that more information was acquired in the direction that the eyes were generally moving through the text. Similarly, Inhoff, Pollatsek, Posner, & Rayner (1989) found that when readers of English were asked to read text backward (i.e., from right to left), then the asymmetry of the perceptual span reversed, so that more information was acquired from locations to the left of the current fixation point. The finding that the direction of the perceptual span changes depending on the direction of reading (Pollatsek et al., 1981), and that this change does not result from long-term learning (Inhoff et al., 1989), suggests that a dynamic attentional component is involved in defining the nature of the perceptual span in reading.

ATTENTION AND EYE MOVEMENT CONTROL IN READING

To account for eye movement control in reading, Morrison (1984) proposed the *parallel programming model* (for variations on the theme, see also Henderson, 1992; Henderson, Pollatsek, & Rayner, 1989; Henderson & Ferreira, 1990; McConkie, 1979; Pollatsek & Rayner, 1990). According to this model, each fixation begins with visual attention focussed on the word currently centred at the fovea. After processing of the foveal word has reached a criterion level of completion, attention shifts to the parafoveal word to the right of the foveal word. The shift of attention gates processing of the word at the newly attended location and signals the eye movement system to prepare a program to move the eyes. The motor program is executed once it is completed, and the eyes then follow attention to the new word. Because there is a time lag between the shift of attention and the movement of the eyes due to the programming latency, information is acquired from the parafoveal word before it is fixated. Attention will sometimes shift again to the word beyond the parafoveal word if the parafoveal word is relatively easy to identify (Morrison, 1984). In these cases, the eye movement program will be changed to send the eyes two words to the right and the parafoveal word will be skipped. Thus, the perceptual span will sometimes include two words to the right of the currently fixated word. Furthermore, because attention precedes the eyes to the word that the eyes will move to next, the asymmetric nature of the perceptual span can be accounted for; information is acquired from locations that are in the direction that the eyes are moving.

The original Morrison model of eye movement control predicted that the amount of information acquired from the parafoveal word to the right of fixation should remain constant regardless of the difficulty of the foveal word. This prediction followed because attention was assumed not to shift to the parafoveal word until the criterion level of processing was reached for the foveal word (see discussion in Henderson, 1992). Thus, if the foveal word were more difficult, then the criterion would take longer to reach and the fixation on the foveal word would be longer. However, because attention would remain on the foveal word, this additional fixation time would not benefit the parafoveal word. When the criterion was finally reached, attention would shift, programming would begin, and the eyes would follow by the constant programming latency.

Initial evidence that the constant preview prediction was wrong was provided by Rayner (1986). Using the moving window paradigm, Rayner (1986) found that the average perceptual span of a beginning reader was about 20% smaller than that of a skilled reader, and that the average size of the perceptual span was further reduced as text difficulty increased. On the assumption that both reading skill and text difficulty increase foveal processing difficulty, these results can be taken to suggest that as foveal load increases (due to less skill or more difficult text), the perceptual span decreases. Unfortunately, a potential problem with this interpretation of the Rayner study is that foveal load and extrafoveal load covaried; for the less skilled readers and for the more difficult text, the difficulty of words appearing both at fixation and beyond fixation increased together. Therefore, it was impossible to determine whether the perceptual span decreased because of increases in foveal difficulty or increases in extrafoveal difficulty.

In order to examine more directly the effect of foveal load on the perceptual span, Henderson and Ferreira (1990) manipulated foveal difficulty in a paradigm that held extrafoveal difficulty constant. In that study, we had subjects read simple sentences for meaning. We asked whether increasing the difficulty of the currently fixated (foveal) word in a sentence would reduce the amount of information acquired from the (parafoveal) word to be fixated next. We employed the *boundary* technique, in which the letter string occupying the target position is changed when the eyes cross an invisible boundary in the text (Rayner, 1975). Using this technique, we were able to manipulate independently foveal difficulty and the availability of a preview of the parafoveal target prior to fixation on the target. We found that increasing the difficulty of the foveal word through either lexical frequency (defined by Kucera and Francis, 1967, norms) or syntactic difficulty (defined by parsing strategies; see Ferreira & Henderson, 1990, this volume) decreased the amount of information acquired from the parafoveal target. This result provided direct evidence that increasing the foveal load decreased the effective size of the perceptual span during reading, contrary to the Morrison model.

There are two ways in which the parallel programming model might be modified in order to account for the effect of foveal load on the preview benefit (Henderson, 1992). First, according to the *parallel allocation* hypothesis, during an eye fixation attention is allocated simultaneously to both the foveal word and the word about to be fixated next. For example, attention might be thought of as an elongated spotlight or gradient covering the foveal and parafoveal words (Eriksen & St. James, 1986; Henderson, 1991). On this view, increasing foveal load decreases the amount of information acquired from the parafoveal word because the spotlight or gradient-peak shrinks as foveal load increases. Second, according to the *sequential allocation with decoupling* hypothesis, attention is normally directed to the foveal word and then the extrafoveal word in a sequential manner, but when foveal processing is difficult, initial programming of the eye movement to the parafoveal word sometimes begins prior to the shift of attention to that word so that the attentional shift and the initiation of eye movement programming are decoupled (Henderson, 1988; Henderson & Ferreira, 1990; Pollatsek & Rayner, 1990). On this view, attention would shift to the parafoveal word after the eye movement programming had already started but prior to the saccade, leading to a reduced time lag between the attentional shift and the saccade, and thus to a reduced preview benefit.

One way to distinguish between the parallel allocation hypothesis and the sequential allocation with decoupling hypothesis would be to determine whether parafoveal processing difficulty affects eye movement behaviour on the currently fixated word. According to the parallel allocation hypothesis, we would expect to observe some effect of parafoveal difficulty, given that attention is being shared between the foveal and parafoveal words (and assuming that parafoveal processing is resource limited). On the other hand, according to the sequential allocation with decoupling hypothesis, parafoveal difficulty should not affect eye movement behaviour on the current word because fixation behaviour on the current word is determined before the next word is attended.

Three previous studies provide some data on the issue of whether parafoveal difficulty affects eye movement behaviour on the current word. First, Rayner (1975) reported that fixations were longer on a word during reading if that word were followed by a non-word than by a regular word, but only if the fixation on the current word was on the final two letters or the space between the words. Second, Blanchard, Pollatsek, and Rayner (1989) reported a study in which they alternated the size of the window of text available to the reader from fixation to fixation. On some fixations the foveal word and the next word were available, while on other fixations only the foveal word was available, while the parafoveal word was replaced with a visual mask. They found that the availability of word information in the parafovea had no effect on the duration of the fixation on the current word. Similarly, in the Henderson and Ferreira (1990) study discussed above, the stimulus available at position $n + 1$ during fixation on word n was either a word or a nonsense letter string. Again, the finding was that parafoveal word information had no effect on the duration of the fixation on the current word. Together, the latter two studies provide evidence against the parallel allocation hypothesis, as does the Rayner study for cases where the fixation is not at the very end of the current word. However, this interpretation depends on the assumption that parafoveal processing difficulty differs as a function of whether there is a word or something else (a mask or nonsense letter string) in the parafovea. Unfortunately, we have no way to know whether or not this assumption is correct. The present experiment seeks to circumvent this problem by manipulating parafoveal difficulty in a more straightforward manner via lexical complexity.

Experiment

The main purpose of the present study was to examine further the degree to which the difficulty of the *next* word (word $n + 1$) would affect eye movement measures during fixation on the current word n. In order to explore this question, we examined the effects of parafoveal difficulty on the processing of the currently fixated word in natural reading. We manipulated parafoveal difficulty using lexical factors, so that the parafoveal stimulus in both the easy and difficult conditions was a word. More specifically, we used two manipulations of parafoveal difficulty. First, we examined the effects of lexical frequency, holding word length and lexical class constant. Second, as a more extreme test, we examined a combination of lexical frequency, lexical class, and length. For this second manipulation, we contrasted short, high frequency, closed class words against longer, lower frequency, open class words. According to the parallel allocation hypothesis, we would expect some effect of the difficulty of word $n + 1$ during the fixation of word n. According to the sequential attention hypothesis, on the other hand, the difficulty of word $n + 1$ should not affect fixation measures during fixation on word n.

We also wanted to ensure that the properties of the currently fixated word were able to affect eye movement behaviour on that word. If we did not find an effect of word $n + 1$ difficulty on word n processing, it would be important to demonstrate that word $n + 1$ difficulty did affect processing of that word itself when it is fixated, in order to show that difficulty was adequately manipulated, and also to show that processing of that word was resource limited. Based on many previous experiments, we expected that the difficulty of the currently fixated word would be reflected in both initial and later processing measures. For example, the lexical frequency of a word has been shown to affect eye movement behaviour on that word (Henderson & Ferreira, 1990; Just & Carpenter, 1980; Rayner, 1977; Rayner & Duffy, 1986). Therefore, we expected that high frequency words would be fixated for less time than low frequency words.

In the present experiment, we will be interested in eye movement behaviour on three words in each sentence. For example, consider the sentences presented in Table 1. In each sentence, *Word 1* refers to the word prior to the first manipulated word, *Word 2* refers to the first manipulated word, and *Word 3* refers to the second manipulated word. The primary question is whether eye movement behaviour on Word 1 is affected by the difficulty (frequency) of Word 2, and whether eye movement behaviour on Word 2 is affected by the difficulty (length, frequency, and syntactic class) of Word 3. Second, in order to test our difficulty manipulations, we will want to examine whether eye movement behaviour on Word 2 is affected by the difficulty of Word 2, and whether eye movement behaviour on Word 3 is affected by the difficulty of Word 3. Finally, we want to determine whether Word 3 will be skipped more when it is short, high-frequency, and closed-class, given that the immediately preceding word is controlled.

METHOD
Subjects
Twenty-four undergraduate and graduate students at the University of Alberta were paid $6.00 to participate in the study. The participants had normal or corrected-to-normal vision. Those with corrected vision wore contact lenses during the study.

TABLE 1
Example sentence frames with each of the two difficulty
manipulations. Word 1 is indicated by underline, *Word 2* by italics,
and **Word 3** by bold.

Easy (high-frequency) Word 2, easy (closed-class) Word 3

I decided to wait until *winter* **to** use my fireplace.

Easy (high-frequency) Word 2, difficult (open-class) Word 3

Working outdoors in the *winter* **cold** is not fun.

Difficult (low-frequency) Word 2, easy (closed-class) Word 3

I decided to wait until *autumn* **to** use my fireplace.

Difficult (low-frequency) Word 2, difficult (closed-class) Word 3

Working outdoors in the *autumn* **cold** is not fun.

Apparatus

Eye movements were monitored via an ISCAN RK-416 eyetracker. Signals from the eyetracker were sampled at a frequency of 60 Hz. Sentences were displayed on a high-resolution, flat-screen monitor, white letters on a black background. At a viewing distance of 36 cm, each letter subtended about 1/3 degree of visual angle. The eyetracker and display were interfaced with an 80386 microcomputer that controlled the experiment. The computer kept a complete eye movement record, including fixation positions and durations.

Materials

Word 2 consisted of 36 pairs of words that varied in lexical frequency, as assessed by the Kucera and Francis (1967) norms. These were the same words used in Experiment 1 of Henderson and Ferreira (1990), and are given in the appendix to that paper. The mean frequencies were 148 and 12 counts per million for the high- and low-frequency words, respectively. The words in each pair were either synonyms or closely related words (e.g., winter, autumn) and were matched on word length. Word 3 consisted of 36 pairs of long, low frequency, open class and short, high frequency, closed class words.

For each Word 2 pair, two sentence frames were constructed. Both members of a Word 2 pair formed a coherent sentence when entered into either frame. One of the two sentence frames contained a short, high frequency, closed class member of a Word 3 pair immediately following the position of Word 2, while the other sentence frame contained the long, low frequency, open class member of that Word 3 pair immediately following the position of Word 2. An example of a Word 2 pair (*winter/autumn*) in the two corresponding sentence frames with the Word 3 pair (*to/cold*) is shown in Table 1.

Two lists of materials were created. In the first list, one of the two members of a Word 2 pair was placed in one of the two sentence frames for that pair, while the other member was placed in the second frame. In the second list, the words in a Word 2 pair were swapped across the sentence frames for that pair. Thus, both members of each Word 2 pair were used in each list, but in a different sentence frame and therefore with a different Word 3. In each list, half of the closed-class members of a Word 3 pair appeared with a high frequency Word 2, and half appeared with a low frequency Word 2. Similarly, half of the open-class members of a Word 3 pair appeared with a high frequency Word 2, and half with a low frequency Word 2. Across lists, both members of each Word 2 pair appeared with both levels of Word 3 class. Each list contained 72 test sentences, the 2 members of each Word 2 pair in 36 pairs of sentence frames.

Procedure

The subject was seated in a comfortable chair and was supported by a chin and forehead rest to minimize body and head movements. At the beginning of the experiment, the eye tracking system was calibrated, a procedure that took under 5 minutes. At the beginning of the session, the subject read several practice sentences until he or she was familiar with the procedure. After the practice sentences, the subject read 72 test sentences. The order of sentence presentation was randomized for each subject.

A trial consisted of the following events: First, the experimenter checked the calibration accuracy of the eye movement system by displaying three check-points (at the beginning, middle, and end of the line on which sentences would appear) and a fourth point that indicated where the system estimated the current fixation position to be. The subject was asked to fixate each check-point, and if the estimated fixation position was within one character position of each check-point, calibration was determined to be accurate. The system was recalibrated whenever the calibration was not accurate by this definition. Second, the subject was asked to fixate a cross on the left side of the CRT when he or she was ready for a sentence. When the subject was ready, a single sentence was presented. The sentence always fit on one horizontal line across the CRT. The subject read each sentence and then pressed a button once it was understood. The button press caused the sentence to disappear and the calibration display to reappear. Subjects were asked a simple yes/no comprehension question at this time on 20% of the trials. Subjects were virtually flawless answering these questions. The entire experimental session lasted for about one hour.

Data Analysis

In the following analyses, the location of a word was defined as beginning at the space immediately to the left of the word and ending at the last letter of the word. Several measures of eye movement behaviour on Words 1, 2, and

3 were analyzed. Four of these measures reflect processing during the initial pass through the sentence: (a) Probability of first-pass fixation: the probability that the eyes landed within the word during the initial pass through the sentence, i.e., excluding fixations following a backward (regressive) eye movement; (b) Gaze duration: the amount of time spent within a word during the initial pass through the sentence, prior to moving off of that word the first time, i.e., total time from initially landing to initially leaving a word but excluding fixations following regressive saccades back to the word[1]; (c) Number of gaze fixations: the number of fixations whose durations are added together to produce the gaze duration; (d) Landing position: the character position on which the initial forward saccade lands. The gaze duration, number of gaze fixations, and landing position measures are contingent on the word being fixated. Because these four measures are assumed to reflect the initial processing of a word, the prediction derived from the parallel allocation hypothesis was that an effect of word $n + 1$ should be observed during fixation on word n, while the sequential allocation hypothesis predicted that no such effect of word $n + 1$ should be observed during fixation on word n.

Three additional measures reflected re-processing time on a word during subsequent passes through the sentence: (e) Percentage of regressions in: The percentage of times that a regressive saccade brought the eyes back to a word from a later point in the sentence; (f) Regressive fixation duration: the amount of time spent on a word following a regression back to that word (with non-regression times scored as zeros); (g) Total reading time: all time spent fixating a word, including refixations back to the word. Because these three measures reflect later processing on a word (following fixations on words that are later in the sentence), they would be expected to show effects of these later words. Such effects would constitute evidence that the manipulations of these later words were successful. For example, the sequential allocation hypothesis would predict no effect of word $n + 1$ on word n initial processing (i.e., before $n + 1$ is fixated), while the parallel allocation hypothesis would predict such an effect. However, an effect of word $n + 1$ on later processing of word n (i.e., after word $n + 1$ has been fixated) could be accommodated by either hypothesis, and would suggest that the manipulation of $n + 1$ had been successful.

Because reporting all of the means from such a large number of regions and measures can be overwhelming, we will concentrate on those effects that were statistically significant. Effects not mentioned had p values greater than .10.

---

1 We also analyzed first fixation durations, defined as the duration of the initial fixation on a word and exclusive of intra-word refixations. The results of this analysis were virtually identical to the gaze duration results. We have chosen to report the gaze durations because this measure offers a more extreme test of the sequential allocation hypothesis.

TABLE 2

Initial processing on Word 1 and Word 2, as a function of the difficulty of the next word (Word N + 1)

	Word N + 1	
Word 1	Easy	Difficult
Probability of Fixation	.67	.69
Gaze Duration	252	244
Number of Gaze Fixations	1.02	1.00
Landing Position	1.8	1.7
Word 2	Easy	Difficult
Probability of Fixation	.81	.84
Gaze Duration	2.64	2.59
Number of Gaze Fixations	1.28	1.36
Landing Position	2.2	2.3

RESULTS AND DISCUSSION

The following analyses excluded trials on which the eyetracker lost track of the eye position. About 1% of the trials were lost in total, and lost trials were randomly distributed across conditions.

Word 1, initial processing. Table 2 summarizes the initial processing measures on Word 1 as a function of the difficulty of Word 2. The mean probability of fixating Word 1 was .68, and was not affected by the difficulty of Word 2, $F < 1$. The mean gaze duration on Word 1 was 248 ms. Importantly, the gaze duration on Word 1 did not increase when Word 2 was more difficult. In fact, gaze durations on Word 1 were 8 ms longer when Word 2 was easier, though this effect was not significant, $F(1,23) = 1.34$, $MS_e = 997$, $p > .25$. The mean number of gaze fixations on Word 1 was 1.01, and also was not affected by the difficulty of Word 2, $F < 1$. The mean landing position was 1.8 characters into the word, and was not affected by the difficulty of Word 2, $F < 1$.

The initial processing data from Word 1 suggest that the difficulty of the next (parafoveal) word does not influence eye movement behaviour during the initial processing of the currently fixated word. This finding offers initial support for a model in which attention is sequentially allocated to the fixated and then the parafoveal word, rather than allocated to both in parallel.

Word 1, re-processing. Table 3 presents re-processing time on Word 1 as a function of Word 2 and Word 3 difficulty. Overall, regressions to Word 1 occurred 12% of the time, and were not affected by either the difficulty of Words 2 or 3, $F<1$ and $F(1,23) = 2.08$, $MS_e = 108$, $p > .15$, respectively. However, the amount of regressive fixation time spent on Word 1 was affected by the difficulty of both Word 2 and Word 3. Regressive fixation

TABLE 3
Re-processing on Word 1 as a function of the difficulty of both the next
two words (Word N + 1 and Word N + 2)

Word 1	Word N + 1	
	Easy	Difficult
Percentage Regressions In	11	13
Regressive Fixation Duration	89	115
Total Time	359	397

Word 1	Word N + 2	
	Easy	Difficult
Percentage Regressions In	12	13
Regressive Fixation Duration	91	112
Total Time	362	395

duration on Word 1 was 26 ms longer when Word 2 was low vs high frequency (115 vs 89 ms), $F(1,23) = 10.5$, $MS_e = 1524$, $p < .005$, and 21 ms longer when Word 3 was a long, low frequency, open class word compared with a short, high frequency, closed class word (112 vs 91 ms), $F(1,23) = 18.7$, $MS_e = 554$, $p < .001$. Similarly, the total time spent on Word 1 was affected by the difficulty of Words 2 and 3. Total time was 38 ms longer when Word 2 was low versus high frequency (397 vs 359 ms), $F(1,23) = 6.13$, $MS_e = 5596$, $p < .05$, and 33 ms longer when Word 3 was a long, low frequency, open class word compared with a short, high frequency, closed class word (395 vs 362 ms), $F(1,23) = 8.50$, $p < .01$, $MS_e = 3185$.

Both the regressive fixation duration and the total reading time on Word 1 give a first indication that our manipulation of Word 2 and Word 3 difficulty was successful: Re-processing time on Word 1 was increased when Words 2 and 3 were more difficult. It therefore appears that the failure to find an effect of Word 2 on Word 1 initial processing measures cannot be explained by an inadequate manipulation of Word 2 difficulty.

Word 2, initial processing. Table 2 presents the initial processing measures on Word 2 as a function of Word 3 difficulty. The mean probability of fixating Word 2 was .82 and was not affected by the difficulty of Word 2 or Word 3 (all p's > .10). Gaze duration on Word 2 was not affected by the difficulty of Word 3, nor was there an interaction between Word 2 and Word 3 difficulty, F's < 1. Similarly, there was no effect of the difficulty of Word 3 on the number of gaze fixations on Word 2, and no interaction, p's > .15.

Table 4 shows the initial processing measures on Word 2 as a function of Word 2 difficulty. Gaze durations were 28 ms faster when Word 2 was high frequency compared with low frequency (247 vs 275 ms), $F(1,23) = 13.2$, $MS_e = 1468$, $p < .005$. The frequency of Word 2 also affected the number of gaze fixations on that word. High frequency words received .2 fewer gaze

TABLE 4

Initial processing on Word 2 and Word 3, as a function of the
difficulty of that word (Word N)

Word 2	Word N	
	Easy	Difficult
Probability of Fixation	.82	.83
Gaze Duration	247	275
Number of Gaze Fixations	1.25	1.39
Landing Position	2.3	2.2
Word 3	Easy	Difficult
Probability of Fixation	.61	.83
Gaze Duration	212	266
Number of Gaze Fixations	.79	1.32
Landing Position	1.7	1.7

fixations than low frequency words (1.2 vs 1.4), $F(1,23) = 6.62$, $MS_e = .0728$, $p < .05$. Finally, the mean landing position within word 2 was 2.2 characters, and was not affected by the difficulty of Word 2 or Word 3, all F's < 1.

These eye movement data support several conclusions. First, the lack of any significant effects of the parafoveal word (Word 3) on initial processing of the currently fixated word (Word 2), in combination with similar findings from Word 1, strongly suggests that the difficulty of a parafoveal word does not affect the duration of the fixation on the current foveal word. Second, these data show that our manipulation of foveal load was successful: Words that had a lower frequency of occurrence were more difficult to process and were therefore fixated more and for a greater amount of time during the first pass through the sentence. Again, this finding makes it difficult to argue that the lack of an effect of Word 2 on the initial processing measures on Word 1 was due to an inadequate manipulation of Word 2 difficulty.

Word 2, re-processing. Table 5 presents re-processing time on Word 2 as a function of Word 2 and Word 3 difficulty. Overall, regressions to Word 2 occurred 13% of the time. There was some tendency for readers to execute more regressions back to a low frequency word compared with a high frequency word (14% vs 11%), but this tendency did not reach significance ($p > .10$). The regressive fixation duration on Word 2 showed a significant effect of the frequency of that word. Subjects spent 44 ms more fixated on a low frequency word following regressions than they did on a high frequency word (141 vs 97 ms, respectively), $F(1,23) = 7.30$, $p < .05$, $MS_e = 6190$. Finally, total reading time on Word 2 was 80 ms longer when it was a low frequency compared with a high frequency word (440 vs 360 ms), $F(1,23) = 15.1$, $MS_e = 10174$, $p < .005$

TABLE 5
Re-processing on Word 2 as a function of the difficulty of both that
word (Word N) and the next word (Word + 1)

Word 2	Word N	
	Easy	Difficult
Percentage Regressions In	11	14
Regressive Fixation Duration	97	141
Total Time	360	440

Word 2	Word N + 1	
	Easy	Difficult
Percentage Regressions In	13	13
Regressive Fixation Duration	120	118
Total Time	394	406

In summary, the re-processing time measures on Word 2 clearly show that the low frequency words were more difficult to process than the high frequency words. Further, the finding that such a difference increased from 28 ms in the gaze duration data to 80 ms in the total time data suggests that at least part of the frequency effect occurs at stages of processing beyond word recognition, such as semantic integration.

Word 3, initial processing. Table 4 presents the initial processing measures on Word 3 as a function of Word 3 difficulty. As expected, there was a main effect of the lexical class of Word 3 on the mean probability that it would be fixated, with short, high frequency, closed class words fixated 22% less often than long, low frequency, open class words, $F(1,23) = 65.7$, $MS_e = 174$, $p < .001$. The long, low frequency, open class words were fixated 83% of the time, while the easier short, high frequency, closed class words were fixated only 61% of the time. There was no effect of the lexical frequency of Word 2 on the percentage of times Word 3 was fixated, $F < 1$, nor did the frequency of Word 2 interact with the difficulty of Word 3, $F (1,23) = 1.17$.

The gaze measures on Word 3 followed the same pattern as the probability of fixation data (see Table 4). First, for mean gaze duration, there was a main effect of the difficulty of Word 3, with gaze durations on short, high frequency, closed class words 54 ms shorter than on long, low frequency, open class words (212 vs 266 ms), $F(1,23) = 35.9$, $MS_e = 1903$, $p <.001$. There was no effect of the frequency of Word 2 on the gaze duration on Word 3, $F(1,23) = 1.36$, $MS_e = 1903$, $p > .25$, and no interaction between Word 2 and Word 3 difficulty, $F(1,23) = 1.06$, $MS_e = 1718$, $p > .30$. Similarly, for the number of gaze fixations there was a significant effect of difficulty, with .54 fewer fixations made on short, high frequency, closed class compared with long, low frequency, open class words (.79 vs 1.32 fixations), $F(1,23) = 112$, $MS_e = .0614$, $p < .001$. Again, there was no effect of the frequency of Word

2, and no interaction, both F's < 1. Finally, there was a significant effect of the difficulty of Word 3 on the initial landing position within the word. Mean landing position was .6 character spaces greater into a long, low frequency, open class compared with a short, high frequency, closed class word (2.3 vs 1.7 characters), $F(1,23) = 33.5$, $MS_e = .3128$, $p < .001$. This effect reflects the fact that a longer saccade would be more likely to miss a shorter word. There was no effect of the frequency of Word 2 on this measure, and no interaction, F's < 1.

The data from the eye movement behaviour on Word 3 support several conclusions. First, short, high frequency, closed class words are skipped more often than are longer, lower frequency, open class words. These data replicate the results reported in earlier correlational studies. In fact, our absolute rates of fixation are very close to those reported by Just and Carpenter (1987) for open and closed class words. Second, the time spent on a short, high frequency, closed class word, given that it was fixated, was less than the time spent on a long, low frequency, open class word, as shown by the shorter gaze durations. Thus, short, high frequency, closed class words are more likely to be skipped, and when they are fixated, they are fixated for less time. Third, there was no effect of Word 2 on any of the initial processing measures on Word 3. Thus, these data suggest that so-called "spillover" effects, in which processing difficulty in one region of a sentence is observed on the initial processing measures of later words (e.g., Ehrlich & Rayner, 1983), are not ubiquitous. At this point, it is not clear when spillover effects will and will not be observed.

Word 3, re-processing. Table 6 presents Word 3 re-processing as a function of Word 2 and Word 3 difficulty. There was a marginal tendency for subjects to regress to a long, low frequency, closed class word more often than to an short, high frequency, open class word (15% vs 12%), $F(1,23) = 3.17$, $MS_e = 74.9$, $p < .10$, but the amount of regressive fixation time spent on the former was 35 ms less than on the latter words (78 vs 113 ms), $F(1,23) = 22.7$, $MS_e = 1292$, $p < .001$. There was a significant interaction of the difficulty of Word 2 and 3 on the regressive fixation duration data on Word 3, $F(1,23) = 4.31$, $MS_e = 1400$, $p < .05$. Refixation time on short, high frequency, closed class words was 26 ms greater when they followed low frequency words compared with high frequency words (91 vs 65 ms); refixation time on long, low frequency, open class words differed by only 6 ms (in the opposite direction) as a function of the frequency of the previous word (110 vs 116 ms).

The total time spent on Word 3 was affected by both the frequency of Word 2 and the class of Word 3. Total time was 33 ms greater when Word 3 followed a low frequency word compared with a high frequency word (361 vs 328 ms), $F(1,23) = 5.51$, $MS_e = 4686$, $p < .05$, and was 114 ms greater when Word 3 was long, low frequency, and open class rather than short, high

TABLE 6
Re-processing on Word 3 as a function of the difficulty of the prior word
(Words N − 1) and that word (Word N)

Word 3	Word N-1	
	Easy	Difficult
Percentage Regressions In	14	13
Regressive Fixation Duration	91	101
Total Time	328	361

Word 3	Word N	
	Easy	Difficult
Percentage Regressions In	15	12
Regressive Fixation Duration	78	113
Total Time	288	402

frequency, and closed class (402 vs 288 ms), $F(1,23) = 67.9$, $MS_e = 4570$, $p < .001$.

In summary, the re-processing time measures on Word 3 further support the adequacy of our manipulation of difficulty for Word 3. There was a tendency for subjects to regress more, spend more time following a regression, and spend more total time on a long, low frequency, open class word compared with a short, high frequency, closed class word. One interesting aspect of these data was the interaction between the frequency of Word 2 and the class of Word 3 on the regressive fixation data. This interaction can be thought of as a complicated type of spillover effect, where processing difficulty on a previous region is observed on *re-processing* time measures on a later region, but only when that later region is itself relatively easy. Given that we did not control the remainder of the sentence following Word 3, it is possible that the effect in our case was due to differences in the difficulty of integrating the remainder of the sentence with the earlier part of the sentence.

General Discussion

The main purpose of the present experiment was to determine whether the difficulty of the parafoveal word to the right of the currently fixated word during reading would affect eye movement behaviour on the current word. This issue is important because it directly bears on two hypotheses concerning the allocation of attention to words during reading. According to the *parallel attention hypothesis*, attention is simultaneously allocated to the currently fixated word and the next, parafoveal word. According to the *sequential attention hypothesis*, on the other hand, attention is allocated first to the currently fixated word, and then to the next one or two words in a sequential manner. If the parallel attention hypothesis were correct, then we would expect that the difficulty of the parafoveal word to the right of the fixated word would affect eye movement behaviour on the fixated word. If the sequential attention hypothesis were correct, we would expect no effect of the upcoming word until that word was fixated.

To contrast the two hypotheses, we constructed sentence frames within which we could vary parafoveal difficulty, holding foveal difficulty constant. One manipulation of difficulty involved lexical frequency, and another involved a combination of syntactic class, lexical frequency, and length. The results from both manipulations were clear. While both types of difficulty produced robust effects on eye movement behaviour once the words were fixated, neither produced even a hint of an effect when the words were in the parafovea. Thus, our results provide strong evidence against the parallel attention hypothesis and instead offer support for the sequential attention hypothesis. It is important to underscore that while the difficulty of the upcoming parafoveal word did not influence processing on the current word, parafoveal information from the upcoming word was acquired during fixation on the present word. This can be seen in the present study by the fact that easy words were more likely to be skipped, and by many previous studies showing that parafoveal preview benefits are obtained from an upcoming parafoveal word (e.g., Henderson & Ferreira, 1990; Rayner, 1975). Our point here is that this parafoveal information acquisition occurs *after* processing of the current word is complete. That is, information is acquired from word *n* and word *n + 1* sequentially during fixation on word *n*.

A secondary issue addressed by this study involved factors that control word skipping in reading. Our data indicated that the short, high frequency, closed class words were fixated about 20% less often than the more difficult long, low frequency, open class words, even though the position in the sentence was controlled. It is important to note that it is still unclear which aspects of a lexical item control whether or not it will be skipped. It has been suggested that lexical class plays a major role in determining word skipping (e.g., Carpenter & Just, 1983; Hogaboam & McConkie, 1981; Just & Carpenter, 1980; O'Regan, 1979). In our study, about 18% of the open class words at Words 2 and 3 were skipped, suggesting that it is not only closed class words that are skipped. Further, lexical class in general is correlated with length and frequency, as it was in our study, so that any or all of these factors may have some influence. In an attempt to tease apart these factors, Stephen Hayduk recently conducted a study in our laboratory in which he contrasted open- and closed-class words of equal length and frequency with the word "the" in identical sentence frames (Hayduk, 1990). For example, consider the sentence frame *Tom told us to install {three/those/the} lights in the basement.* In this case, "three" is open-class, "those" is closed-class of the same length and frequency, while "the" is much higher in frequency and shorter. In this study, Hayduk found that the probability of skipping the open-

and closed-class words was identical (27%), while the probability of skipping "the" was much higher, at 65%. These data suggest that it is frequency and/or length that determines whether a word is skipped, rather than the lexical class per se.

Another aspect of the skipping data worth noting is that the likelihood of skipping a word is markedly reduced when the word immediately before had been skipped. For example, overall, the Word 3 difficult words were skipped 17% of the time versus 39% of the time for the easier words. However, when the word immediately before had not been fixated, the values changed to 4% of the difficult words skipped versus 12% for the easy words $F(1,23) = 20.9$, $MS_e = .0067$, $p < .001$. Thus, it appears that the majority of skips occur when the previous word had been fixated, as we would expect if words are skipped only when they have been parafoveally processed from an earlier position in the text.

ATTENTION AND EYE MOVEMENT CONTROL REVISITED

In this section, we briefly outline our view of eye movement control in reading. First, we take as our starting point Morrison's (1984) parallel programming model, as outlined in the Introduction. The main feature of the parallel programming model is that overlapping motor programs can sometimes exist simultaneously (hence parallel programming). Because our focus has been on the sequential nature of attentional allocation during fixations rather than on parallel programming, we have called our version of the basic model the sequential attention model (Henderson, 1988; Henderson, 1992; Henderson et al., 1989; Henderson & Ferreira, 1990). Perhaps the best moniker would be the *sequential attention – parallel programming model*. In any case, we make the following basic assumptions: First, at the beginning of a fixation on a new stimulus, attention is allocated to that stimulus. In reading, the stimulus would generally be the currently fixated word, though the reader would presumably have some control over whether attention were directed at the word, letter, or even page level (McConkie & Zola, 1987). Second, attention is redirected to a new word when processing on the fixated word is completed. Given that factors at the lexical (Henderson & Ferreira, 1990; Just & Carpenter, 1980; Rayner and Duffy, 1986), syntactic (Ferreira & Henderson, 1990, 1993; Frazier & Rayner, 1982), and semantic (Ehrlich & Rayner, 1983) levels can all exert an influence on first-pass processing on a word, completion probably entails at least partial analysis of the fixated word at all of these levels. Third, the reallocation of attention coincides with the signal to generate an eye movement to the new word, and the word toward which the eyes are programmed is the word to which attention is directed. Whether this relationship is structurally necessary or functionally convenient is an empirical issue yet to be resolved, though our bias at the present time is toward the former view (see Henderson, 1992, and Klein et al., 1992, for discussion of this issue). Fourth, the allocation of attention to the new word gates higher-level analysis of that word. By higher-level analysis, we mean acquisition of information beyond that which can be obtained preattentively, such as simple features (e.g., Treisman, 1988). Fifth, a saccade brings the eyes to the attended word following the eye movement programming latency. This latency would include the time to compute the eye movement parameters plus the neural transmission time to the ocular muscles, probably no less than 100 ms, and probably closer to 150 ms. Sixth, the preview benefit derived from the parafoveal word is assumed to be a function of the latency between the shift of attention and the saccade to that word (as well as other factors such as the visual eccentricity of the word, its size, etc.)

While the above model can account for a great deal of eye movement behaviour in reading, and with slight modification, in scene viewing (Henderson, 1992), it does have some difficulty accounting for one recent finding; the parafoveal preview benefit is reduced when word n is more difficult (Henderson and Ferreira, 1990). One way to deal with this finding would be to assume that attention is normally allocated to both the foveal and parafoveal word, as described in the Introduction. However, given that we can find no effect of the parafoveal word on foveal word processing in the current study, this approach does not seem viable. The alternative is to maintain the sequential attention assumption, but to suggest that when foveal processing is difficult, computations on an eye movement program can begin prior to the shift of attention, so that the latency between the shift of attention and the movement of the eyes is reduced. This is essentially the view taken by Henderson & Ferreira (1990; Henderson, 1992), and by Pollatsek and Rayner (1990), though the particulars differ in the two cases. In our view, the eye movement system imposes a deadline on the amount of time it is willing to devote to a particular fixation during reading. If the deadline is reached, the system will begin to program an eye movement even though attention has not yet been reallocated away from the currently fixated word. In the extreme case, this will lead to a refixation on a new part of the fixated word, which should aid further analysis. However, if processing on the fixated word is subsequently finished and attention shifts to the next word, the latency between the attentional shift and the eye movement will be reduced, due to savings in programming time (Morrison, 1984). Because parafoveal preview benefit is assumed to be a function of this latency, and because the latency is reduced, the preview benefit will also be reduced.

The research reported here was supported by the Natural Sciences and Engineering Research Council of Canada. We would like to thank Kate Murie for her assistance with subject running, Michael Anes and Vic Ferreira for their aid in data analysis, and Keith Rayner and Murray Singer for helpful comments. Correspondence concerning this article should be addressed to John M. Henderson, Department of Psychology, 129 Psychology Research Building, Michigan State University, East Lansing, MI, 48824, USA. Send electronic mail to: johnh@msu.edu.

References

Blanchard, H.E., Pollatsek, A., & Rayner, K. (1989). Parafoveal processing during eye fixations in reading. *Perception & Psychophysics, 46,* 85-94.

Bryden, M.P. (1961). The role of post-exposural eye movements in tachistoscopic perception. *Canadian Journal of Psychology, 15,* 220-225.

Carpenter, P.A., & Just, M.A. (1983). What your eyes do while your mind is reading. In K. Rayner (Ed.), *Eye movements in reading: Perceptual and language processes.* New York: Academic Press.

Crovitz, H.F., & Daves, W. (1962). Tendencies to eye movement and perceptual accuracy. *Journal of Experimental Psychology, 63,* 495-498.

Ehrlich, K., & Rayner, K. (1983). Pronoun assignment and semantic integration during reading: Eye movements and immediacy of processing. *Journal of Verbal Learning and Verbal Behavior, 20,* 641-655.

Eriksen, C.W., & St James, J.D. (1986). Visual attention within and around the field of focal attention: A zoom lens model. *Perception & Psychophysics, 40,* 225-240.

Ferreira, F., & Henderson, J.M. (1993). Reading processes during syntactic analysis and reanalysis. *Canadian Journal of Experimental Psychology, 47,* 247-275.

Ferreira, F., & Henderson, J.M. (1990). The use of verb information in syntactic parsing: Evidence from eye movements and word-by-word self-paced reading. *Journal of Experimental Psychology: Learning, Memory, and Cognition, 16,* 555-569.

Frazier, L., & Rayner, K. (1982). Making and correcting errors during sentence comprehension: Eye movements in the analysis of structurally ambiguous sentences. *Cognitive Psychology, 14,* 178-210.

Hayduk, S. (1990). *Do people process function words and content words different-ly?* Unpublished Honours Thesis, University of Alberta, Edmonton, Canada.

Henderson, J.M. (1988). *Visual attention and the acquisition of extrafoveal information during eye fixations.* Unpublished doctoral dissertation, University of Massachusetts, Amherst, MA.

Henderson, J.M. (1991). Stimulus discrimination following covert attentional orienting to an exogenous cue. *Journal of Experimental Psychology: Human Perception and Performance, 17,* 91-106.

Henderson, J.M. (1992). Visual attention and eye movement control during reading and picture viewing. In K. Rayner (Ed.), *Eye movements and visual cognition: Scene perception and reading.* New York: Springer-Verlag.

Henderson, J.M. (1993). Visual attention and saccadic eye movements. In G. d'Ydewalle and J. van Rensbergen (Eds.), *Perception and cognition: Advances in eye movement research.* Amsterdam: North-Holland.

Henderson, J.M., & Ferreira, F. (1990). Effects of foveal processing difficulty on the perceptual span in reading: Implications for attention and eye movement control. *Journal of Experimental Psychology: Learning, Memory, and Cognition, 16*, 417-429.

Henderson, J.M., Pollatsek, A., & Rayner, K. (1989). Covert visual attention and extrafoveal information use during object identification. *Perception & Psychophysics, 45*, 196-208.

Hogaboam, T.W., & McConkie, G.W. (1981). *The rocky road from eye fixations to comprehension*. Technical Report No. 207, Urbana-Champaign: University of Illinois, Center for the Study of Reading.

Inhoff, A.W., Pollatsek, A., Posner, M.I., & Rayner, K. (1989). Covert attention and eye movements in reading. *Quarterly Journal of Experimental Psychology, 41A*, 63-89.

Just, M.A., & Carpenter, P.A. (1980). A theory of reading: From eye fixations to comprehension. *Psychological Review, 87*, 329-354.

Just, M.A., & Carpenter, P.A. (1987). *The psychology of reading and language comprehension*. Newton, MA: Allyn and Bacon.

Klein, R.M., Kingstone, A., & Pontefract, A. (1992). Orienting of visual attention. In K. Rayner (Ed.), *Eye movements and visual cognition: Scene perception and reading*. New York: Springer-Verlag.

Kucera, H., & Francis, W.N. (1967). *Computational analysis of present-day American English*. Providence, RI: Brown University Press.

McConkie, G.W. (1979). On the role and control of eye movements in reading. In P.A. Kolers, M.E. Wrolstad, & H. Bouma (Eds.), *Processing of visible language*, Vol. 1, (pp. 37-48). New York: Plenum Press.

McConkie, G.W., & Rayner, K. (1975). The span of the effective stimulus during a fixation in reading. *Perception & Psychophysics, 17*, 578-586.

McConkie, G.W., & Rayner, K. (1976). Asymmetry of the perceptual span in reading. *Bulletin of the Psychonomic Society, 8*, 365-368.

McConkie, G.W., & Zola, D. (1987). Visual attention during eye fixations in reading. *Attention and Performance XII* (pp. 327-362). London: Erlbaum.

Morrison, R.E. (1984). Manipulation of stimulus onset delay in reading: Evidence for parallel programming of saccades. *Journal of Experimental Psychology: Human Perception and Performance, 10*, 667-682.

O'Regan, J.K. (1979). Moment to moment control of eye saccades as a function of textual parameters in reading. In P. A. Kolers, M. E. Wrolstad, & H. Bouma (Eds.), *Processing of visible language*, Vol. 1. New York: Plenum Press.

Pollatsek, A., Bolozky, S., Well, A.D., & Rayner, K. (1981). Asymmetries in the perceptual span for Israeli readers. *Brain and Language, 14*, 174-180.

Pollatsek, A., and Rayner, K. (1990). Eye movements and lexical access in reading. In. D.A. Balota, G.B. Flores d'Arcais, and K. Rayner (Eds.), *Comprehension processes in reading*. Hillsdale, N.J.: Erlbaum.

Rayner, K. (1975). The perceptual span and peripheral cues in reading. *Cognitive Psychology*, *7*, 65-81.

Rayner, K. (1977). Visual attention in reading: Eye movements reflect cognitive processes. *Memory & Cognition*, *4*, 443-448.

Rayner, K. (1986). Eye movements and the perceptual span in beginning and skilled readers. *Journal of Experimental Child Psychology*, *41*, 211-236.

Rayner, K., & Duffy, S.A. (1986). Lexical complexity and fixation times in reading: Effects of word frequency, verb complexity, and lexical ambiguity. *Memory & Cognition*, *14*, 191-201.

Rayner, K., McConkie, G.W., & Ehrlich, S.F. (1978). Eye movements and integrating information across fixations. *Journal of Experimental Psychology: Human Perception and Performance*, *4*, 529-544.

Rayner, K., Inhoff, A.W., Morrison, R.E., Slowiaczek, M.L., & Bertera, J.H. (1981). Masking of foveal and parafoveal vision during eye fixations in reading. *Journal of Experimental Psychology: Human Perception and Performance*, *7*, 167-179.

Rayner, K., & Pollatsek, A. (1989). *The psychology of reading*. Englewood Cliffs, NJ: Prentice Hall.

Rayner, K., Well, A.D., & Pollatsek, A. (1980). Asymmetry of the effective visual field in reading. *Perception & Psychophysics*, *27*, 537-544.

Remington, R.W. (1980). Attention and saccadic eye movements. *Journal of Experimental Psychology: Human Perception and Performance*, *6*, 726-744.

Shepherd, M., Findlay, J.M., & Hockey, R.J. (1986). The relationship between eye movements and spatial attention. *Quarterly Journal of Experimental Psychology*, *38A*, 475-491.

Treisman, A. (1988). Features and objects: The 14th Bartlett memorial lecture. *Quarterly Journal of Experimental Psychology*, *40*, 201-237.

Underwood, N.R., & McConkie, G.W. (1985). Perceptual span for letter distinctions during reading. *Reading Research Quarterly*, *20*, 153-162.

6 Thematic Roles in Sentence Parsing

CHARLES CLIFTON, JR.
University of Massachusetts/Amherst

Abstract   Two eyetracking experiments examined the reading of sentences like "While the police/truck stopped the Datsun disappeared into the night." A paper by L. Stowe (Thematic structures and sentence comprehension. In G. N. Carlson and M. K. Tanenhaus (Eds.), *Linguistic structure in language processing*, 1989) indicated that an *inanimate* subject ("truck" in "After the truck stopped the Datsun disappeared...") is taken as theme of the ergative verb ("stop"), preventing the assignment of the postverbal noun phrase ("the Datsun") as direct object. This eliminates the disruption of reading that is normally observed on the disambiguating verb ("disappear"). The present experiments found the pattern of results reported by Stowe when looking at the disambiguating region of a sentence. However, the results for earlier regions suggest that the postverbal noun phrase was initially taken as direct object of an ergative verb even when the subject was inanimate. It appears that the inanimacy of the subject may not have guided the initial syntactic analysis, but rather facilitated the revision of an initial misanalysis.

Résumé   Deux expériences permettant de capter les mouvements oculaires ont porté sur la lecture de phrases telles «While the police/truck stopped the Datsun disappeared into the night». Dans un document de L. Stowe (Thematic structures and sentence comprehension. G.N. Carlson and M.K. Tanenhaus (Eds.), *Linguistic structure in language processing*, 1989), il est indiqué qu'un sujet *inanimé* («truck» dans «After the truck stopped the Datsun disappeared (...)»), est considéré comme le thème du verbe ergatif («stop»), empêchant ainsi d'attribuer au syntagme nominal postverbal («the Datsun») le rôle d'objet direct. Cette approche élimine la perturbation de la lecture qu'on observe normalement lorsqu'intervient le mot désambiguisant («diseappear»). Les expériences que nous avons menées ont conduit aux résultats signalés par Stowe pour ce qui est du segment désambiguisant de la phrase. Par contre, les résultats se rapportant aux premiers segments nous portent à croire que le syntagme nominal postverbal était d'abord vu comme le complément d'objet direct d'un verbe ergatif même quand le sujet était inanimé. Il semble donc que le caractère inanimé du sujet n'ait peut-être pas guidé l'analyse syntaxique initiale, mais qu'il ait plutôt facilité la révision de l'analyse initiale erronée.

Two of the principal questions that have driven research on sentence comprehension during the past decade concern (a) the role that discourse information, meaning, and world knowledge play in assigning a structural analysis to a sentence, and (b) the role that lexically specific information plays in such structural analysis. These questions have seemed particularly important to researchers who are interested in questions of modularity and interactive processing (e.g., Fodor, 1983; Marslen-Wilson, 1987). Some have argued for a strongly interactive system that makes decisions, efficiently and without delay, on the basis of any relevant information as soon as it becomes available (Marslen-Wilson, 1987). Others have argued for a more weakly interactive system that, for instance, initially builds several possible analyses on the basis of purely syntactic information but quickly uses discourse information to select among them (Crain & Steedman, 1985; Altmann & Steedman, 1988). Still others have argued for a highly modular system in which initial decisions about what structures to build are based solely on grammatical information, and in which other sources of information are used to evaluate these decisions and to guide reanalysis (Frazier, 1987).

The role of extragrammatical information (including discourse information, meaning, and world knowledge) in sentence comprehension bears on these distinctions. Any language processing system *must* have some way of using all relevant information if it is to be an adequate model of the human system. Existing models differ primarily in how and when different information sources are used. Some claim that all sources of information are used at the same time, limited only by differences in the speed with which different types of information become available. Others claim that some types of information are used to make initial decisions, while other types are used only to evaluate and revise the products of these initial decisions. Experimental evidence does not yet permit clear answers to these questions. Clearly, a wide variety of information is used very quickly (Altmann, 1988; Marslen-Wilson, 1989; Marslen-Wilson, Brown, & Tyler, 1988; Tanenhaus, Garnsey, & Boland, 1991; Taraban & McClelland, 1988). However, being used quickly does not entail being used initially and indifferently. Some research strongly suggests that if one examines an early enough stage of processing, one can find evidence for decisions made solely on the basis of grammatical information, with other sources of information coming into play only later (Ferreira & Clifton, 1986; Mitchell, 1989; Rayner, Carlson, & Frazier, 1983). Exactly how and when various information sources are used is not likely to be answered by any single experiment. If one's experimental technique has inadequate resolving power, one can easily obtain evidence consistent with the interactive or at least simultaneous use of different sources of information. Conversely, one can always protect a noninteractive modular position by claiming one could have found evidence for modularity if one could look more closely.

The role of lexically specific information (such as subcategorization, argument, thematic role, or control structure) in sentence parsing is less central to the choice between modular and interactive models. While a model that claims all information is used interactively must permit lexically specific information to be used as soon as it becomes available, a fully modular model can permit the same thing. While some modular theorists have proposed that such lexically specific information is used to guide initial parsing decisions (e.g., Abney, 1989; Holmes, Stowe, & Cupples, 1989; Pritchett, 1991; Shapiro, Zurif, & Grimshaw, 1987), others have suggested that it may not be used in such a manner (Clifton, Speer, & Abney, 1991; Ferreira & Henderson, 1990; Frazier, 1987; Frazier, 1989).

The choice of a position within a modular account seems to be determined by a variety of considerations. For instance, theorists who are concerned with the processing of head-final languages (Frazier, 1989) are forced to de-emphasize the role that lexically specific information plays in initial parsing decisions. If the head of a phrase provides information that is crucial to making the initial analysis of a sentence, a language in which the head appears only at the end of its phrase would seem to be poorly designed. More general considerations are relevant as well. There is current interest in whether the parser directly uses grammatical information expressed in the form of principles (e.g., X-bar syntax, case theory, etc; cf. Berwick, 1991) or whether the grammatical information it uses has been "precompiled" into, for example, phrase-structure rules or templates suited for rapid parsing (Frazier, 1989). Principle-based parsing theorists may not have a natural way of ensuring that the parser uses just a subset of the grammatical information associated with a lexical item. Theorists who propose that the parser uses precompiled, rule-like information, on the other hand, can very naturally claim that the parser uses phrase structure rules, which express relations determined just by the major category (part of speech) information associated with a word.

The evidence about just how lexically specific information is used in parsing is mixed, just as we saw in discussing the use of extragrammatical information. Such information is used quite quickly (Clifton, Frazier, & Connine, 1984; Marslen-Wilson, Brown, & Tyler, 1988; Mitchell & Holmes, 1985; Holmes, Stowe, & Cupples, 1989). However, it may not be used in as immediate and obligatory a fashion as major category information (Ferreira & Henderson, 1990; Mitchell, 1987; Mitchell, 1989; but cf. Trueswell, Tanenhaus, & Kello, in press).

Stowe (1989) combined questions about the use of extragrammatical and lexically specific information in a very interesting series of experiments. She concluded that the parser's initial decisions are guided by semantic information about thematic structure of particular verbs and by world knowledge information about the possible roles animate vs. inanimate entities can play. She studied sentences like those in Table 1 which, in their (a) form, have a

TABLE 1
Example of Sentences used by Stowe (1989)

ANIMATE, TEMPORARILY AMBIGUOUS
1a.   As the children rolled the ball fell off the table.

ANIMATE, DISAMBIGUATING ADVERBIAL PHRASE
1b.   As the children rolled across the floor the ball fell off the table.

INANIMATE, TEMPORARILY AMBIGUOUS
2a.   As the pennies rolled the ball fell off the table.

INANIMATE, DISAMBIGUATING ADVERBIAL PHRASE
2b.   As the pennies rolled across the floor the ball fell off the table.

---

temporary ambiguity between a late closure interpretation (in which *the ball* is the direct object and theme of *roll*) and an early closure interpretation (in which *the ball* is subject of the main clause of the sentence and theme of the main verb, *fall*). In general, the late closure interpretation is preferred; reading times in a region that disambiguates the sentence to an early closure interpretation (*fell* in the example) are long compared to times in a region that permits a late closure interpretation (e.g., *it fell*) or in sentences with earlier disambiguation (e.g., (1b)). Some theorists have suggested the operation of a parsing strategy in which each incoming phrase is attached into the phrase currently being processed if consistent with phrase structure rules (Frazier, 1978; Frazier & Rayner, 1982; Kimball, 1973).

Stowe used a word-by-word ungrammaticality decision task to measure reading difficulty in sentences like those in Table 1. She found slow reading times for the disambiguating verb (*fell*) in temporarily ambiguous sentences with an animate initial noun (1a) compared to an initially disambiguated sentence like (1b), but no corresponding penalty for sentences with an inanimate initial noun like (2). She suggested that her readers used the inanimacy of the initial noun (*pennies* in (2)) to determine that it could not plausibly be the agent of the causative/ergative verb *roll* but instead had to be its theme. Since such an analysis fills the lexically-specified thematic role "theme" of *roll*, the verb in (2) cannot be followed by a direct object carrying such a thematic role. Readers thus would not make the late closure analysis of *the ball* but instead would interpret it as the subject of the main clause, eliminating comprehension difficulty at the word *fell*.

This conclusion may be exactly correct for Stowe's ungrammaticality judgement task, but may not be correct in a normal reading situation. Reading in Stowe's task was very slow, 700-800 ms/word (and up to 1400 ms/word at the disambiguating point), and the constant requirement to judge the grammaticality of each added word certainly placed unfamiliar demands on the reader. Readers in this task may well have evaluated the plausible thematic relations for each word before moving on. What is at stake, though, is whether such immediate evaluation is needed for language comprehension. Is it a part of normal, efficient reading?

Some evidence suggests that it is not. Clifton (1992) reported a replication of Stowe's experiment, using her experimental materials, but measured eye movements during normal reading rather than grammaticality judgements. His 24 subjects read sentences with the requirement that they answer simple questions after some of the sentences. No sentences were ungrammatical. He reported two primary measures of reading time. Mean total reading time[1] replicated Stowe's results very well. For temporarily ambiguous sentences with an animate initial noun (e.g., 1a of Table 1), reading time was a very long 76.3 ms/character in the region of the disambiguating verb (*fell* in Table 1). It ranged between 50 and 60 ms/character in this region for all other conditions, including the temporarily ambiguous sentence with an inanimate initial noun. Gaze duration (see footnote 1), however, showed very different results for the disambiguating region. Gaze duration in this region was 516 and 518 ms for the animate and inanimate ambiguous sentences, respectively (1a and 2a), while it was 414 and 441 for the two disambiguated sentences (1b and 2b).

The total reading time results indicate that thematic role and animacy information play a part in how readers eventually figure out what a sentence means. The gaze duration results suggest that their role in assigning an initial structure to a sentence is limited. Rather, it seems reasonable to propose that the postverbal NP (*ball*) is always initially assigned as object of the verb (*roll*) in the temporarily ambiguous sentences. When the disambiguating verb (*fall*) is read, it forces a revision of the analysis, slowing reading time. The total reading times show that this disruption is less severe when the initial noun is inanimate than when it is animate. The inanimate initial noun is a highly plausible candidate for the theme role of the first verb (*roll*), and this plausibility facilitates reanalysis.

Some aspects of the experiment, however, are less than satisfying. Many of the postverbal noun phrases (*the ball* in our example) were implausible as objects of the first verb when the initial noun was inanimate (but not when it was animate). Forty-seven undergraduates at the University of Massachusetts rated simple subject-verb-object sentences based on Stowe's (1989) sentences (e.g., *The children rolled the ball* or *The pennies rolled the ball*) on a 7-point plausibility scale. Such sentences with an animate subject averaged 6.09 (7 = maximum plausibility), but sentences with an inanimate subject averaged

---

1 Total reading time is the sum of all fixation durations in a region, including time spent refixating the region after initially leaving it. Gaze duration is the initial time spent in a region before leaving it and before reading any material that follows the region. As calculated here, it included time spent fixating up to three characters to the left of the region if no fixation was otherwise made in the region (cf. Rayner, Sereno, Morris, Schmauder, & Clifton, 1989).

only 2.95. The sheer implausibility of the inanimate sentences, rather than effects of animacy on thematic role preferences, may have been behind the observed effects. Stowe (1989) reported a second experiment in which she attempted to manipulate the plausibility of the postverbal noun phrase as an object of the initial verb. Plausibility had substantial effects of grammaticality judgement time. Implausible postverbal noun phrases were read slowly regardless of the animacy of the initial noun, but resulted in relatively fast reading times on the disambiguating verb. However, these results show only that plausibility as well as thematic role appropriateness may contribute to ungrammaticality judgements. Any interpretation is complicated by the fact that many of Stowe's supposedly acceptable postverbal nouns were actually anomalous when used with inanimate subjects (14/20 in this author's judgement), and further, that many of her implausible nouns were abstract (hence, perhaps, read slowly; cf. Schwanenflugel and Shoben, 1983) while the plausible ones were concrete. Finally, Stowe did not have a disambiguated control condition, which makes any evaluation of the effects she observed incomplete.

The two experiments reported here (which are briefly described in Clifton, 1992) measured eye movements to study the reading of sentences which met the basic criteria set out by Stowe but in which the plausibility of the direct object (late closure) interpretation was explicitly varied. Experiment 1 was designed to examine the effects that would be observed where all postverbal NPs are highly implausible as direct objects, and Experiment 2 was designed to study the effects when all postverbal NPs are reasonably plausible as direct objects. Each contained, as a baseline, control sentences in which the late closure interpretation was blocked by a comma (cf. Frazier & Rayner, 1982; Underwood and Everatt, 1992). Jointly, they were designed to examine the interaction among syntactic parsing preferences, thematically-based comprehension preferences, and plausibility in the early stages of reading a sentence.

Experiment 1
METHOD
Materials

Sixteen sets of four sentences each were constructed, as illustrated in Table 2. The four forms of a sentence were defined by the factorial combination of animate vs inanimate subject and presence vs. absence of a disambiguating comma. The sentences had ergative verbs, permitting an agent/theme ambiguity for their subjects. All sentences used in Experiment 1 appear in Appendix 1.

The sentences were fairly closely modeled on those used by Stowe except that *all* postverbal NPs were anomalous (or at least, highly implausible) as direct objects. They were embedded in 104 other sentences of a variety of constructions. Thirty of the sentences were followed by true/false questions

TABLE 2
Example of Sentences used in Experiment 1 (Analysis Regions Indicated by '/' and Labeled)

ANIMATE, DISAMBIGUATING COMMA (DISAMBIGUATED)

Before the police/	stopped, /	the moon/	had risen/	over the ocean./
Region 1	v1	NP	D	Post-D

ANIMATE, NO DISAMBIGUATING COMMA (AMBIGUOUS)

Before the police/	stopped/	the moon/	had risen/	over the ocean./
Region 1	v1	NP	D	Post-D

INANIMATE, DISAMBIGUATING COMMA (DISAMBIGUATED)

Before the truck/	stopped, /	the moon/	had risen/	over the ocean./
Region 1	v1	NP	D	Post-D

INANIMATE, NO DISAMBIGUATING COMMA (AMBIGUOUS)

Before the truck/	stopped/	the moon/	had risen/	over the ocean./
Region 1	v1	NP	D	Post-D

to ensure comprehension. Ten sentences of a variety of constructions, but dissimilar to the experimental sentences, were written as practice sentences.

Subjects and Procedure

Forty members of the University of Massachusetts community were tested, ten in each of four counterbalancing conditions. They received course credit or $5.00 payment. Their reading was measured using a Generation V SRI Eyetracker and a Sony 1302 video display displaying text generated by a Targa 16 video board. The display presented a maximum of 72 characters in each line, with approximately 4 characters per degree of visual angle. The experimental sentences were one or two lines long on the screen. In the latter cases, all critical material through the disambiguating verb (plus, for most sentences, a few additional words) appeared on the first line.

A bite bar was prepared for each subject and the functioning of the eyetracker was explained. Subjects were told that they should read in a normal fashion, attempting to understand each sentence so that they could answer straightforward questions about it, and that they should press a button when they had read it to their satisfaction. After an initial calibration period, the ten practice sentences were presented in an individually-randomized order. Subjects read them at a comfortable rate, pressing a button after each sentence had been read. Before each sentence, a brief calibration check was performed, and the eyetracker recalibrated if necessary. During each sentence, an Epson Equity III microcomputer, interfaced with the Eyetracker, sampled the eye position each ms, determining when and where each fixation began and ended. One question was visually presented after each sentence, and the subject answered by pressing one of two buttons for "yes" or "no." After practice, the

TABLE 3
Measures of Eye Fixation in Experiment 1

Condition	Measure				
	First Fixation Time, ms	First Pass Time, ms/ch	Total Time, ms/ch	Second Pass Times ms/ch	Percentage Regressions Out
Region 1					
An/D	224	33.0	42.5	9.5	...
An/A	217	33.1	40.3	7.1	...
In/D	218	35.6	40.0	4.4	...
In/A	223	36.0	40.7	4.6	...
Region v1					
An/D	254	34.2	42.4	5.0	14
An/A	250	35.4	45.6	9.3	6
In/D	246	30.7	33.3	1.5	8
In/A	244	35.9	42.5	6.7	3
Region NP					
An/D	252	28.2	32.2	3.7	8
An/A	250	32.6	45.0	10.1	9
In/D	239	28.0	30.9	3.2	1
In/A	256	31.9	37.2	4.0	6
Region D					
An/D	244	32.2	37.0	3.5	11
An/A	275	37.3	48.8	5.4	22
In/D	255	33.1	37.6	4.0	10
In/A	254	34.7	40.4	3.7	7
Region Post-D					
An/D	233	28.6	30.7	1.1	30
An/A	250	32.2	35.9	1.5	19
In/D	238	28.9	31.3	1.6	22
In/A	249	30.7	34.2	1.5	23

Note: An/D = animate subject, disambiguated by comma; An/A = animate, ambiguous; In/D = inanimate, disambiguated; In/A = inanimate, ambiguous.

eyetracker was recalibrated, and the 120 experimental and distractor sentences were presented in individually randomized order, just as in the practice list. The entire session took approximately half an hour.

Each subject was tested in one of four different counterbalancing conditions, to ensure that each experimental sentence was tested equally often in

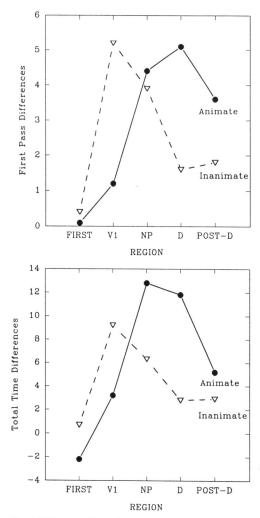

Fig. 1 Differences in reading time between ambiguous
and disambiguated sentences, Experiment 1. Top panel:
First Pass Time differences (ms/character). Bottom
panel: Total Time differences (ms/character).

each of the four forms, and that each subject received an equal number of
sentences in each form.

RESULTS

Table 3 presents the basic eyetracking data, after dividing the sentences into
regions 1, V1, NP, D, and post-D (as illustrated in Table 2). The various
measures presented were calculated from a record of fixation positions and

durations, after eliminating all individual fixations over 1000 or under 100 ms in length. Figure 1 also presents the differences between ambiguous and disambiguated forms in terms of first pass and total time data for these regions (including post-D, although not all sentences yielded scorable data for this position).

In the preliminary experiment described earlier (cf. Clifton, 1992), the total time measure indicated disruption in the disambiguating region only for animate subject sentences (as reported by Stowe) while gaze duration indicated equivalent disruption for both animate and inanimate subject sentences. In contrast, the total time and first pass measures in the present experiment yielded similar patterns of results. However, the regions of the sentence differed in the extent to which they produced results congruent with Stowe's. Therefore, the data will be analyzed region by region.

Consider the critical D region. All data indicate clear disruption of reading in the ambiguous-animate condition, compared to the disambiguated-animate condition, but relatively little disruption for inanimate subject sentences. (Disruption in an ambiguous condition compared to a disambiguated condition can be seen in Figure 1 as reading time differences greater than zero.) First fixation durations were selectively long in the ambiguous-animate condition, yielding a significant interaction between animacy and ambiguity ($F_1(1,39) = 7.47$, $p < .01$; $F_2(1,15) = 7.09$, $p < .01$) as well as a significant main effect of ambiguity ($p < .02$). First pass times exhibited a similar pattern, with a mean of 37.3 ms/char in the ambiguous-animate condition against a mean of 33.5 ms/char in the other three conditions, but here the interaction was significant by items but not by subjects ($F_1(1,39) = 1.71$, $p > .15$; $F_2(1,15) = 5.35$, $p < .04$). The main effect of ambiguity was significant ($F_1(1,39) = 7.83$, $p < .01$; $F_2(1,15) = 15.71$, $p < .01$). An analysis of gaze duration (see Footnote 1) produced comparable results, with significant effects of ambiguity ($p < .01$) and a nearly-significant interaction ($F_1(1,23) = 3.49$, $p < .07$; $F_2(1,15) = 6.67$, $p < .02$).

The analysis of total times in the D region yielded significant effects for both factors and the interaction (animate > inanimate, $F_1(1,39) = 7.58, p < .01$, $F_2(1,15) = 4.45$, $p < .05$; ambiguous > disambiguated, $F_1(1,39) = 28.86$, $F_2(1,15) = 11.71$, $p < .01$; interaction, $F_1(1,39) = 5.89$, $F_2(1,15) = 5.94$, $p < .05$). Finally, the frequency of regressions out of Region D was higher in the animate-ambiguous condition than in the others (interaction $F_1(1,39) = 5.53$, $p < .03$, but $F_2(1,15) = 2.93$, $p = .10$) as well as being higher for ambiguous than disambiguated sentences $F_1(1,39) = 10.66, p < .01; F_2(1,15) = 4.58$, $p < .05$).

The data from the disambiguating region are thus totally compatible with the description Stowe (1989) gave to her data: substantial disruption in the ambiguous-animate condition, but not in the ambiguous-inanimate condition. There is little or no sign of the early disruption for the ambiguous-inanimate condition that was observed in the gaze duration data obtained in the preliminary experiment described earlier. Considered by itself, this suggests that Stowe was correct in her conclusions; default thematic role information can guide initial parsing decisions.

However, close examination of the reading of the preceding regions places severe qualifications on this conclusion. Consider first the NP region, containing the NP that was temporarily ambiguous as a direct object but anomalous (or at least implausible) in all conditions. Here, although there were no significant differences in first fixation durations, first pass times were longer for ambiguous than disambiguated NPs (32.3 vs 28.1 ms/character; $F_1(1,39) = 11.06$, $F_2(1,15) = 13.79$, $p < .01$). There was no interaction involving animacy of the subject (interaction $F < 1$). Gaze duration in the NP region patterned in the same way (38.8 vs 34.2 ms/char for ambiguous vs. disambiguated sentences; $F_1(1,39) = 9.70, p < .01; F_2(1,15) = 12.55, p < .01$), with no sign of an interaction ($F = 0$). More first-pass fixations were made in the NP region of ambiguous than disambiguated sentences (1.50 vs 1.31 for animate subjects, 1.58 vs 1.35 for inanimate subjects; $F_1(1,39) = 15.65$, $p < .01; F_2(1,15) = 13.60, p < .01$).

Total reading times were similarly longer for ambiguous than disambiguated sentences (41.1 vs 31.5 ms/char, $F_1(1,39) = 22.98$, $F_2(1,15) = 33.77$, $p < .01$). Here, however, the effect of ambiguity was greater for animate than inanimate subject sentences, although present for each (interaction $F_1(1,39) = 3.54, p = .06; F_2(1,15) = 6.34, p < .03$), and animate sentences yielded slower reading overall than inanimate sentences ($F_1(1,39) = 8.54$, $p < .01, F_2(1,15) = 7.39, p < .02$).

Before interpreting this pattern of results, consider briefly the first pass times in the previous region, V1. Figure 1 suggests a markedly larger effect of ambiguity for inanimate than for animate subjects, but the interaction between ambiguity and animacy was of questionable significance ($F_1(1,39) = 2.11$, $p = .15$, $F_2(1,15) = 5.00$, $p < .04$). Inspection of Table 3 seems to indicate that this difference is due to notably fast reading time for the disambiguated sentences with inanimate subjects rather than slow times for the ambiguous inanimate subject sentences. However, it is possible that the proper description of the questionably significant interaction should focus on the animate subject sentences. The V1 region included a comma in the disambiguated condition, and counting this comma as an additional character in calculating the ms/char data (as was done) may make these values artifactually small in the disambiguated condition. In fact, the raw first pass reading times for Region V1 indicated long times for the *animate* subject disambiguated condition, 334 ms, and roughly equal times for the other three conditions (305, 312, and 301 ms).[2]

---

2 All regions other than Region V1 were the same length in the ambiguous and unambiguous

Regardless of the proper description of the interaction, it essentially disappeared (actually reversing numerically) when the data were scored with the right boundary of the V1 region moved left to three characters from the end of the verb. Such a scoring procedure presumably eliminates most trials on which useful preview of the disambiguating comma and the word after V1 is obtained during the fixation on V1. First pass times were 48 vs 44 ms/char for the disambiguated and ambiguous animate subject sentences, and 52 vs 49 ms/char for the corresponding inanimate subject sentences. An interpretation for this pattern of results will be offered in the Discussion section.

DISCUSSION
The data from Region D seem to tell a clear story: Readers apparently take a temporarily ambiguous postverbal NP as direct object of an ergative verb when the subject is animate. Disambiguating material that forces the NP to be subject of a complement sentence is read slowly in this case. When the subject is inanimate, readers presumably take the NP to be subject of a complement sentence. Reading of the following disambiguating material is not then disrupted.

However, this simple and attractive story is inadequate. First, it is inconsistent with the data from the preliminary experiment, which strongly suggested that subject animacy did not guide initial analysis but rather affected reanalysis. Second, and more crucially, it fails to take into account the effects of ambiguity and animacy in the region preceding the disambiguating region. Ambiguity slowed all sentences equally in the NP region itself on the first pass reading time measure. Recall that the NPs in Experiment 1 were anomalous or implausible as direct object of the verb. The finding of slow reading times in the ambiguous condition would be expected if readers were in fact taking the postverbal NP to be direct object and reacting quickly to its implausibility (Stowe, 1989, actually raises this possibility; cf. Tanenhaus, Stowe, & Carlson, 1985; for a similar argument).

Under this interpretation, the animate and inanimate subject conditions differ because an inanimate subject is easily taken as the theme of the main verb, displacing the postverbal NP from this role. However, the present interpretation does not claim that the subject is *initially* analyzed as theme of the verb. If it were the first analysis, the postverbal NP could not be taken as

---

conditions, and resulted in the same pattern of results regardless whether they were analyzed in terms of either ms/char or raw uncorrected ms. This is fortunate, because neither measure adequately adjusts for differences in region length (cf. Ferreira & Clifton, 1986). However, when both measures yield the same results, these results cannot be attributed to length differences. As indicated in the text, neither measure allows an unambiguous comparison of the time to read a region with a comma and a region without a comma. This comparison is not a crucial one from the theoretical perspective adopted in this paper, although it may be from other perspectives.

a direct object or theme, implausible or otherwise. The apparent disruption in reading the NP would have to be attributed to some factor other than its implausibility as direct object. Rather, the subject is taken as theme of the main verb as the result of a reanalysis that is triggered by the implausibility of the postverbal NP as direct object. This reanalysis succeeds more quickly in the inanimate subject condition than in the animate subject condition. Time to read the syntactically disambiguating material is less in the inanimate subject condition than in the animate subject condition because the initial direct object (late closure) analysis was already rejected in the former but not in the latter condition.

Alternative accounts of the generally-slow reading times for ambiguous sentences in the postverbal NP region do not seem able to account for the entire pattern of results. For instance, one might suggest that the slow reading in the NP region comes about from the complexity of building a new clause, not from the need to revise an initial NP-object analysis. However, this seems inconsistent with the failure to find slow reading time in the V1 region of disambiguated sentences, where the comma forces the presumably-complex operation of building a new clause. It also seems inconsistent with the finding of slow reading time in the disambiguating verb region of ambiguous-animate sentences, which should be read quickly if the postverbal NP had been taken as subject of a new clause.

Two puzzling results remain. First, there was a possible interaction between subject animacy and ambiguity at V1. At first glance, this effect seems to suggest that information from the verb is used very quickly, before the following NP is assigned as its direct object. However, the fact that the interaction reflects selectively slow reading times for the disambiguated animate subject sentences (or fast times for the disambiguated inanimate subject sentences) means that readers were influenced by the comma that follows the verb in the disambiguated condition. This comma forces the construction of an interpretation in which the postverbal NP serves as subject of the matrix clause, a task which is easy when an inanimate subject can fill the obligatory theme role of V1 but harder when an animate subject must be taken as theme. Thus, verb information by itself (in conjunction with subject animacy) does not guide the initial analysis of a sentence; rather, it is used to facilitate an analysis process triggered by reading the comma (and perhaps the following NP). When the comma and the NP were probably not read during the fixation on V1 (by eliminating trials on which the last three letters of V1 were fixated), no interaction between animacy and ambiguity was seen on reading time for V1.

Second, there was little evidence of the distinctly different pattern of results between first pass and total time measures that was observed in the preliminary experiment (see Clifton, 1992). An analysis of second pass times in regions V1, NP, and D (the time spent re-reading these regions; see Table 3) indicated that although the effect of disambiguation on second pass times seemed greater for animate than for inanimate sentences (4.21 vs 1.94 ms/item), the interaction that tests this difference was nonsignificant ($p > .10$). Second-pass times in these regions were longer for animate than inanimate sentences (6.2 vs 3.9 ms/char; $F_1(1,39) = 6.17$, $p < .02$; $F_2(1,15) = 11.78$, $p < .01$) and for ambiguous than for disambiguated sentences (6.5 vs 3.5 ms/char; $F_1(1,39) = 15.98$, $p < .01$; $F_2(1,15) = 14.74$, $p < .01$). A significant interaction between ambiguity and region ($p < .01$) indicated that the differences in second pass time disappeared by Region D. Thus, while reanalysis appeared to be needed in the ambiguous sentences, and re-reading time was longer for animate than inanimate subject sentences, the difference between such sentences cannot be attributed solely to re-reading time. These sentences also differed in first pass time, a difference that was most apparent in Region D where the difference in second pass time had disappeared.

Experiment 2

The interpretation given for the Experiment 1 results relies on the implausibility of the postverbal NPs as direct objects. Their implausibility was claimed to be noted very quickly in ambiguous sentences, provoking an attempt at reanalysis. This reanalysis was claimed generally to succeed before Region D was read in the inanimate subject condition, but not in the animate subject condition. Making this argument assumes that thematic role information does not guide analysis in the strongest sense considered by Stowe (else there should have been no disruption on the noun in the inanimate subject condition), but that such information can guide reanalysis (cf. Frazier, 1987). If thematic role information did guide analysis in the strong sense, then plausibility of the postverbal NP as direct object should not matter, given an inanimate subject of an ergative verb. Such a subject should be taken as theme, blocking the direct object interpretation of the postverbal NP.

To test this account, the sentences used in Experiment 1 were modified so that the postverbal NP could be reasonably plausible as object of V1 for both the animate and the inanimate subject sentence. The sentences used in Experiment 2 were identical to those used in Experiment 1 up through the VP (except for one sentence, where an embedding clause was added before this point to allow the sentence to be plausible). The same postverbal NP was used in all four versions of each sentence, and was chosen to be as plausible a direct object as possible in all four versions. An example sentence appears in Table 4.

Minor differences in plausibility probably still exist between animate and inanimate subject sentences (it was much harder to create fully natural transitive initial clauses with inanimate subjects), but are not crucial for the logic of Experiment 2. No instances of the anomaly apparent in Experiment 1 exist in Experiment 2. There is no reason to expect plausibility-based

TABLE 4
Example of Sentences used in Experiment 2 (Analysis Regions Indicated by '/'
and Labeled)

ANIMATE, DISAMBIGUATING COMMA (DISAMBIGUATED)				
Before the police/	stopped, /	the Datsun/	disappeared/	into the night./
Region 1	v1	NP	D	Post-D
ANIMATE, NO DISAMBIGUATING COMMA (AMBIGUOUS)				
Before the police/	stopped/	the Datsun/	disappeared/	into the night./
Region 1	v1	NP	D	Post-D
INANIMATE, DISAMBIGUATING COMMA (DISAMBIGUATED)				
Before the truck/	stopped, /	the Datsun/	disappeared/	into the night./
Region 1	v1	NP	D	Post-D
INANIMATE, NO DISAMBIGUATING COMMA (AMBIGUOUS)				
Before the truck/	stopped/	the Datsun/	disappeared/	into the night./
Region 1	v1	NP	D	Post-D

disruption on the postverbal NP in animate subject sentences. Thus, in the animate subject condition, reading times for ambiguous sentences should not be slow at the postverbal NP (as they were in Experiment 1), but should slow in the following disambiguating region. Inanimate subject sentences may show disruption on the postverbal NP if readers can use evidence of relatively minor implausibility together with thematic role information to revise an initial analysis of the postverbal NP as a direct object and substitute a thematically-based reanalysis. However, if this initial direct object is not always rejected (as it seemed to be in Experiment 1, when the direct object analysis was anomalous) then there should be some evidence of disruption in the disambiguating region for inanimate subject sentences.

METHOD

The sixteen sentences used in Experiment 1 were modified by changing them from the postverbal NP onwards, attempting to maintain plausibility of the direct object interpretation up to the syntactically disambiguating region. An example appears in Table 4, and all sentences appear in Appendix 2. As in Experiment 1, four forms of each sentence were constructed. The experimental sentences were embedded into a list of 102 sentences of various forms, each of which was followed by a simple yes/no question. Twenty-four University of Massachusetts subjects (most of whom had had previous eyetracking experience, but none of whom had served in Experiment 1) were tested using the same procedures as in Experiment 1.

RESULTS

The basic eyetracking results appear in Table 5 and a figure of difference scores appear in Figure 2. The theoretically interesting NP and D regions

TABLE 5
Measures of Eye Fixation in Experiment 2

Condition	Measure				
	First Fixation Time, ms	First Pass Time, ms/ch	Total Time ms/ch	Second Pass Time, ms/ch	Percentage Regressions Out
Region 1					
An/D	230	33.4	39.5	6.7	...
An/A	224	32.2	39.9	7.7	...
In/D	226	34.2	38.2	4.2	...
In/A	222	35.3	39.7	4.8	...
Region V1					
An/D	244	31.4	38.2	3.2	11
An/A	244	35.2	45.4	9.7	5
In/D	237	28.8	32.7	1.0	9
In/A	250	36.2	44.9	5.9	3
Region NP					
An/D	243	28.5	32.8	3.0	4
An/A	258	28.7	37.8	7.9	11
In/D	238	25.7	27.6	1.1	3
In/A	250	29.7	36.1	4.7	7
Region D					
An/D	269	35.0	39.9	4.2	6
An/A	286	46.2	58.9	9.3	9
In/D	243	35.7	37.4	1.0	4
In/A	256	37.7	45.0	5.9	7
Region Post-D					
An/D	257	31.5	37.2	4.2	14
An/A	260	34.9	43.6	4.6	28
In/D	254	32.7	33.8	1.9	1
In/A	255	31.9	38.0	3.8	18

Note: An/D = animate subject, disambiguated by comma; An/N = animate subject, ambiguous; In/D = inanimate subject, disambiguated; In/A = inanimate subject, ambiguous.

showed different patterns of results for the different eye movement measures. An analysis of variance indicated that first fixation durations in Region NP were marginally faster for disambiguated than ambiguous sentences ($F_1(1,23) = 2.89, p < .10; F_2(1, 15) = 3.07, p < .10$) while no other differences approached significance. In Region D, first fixations were faster for sentences

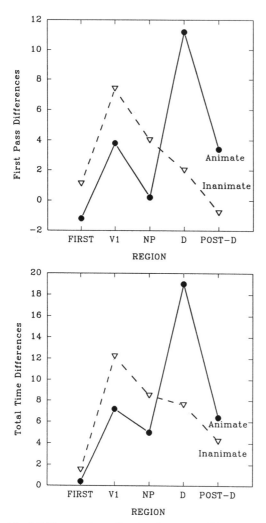

Fig. 2 Differences in reading time between ambiguous and disambiguated sentences, Experiment 2. Top panel: First Pass Time differences (ms/character). Bottom panel: Total Time differences (ms/character).

with inanimate than with animate subjects ($F_1(1,24) = 9.90, p < .01; F_2(1,15) = 5.32, p < .05$), and they were again marginally faster for disambiguated than ambiguous sentences ($F_1(1,24) = 2.79, p < .15; F_2(1,15) = 5.71, p < .05$). The interaction did not approach significance.

First pass times were faster in analyses of Regions NP and D for disambiguated than for nondisambiguated sentences ($F_1(1,23) = 5.27, p < .05$ and $F_2(1, 15) = 5.36, p < .05$ for Region NP; $F_1(1,23) = 15.0, p < .01$ and $F_2(1, 15) =$

9.86, $p < .01$ for Region D). However, nearly-significant interactions qualify this consistent pattern ($F_1(1,23) = 2.96$, $p < .10$ and $F_2(1, 15) = 3.02$, $p < .10$ for Region NP; $F_1(1,23) = 4.61$, $p < .05$ and $F_2(1, 15) = 6.41$, $p < .05$ for Region D). In Region NP, the disambiguating comma facilitated reading for sentences with an inanimate subject (25.7 vs 29.7 ms/char) but not for sentences with an animate subject (28.7 vs 28.5 ms/char). In Region D, however, the comma facilitated reading sentences with an *animate* subject (46.2 vs 35.0 ms/char), but did not significantly facilitate sentences with an inanimate subject (37.7 vs 35.7 ms/char). This difference in pattern is confirmed by a three-way interaction in an analysis combining presence or absence of a comma, subject animacy, and region (NP vs D: $F_1(1,23) = 5.66$, $p < .03$; $F_2(1,15) = 11.53$, $p < .01$). An analysis of gaze durations, as used in Experiment 1, showed essentially the same results.

The first pass times from Region V1 indicated longer ms/char times for ambiguous than for disambiguated sentences ($p < .05$). However, as was noted earlier, this difference may be due to the inclusion of one more character (the comma) in the ms/char adjustment. The difference disappeared in the uncorrected reading time data (302 vs 306 msec for disambiguated vs ambiguous sentences). No interaction between ambiguity and subject animacy was apparent.

Second pass times were analyzed by treating Regions V1, NP, and D as a factor. They were longer for ambiguous than disambiguated sentences (7.7 vs 2.4 ms/char; $F_1(1,39) = 16.35$, $p < .01$; $F_2(1,15) = 17.90$, $p < .01$). In addition, second pass times were longer for animate than inanimate subject sentences (6.2 vs 3.9 ms/char; $F_1(1,39) = 5.28$, $p < .03$; $F_2(1,15) = 5.62$, $p < .04$). No interactions approached significance. Second pass times (and total reading times) were long in Region D (as well as in the earlier regions) for ambiguous sentences compared to unambiguous ones, both for animate subject and inanimate subject sentences. Regressions from Regions NP and D were more frequent (in an analysis treating regions as a factor) for ambiguous than for disambiguated sentences (8.8 vs 4.2; $F_1(1,39) = 7.40$, $p < .02$; $F_2(1,15) = 10.07$, $p < .01$); the difference held for both animate and inanimate subject sentences. No other effects were significant.

DISCUSSION

When the subject of a sentence was animate, reading was disrupted at the disambiguating matrix verb, Region D. However, when the subject was inanimate, disruption was most notable at an earlier point, the postverbal NP, but there was evidence in the second pass times, total reading times, and pattern of regressive eye movements for disruption in Region D. The disruption at the postverbal NP, in conjunction with the other data presented here, suggests that the postverbal NP *was* initially taken as direct object even when the subject was inanimate, but the modest implausibility of the postverbal NP as direct object together with a preference to take an inanimate subject as theme caused readers to reconsider the analysis. The disruption in Region D suggests that the preference to take the postverbal NP as direct object persisted until the disambiguating region. Such a late closure analysis was apparently maintained more frequently when the subject of the initial clause was animate than when the subject was inanimate. The persistence of the late closure analysis in the latter case contrasts with Experiment 1, where there was little or no evidence that a direct object interpretation (anomalous in Experiment 1, merely mildly implausible in Experiment 2) was ever maintained in the inanimate subject condition.

Conclusions

Stowe's (1989) results suggested that readers could use the inanimacy of the subject of an ergative verb to assign it the thematic role of "theme." This assignment would force the verb to be intransitive, prohibiting a direct object reading of a noun phrase after the verb. Instead, the postverbal noun phrase would have to be the subject of the following clause. Since this was the correct analysis of the temporarily ambiguous sentences Stowe used, no "garden path" disruption should be observed. Stowe's findings were congruent with this account, suggesting that readers use plausibility information (specifically, the relative plausibility of animate and inanimate noun phrases as agents vs. themes of ergative verbs), thematic role structure, and subcategorization possibilities in computing the initial analysis of a temporarily ambiguous sentence.

The present results show that this interpretation is at least premature. Stowe's pattern of results appear in portions of the data presented here, but most likely reflect processes that operate rather late in parsing. The eye movement measures reported here provide evidence that a noun phrase following an ergative verb with an inanimate subject *is* initially taken as the object of that verb, if one looks early enough in the eye movement record (initial fixations on the disambiguating verb, in the preliminary study; sentence regions before the disambiguating verb, in the experiments reported here).

The plausibility of the initial analysis has a quick and substantial effect on parsing. A noun phrase that is implausible as the direct object of a particular verb (as in "stopped the moon") or an unusual assignment of thematic role to a noun phrase (as in "the truck [as agent] stopped the Datsun") results in slow reading times on the postverbal noun phrase. Presumably, the reader forms and evaluates a representation of the meaning of the sentence while looking at the postverbal noun phrase, and this representation is based upon the interpretation of that noun phrase as direct object of the verb. Thematic role assignment possibilities seem to guide reanalysis in a way that implausibility does not; an inanimate subject of an ergative verb puts constraints on likely thematic relations, which speeds reanalysis (cf. Frazier, 1989; Frazier, 1990). The results reported by Stowe very likely reflect the speed of reanalysis rather than choices made in initial analysis, especially given the slow reading rates imposed by her experimental technique. The Stowe-like results found in the disambiguating region of the present experiments presumably reflect the same thing. The actual initial analysis of a sentence can only be determined by looking at earlier points in the processing of the types of sentences used here.

This interpretation supports an almost ascetic modular view in which the initial analysis of a sentence is based only on information that is guaranteed to be relevant to all sentences, namely, major category information and phrase structure rules. Subcategorization preferences, thematic role possibilities, plausibility, etc. are used quickly, but only to evaluate and correct the initial analysis.[3] Such a view of the processor is not the only one that could account for the present data. An interesting approach currently being considered by several researchers attributes slow reading time at points of implausibility and/or thematic role inappropriateness to competition between alternative analyses (e.g., MacDonald, unpublished; MacWhinney, 1987; Trueswell, Tanenhaus, & Kello, in press). The animacy of the initial subject, the thematic role structure of the verb, the canonical nature of a postverbal NP as direct object, the plausibility of this NP as direct object, and the presence or absence of the comma itself all provide different amounts of evidence for various possible analyses of a sentence. A uniform process of competition resolves any conflict among the sources of information, and will take longer when the conflict is greater. Reading time will be slow, for example, when an ergative verb with an inanimate subject is followed directly by an NP (with no intervening comma). The inanimate subject and thematic role structure of the verb point to an intransitive clause analysis, but the absence of the comma after the verb points to an analysis in which the clause must continue, for example with a direct object. Conflict between these intransitive and transitive analyses slows reading time on the postverbal NP.

Such competition-based analyses must be developed further before they provide predictive accounts of data such as those reported here. For instance, existing competition-based accounts do not explain why the conflict discussed at the end of the previous paragraph would be reflected in reading time effects of similar size when the postverbal NP is anomalous as direct object (Experiment 1) vs when it is merely implausible (Experiment 2). This equivalence is especially surprising since the disruption seems to be much

---

3 A somewhat different view is advanced by Frazier (1990), who proposes that information such as subcategorization preferences and thematic role possibilities is used as soon as it becomes available, but that the parser can make its initial attachments based on phrase structure rules and major category information without waiting for such information to become available.

longer-lasting in the latter case than in the former case, spilling over into following regions and arguably reflecting greater conflict in Experiment 2 than in Experiment 1. However, if conflict really were greater in Experiment 2 than in Experiment 1, the disruption on the postverbal NP should have been greater as well. (From the modular perspective adopted here, this pattern of results is not surprising; the disruption on the NP reflects the cost of rejecting an initial analysis, and the persistence of disruption reflects the difficulty of replacing it with an alternative analysis.)

Another instance where a competition-based approach may fall short concerns the role played by the comma. From the modular perspective, presence of a comma provides grammatical evidence that a clause has ended (perhaps because an intonational phrase break in a spoken sentence is optional after the initial subordinate clause, but generally is not allowed between a verb and its direct object), while absence of a comma does not provide clear evidence about grammatical structure. A competition-based theory could be developed in which statistical information about the presence of commas in different structures is taken as evidence about the likelihood of a structure. However, it may not be easy for the theory to deal with evidence such as that provided by Adams, Clifton, & Mitchell (1992) that the absence of a comma does not affect reading time when the comma is merely stylistically preferred and does not carry disambiguating grammatical information. The simple lack of a comma that is presumably generally present does not seem to constitute evidence against an otherwise acceptable structure.

Competition-based accounts need to be developed further to become truly predictive accounts of sentence processing. Even if such development results in accounts of data that are equivalent in descriptive adequacy to a modular model such as that advocated here, there are reasons to prefer the modular proposal. Rather than assessing processing difficulty as a parametrically-determined function of the number and relative frequencies of alternative possible analyses, the modular proposal has the advantage of accounting for the processing of a wide range of sentence constructions with a very small number of principles that have cognitive and linguistic motivation (cf. Clifton & Ferreira, 1989). The proposal also encourages the theorist to search for universal cognitive constraints on sentence processing rather than attribute psycholinguistic phenomena to the vagaries of experience. The present results suggest that, if one looks closely enough, it is possible to find evidence for the operation of a specialized grammatical processor, distinct from the operation of whatever processes evaluate the entire range of information that must eventually be considered in arriving at the correct interpretation of a sentence.

This research was supported by grant HD 18708 to the author and Lyn Frazier.
Correspondence can be directed to Charles Clifton, Department of Psychology,

University of Massachusetts, Amherst, MA 01003. The author would like to thank John Huitema and René Schmauder for their help in collecting and analyzing the data reported here, and Lyn Frazier, Shelia Kennison, Sara Sereno, Shari Speer, Mike Tanenhaus, and the editors of this special issue for valuable comments on earlier drafts of this paper.

References

Abney, S. (1989). A computational model of human parsing. *Journal of Psycholinguistic Research, 18*, 129-144.

Adams, B., Clifton, C., Jr., & Mitchell, D. (1992). Syntactic guidance in sentence processing. Poster presented at Psychonomic Society, St. Louis, November, 1992.

Altmann, G. (1988). Ambiguity, parsing strategies, and computational models. *Language and Cognitive Processes, 3*, 73-98.

Altmann, G., & Steedman, M. (1988). Interaction with context during human sentence processing. *Cognition, 30*, 191-238.

Berwick, R.C. (1991). Principles of principle-based parsing. In R.C. Berwick, S.P. Abney, & Carol Tenny (Eds.), *Principle-based parsing: Computation and psycholinguistics*, pp. 1-39. Dordrecht: Kluwer.

Clifton, C., Jr. (1992). Tracing the course of sentence comprehension: How lexical information is used. In K. Rayner (Ed.), *Eye movements in visual cognition: Scene perception and reading*, pp. 397-414. New York: Springer-Verlag.

Clifton, C., Jr., & Ferreira, F. (1989). Ambiguity in context. *Language and Cognitive Processes, 4*, SI 77-104.

Clifton, C. Jr., Frazier, L., & Connine, C. (1984). Lexical expectations in sentence comprehension. *Journal of Verbal Learning and Verbal Behavior, 23*, 696-708.

Clifton, C., Jr, Speer, S., & Abney, S. (1991). Parsing arguments: Phrase structure and argument structure as determinants of initial parsing decisions. *Journal of Memory and Language, 30*, 251-271.

Crain, S., & Steedman, M. (1985). On not being led up the garden path: The use of context by the psychological parser. In D. Dowty, L. Kartunnen, and A. Zwicky (Eds.), *Natural language parsing*. Cambridge: Cambridge University Press.

Ferreira, F., & Clifton, C., Jr. (1986). The independence of syntactic processing. *Journal of Memory and Language, 25*, 348-368.

Ferreira, F., & Henderson, J. (1990). The use of verb information in syntactic parsing: Evidence from eye movements and word-by-word self-paced reading. *Journal of Experimental Psychology: Learning, Memory, and Cognition, 16*, 555-568.

Fodor, J.A. (1983). *Modularity of mind*. Cambridge, MA : MIT Press.

Frazier, L. (1978). *On comprehending sentences: Syntactic parsing strategies*. Unpublished doctoral dissertation, University of Connecticut.

Frazier, L. (1987). Sentence processing: A tutorial review. In M. Coltheart (Ed.), *Attention and Performance, XII*, Hillsdale, (pp. 559-586). N.J.: Lawrence Erlbaum Associates.

Frazier, L. (1989). *Parsing with chains*. Paper presented at Second Annual CUNY Conference on Human Sentence Processing, March, 1989.

Frazier, L. (1990). Exploring the architecture of the language system. In G. Altmann (Ed.), *Cognitive Models of Speech Processing: Psycholinguistic and Computational Perspectives*, Cambridge, MA: MIT Press.

Frazier, L., & Rayner, K. (1982). Making and correcting errors during sentence comprehension: Eye movements in the analysis of structurally ambiguous sentences. *Cognitive Psychology, 14*, 178-210.

Holmes, G.M., Stowe, L., & Cupples, L. (1989). Lexical expectations in parsing complement-verb sentences. *Journal of Memory and Language, 28*, 668-689.

Kimball, J. (1973). Seven principles of surface structure parsing in natural language. *Cognition, 2*, 15-47.

MacDonald, M. (unpublished). *Probabilistic constraints and syntactic ambiguity resolution*.

MacWhinney, B. (1987). The competition model. In B. MacWhinney (Ed.), *Mechanisms of language acquisition*. Hillsdale, NJ: Erlbaum.

Marslen-Wilson, W.D. (1987). Functional parallelism in spoken word-recognition. *Cognition, 25*, 71-102.

Marslen-Wilson, W. (1989). Access and integration: Projecting sound onto meaning. In W. Marslen-Wilson (Ed.), *Lexical representation and process.* (pp. 3-24). Cambridge, MA: MIT.

Marslen-Wilson, W., Brown, C.M., & Tyler, L.K. (1988). Lexical representations in spoken language comprehension. *Language and Cognitive Processes, 3*, 1-16.

Mitchell, D.C. (1987). Lexical guidance in human parsing: Locus and processing characteristics. In M. Coltheart (Ed.), *Attention and Performance XII*, (pp. 601-618). Hillsdale, NJ: Erlbaum.

Mitchell, D.C. (1989). Verb-guidance and other lexical effects in parsing. *Language and Cognitive Processes, 4*, SI 123-154.

Mitchell, D.C., & Holmes, V.M. (1985). The role of specific information about the verb in parsing sentences with local structural ambiguity. *Journal of Memory and Language, 24*, 542-559.

Pritchett, B.L. (1991). Head position and parsing ambiguity. *Journal of Psycholinguistic Research, 20*, 251-270.

Rayner, K., Carlson, M., & Frazier, L. (1983). The interaction of syntax and semantics during sentence processing: Eye movements in the analysis of semantically biased sentences. *Journal of Verbal Learning and Verbal Behavior, 22*, 358-374.

Rayner, K., Sereno, S.C., Morris, R.K., Schmauder, A.R., & Clifton, C., Jr. (1989). Eye movements and on-line language comprehension processes. *Language and Cognitive Processes, 4*, SI 21-49.

Schwanenflugel, P.J., & Shoben, E.J. (1983). Differential context effects in the comprehension of abstract and concrete verbal materials. *Journal of Experimental Psychology: Learning, Memory, and Cognition, 9*, 82-102.

Shapiro, L.P., Zurif, E., & Grimshaw, J. (1987). Sentence processing and the mental representation of verbs. *Cognition, 27,* 219-246.

Steedman, M., J., & Altmann, G.T.M. (1989). Ambiguity in context: A reply. *Language and Cognitive Processes, 4,* SI 77-105.

Stowe, L. (1989). Thematic structures and sentence comprehension. In G.N. Carlson and M.K. Tanenhaus (Eds.), *Linguistic structure in language processing,* Dordrecht: Kluwer Academic Publishers.

Tanenhaus, M., Garnsey, S., & Boland, J. (1991). Combinatory lexical information and language comprehension. In G. Altmann (Ed.), *Cognitive models of speech processing.* (pp. 383-408). Cambridge, MA: MIT Press.

Tanenhaus, M.K., Stowe, L.A., & Carlson, G.N. (1985). *The interaction of lexical expectation and pragmatics in parsing filler-gap constructions.* Proceedings of the Seventh Annual Cognitive Science Society Conference, Irving, CA.

Trueswell, J.C., Tanenhaus, M.K., & Kello, C. (in press). Verb-specific constraints in sentence processing: Separating effects of lexical preference from garden-paths. *Journal of Experimental Psychology: Learning, Memory, and Cognition.*

Taraban, R., & McClelland, J.R. (1988). Constituent attachment and thematic role assignment in sentence processing: Influences of content-based expectations. *Journal of Memory and Language, 27,* 597-632.

Underwood, G., & Everatt, J. (1992). The role of eye movements in reading: Some limitations of the eye-mind assumption. In E. Chekaluk and K.R. Llewellyn (Eds.), *The role of eye movements in perceptual processes.* Amsterdam: Elsevier Science Publishers.

Appendix 1: Sentences used in Experiment 1

1. While the batherIwet towel was drying[,] the sun went behind a cloud.
2. After the partnersImarriage split up[,] the judge awarded the property to Mr. Joyce.
3. After the driverIcar turned[,] the scenery suddenly became much more beautiful.
4. Even after the singerImusic ended[,] the dancers stayed on the stage.
5. After the teacherIlecture began[,] the auditorium erupted with boos and catcalls.
6. Before the policeItruck stopped[,] the moon had risen over the ocean.
7. While the knightIrope was swinging[,] the hangman laughed sadistically.
8. After the soldiersIbombs dropped[,] the women and children started coming out of their houses.
9. When the captainIyacht was about to sail[,] the Coast Guard began to search for cocaine.
10. Although the apprenticeIsituation improved[,] the foreman took over the important job.
11. After the businessmanIreport returned[,] the police decided not to press charges.
12. As the pirateIboat sank[,] the bubbles floated up to the surface.
13. When the whole crewIbig tent collapsed[,] the onlookers all started screaming.

14. While the majorettes|batons twirled[,] the band kept playing as loud as it could.
15. Long before the actor|play finished[,] the crowd became very restless.
16. When the dancer|curtain shifted[,] the stage suddenly collapsed.

Appendix 2: Sentences used in Experiment 2

1. While the bather/wet towel was drying[,] the dog jumped back into the water.
2. After the partners/marriage split up[,] the friendship remained as strong as ever.
3. After the driver/car turned[,] the wheels fell off with a loud crash.
4. Even after the singer/music ended[,] the celebration went on for a long time.
5. After the teacher/lecture began[,] the meeting became much more exciting.
6. Before the police/truck stopped[,] the Datsun disappeared into the night.
7. The passerbys noticed that, while the man who was dressed as a knight/the sword on the end of the rope was swinging[,] the children refused to go near the playground.
8. After the soldiers/bombs dropped[,] the high explosives killed hundreds of people.
9. When the captain/yacht was about to sail[,] the calm channel turned dark and stormy.
10. Although the apprentice/situation improved[,] everybody's mood remained as unhappy as ever.
11. After the businessman/report returned[,] the job applications were processed much more quickly.
12. As the pirate/boat sank[,] the enemy ship raised its anchor and sailed away.
13. When the whole crew/big tent collapsed[,] the scaffolding began to topple over.
14. While the majorettes/batons twirled[,] the flags kept waving in the strong wind.
15. Long before the actor/play finished[,] the last act became extremely tedious.
16. When the dancer/curtain shifted[,] the microphone tumbled over with a loud crash.

7 Reading Processes During Syntactic Analysis and Reanalysis

FERNANDA FERREIRA and JOHN M. HENDERSON
Michigan State University

Abstract   We conducted two experiments to examine the process-ing of garden path sentences such as *While the boy scratched the dog yawned loudly.* We varied the ambiguous phrase of such sentences so that it was either short (*the dog*), long due to the inclusion of a relative clause (*the dog that was hairy*), or long due to the inclusion of prenominal adjectives (*the big and hairy dog*). The subjects' task was to read each sentence while their eye movements were monitored and then judge whether the sentence was grammatical. We found that early closure sentences were judged grammatical less often than were late closure sentences, and sentences with a long ambiguous phrase, particularly one made long through the insertion of a relative clause, were judged grammatical less often than were those with a short ambiguous phrase. The reading time data, however, showed a curious pattern. Reading times on the disambiguating word of the sentences (*yawned* in the above example) were longer for early closure than for late closure sentences, as expected, but reading times were shorter for sentences with a long ambiguous phrase. We argue that the latter finding reflects subjects' tendency to read more quickly as they proceed through a sentence. We suggest that researchers interpret any studies showing differences in the processing of syntactically easy and difficult constructions with extreme caution, unless the words being compared in these studies are preceded by the same number of words in the different experimen-tal conditions.

Résumé   Nous avons effectué deux expériences sur le traitement des phrases trompe-l'oeil telles *While the boy scratched the dog yawned loudly.* Nous avons varié la formulation ambiguë de ces phrases pour qu'elle soit brève (*the dog*), longue en raison de l'insertion d'une proposition relative (*the dog that was hairy*) ou longue par l'insertion d'adjectifs antéposés (*the big and hairy dog*). Les sujets devaient lire chacune des phrases pendant que leurs mouvements oculaires étaient enregistrés, puis ils devaient juger de leur grammaticalité. Nous avons constaté que les phrases à clôture hâtive étaient jugées moins souvent grammaticales que les phrases reposant sur le principe de clôture tardive. Nous avons également constaté que les phrases ayant une formulation longue et ambiguë,

en particulier lorsqu'une proposition relative y était insérée, étaient jugées grammaticales moins souvent que celles dont la formulation était courte et ambiguë. Un
patron étrange ressort des temps de lecture. Comme prévu, les temps de lecture
enregistrés pour le terme désambiguisant des phrases (*yawned* dans l'exemple ci-
dessus) étaient plus longs dans le cas des phrases à clôture hâtive; en revanche, ils
étaient plus courts pour les phrases longues et ambiguës. Ce résultat montre, à notre
avis, que la vitesse de lecture des sujets tend à s'accroître d'un bout à l'autre de la
phrase. Nous invitons les chercheurs à interpréter avec force circonspection toutes
les études révélant des différences dans le traitement des constructions syntaxique-
ment complexes et simples, à moins que les mots qui y sont comparés soient
précédés du même nombre de mots dans les différentes conditions expérimentales.

Reading involves a number of inter-related processes. Readers must access the
lexical reprentations of words and combine them so as to reflect the overall
meaning of the sentence. For example, consider the ambiguous sentence *Mary
saw the boy with binoculars*. The phrase *with binoculars* could function either
as the modifier of the verb phrase that includes *saw*, indicating that Mary was
the one in possession of the binoculars, or as the modifier of *boy*, in which
case the boy is the one with the binoculars. These different syntactic
attachments of the phrase *with binoculars* have different semantic consequences, resulting in different truth conditions for the two possible semantic
interpretations of the ambiguous sentence. An important process during
reading, then, is to create phrases and assign them to their appropriate
grammatical roles, a process we will refer to as *parsing*.

Partially or fully ambiguous sentences have proven to be a useful tool for
examining how parsing operates, particularly during reading. Frazier and her
colleagues (Frazier, 1987; Frazier & Rayner, 1982; Rayner, Carlson, &
Frazier, 1983; Rayner & Frazier, 1987) have found that the parser obeys two
fundamental principles when deciding how to attach phrases into the ongoing
syntactic representation. The first is the *minimal attachment* principle, which
states that readers assign the simplest syntactic structure possible for a
sentence consistent with the well-formedness rules of the language. For
example, for the above sentence *Mary saw the boy with binoculars*, the
parser's initial preference would be to assign the phrase *with binoculars* as the
modifier of the verb phrase dominating *saw*, because on at least some
syntactic analyses, that assignment results in a less complex syntactic structure
than does the alternative assignment (Ferreira & Clifton, 1986; Frazier, 1990;
Rayner, Carlson, & Frazier, 1983; but see Britt, Perfetti, Garrod, & Rayner,
1992; Perfetti, 1990; Taraban & McClelland, 1988).

The second principle is *late closure*, which states that the parser prefers to
assign a constituent to the current phrase or clause that is already open, rather
than constructing a new phrase or clause to accommodate the new constituent.

For example, given an ambiguous sequence such as *Because the boy left the room*, most readers would initially assign the phrase *the room* to the role of direct object of *left* rather than assuming that the phrase is the subject of a new clause, as in *Because the boy left the room seemed empty* (Frazier, 1978). The phrase *the room* is initially assigned to the role of direct object because that assignment allows the phrase to be incorporated into the currently open clause, whereas the alternative assignment requires the postulation of a new clause. One might expect, therefore, that sentences such as *Because the boy left the room seemed empty* would be difficult to process, particularly upon encountering the word *seemed*, which disambiguates the assignment of the previous phrase. This prediction has been borne out in several studies (Ferreira & Henderson, 1991a, 1991b; Frazier & Rayner, 1982; Mitchell, 1987), which have generally shown long reading times in the disambiguating region of such sentences. Sentences such as these that tend to be initially syntactically misanalyzed have been termed *garden-path sentences*, because they send the parser down the wrong syntactic path or parse; when a subject misanalyzes such a sentence, the subject is said to have been *garden-pathed.*

Much debate has centered on the question of how robust the minimal attachment and late closure preferences are, and particularly on the question of whether nonsyntactic sources of information can modify these preferences. One source of information that has been extensively studied is discourse context. Researchers have proposed that if a syntactically difficult sentence (a nonminimal attachment or early closure sentence) were to occur in an appropriately biased context, the difficulty of parsing that sentence might be reduced or even eliminated. Most studies have found evidence for this prediction, with differences centering on whether the garden-path effect is entirely eliminated in context (Altmann & Steedman, 1988; Crain & Steedman, 1985; Spivey-Knowlton, Trueswell, & Tanenhaus, 1993) or reduced (Britt et al., 1992; Ferreira & Clifton, 1986).

Another source of information that has been of interest concerns verbs' tendencies to take different kinds of arguments. For example, one might expect that given a sequence such as *Because the boy smiled the room*, the tendency to take the second noun phrase *the room* to be an object would be attenuated, because the verb *smiled* cannot take one. Some models, which we have previously termed verb guidance models (Holmes, 1987; Holmes, Stowe, & Cupples, 1990), go so far as to claim that all parsing preferences reflect the subcategorization preferences of the verbs used in the sentences. For example, if a verb such as *left* were used, evidence in support of the late closure principle would be found, because such a verb tends to occur with a direct object; in contrast, a verb such as *smiled* would yield no such evidence. According to these models, then, sentences are parsed in accordance with the main verb's preference to take various syntactic arguments, not according to general purpose principles such as minimal attachment and late closure.

Although one can adduce evidence to support both sides, we believe the bulk of the evidence is inconsistent with the verb guidance model. We have reviewed the relevant experiments in detail (Ferreira & Henderson, 1991b), and in a recent study employing eye movement monitoring (Ferreira & Henderson, 1990), we obtained evidence that verb information does not influence the initial parse of a garden-path sentence. The purpose of one of the experiments we will describe here was to examine this issue further by presenting readers with garden-path sentences and varying the characteristics of the sentences' critical verb.

Recently, we have started to examine how readers are able to recover from syntactic errors they might initially make during the processing of a sentence. Our logic is that if it turns out that nonsyntactic sources of information can influence the initial syntactic parse of a sentence and therefore prevent garden-pathing, readers will still occasionally misanalyze sentences and have to revise their interpretation. We have been interested in examining how these revisions are made, both because we believe it that is an important question in and of itself, and because the answer to this question might indicate how information from a variety of different sources is integrated during sentence processing.

To examine this issue, we have conducted experiments in which we varied the characteristics of the ambiguous phrase in garden-path sentences. For example, compare the three sentences shown below:

(1) Because the boy left the room seemed empty.
(2) Because the boy left the room that's hot and stuffy seemed empty.
(3) Because the boy left the hot and stuffy room seemed empty.

Intuitively, the second sentence with the longer ambiguous phrase seems the most difficult. We have verified this intuition in experiments showing that subjects judge sentences such as (2) to be grammatical much less often that sentences such as (1) or (3) (Ferreira & Henderson, 1991a; Ferreira & Henderson, 1991b). In Ferreira and Henderson (1991a), we conducted a number of studies to determine the reason for this effect. We found that length alone did not matter; a sentence such as (3) was judged grammatical as often as (1) and far more often than (2). (Those experiments also ruled out the possibility that (2) is difficult because of the complexity of the relative clause construction.) It appears instead that the further the head of the ambiguous phrase (the word *room* in these examples) from the disambiguating word (*seemed*), the less likely a subject is to parse the sentence successfully.

In the two experiments that we will report here, we sought to extend this finding by examining reading times for early closure sentences such as (1) through (3) compared to their late closure counterparts. Subjects' eye movements were monitored as they read each sentence, for the purpose of determining whether it was grammatical or ungrammatical. We expected that reading times for early closure sentences would be longer than for late closure sentences. As will be seen below, this prediction was supported. In addition, because early closure sentences with a long ambiguous region (such as (2)) are judged ungrammatical more often than the other early closure versions, we expected that reading times for such sentences would also be longer. However, as will be seen below, we did not obtain this expected pattern. Instead, paradoxically, we found that reading times were *shorter* for sentences with a long ambiguous region than for those with a short ambiguous region. In the General Discussion, we offer some possible explanations for this surprising pattern.

Experiment 1

The goal of the first experiment was to examine eye movement behaviour during the processing of garden-path sentences. We were particularly interested in the question of how varying the length of the ambiguous region of these sentences would influence fixation times and patterns, because we already had evidence from grammaticality judgements that increasing the length of the ambiguous region caused subjects to judge garden-path sentences to be ungrammatical (Ferreira & Henderson, 1991a, 1991b). In addition, we wished to examine how verb information would influence the processing of garden-path sentences. We presented subjects with sentences in which the verb either matched the ultimate form of the sentence (intransitive verbs with early closure sentences; transitive verbs with late closure sentences) or did not. Following our other work (Ferreira & Henderson, 1990), we expected that verb information would not influence reading time measures reflecting the initial processing of the garden-path sentences, but instead would affect reanalysis measures and grammaticality judgements.

METHOD
Subjects
The participants were 40 undergraduates from the University of Alberta who participated in the experiment in exchange for partial credit towards their introductory psychology courses. All were native speakers of Canadian English and had either normal or corrected-to-normal vision. None was aware of the hypotheses under investigation in the experiment.

Materials
Each subject read 104 sentences, 32 of which were experimental items, and 72 were filler items (half grammatical, half ungrammatical). Table 1 gives an example of an experimental item in each of the eight conditions. For each sentence, the ambiguous region was either short, consisting of just a determiner-noun sequence, or long, consisting of a determiner and noun

TABLE 1
Example of an Experimental Item, Experiment 1

Early Closure Versions

Intransitive Verb, Short Region
Because Jeff walked the dog got upset.

Intransitive Verb, Long Region
Because Jeff walked the dog who was very obese got upset.

Transitive Verb, Short Region
Because Jeff pulled the dog got upset.

Transitive Verb, Long Region
Because Jeff pulled the dog who was very obese got upset.

Late Closure Versions

Intransitive Verb, Short Region
Because Jeff walked the dog his wife got upset.

Intransitive Verb, Long Region
Because Jeff walked the dog who was very obese his wife got upset.

Transitive Verb, Short Region
Because Jeff pulled the dog his wife got upset.

Transitive Verb, Long Region
Because Jeff pulled the dog who was very obese his wife got upset.

---

followed by a relative clause. We also varied the verb of the first clause of each experimental sentence, so that the verb was one that either tends to be used intransitively or transitively in English, as assessed by norms collected by Connine, Ferreira, Jones, Clifton, and Frazier (1984). Finally, we varied whether the sentence was early or late closure.

Procedure

Upon arrival for the experimental session, the subject was seated in a comfortable chair and asked to place his or her head in a chinrest to minimize head and body movements. The eye tracking system (an ISCAN RK-416 eyetracker) was then calibrated, a procedure that generally took under 5 minutes. Ten practice sentences were then shown on a high-resolution flat-screen monitor to familiarize subjects with reading on the eyetracker. Any questions from the subject were answered, and then the subject proceeded to read on the monitor the 104 items that made up the experiment. Each subject received a different random order of the items. The eyetracker and monitor were interfaced with an 80386 microcomputer, which controlled the presentation of sentences and kept a complete eye movement record, including fixation positions and durations.

TABLE 2
Data Analysis Segments, Experiment 1

Segment	Example
Unambiguous Segment	Because Jeff walked Because Jeff pulled
Ambiguous Region	the *dog* the *dog* who was very obese
Disambiguating Segment	got
Rest of Sentence	upset

Note: The head noun of the ambiguous region is italicized.

A trial consisted of the following events: First, the experimenter checked the calibration accuracy of the eye movement system (see Henderson & Ferreira, 199, for details). Second, the subject was asked to fixate a cross on the left side of the CRT when he or she was ready for a sentence. A single sentence was then presented. The sentence always fit on a single horizontal line across the CRT. The subjects read the sentence and, when ready, indicated their grammaticality decision by pushing one button on a button panel in front of them to indicate that the sentence was grammatical and another button to indicate that the sentence was ungrammatical. The entire experimental session lasted about one hour.

Data Analysis and Design

For the analysis of the reading time data, each sentence was divided into a number of scoring segments, as shown in Table 2. The first segment is the *unambiguous* segment, and includes all the material up to the ambiguous noun phrase. Reading times for this segment are given in ms per character to control for variations in segment length (reading time for the segment is divided by the number of characters in the segment). Next is the *ambiguous* segment, which consists of the ambiguous noun phrase. Reading times here are also given in ms per character. Within the ambiguous segment we also separately analyzed just the *head* noun of the phrase. For this segment and the remaining segments, we will report raw reading times rather than reading times per character, because these segments are identical across all conditions. The next segment, the *disambiguating* segment, was always one word long, and consisted of the second verb of the sentence. This segment is the crucial one for revealing any garden-path effects, and so we will discuss the results for this region before the others. Finally, the *rest of sentence* segment consisted of the last one or two words of the sentence. This segment also may show garden-path effects spilling over from the disambiguating segment, and so we will discuss the results for this segment following our consideration of the disambiguating segment.

The measures we will report for these segments were divided into two types: *initial analysis* and *reanalysis* measures. This distinction reflects the theoretical distinction between reading processes that occur when a reader first encounters some portion of a sentence, and later processes that occur when the reader corrects any errors made during initial processing and integrates all the information contained in the sentence. For example, the garden-path model of sentence processing assumes that when readers first encounter an ambiguous string such as *Because Jeff walked the dog*, they misanalyze the ambiguous noun phrase as the object of the first clause and detect their error upon encountering the sentence's disambiguating word. These initial processes would be primarily reflected in the measure *first pass reading time* (the total reading time spent in a sentence segment before exiting that segment), but in a few cases we will also report *first fixation duration* (the duration of just the initial fixation in a region before exiting that segment) and *number of fixations* (the number of fixations in a segment before exiting that segment). Reanalysis of the misanalyzed material might require reassigning the ambiguous NP to the role of subject of the second clause, and computing the semantic consequences of this different phrasal attachment. These reanalysis processes are captured by the *total reading time* measure, which is the sum of all fixation durations in a segment. In addition, reanalysis is reflected in the frequency of regressive eye movements. We will analyze regressive eye movements from the disambiguating segment and rest of sentence to the unambiguous segment, the ambiguous segment, and the head noun.

The experiment was analyzed as a $2 \times 2 \times 2$ factorial. The first variable was verb transitivity; the first verb of each experimental sentence was either one that tends to be used intransitively in English, or transitively. The second variable concerned the characteristics of the ambiguous region; the region was either short, consisting of only a determiner and a noun, or long, consisting of a determiner, noun, and a relative clause. The final variable was whether the sentence was early or late closure. Analyses were conducted treating both subjects and items as random effects ($F1$ and $F2$ respectively). All effects were significant at an α level of .05 unless otherwise noted.

RESULTS

Grammaticality Judgements

The data over all conditions are shown in Figure 1. Grammaticality judgements were significantly affected by region type, $F1(1,39) = 47.94$, $MS_e = 2.84$, $F2(1,31) = 36.34$, $MS_e = 2.21$, and closure, $F1(1,39) = 77.55$, $MS_e = 4.86$, $F2(1,31) = 34.16$, $MS_e = 3.96$. These two variables interacted, $F1(1,39) = 15.42$, $MS_e = .83$, $F2(1,31) = 12.87$, $MS_e = .61$. With a short ambiguous region, 64% of early closure sentences and 79% of late closure sentences were judged grammatical; with a long ambiguous region, 35% of

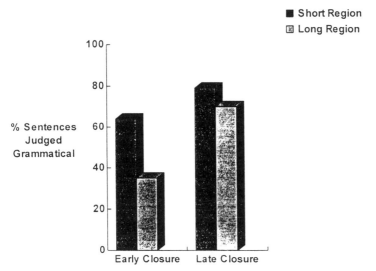

Fig. 1 Grammaticality judgements, Experiment 1.

early closure sentences and 70% of late closure sentences were judged grammatical. Thus, the nature of the interaction seems to be that the difference between early and late closure sentences is exaggerated when the ambiguous region is long. There was no three-way interaction, both F's < 1.

The verb by closure interaction was marginal by subjects, $F1(1,39) = 3.68$, $MS_e = .17$, but not significant by items, $F2(1,31) = 1.73$, $MS_e = .19$. With early closure sentences, sentences with intransitive verbs were judged grammatical 51% of the time and those with transitive verbs were judged grammatical 48% of the time; with late closure sentences, the percentage judgements for the same two conditions were 71% and 77%. Thus, the pattern is that with early closure sentences, intransitive verbs are slightly preferred; with late closure sentences, transitive verbs are preferred. This pattern makes sense: Early closure sentences in this experiment were sentences that ultimately did not take a direct object argument, and the intransitive verbs preferred not to take a direct object. Thus, the verb and closure types match. Similarly, late closure sentences ultimately did take a direct object, and transitive verbs prefer to take a direct object. Again, the verb and closure types match.

Eye Movement Measures[1]
Table 3 shows the results for first-pass reading time, total reading time, and

---

1 The eye movement measures are based on data from both correct and incorrect trials. The results for some measures are somewhat different when only correct trials are analyzed, but these differences do not bear on the interpretation of the results reported here. Information about the results from correct trials only can be obtained from either author.

TABLE 3
Measure of Eye Fixation, Experiment 1

Condition	First Pass	Total	Proportion In	Proportion Out
	Unambiguous Segment (ms/char)			
Short-EC	36.2	59.2	27	...
Long-EC	39.2	56.1	16	...
Short-LC	38.8	55.5	22	...
Long-LC	37.1	49.4	15	...
	Ambiguous Region (ms/char)			
Short-EC	34.9	74.1	27	...
Long-EC	30.5	52.1	21	...
Short-LC	34.1	64.4	28	...
Long-LC	28.4	46.0	10	...
	Head of Ambiguous Region (ms)			
Short-EC	248	485	22	...
Long-EC	244	371	19	...
Short-LC	249	440	25	...
Long-LC	245	340	14	...
	Disambiguating Segment (ms)			
Short-EC	266	403	...	25
Long-EC	225	302	...	22
Short-LC	246	345	...	23
Long-LC	223	278	...	14
	Rest of Sentence (ms)			
Short-EC	243	363	...	24
Long-EC	259	360	...	25
Short-LC	251	313	...	19
Long-LC	302	396	...	18

Note: Short-EC = Short region, early closure; Long-EC = Long region, early closure; Short-LC = Short region, late closure; Long-LC = Long region, late closure.

proportion regressions into or out of a segment for each segment of the sentences. We will begin with the **disambiguating segment** of the sentence, and we will report results for three initial analysis measures: first pass reading times, first fixation durations, and number of fixations (note that only first pass reading times are shown in the table). We conducted analyses on all three of these measures in order to maximize the chances of finding evidence for garden-pathing on the disambiguating word of these sentences. As we will see, however, there is little evidence for longer initial processing time on the disambiguating word.

First pass reading times on the disambiguating segment were unaffected by closure (p's > .25), but were influenced by region length; reading times were longer when the ambiguous region had been short (256 ms) rather than long (225 ms), $F1(1,39) = 7.32$, $MS_e = 78970$, $F2(1,31) = 6.99$, $MS_e = 45076$. With number of fixations as the dependent measure, region length again had an effect (.99 fixations on the disambiguating word in the short condition and .82 in the long condition), $F1(1,39) = 9.11$, $MS_e = 2.35$, $F2(1,31) = 14.99$, $MS_e = 2.07$. Closure had a marginal effect in the expected direction (expected from the point of view of the garden-path model), $F1(1,39) = 2.16$, $MS_e = .44$, $p > .10$, $F2(1,31) = 3.10$, $MS_e = .35$, $p < .10$, with .94 fixations in the early closure condition and .87 in the late closure condition. Finally, with first fixation duration as the dependent measure, no effects were evident, all p's > .15.

For the segment consisting of the **rest of the sentence**, there was a significant verb type by closure interaction, $F1(1,39) = 4.12$, $MS_e = 90382$, $F2(1,31) = 10.54$, $MS_e = 143546$. With intransitive verbs, reading times at the end of the sentence were longer for early closure sentences (261 ms) than late closure sentences (252 ms); with transitive verbs, the opposite pattern was obtained (241 vs. 300 ms for the early and late closure conditions respectively). This pattern does not reflect any effects of garden-pathing, but instead indicates that the end of a sentence containing more phrases is read for a longer period of time than the end of a sentence containing fewer phrases. We will see when we report the results of the next experiment (in which only transitive verbs were used) this same finding that sentences with a greater number of arguments are associated with longer end-of-sentence reading times.

Thus far, we have found little evidence that readers were garden-pathed by the early closure sentences. However, the reanalysis measures that we will report next indicate that readers spent much more time rereading the early closure than the late closure sentences, consistent with the idea that they had been garden-pathed by the former sentence type. The longer re-reading times for early closure sentences held for each sentence segment, and so we will report results for the reanalysis measures beginning with the left-most segment (the unambiguous segment) and continuing to the end of the sentence.

Total reading time on the **unambiguous segment** was longer in the early closure condition than the late closure condition (57.7 vs. 52.5 ms per character), $F1(1,39) = 15.16$, $MS_e = 2151$, $F2(1,31) = 16.70$, $MS_e = 1877$. Reading times were also longer when the ambiguous region of the sentence was short rather than long (57.4 vs. 52.8 ms per character), $F1(1,39) = 7.87$, $MS_e = 1711$, $F2(1,31) = 7.84$, $MS_e = 1389$. Regressions to this same region appeared to be more common in the early closure than the late closure condition (21% of trials vs. 19%), but this effect was not significant, $F1(1,39) = 1.65$, $MS_e = 578$, p > .20, $F2(1,31) = 1.14$, $MS_e = 454$, p > .20. The percentage of regressions to the unambiguous segment was influenced by region length, $F1(1,39) = 14.74$, $MS_e = 6643$, $F2(1,31) = 17.91$, $MS_e = 5338$, with regressions being more common in the short (25%) than the long (16%) ambiguous region condition. This finding that subjects are more likely to make a regression to the unambiguous segment when the ambiguous region (the one immediately following) is short may occur because it is easier to execute a regression from the latter half of the sentence to the beginning of the sentence with less intervening material.

On the **ambiguous region**, total reading time was longer in the early closure than the late closure condition (63.1 vs. 55.2 ms per character), $F1(1,39) = 16.32$, $MS_e = 5029$, $F2(1,31) = 18.92$, $MS_e = 4176$. Total reading time was also longer when the ambiguous region was short rather than long (69.2 vs. 49.0 ms per character), $F1(1,39) = 70.32$, $MS_e = 32728$, $F2(1,31) = 127.77$ $MS_e = 26978$. Regressions showed a similar pattern: Regressions to the ambiguous region were more frequent when the sentence turned out to be early closure rather than late closure (24% vs. 19%), $F1(1,39) = 5.13$, $MS_e = 1945$, $F2(1,31) = 3.48$, $MS_e = 1492$, $p < .10$, and when the ambiguous region was short rather than long (28 vs. 16%), $F1(1,39) = 19.16$, $MS_e = 11725$, $F2(1,31) = 27.50$, $MS_e = 9900$.

Focussing on just the **head** noun of the ambiguous region, total reading time was longer when the sentence was early closure rather than late closure (428 vs. 390 ms), $F1(1,39) = 5.68$, $MS_e = 114268$, $F2(1,31) = 6.26$, $MS_e = 92040$, and when the ambiguous region of the sentence was short rather than long (462 vs. 355 ms), $F1(1,39) = 36.61$, $MS_e = 920100$, $F2(1,31) = 44.02$, $MS_e = 753428$. Regressions to the head noun were more common when the ambiguous region was short rather than long (24% vs. 16%), $F1(1,39) = 12.07$, $MS_e = 4530$, $F2(1,31) = 6.29$, $MS_e = 3263$.

A similar pattern was found for the **disambiguating** segment. Total reading time was longer in the early closure than the late closure condition (353 vs. 311 ms), $F1(1,39) = 7.42$, $MS_e = 135384$, $F2(1,31) = 16.98$, $MS_e = 162610$, and with a short ambiguous region rather than a long ambiguous region (374 vs. 290 ms), $F1(1,39) = 26.14$, $MS_e = 567172$, $F2(1,31) = 45.96$, $MS_e = 521644$. Regressions showed a similar pattern: Regressions occurred more often in the early closure (24%) than the late closure (19%) condition, $F1(1,39) = 3.84$, $MS_e = 1990$, $p < .10$, $F2(1,31) = 4.12$, $MS_e = 3292$, and when the ambiguous region was short (25%) rather than long (18%), $F1(1,39) = 6.05$, $MS_e = 3672$, $F2(1,31) = 3.67$, $MS_e = 3675$, $p < .10$.

For the **rest of sentence** segment, total reading times did not differ among the experimental conditions, all p's > .20. However, regressions were more frequent for early closure than late closure sentences (24% vs. 19%), $F1(1,39) = 4.63$, $MS_e = 2387$, $F1(1,31) = 6.35$, $MS_e = 5220$.

Thus far, the data indicate that early closure sentences require more rereading than do late closure sentences, consistent with the notion that early closure sentences lead the parser down the garden-path and require syntactic reanalysis. However, there is no evidence in the reading time data that increasing the length of the ambiguous region of these sentences made the sentences any more difficult to reanalyze. Instead, what the results reported to this point indicate is that sentences with a *short* ambiguous region elicit more rereading time and more regressions than do sentences with a long ambiguous region. This finding is the opposite of what we expected given the results from grammaticality judgements, where we found that sentences with a short ambiguous region are judged grammatical more often than those with a long ambiguous region. To determine the nature of this effect, we analyzed the first-pass reading times for the segments preceding the disambiguating segment. Any reading time effects on these segments from initial analysis measures such as first-pass reading times cannot reflect processes related to garden-pathing, because the garden-path is not detected until the disambiguating segment of the sentence.

First pass reading times on the **unambiguous segment** showed a significant length by closure interaction, $F1(1,39) = 9.34$, $MS_e = 433$, $F2(1,31) = 5.75$, $MS_e = 372$. In the early closure, short region condition, first pass reading times were 36.2 ms per character; in the early closure, long region condition, 39.2 ms per character; in the late closure, short region condition, 38.8 ms per character; and in the late closure, long region condition, 37.1 ms per character. This is a puzzling finding, because at this point the sentences do not differ among the various conditions of the experiment, and the subjects had not yet fixated the material that distinguishes the different sentence versions. One possibility is that during readers' first pass through the unambiguous segment, they are able to detect extrafoveally how much material was left to process in the sentence, and subjects may fixate less time on the unambiguous segment in the condition in which they have the least amount of material to process later.

First pass reading times on the **ambiguous segment** were sensitive to just region length: Reading times per character were longer when the ambiguous region was short (34.5 ms) rather than long (29.4 ms), $F1(1.39) = 25.89$, $MS_e = 2064$, $F2(1,31) = 48.02$, $MS_e = 1638$. Thus, it appears that readers spend more time per character on a phrase the shorter that phrase is, a finding which we will replicate in the next experiment.

Turning now to the **head** of the ambiguous phrase, we found no effects on first pass reading times, all p's > .20. However, there was a marginal tendency for first fixation durations to be longer with a long region compared with a short region (173 vs. 167 ms), $F1(1,39) = 2.79$, $MS_e = 3394$, $p < .10$, $F2(1,31) = 2.62$, $MS_e = 1541$, $p > .10$. In addition, there was a significant verb by region length interaction, $F1(1,39) = 4.52$, $MS_e = 6623$, $F2(1,31) = 8.51$, $MS_e = 6301$. With an intransitive verb, region length had little effect on first fixation durations (171 vs. 168 ms); but with a transitive verb, first fixation durations were 163 ms in the short condition and 179 ms in the long condition. Thus, the main effect of region length seems to hold only for sentences with a transitive verb.

SUMMARY AND DISCUSSION

The grammaticality judgements nicely complement the data we reported in Ferreira and Henderson (1991a, 1991b). Early closure sentences were judged grammatical less often than late closure sentences, and sentences with a long ambiguous region were judged grammatical less often than those with a short ambiguous region. In addition, as we observed in our previous work, the effect of region length was much larger with early closure sentences than with late closure sentences. Furthermore, subjects were more likely to label a sentence as grammatical when the closure and verb types matched; early closure sentences preferred intransitive verbs, and late closure sentences preferred transitive verbs.

The reading time data provide some evidence that subjects were garden-pathed by the early closure sentences, but the results were more compelling from the reanalysis than from the initial analysis measures. None of the initial analysis measures showed any compelling effects of garden-pathing in the disambiguating segment (although the situation will improve somewhat in the next experiment). However, the total amount of time spent in virtually every segment of the sentences was longer when the sentences were early closure rather than late closure, and regressions from the disambiguating and end-of-sentence segments to the earlier segments were more common with early closure sentences.

We found little evidence for any influence of verb transitivity, except in the data from grammaticality judgements. The grammaticality judgements showed the expected pattern that early closure sentences were judged grammatical more often with intransitive verbs, and late closure sentences with transitive verbs (these results have recently been replicated by Anes & Ferreira, in progress, with more strongly biased verbs). The characteristics of the ambiguous region had no effect on this pattern. The absence of any effects in the reading time measures does not necessarily indicate that verb information has little effect on sentence processing, especially in light of the numerous studies providing strong evidence for such effects (e.g., Holmes et al., 1989). It is possible that our verb manipulation was too weak to influence reading time and regressions, and that the other manipulations of closure and ambiguous region length were so powerful as to swamp out any effect of verb. We are currently conducting research in our laboratory to examine further the effects of verb information on reading time for early and late closure sentences (Anes & Ferreira, in progress; McClure & Ferreira, in progress).

The length of the ambiguous region had a powerful effect on reading times and the probability of a regression. However, contrary to our expectations, readers spent more time on segments of the sentence other than the ambiguous phrase when that phrase was short. This finding did not interact with closure in any analysis, suggesting that it does not reflect parsing processes. We can only speculate about what might account for such a finding. One possibility is that as subjects proceed through a sentence, their reading speed increases. With the longer ambiguous phrase, subjects would have processed more material, and so might have been going faster as they first encountered the various segments after the ambiguous region, and as they reread any of the sentence segments. Gernsbacher (1990) has summarized a variety of evidence indicating that processing speed increases as comprehenders proceed through a sentence or text: The initial sentence of a passage is read more slowly than subsequent sentences; the initial words of a sentence are read more slowly than later words; phoneme monitoring times are shorter the later the position of the phoneme in the sentence; and event-related potentials indicating difficulty of processing are less pronounced for later words than for earlier words. This tendency is even evident in the processing of nonverbal materials: The initial picture of a series of pictures comprising a story is examined longer than later pictures. Thus, it seems quite likely that reading speed increases throughout a sentence, at least until the sentence-final word is encountered.

Other results obtained in this experiment pertain more to basic reading processes. First, we found that short phrases were read more slowly than long phrases on a per character basis. As we will see, this result was also obtained in Experiment 2. This finding is difficult to interpret, however. It is possible that subjects do indeed read short phrases more carefully than long phrases. Another possibility, however, is that the longer phrases were made up proportionally of more function words than content words, and because function words are often skipped during reading and are read extremely quickly when fixated (Henderson & Ferreira, 1993; Just & Carpenter, 1980; Rayner & Pollatsek, 1989), reading times overall might have been inflated for the short phrases. Second, we found that the first fixation duration on the head of a phrase appears to be shorter when the phrase is long. This result may indicate that readers spend more time on the head of a phrase when it is modified. Finally, end-of-sentence reading times are longer for late closure than early closure sentences, indicating that the more material in a sentence to be integrated, the longer the end-of-sentence integration process takes.

Experiment 2

The purpose of the second experiment was to examine more carefully how the characteristics of the ambiguous region of a garden-path sentence influence the processing of early and late closure sentences. As in the previous experiment, we varied whether the ambiguous region was short or long. However, we also varied whether the region was lengthened by inserting a relative clause after the head noun of the ambiguous phrase, or by inserting

TABLE 4
Example of an Experimental Item, Experiment 2

Early Closure Versions

Short Region
While the boy scratched the dog yawned loudly.

Long Region – Relative Clause
While the boy scratched the dog that is hairy yawned loudly.

Long Region – Prenominal Adjectives
While the boy scratched the big and hairy dog yawned loudly.

Late Closure Versions

Short Region
While the boy scratched the dog the girl yawned loudly.

Long Region – Relative Clause
While the boy scratched the dog that is hairy the girl yawned loudly.

Long Region – Prenominal Adjectives
While the boy scratched the big and hairy dog the girl yawned loudly.

---

adjectives in front of the head noun. The former manipulation has the effect of distancing the head of the ambiguous phrase from the disambiguating word of the sentence, while the latter manipulation lengthens the phrase while still leaving the head and the disambiguating word adjacent to each other. Recall that we found in our earlier studies (Ferreira & Henderson, 1991a, 1991b) that distancing the head of the ambiguous phrase from the disambiguating word resulted in much poorer comprehension of early closure sentences (and even somewhat of late closure sentences) than was observed either with a short ambiguous region or with an ambiguous region lengthened through the insertion of prenominal adjectives. We therefore expected that reading times might be longer and regressions more frequent in the long-relative clause condition, particularly with early closure sentences. (Of course, the results of the first experiment showed just the opposite pattern.) In addition, we eliminated the verb manipulation from this experiment, because it had such a weak effect in the previous study, and because we wanted to minimize the complexity of our experiment while still being able to examine closely the influence of the characteristics of the ambiguous region.

METHOD
Subjects
Twenty-four subjects participated in this experiment, obtained from the same pool as in Experiment 1.

TABLE 5
Data Analysis Segments, Experiment 2

Segment	Example
Unambiguous Segment	While the boy scratched
Ambiguous Region	the *dog* the *dog* that was hairy the big and hairy *dog*
Disambiguating Segment	yawned
Rest of Sentence	loudly.

Note: The head noun of the ambiguous region is italicized.

Materials

Each subject read 108 sentences, 36 of which were experimental items, and 72 were filler items (half grammatical, half ungrammatical). Table 4 gives an example of one of the experimental items in each of the six conditions. As before, we manipulated closure, and we also varied the characteristics of the ambiguous region. The region was either short, long due to the insertion of a relative clause following the head noun of the ambiguous phrase, or long due to the insertion of adjectives in front of the head noun of the ambiguous phrase. We equated the two long region conditions on number of words (*the dog that is hairy* vs. *the big and hairy dog*), which necessitated dropping one of the adjectives in the relative clause condition. Removing that adjective could have made the relative clause condition semantically less complex, but this would work against our hypothesis that the long, relative clause condition should be more difficult than the long, prenominal adjective condition.

Procedure

The procedure was the same as in the first experiment.

Data Analysis and Design

As before, for the purposes of data analysis, we divided the experimental sentences into scoring segments: the unambiguous segment, the ambiguous noun phrase, the head noun of the ambiguous noun phrase, the disambiguating segment, and the rest of sentence. Table 5 shows an example sentence from the experiment divided into these segments. The experiment was analyzed as a 3 × 2 factorial. The first variable was ambiguous region type; the ambiguous noun phrase was either *short*, long due to the inclusion of a relative clause (*long-relative clause*), or long due to the inclusion of prenominal adjectives (*long-adjectives*). The second variable was closure (*early closure* vs. *late closure*).

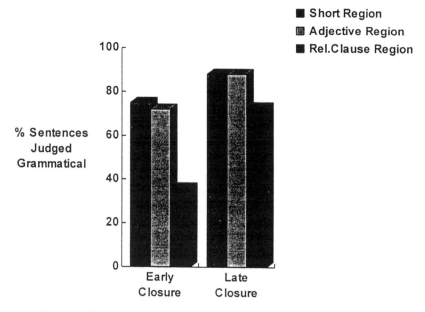

Fig. 2 Grammaticality judgements, Experiment 2.

RESULTS

Grammaticality Judgements

The percentage of sentences judged to be grammatical in each condition of the experiment was analyzed. Early closure sentences were judged grammatical less often than late closure sentences (61 vs. 83%), $F1(1,23) = 47.12$, $MS_e = 1.70$, $F2(1,35) = 29.15$, $MS_e = 2.53$. There was also a main effect of region type, $F1(2,46) = 41.95$, $MS_e = 1.08$, $F2(2,70) = 41.02$, $MS_e = 1.60$. Sentences were judged grammatical 81%, 55%, and 80% in the short, long-relative clause, and long-adjective conditions respectively. These two variables also interacted, $F1(2,46) = 5.73$, $MS_e = .21$, $F2(2,70) = 7.12$, $MS_e = .32$. The pattern is shown in Figure 2. For early closure sentences, grammaticality judgements were about the same in the short and the long-adjective conditions (75% and 72%), but much lower in the long-relative clause condition (36%), $F1(2,46) = 39.80$, $MS_e = 1.12$, $F2(2,70) = 36.63$, $MS_e = 1.68$. A similar pattern held for the late closure sentences (88%, 88%, and 73% for the short, long-adjective, and long-relative clause conditions respectively), $F1(2,46) = 4.39$, $MS_e = .19$, $F2(2,70) = 4.96$, $MS_e = .17$. The nature of the interaction is that the drop for the long-relative clause condition is much larger for early closure sentences than for late closure sentences (36% vs. 73%).

These findings replicate the pattern found in Ferreira and Henderson (1991a, 1991b), and can be described as follows: The short region condition and the long-adjective region condition share the characteristic that the head of the ambiguous phrase is adjacent to the disambiguating word. In the long-relative clause condition, the head of the phrase is separated from the disamb-iguating word by a few words. As we argued in our earlier papers, the further the head of the ambiguous region from the disambiguating word, the more difficult it is for subjects to arrive at a coherent interpretation of the sentence.

Eye Movement Measures
Table 6 gives the results for first-pass reading time, total reading time, and proportion of regressions either into or out of a segment for each segment of the sentences. In the **disambiguating segment** of the sentence, first pass reading times were marginally affected by closure, $F1(1,23) = 3.15$, $MS_e = 11773$, $p < .10$, $F2(1,35) = 2.39$, $MS_e = 18984$, $p > .10$. First pass reading times were 285 ms in the early closure condition and 267 ms in the late closure condition. There was no effect of the region type variable, both F's < 1, and no interaction, $F1(2,46) = 1.48$, $MS_e = 5487$, $p > .20$, $F2 < 1$. Number of fixations also revealed a strong effect of closure, $F1(1,23) = 9.31$, $MS_e = 1.98$, $F2(1,35) = 16.39$, $MS_e = 3.30$, with more fixations occurring on the disambiguating word in the early closure condition (1.45) compared with the late closure condition (1.21). In addition, more fixations occurred when the ambiguous phrase had been short (1.41) than when it had been long due to a relative clause (1.28) or long due to prenominal adjectives (1.30), but this effect was only marginal by subjects, $F1(2,46) = 9.31$, $MS_e = 1.98$, and not significant by items, $F2(2,70) = 1.42$, $MS_e = .37$, $p > .20$. First fixation durat-ions were virtually unaffected by the experimental variables, all p's $> .10$.

In this experiment, in contrast to Experiment 1, we have found evidence that readers were garden-pathed during their initial pass of the disambiguating segment of the early closure sentences. In addition, as in Experiment 1, results from the reanalysis measures reinforce this conclusion further. We will report total reading time and regression data from each segment of the sentence, moving from left to right. The total amount of time spent reading the **unambiguous segment** of the sentence was longer in the early closure condition (85.6 ms per character) than in the late closure condition (76.5 ms per character), $F1(1,23) = 12.05$, $MS_e = 2965$, $F2(1,35) = 9.36$, $MS_e = 4233$. Region type produced a marginal effect, $F1(2,46) = 2.41$, $MS_e = 636$, $p < .10$, $F2(2,70) = 2.74$, $MS_e = 874$, $p < .10$. Total reading times were 85.0, 80.3, and 77.8 ms per character in the short, long-relative clause, and long-adjective conditions respectively. The two variables did not interact, both F's < 1.

In the **ambiguous region**, total reading times were longer in the early closure (77.9 ms per character) than the late closure (64.9 ms per character) condition, $F1(1,23) = 33.45$, $MS_e = 6093$, $F2(1,35) = 14.33$, $MS_e = 9121$. Similarly, the percentage of trials on which a regression to the ambiguous region occurred was greater in the early closure (26%) than the late closure (19%) condition, $F1(1,23) = 6.53$, $MS_e = 1613$, $F2(1,35) = 5.37$, $MS_e = 2474$.

TABLE 6
Measures of Eye Fixation, Experiment 2

Condition	First Pass	Total Time	Proportion In	Proportion Out
	Unambiguous Segment (ms/char)			
Short-EC	47.8	89.7	24	...
RC-EC	48.8	84.2	29	...
Adj-EC	46.6	82.8	22	...
Short-LC	47.2	80.2	28	
RC-LC	48.2	76.4	18	
Adj-LC	47.7	72.8	20	...
	Ambiguous Region (ms/char)			
Short-EC	34.9	87.0	29	...
RC-EC	29.5	77.2	27	...
Adj-EC	28.4	69.5	22	...
Short-LC	33.5	74.7	31	
RC-LC	30.0	62.7	14	
Adj-LC	29.9	57.2	13	...
	Head of Ambiguous Region (ms)			
Short-EC	230	486	26	...
RC-EC	257	464	23	...
Adj-EC	255	479	21	...
Short-LC	222	445	29	
RC-LC	234	404	21	
Adj-LC	251	381	10	...
	Disambiguating Region (ms)			
Short-EC	273	570	...	19
RC-EC	292	531	...	20
Adj-EC	290	507	...	16
Short-LC	279	519		11
RC-LC	263	407		5
Adj-LC	257	408	...	9
	Rest of Sentence (ms)			
Short-EC	236	403	...	42
RC-EC	289	462	...	25
Adj-EC	300	463	...	29
Short-LC	325	459		24
RC-LC	392	551		23
Adj-LC	380	512	...	21

Note: Short-EC = Short region, early closure; RC-EC = Long relative clause region, early closure; Adj-EC = Long adjective region, early closure; Short-LC = Short region, late closure; RC-LC = Long relative clause, late closure; Adj-LC = Long adjective region, late closure.

These findings are consistent with the notion that subjects had difficulty during their initial analysis of the ambiguous noun phrase, although the relatively high number of regressions in the late closure condition indicates that the sentences were somewhat difficult to comprehend regardless of closure. (This suggestion is supported also by the data from grammaticality judgements; subjects considered more than 10% of the sentences in the two long late closure conditions to be ungrammatical.)

The total time spent in the ambiguous region was also significantly affected by its own characteristics (that is, by the region variable). The total amount of time spent reading the ambiguous noun phrase when it was short was 80.8 ms per character; when it was long due to the inclusion of a relative clause, total reading time was 70.0 ms per character; and when the ambiguous noun phrase was long due to the inclusion of prenominal adjectives, the total reading time was 63.4 ms per character. This pattern resulted in a significant effect of region, $F1(2,46) = 10.45$, $MS_e = 3729$, $F2(2,70) = 10.74$, $MS_e = 5143$. As we saw in Experiment 1, reading times per character appear to be longer for short phrases than for longer phrases. Interestingly, regressions to the ambiguous region occurred on a greater percentage of trials when the region was short (30%) compared to the long-relative clause (20%) and long-adjective (18%) conditions. It appears that not only are short phrases read more slowly on a per character basis, but they are also more likely to receive a regressive eye movement.

Turning now to the **head** of the ambiguous noun phrase, total reading time was longer in the early closure than the late closure condition (476 vs 410 ms), $F1(1,23) = 9.57$, $MS_e = 159000$, $F2(1,35) = 7.10$, $MS_e = 232264$. There was no effect of region and no interaction between the two variables, all F's < 1.

Next we will consider total reading time in and regressions to the **disambiguating segment**. Total reading times were longer in the early closure (536 ms) than in the late closure condition (444 ms), $F1(1,23) = 11.43$, $MS_e = 300484$, $F2(1,35) = 12.13$, $MS_e = 542104$. Region also affected total reading times on the disambiguating word, $F1(2,46) = 5.74$, $MS_e = 106476$, $F2(2,70) = 5.71$, $MS_e = 138558$. Reading times were 544, 469, and 457 ms in the short, long-relative clause, and long-adjective conditions. No interaction was evident, all p's $> .30$. Regressions to the disambiguating segment were more frequent in the early closure than the late closure condition, $F1(1,23) = 11.21$, $MS_e = 3083$, $F2(1,35) = 11.17$, $MS_e = 4874$ (18% vs. 8%).

Thus far, the data from both initial and reanalysis measures indicate that readers were garden-pathed during their initial analysis of early closure sentences, and spent more time rereading such sentences. In addition, the reanalysis measures have consistently shown that total reading times are longer and regressions more frequent for sentences with a short rather than a long ambiguous region. It appears that readers spend more time reprocessing a sentence if it contains a shorter ambiguous phrase. The next analyses will show that readers also spend more time in their initial processing of the ambiguous region (including its head noun) if that region is short rather than long.

First-pass reading times for the **ambiguous noun phrase** were 34.2 ms per character when the phrase was short, 29.8 when it was long, due to the inclusion of a relative clause, and 29.1 when it was long, due to the inclusion of prenominal adjectives, $F1(2,46) = 8.87$, $MS_e = 369$, $F2(2,70) = 3.57$, $MS_e = 485$. The finding that the two long region conditions are about equivalent suggests that one account we suggested in our explanation of the results from Experiment 1 is not plausible. We suggested there that perhaps reading times per character were shorter with the longer phrase because of the greater proportion of function word material in those longer phrases. However, the finding that the long-relative clause and long-adjective conditions were equivalent is inconsistent with this argument, because the long-adjective region contains more content words than the long-relative clause condition, and so should have been read more slowly on this account. Therefore, the conclusion that short phrases are read more slowly than long phrases is reinforced. No other effects were evident, all F's < 1.

Focussing specifically on the **head** of the ambiguous noun phrase, we found that first-pass reading times were unaffected by the variables, all p's $> .10$. However, first fixation durations revealed an effect of region type, $F1(2,46) = 4.36$, $MS_e = 6302$, $F2(2,70) = 6.15$, $MS_e = 13812$. First fixation duration on the head was 201 ms in the short condition, 221 ms in the long-relative clause condition, and 220 ms in the long-adjective condition. It appears that readers spent more time on the head of a phrase when that phrase was modified in some way, either through the use of adjectives or a relative clause. It is particularly interesting that this tendency was evident in the long relative clause condition. In relative clauses, the modifier follows the head noun, and so subjects are not likely to see much of the semantic content of the modification when they fixate the head. The finding that reading times are about as long when a head is preceded or followed by modifiers suggests that it is not the semantic integration of modifiers and head information that takes extra time, but instead, something about the presence of modification that causes subjects to read carefully the word to be modified. Of course, it is possible that some subjects on some trials were able to acquire enough parafoveal information to process the modifer semantically in the relative clause condition. However, readers normally do not acquire semantic information from beyond the word to the right of the currently fixated word and so it is not likely that, given a phrase such as *the dog that is hairy*, subjects would be able to acquire much semantic information from beyond the word *that*.

Finally, we will report results for the segment consisting of the **rest of the sentence**, for both first-pass and reanalysis measures. First pass reading times were affected both by region type, $F1(2,46) = 8.02$, $MS_e = 57444$, $F2(2,70) = 5.88$, $MS_e = 93608$, and by closure, $F1(1,23) = 30.24$, $MS_e = 295210$, $F2(1,35) = 27.37$, $MS_e = 412914$. (There was no interaction, both F's < 1.) The pattern appears to be that the longer the sentence, the longer the reading time at the end of the sentence. Reading times were 281, 341, and 340 ms in the short, long-relative clause, and long-adjective conditions respectively, indicating that subjects took longer to read the last word of the sentence the more material that had been in the ambiguous noun phrase. Reading times were 275 ms in the early closure condition and 366 ms in the late closure condition, similarly suggesting that reading times at the end of a sentence are longer in the condition in which more material has to be integrated. Note that for early closure sentences, the first clause consists of just one argument (since the verb is used intransitively) and the second clause consists of two arguments (subject and object of the second verb). For late closure sentences, each clause consists of two arguments. Thus, late closure sentences contain more information to be integrated. These two main effects together suggest that end-of-sentence wrap-up effects (Just & Carpenter, 1980) are more pronounced the longer the sentence.

Reanalysis measures strengthen this argument

Total reading time was longer in the late closure (507 ms) than the early closure (443 ms) condition, and longer when the ambiguous region was long (431, 507, and 487 ms for the short, long-relative clause, and long-adjective conditions respectively). There was no interaction, both F's < 1. As before, it appears that the longer the sentence, the more time subjects spend at the end of the sentence. Regressions from the end of sentence were more frequent with early closure (32%) than late closure (23%) sentences, $F1(1,23) = 10.02$, $MS_e = 2925$, $F2(1,35) = 6.20$, $MS_e = 4779$. Frequency of regressions out was also significantly affected by region type; regressions occurred on 33%, 24%, and 25% of all trials in the short, long-relative clause, and long-adjective conditions, $F1(2,46) = 3.65$, $MS_e = 1075$, $F2(2,70) = 3.44$, $MS_e = 2128$. Thus, it appears that regressions occurred most frequently in the short condition.

SUMMARY AND DISCUSSION

The data from grammaticality judgements replicate the results of Experiment 1 and the results we reported in Ferreira and Henderson (1991a, 1991b). Sentences with a long ambiguous region due to the inclusion of a relative clause were judged grammatical less often than those with a short ambiguous region or those with an ambiguous region made long through the insertion of prenominal adjectives. Therefore, as we argued previously, it is not the actual *length* of the ambiguous region that causes syntactic reanalysis to be difficult, it is the distance from the head of the misanalyzed phrase to the disambiguating word.

The reading time data in this experiment provided more convincing evidence for garden-path effects during initial analysis than did the previous experiment. Reading measures reflecting initial processing showed that the disambiguating segment was more difficult in the early closure than the late closure condition. We also saw that the total amount of time spent in a segment was longer in the early closure conditions, and regressions from the disambiguating segment of the sentence and beyond to earlier portions of the sentence were more frequent with early closure sentences. As in the previous experiment, the region variable did not seem to interact with closure, indicating that whatever processes are involved in processing the different types of ambiguous region do not seem to be the same ones involved in sentence parsing. Instead, as before, we found that sentences with a short ambiguous region were read more slowly and were associated with more regressions than those with a long region.

Finally, as with Experiment 1, we found a few effects related to basic reading processes. First, we replicated our previous finding that short phrases are read more slowly on a per character basis than are long phrases. Second, it appears that reading speed across a sentence may increase as a sentence becomes longer. Third, we replicated the finding from the first experiment that first fixation duration is longer on the head of a phrase when that phrase is modified. The current experiment extended that finding by showing that it is not the presence of an upcoming modifier that increases reading times on the head, or the integration of previously occurring modifying material. Instead, it appears that the mere presence of modification, whether it has occurred upon encountering a head or not, increases the processing time on the head of a phrase. Interestingly, this finding only obtains in both experiments with first fixation duration as the measure, suggesting that this tendency reflects early, quasi-perceptual processes during reading. Finally, we again found that end-of-sentence reading times were longer with late closure sentences than with early closure sentences and, in addition, we found the same result for sentences with a long ambiguous phrase. It appears that the more material that has to be integrated at the end of a sentence, the more time it takes to perform that integration; that is, end-of-sentence wrap-up effects (Just & Carpenter, 1980) are greater the more phrases in the sentence.

General Discussion

The results of the two experiments presented here have implications both for issues in parsing and reading. Consistent with our previous work, we found that early closure sentences are judged grammatical less often than late closure sentences. Early closure sentences are also read more slowly, particularly after subjects have encountered the disambiguating word and have to reread the sentence. However, contrary to our expectations, we found that sentences with a *short* ambiguous region were read more slowly than were sentences with a long ambiguous region. This result is surprising because it does not fit with the grammaticality judgement data, which consistently show that sentences with a short region are judged grammatical more often than are sentences with a long region. Generally, one would expect that the factors that make a sentence sensible and interpretable would also tend to make the sentence easier to read.

To begin to account for this finding, let us review the circumstances in which it was observed in both experiments. First, recall that even within the ambiguous region itself, reading times per character were longer when that region was short. Second, reading times on the disambiguating segment of the sentence were longer when the ambiguous phrase had been short. Third, total reading time on the unambiguous, the ambiguous, and the disambiguating segment were all longer when the ambiguous region had been short. Note that these effects on total reading time would all have taken place *after* the ambiguous phrase had been encountered. In addition, it may be useful to note in which circumstance we did not find longer reading times given a short ambiguous phrase, and that was when we examined reading times on the final word of the sentence (the end-of-sentence segment). There, we found that reading times were longer when the ambiguous region had been long, and longer when the sentence was late closure.

Thus, the overall pattern seems to be the following: On every part of the sentence except for the final word, reading times are longer when the sentence has a short ambiguous phrase and is early closure; on the final word, reading times are longer when the sentence has a long ambiguous phrase and is late closure. This pattern makes more sense than at first appears. The effect of having a short phrase and of being early closure is to make the sentence short; the effect of having a long phrase and of being late closure is to make the sentence long. Perhaps, as we suggested in the results sections of both experiments, readers increase their reading speed as they proceed through a sentence. Consider what will happen to first pass reading times on the disambiguating word given, say, an early closure sentence with a short vs a long ambiguous region. With a short region, subjects will have read less material when they encounter the disambiguating word, and so will be reading at a slower speed; with a long region, subjects will have read more material, and so will be reading faster. As a result, reading times on the disambiguating word will be longer when the ambiguous phrase had been short.

This finding has important implications for the closure effects we observed in this experiment, and perhaps for many other studies examining the processing of garden-path sentences. In our studies, the early closure and late closure sentences differed from each other only in that the former did not include a direct object for the first clause of the sentences. Therefore, if we are correct in our suggestion that readers speed up as they proceed through a sentence, then when subjects encounter the disambiguating word of the sentence, they will be reading more slowly in the early closure than the late closure condition. Therefore, at least some of the effects that we have attributed to garden-pathing may in part be attributable to the subjects' reading at a slower speed when they encounter the disambiguating segment of the early closure sentences.

It appears, therefore, that much more caution has to be exercised in interpreting the results of studies such as ours than we would have hoped. In an effort to evaluate how extensive this problem might be, we reviewed the results of a number of published studies designed to examine the processing of garden-path sentences. The sentences used in these studies all had the characteristic that, prior to the disambiguating segment, a syntactically easier construction – a minimal attachment or late closure sentence – had more words than the syntactically more difficult construction (e.g., Ferreira & Clifton, 1986; Ferreira & Henderson, 1990; Frazier & Rayner, 1982; Mitchell, 1987; Rayner & Frazier, 1987; Spivey-Knowlton et al., 1993; Trueswell, Tanenhaus, & Kello, in press). We will take just one example, Experiment 1 by Ferreira and Clifton (1986) who measured reading time for sentences such as the following:

(4)
a. The evidence examined by the lawyer turned out to be unreliable.
(reduced version)
b. The evidence that was examined by the lawyer turned out to be unreliable.
(unreduced version)

Ferreira and Clifton (1986) created the more difficult construction (4a) by omitting the words *that was*. As a result, (4a) is ambiguous up to the phrase *by the lawyer*, and Ferreira and Clifton found that reading times on that phrase were longer in (4a) than in (4b). However, their data also show that first pass reading times on the word *examined* were longer in (a) than (b), even though the subjects had not yet encountered the disambiguating word. This result is consistent with our argument that readers speed up as they process material in a sentence. Having encountered the words *that was* in (b), they will have increased their reading speed when they encountered the word *examined* and the subsequent words. As a result, reading time on those words will be lower in the unreduced version than in the reduced version.

Similar patterns can be found in numerous studies, such as the ones cited above. The critical question is whether all the results that have been taken to indicate garden-pathing are now called into question. To address this question, we examined the results of studies in which researchers equated the syntactically easy and difficult constructions in number of words. One such study was recently conducted by Britt et al. (1992), who compared sentences such as (5):

(5)
a. The coffee spilled on the rug was difficult for her to conceal.
b. The coffee spilled on the rug and even marked the new wallpaper.

Here, we can see that the disambiguating words (*was* and *and*) line up across the two conditions, and so reading speed should not be a factor when subjects encounter the disambiguating words. Reassuringly, Britt et al. still found longer reading times on the disambiguating word in sentences such as (5a). Other studies showing garden-path effects with overall sentence length equated include Clifton (1993) and Rayner et al. (1983). These studies indicate that not all garden-path effects observed in studies of parsing up to this point can be attributed to the reading speed variable we have identified. Nevertheless, it is also clear that measures must be taken in the future to avoid comparing reading times for sentences of different lengths. A similar point has been made recently by Trueswell et al. (in press), who found that the pattern of fixations differs between sentences of different word lengths.

We also observed in the two experiments that longer sentences were associated with longer end-of-sentence reading times. Reading times were longer for late closure sentences than for early closure sentences, and for sentences with a long ambiguous region than for sentences with a short region. Thus, it appears that the more modifiers and phrases a sentence contains, the more work it takes to integrate all the material in the sentence. In addition, the reading speed factor that we identified in this study may also be at work: Subjects read the longer sentences faster, and so at the end of the sentence they have two strikes against them: they have more material to integrate but they read the sentence less carefully. Therefore, end-of-sentence wrap-up may be especially time-consuming.

We believe that the most important conclusion that emerges from this work is that researchers in psycholinguistics can no longer confidently compare reading times for sentences of various lengths. Trueswell et al. (in press) have recently shown the effect sentence length has on fixation patterns, and we have observed that sentence length seems to affect reading speed. The moral seems to be that when subjects process visually presented sentences, they are not just parsing – they are also reading, and so basic reading processes will necessarily become engaged. The challenge then becomes to realize which effects should be attributed to parsing processes, which to reading processes, and which reflect an interaction of the two.

The research reported here was supported by grants to each author from the Natural Sciences and Engineering Research Council. We would like to thank Kate Murie for her assistance with the testing of subjects and data analysis, and Murray Singer and an anonymous reviewer for helpful comments on a previous version of this manuscript. Correspondence concerning this article should be addressed to Fernanda Ferreira, Department of Psychology, 129 Psychology Research Building, Michigan State University, East Lansing, MI 48824, USA. Send electronic mail to: fernanda@msu.edu.

References

Altmann, G., & Steedman, M. (1988). Interaction with context during human sentence processing. *Cognition, 30*, 191-238.

Anes, M., & Ferreira, F. (in progress). Verb transitivity and parsing preferences.

Britt, M.A., Perfetti, C.A., Garrod, S., & Rayner, K. (1992). Parsing in discourse: Context effects and their limits. *Journal of Memory and Language, 31*, 293-314.

Clifton, C. (1993). Thematic Roles in Sentence Parsing. *Canadian Journal of Experimental Psychology, 47*, 222-246.

Clifton, C.E., & Ferreira, F. (1990). Ambiguity in context. *Language and Cognitive Processes, 4*, 77-103.

Connine, C.M., Ferreira, F., Jones, C., Clifton, C.E., & Frazier, L. (1984). Verb frame preferences. *Journal of Psycholinguistic Research, 13*, 307-319.

Crain, S., & Steedman, M. (1985). On not being led up the garden path: The use of context by the psychological parser. In D. Dowty, L. Kartunnen, and A. Zwicky (Eds.), *Natural language parsing*. Cambridge: Cambridge University Press.

Ferreira, F., & Clifton, C.E. (1986). The independence of syntactic processing. *Journal of Memory and Language, 25*, 348-368.

Ferreira, F., & Henderson, J.M. (1990). The use of verb information in syntactic parsing: A comparison of evidence from eye movements and word-by-word self-paced reading. *Journal of Experimental Psychology: Learning, Memory, and Cognition, 16*, 555-568.

Ferreira, F., & Henderson, J.M. (1991a). Recovery from misanalyses of garden-path sentences. *Journal of Memory and Language, 30*, 725-745.

Ferreira, F., & Henderson, J.M. (1991b). How is verb information used during syntactic parsing? In G.B. Simpson (Ed.), *Understanding word and sentence*. North-Holland: Elsevier Science Publications.

Frazier, L. (1978). *On comprehending sentences: Syntactic parsing strategies*. Unpublished doctoral dissertation, University of Connecticut.

Frazier, L. (1987). Sentence processing. In M. Coltheart (Ed.), *Attention and Performance XII*. Hillsdale, N.J.: Erlbaum.

Frazier, L. (1990). Parsing modifiers: Special purpose routines in HSPM? In D.A. Balota, G.B. Flores d'Arcais, & K. Rayner (Eds.), *Comprehension processes in reading*. Hillsdale, N.J.: Erlbaum.

Frazier, L., & Rayner, K. (1982). Making and correcting errors during sentence comprehension: Eye movements in the analysis of structurally ambiguous sentences. *Cognitive Psychology, 14*, 178-210.

Gernsbacher, M.A. (1990). *Language comprehension as structure building.* Hillsdale, NJ: Erlbaum.

Henderson, J.M., & Ferreira, F. (1990). Covert attention and eye movement control: The effects of foveal processing difficulty on the perceptual span in reading. *Jour-nal of Experimental Psychology: Learning, Memory, and Cognition, 16*, 417-429.

Henderson, J.M., & Ferreira, F. (1993). Eye movement control during reading: Fixation measures reflect foveal but not parafoveal processing difficulty. *Canadian Journal of Experimental Psychology, 47*, 201-221.

Holmes, V.M. (1987). Syntactic parsing: In search of the garden path. In M. Coltheart (Ed.), *Attention and Performance XII.* Hillsdale, N.J.: Erlbaum.

Holmes, V.M., Stowe, L., & Cupples, L. (1989). Lexical expectations in parsing complement-verb sentences. *Journal of Memory and Language, 28*, 668-689.

Just, M.A., & Carpenter, P.A. (1980). A theory of reading: From eye fixations to comprehension. *Psychological Review, 87*, 329-354.

McClure, K., & Ferreira, F. (in progress). *Reciprocal verbs and the parsing of garden-path sentences.*

Mitchell, D.C. (1987). Lexical guidance in human parsing: Locus and processing. In M. Coltheart (Ed.), *Attention and Performance XII.* Hillsdale, N.J.: Erlbaum.

Perfetti, C.A. (1990). The cooperative language processors: Semantic influences in an autonomous syntax. In D.A. Balota, G.B. Flores d'Arcais, & K. Rayner (Eds.), *Comprehension processes in reading.* Hillsdale, N.J.: Erlbaum.

Rayner, K., Carlson, M., & Frazier, L. (1983). The interaction of syntax and semantics during sentence processing: Eye movements in the analysis of semantically ambiguous sentences. *Journal of Verbal Learning and Verbal Behavior, 22*, 358-374.

Rayner, K., & Frazier, L. (1987). Parsing temporarily ambiguous complements. *Quarterly Journal of Experimental Psychology, 39A*, 657-673.

Rayner, K. & Pollatsek, A. (1989). *The psychology of reading.* Englewood Cliffs, N.J.: Prentice Hall.

Spivey-Knowlton, M.J., Trueswell, J.C., & Tanenhaus, M.K. (1993). Context effects in parsing reduced relative clauses. *Canadian Journal of Experimental Psychology, 47*, 276-309.

Taraban, R., & McClelland, J.L. (1988). Constituent attachment and thematic role assignment in sentence processing: Influences of content-based expectations. *Journal of Memory and Language, 27*, 597-632.

Trueswell, J.C., Tanenhaus, M.K., & Kello, C. (in press). Verb-specific constraints in sentence processing: Separating effects of lexical preference from garden-paths. *Journal of Experimental Psychology: Learning, Memory, and Cognition.*

8 Context Effects in Syntactic Ambiguity Resolution: Discourse and Semantic Influences in Parsing Reduced Relative Clauses

MICHAEL J. SPIVEY-KNOWLTON,
JOHN C. TRUESWELL, and MICHAEL K. TANENHAUS
University of Rochester

Abstract   This article examines how certain types of semantic and discourse context affect the processing of relative clauses which are temporarily ambiguous between a relative clause and a main clause (e.g., *"The actress selected by the director…"*). We review recent results investigating local semantic context and temporal context, and we present some new data investigating referential contexts. The set of studies demonstrate that, contrary to many recent claims in the literature, all of these types of context can have early effects on syntactic ambiguity resolution during on-line reading comprehension. These results are discussed within a "constraint-based" framework for ambiguity resolution in which effects of context are determined by the strength and relevance of the contextual constraint and by the availability of the syntactic alternatives.

Résumé   Le présent article porte sur les effets qu'ont certains types de contextes sémantiques et propres au discours sur le traitement de propositions relatives qui sont temporairement ambiguës (p. ex. «*The actress selected* by the director…»). Nous examinons les résultats obtenus récemment au sujet du contexte sémantique et du contexte temporel et nous présentons de nouvelles données sur les contextes référentiels. Il ressort de la série d'études que, contrairement à maintes affirmations récentes dans la littérature, tous ces types de contextes peuvent influer dès le début sur la résolution d'ambiguïtés syntaxiques pendant la lecture en temps réel. Les résultats sont traités selon un cadre basé sur des contraintes pour la résolution d'ambiguïtés, dans lequel les effets contextuels sont déterminés par la force et la pertinence des contraintes liées au contexte ainsi que par la présence de choix syntaxiques.

Language comprehension takes place rapidly and, to a first approximation, incrementally. As the linguistic input is received, readers and listeners update representations that take into account information from the sentence and information from the discourse (Marslen-Wilson, 1973). The on-line nature of comprehension has important consequences for syntactic processing. First, developing even a provisional interpretation requires making some syntactic commitments. Thus, readers will have to make at least partial syntactic commitments at points in a sentence where the input underdetermines the syntactic structure. These commitments will have to be revised if they turn out to be inconsistent with subsequent input. Clear examples arise when readers experience a conscious confusion or "garden-path", as in Bever's (1970) famous sentences with reduced relatives, examples of which are illustrated in:

1. a. The horse raced past the barn fell
   b. The boat floated down the river sank.

A second consequence of on-line interpretation is that readers will have information available from the preceding context that could be used to constrain the syntactic alternatives at points of local indeterminacy. How and when the language processing system makes use of this information is currently the focus of extensive research. The underlying theoretical question is often cast as one about the architecture of the language processing system. In particular, does the architecture of the system restrict the types of information that can be used in syntactic ambiguity resolution?

The research reported here uses sentences with reduced relative clauses to investigate how different types of contextual information are used in ambiguity resolution. We will be summarizing some recent results and reporting new experimental data on the use of (a) local semantic constraints on verb arguments; and (b) pragmatic/referential information from the discourse. Each of these types of information has played an important role in current discussions of parsing and, more generally, about the architecture of the language processing system. Contrary to many findings in the literature, we report evidence that both types of information have clear and immediate effects on ambiguity resolution. However, these effects depend upon the bottom-up availability of the syntactic alternatives. This helps explain why the literature on these topics has produced somewhat inconsistent results. Before we turn to the details of this research, we will first describe the reduced relative clause ambiguity and the types of contextual information that we will be exploring. We then present a brief overview of the different types of approaches to syntactic ambiguity resolution that are currently being explored in the literature.

Reduced Relative Clauses

In English, reduced relative clauses are frequently ambiguous because the same verb form, usually verb + "ed", is used for both the past tense and the participial forms of most verbs. Thus, a fragment beginning with a noun followed by a verb + "ed" will be ambiguous between the start of a main clause and the start of a relative clause. In a main clause, the noun phrase is the subject of the verb, whereas in a relative clause, the noun phrase is the logical object of the verb.

As the examples in (2) illustrate, readers have a clear bias in favour of treating an ambiguous fragment as a main clause. Numerous empirical studies have demonstrated that readers experience difficulty as soon as they encounter syntactic information that disambiguates the fragment as a relative clause (e.g., Ferreira & Clifton, 1986; Rayner, Carlson, & Frazier, 1983). For example, reading times will be longer to the disambiguating agentive "by"-phrase in (2a) than in the unambiguous (2b) or (2c).

2. a. The scientist selected by the committee was later fired.
   b. The scientist who was selected by the committee was later fired.
   c. The scientist chosen by the committee was later fired.

There are a variety of explanations for why this preference exists. Bever (1970) proposed that readers and listeners adopt frequency-based perceptual strategies for predicting clause boundaries and recovering deep-structure relationships. A verb + "ed" form that immediately follows a noun is far more likely to be a past tense verb than a participial, especially at the beginning of a sentence (cf. Tabossi, Spivey-Knowlton, McRae, & Tanenhaus, 1993). Frazier (1978) accounts for the main clause preference in terms of syntactic simplicity using the Minimal Attachment Principle, which states that the parser prefers to attach a word using the fewest possible nodes consistent with the phrase structure rules of the language. A relative clause has more nodes because it is a sentence embedded within a noun phrase, whereas a main clause is just a simple sentence. Crain and Steedman (1985) propose an explanation in terms of conceptual simplicity. In the absence of specific information in the discourse, the pragmatic presuppositions associated with a restrictive relative clause are more complex than those for a main clause.

The reduced relative clause has been a useful structure for examining the role of context in ambiguity resolution for several reasons. First, as we have seen, it has a clear unambiguous baseline condition, either a full (unreduced) relative clause, such as (2b), or preferably an unambiguous relative clause such as (2c). Second, the ambiguity is local, as is the point at which the sentence is disambiguated. Third, in the absence of context, there is a strong preference for one of the syntactic alternatives. This would make evidence for context effects quite compelling. Finally, using relative clauses allows one to explore a variety of different types of context using the same structure, and in some cases the same sentences. This makes it possible to compare the time course with which different types of information are used in sentence processing, while holding local factors constant.

There are two broad classes of constraint that are directly relevant to the reduced relative/main clause ambiguity. Each of these types of constraint is quite general, i.e., relevant to a wide range of syntactic ambiguities. The first is the semantic fit of a noun phrase to a potential argument position. The subject noun phrase in a main clause typically plays the thematic role of Agent in the event denoted by the verb, whereas the noun phrase in a reduced relative clause is the Theme or Patient. Thus, the semantic fit of the noun as an Agent and as a Patient of the ambiguous verb would be a relevant source of constraint. Consider, for example the fragments in (3):

3. a. The evidence examined...
   b. The scientist examined...

"Evidence" is an implausible Agent of an "examining" event, but a plausible Theme, whereas "scientist" is a highly plausible Agent and a less plausible Theme. Therefore the fragment in (3a) is more likely to begin a reduced relative clause, whereas the fragment in (3b), is more likely to begin a main clause.

The second type of constraint is the relationship between the sentence and the prior discourse. Definite noun phrases typically refer to entities that have already been introduced into a discourse. Main clauses introduce new events into the discourse, whereas restrictive relative clauses often disambiguate among a set of possible referents. A processing system that is incrementally updating a model of the events and entities in the discourse might attempt to immediately establish the referent of the noun phrase. Whether a unique referent or a set of possible referents was available would then be relevant to the likelihood that the ambiguous structure was a main clause or a relative clause. Note that a fragment that has a main clause bias when it is preceded by a context with a unique referent (e.g., one scientist) has a strong relative clause bias when it is preceded by a context that introduces a set of referents (e.g., two scientists) (Crain, 1980; Crain & Steedman, 1985).

Current approaches to ambiguity resolution differ in how they make use of contextual information. For purposes of simplicity, we will divide recent proposals into three categories: Two-stage approaches, discourse-based approaches, and constraint-based approaches.

Two-stage models

Two-stage models assume that parsing proceeds serially, with only one structure under active consideration. During the first stage of parsing, a *restricted* domain of syntactically-relevant information is used to posit an initial structure. This structure is then evaluated and, if necessary, revised. The evaluation and revision stage can make use of information that was not used in initial structure building. The best-known model in this category is the "garden-path" model originally proposed by Frazier and Rayner (1982). In the most current version of the model, initial structure building is guided by a small set of maximally general attachment principles (Minimal Attachment and Late Closure) which are defined over syntactic categories. Thus, an initial structure can be built rapidly using a limited domain of information. Garden-paths occur whenever the structure of a sentence turns out to be inconsistent with the attachment principles. According to this model, both local semantic constraints and discourse constraints, as well as lexically-specific syntactic constraints, can affect the evaluation and revision stage of parsing, but not the initial structure building stage. Thus, the garden-path model would predict that the effects of either semantic fit or discourse context would be delayed for architectural reasons.

Discourse-based models

According to this class of models, ambiguity resolution is guided by syntactically-relevant information from the discourse. This information is pragmatic in that it is tied to the discourse function of syntactic structures. Discourse-based constraints can guide ambiguity resolution because the discourse model is being continuously updated as the information in a sentence is processed. The best developed model in this category is the referential theory originally proposed by Crain and Steedman (1985) and further developed by Altmann and Steedman (1988) and Ni and Crain (1990). According to the referential theory, syntactic analyses are developed in parallel. The structure whose pragmatic presuppositions are best satisfied by the discourse is then rapidly selected. In the absence of appropriate information in the discourse model, the structure requiring the fewest additional presuppositions is chosen. Most of the work in the theory is accomplished by referential mechanisms, as will be developed in more detail later. Garden-paths occur whenever a local ambiguity is resolved in favour of the alternative requiring the most additional presuppositions. The referential theory predicts that appropriate discourse contexts can reverse syntactic preferences. Thus, it predicts immediate effects of discourse context. However, local factors, such as argument fit, are not assigned any weight by the theory.

Constraint-based approaches

Constraint-based, or "evidential", approaches treat syntactic ambiguity resolution as a constraint-satisfaction problem (e.g., Bates & MacWhinney, 1989; McClelland, St. John, & Taraban, 1989) in which different constraints provide evidence in support of partially activated alternatives. In current structurally-driven variants, in which "bottom-up" information defines the "search" space, syntactic alternatives will be more or less active depending upon how consistent they are with the input (e.g., MacDonald, 1992; Tabossi, et al., 1993; Trueswell, Tanenhaus, & Garnsey, 1992). For example, the more frequent alternative given the input will become activated more rapidly.

Salient (currently active) contextual information that is correlated with the alternatives can provide biasing evidence. Ambiguity resolution is viewed as continuous. Both local semantic context and discourse context will have strong and immediate effects when the relevant alternatives are active and the constraint is strong. They will have weak and/or delayed effects when the constraints are weak or when the alternative that they are biased in favour of is only weakly activated. Conscious garden-paths occur when an alternative that is strongly supported by the initial evidence later turns out to be incorrect and the correct alternative is no longer active.

Each class of model makes different predictions about the processing of fragments that are temporarily ambiguous between a main clause and a relative clause. Two-stage models, such as the garden-path model, predict that the main clause structure will be the only structure initially computed because it is the syntactically simplest alternative. The referential theory predicts that both alternatives will be equally available. The alternative that best fits the context or involves the fewest presuppositions will be chosen. Finally, the constraint-based approach predicts that the main clause alternative will be more active initially, because it is the more frequent structure given the input; however, strong contextual constraints will come into play immediately.

LOCAL SEMANTIC CONTEXT

The issue of whether the semantic content of words influences initial parsing decisions plays an important role in distinguishing among various approaches to sentence processing. Proponents of constraint-based models would argue that when this kind of information places clear restrictions on grammatical relations among constituents, these restrictions could in turn constrain on-line parsing commitments. For example, verbs often place semantic constraints on the nouns that they allow in subject and object positions. The question arises: will such constraints determine which alternative is computed in the case of a syntactic ambiguity? Ferreira & Clifton (1986, Experiment 1) monitored eye-movements while subjects read sentences with relative clauses such as (4):

4. a. The defendant examined by the lawyer turned out to be unreliable.
   b. The defendant that was examined by the lawyer turned out to be unreliable.
   c. The evidence examined by the lawyer turned out to be unreliable.
   d. The evidence that was examined by the lawyer turned out to be unreliable.

The first noun in the sentence was either animate or inanimate. Recall that animate nouns are typically plausible Agents, whereas inanimate nouns are implausible Agents but plausible Themes. The first noun in a main clause is likely to be the Agent whereas, the first noun in a reduced relative clause is likely to be the Theme. Therefore, the animacy of the noun provides information that would be relevant to resolving the ambiguity.

A two-stage restricted domain processor, or a *pure* discourse-based processor, would ignore constraints of this kind. In (4a) and (4c), the simplest structure, and the structure having the least discourse presuppositions, is the main clause rather than the relative clause. Thus, on either approach, the processor would be equally likely to incorporate "The defendant" or "The evidence" as the subject (or Agent) of "examined".

Ferreira and Clifton (1986) found two important results. First, reading times to the verb following an inanimate noun were elevated for the reduced relatives, suggesting that the animacy information was available. Second, both first and second pass reading times in the "by"-phrase region were elevated in the reduced relatives (4a & 4c) as compared to the unambiguous unreduced relative clauses (4b & 4d) regardless of animacy. This reduction effect suggests that the semantic information was not used in parsing. While these results would appear to provide definitive evidence in support of two-stage models in which initial commitments are made without reference to semantic information, recent work from our laboratory suggests a different story.

Trueswell et al. (1992) conducted two eye-tracking experiments that were similar in design to Ferreira and Clifton (1986), but with modified materials. Ferreira and Clifton's materials included inanimate nouns that did not rule out a main clause continuation with the ambiguous verb (e.g., "the trash smelled..." or "the car towed..."), and a variety of different types of prepositional phrases. In Trueswell et al.'s first experiment, only inanimate nouns that ruled out a congruous main clause continuation were used. In addition, the disambiguating prepositional phrase was always an agentive "by"-phrase, providing an explicit Agent for every relative clause. Trueswell et al. found clear effects of animacy. First pass and second pass reading times to the "by"-phrase were longer to reduced relative clauses compared to unambiguous controls when the noun was animate but not when it was inanimate.

This pattern of results was then replicated using materials developed by Burgess (1991). Burgess (Burgess, 1991; Burgess & Tanenhaus, 1992) used completion norms to select inanimate noun-verb fragments that were typically completed as relative clauses (e.g., The evidence examined...). In a self-paced reading study in which *two word* segments were presented using a moving window (e.g., /The evidence/ /examined by/), Burgess found the same pattern of results as Trueswell et al., namely an interaction between animacy and clause type. However, with a *one word* moving window, Burgess found exactly the same pattern of results as Ferreira and Clifton (1986), that is, longer reading times at the verb for inanimates with reduced relative clauses and no interaction between animacy and reduction at the "by"-phrase. In addition, Burgess did not find an interaction with animacy using either a one-word window or a two-word window with Ferreira and Clifton's materials.

The pattern of data across studies can be explained by a simple general-ization. Animacy had clear effects when (a) it provided a strong constraint and (b) both the past-tense and the participial forms of the ambiguous verb were sufficiently activated. The participial form was substantially available, however, only when the reader could see the "by", either parafoveally in unrestricted reading, where a short high frequency function word such as "by" typically does not require a separate fixation (Trueswell et al., 1992), or with a two-word window in which the verb and "by" were presented together. The parafoveal preview of "by" during fixation of the verb provides probabilistic information (the Agentive use of "by") that supports a relative clause structure. This information counteracts the strong asymmetry in availability between the highly frequent main clause structure and the less frequent reduced relative clause structure.

Note also that the segmentation that Burgess used with the relative clause structure, which pairs a function word and a content word, groups together just those words that would normally be processed on the same fixations.[1] This similarity in segmentation and the similarity in experimental results support the claim that, with the reduced relative ambiguity, two-word self-paced reading better simulates free-field reading during eye-tracking than one-word self-paced reading.

Why then did Ferreira and Clifton (1986) not find a suggestion of an interaction with animacy since some of their inanimate noun phrases were strongly constraining and some of their sentences contained agentive "by"-phrases? The likely explanation has to do with the particular set of materials. Many of the sentences with "by"-phrases had only weakly biasing nouns and many of the sentences with strongly biasing nouns had long prepositions, which would normally require a separate fixation to be recognized (see Burgess & Tanenhaus, 1992).

Maryellen MacDonald and Neal Pearlmutter (MacDonald, 1992; Pearlmutter & MacDonald, 1992) have presented a constellation of results with relative clauses that are similar to the results described here. For example, MacDonald (1992) manipulated several different kinds of constraining information, including animacy, verb subcategorization information, and "post-ambiguity" constraints associated with point of disambiguation. All three kinds of information independently decreased reading times for reduced relatives. When the constraints were combined, reduction effects were almost complete-ly eliminated. The results indicate that the presence of information that correlates highly with the relative clause construction can be coordinated to constrain parsing decisions for this structural ambiguity.

Pearlmutter and MacDonald (1992) show that even weak semantic

---

1 Note that we are not claiming that self-paced reading with a two-word window is as natural as normal reading, or that it is *generally* preferable to one-word presentation.

constraints can affect the time course of ambiguity resolution with reduced relatives. In particular, ambiguity resolution is faster for animate noun phrases that are atypical agents for the following verb (e.g., The prisoner captured...). While these effects occur relatively late in the relative clause as measured by standard analysis of variance techniques, regression analyses show that the effects actually begin at, or shortly after, the ambiguous verb. A recent replication of these results conducted in our laboratory is reported in Tabossi et al. (1993).

In sum, semantic constraints that are relevant to argument assignment have clear and immediate effects on ambiguity resolution. However, the effects are restricted to conditions under which the relevant alternatives would both be active. This pattern of results is clearly consistent with the constraint-based framework.

While the set of results we have described are naturally accommodated by constraint-based models, they could be accounted for within a two-stage parsing framework in one of two ways. The first alternative would be to incorporate syntactically-relevant features such as animacy within the domain of the first-stage parser. However, this move cannot naturally accommodate the effects that are seen with animate noun phrases that are atypical agents. The second approach would be to argue that all of the effects observed in these studies are revision effects. On this view, the initial attachment stage is difficult to observe under conditions where potentially disambiguating information is available parafoveally because the attachment is extremely rapid and evaluation and revision begins almost immediately. We will return to this alternative in more detail in the general discussion.

DISCOURSE CONTEXT

Discourse-based models assume that a mental model of the events and entities being discussed in the discourse is continuously updated during sentence comprehension (e.g., Crain & Steedman, 1985; Marslen-Wilson & Tyler, 1987; Altmann & Steedman, 1988). Since many linguistic expressions can only be interpreted by making reference to information in the discourse model, it might be expected that the 'referential context' of these expressions could impose constraints on subsequent syntactic ambiguity resolution (Crain & Steedman, 1985; Altmann & Steedman, 1988). For example, consider what needs to be present in a discourse to make felicitous either a main clause interpretation or a relative clause interpretation of the following ambiguous fragment:

5. The student spotted...

If (5) is taken to be part of a main clause (e.g., "The student spotted the proctor and ..."), "The student" is an anaphoric noun phrase. Thus, there needs to be at least one 'student' in the discourse context which this expression can refer to (i.e., there must be an antecedent that is in discourse focus). In addition, the verb "spotted" is a past tense verb which introduces a new event into the immediate discourse. As pointed out in Trueswell and Tanenhaus (1991, 1992), the introduction of a new past event requires the current discourse segment to have a temporal relation that is consistent with past events (i.e., other events in the discourse segment must also be in the past, otherwise a separate discourse segment that is consistent with past events must be established). Thus, even the past tense verb "spotted" has certain contextual dependencies which make presuppositions about the discourse.

If (5) is taken to be part of a relative clause (e.g., "The student spotted by the proctor was expelled."), the entire phrase is part of a complex anaphoric expression which refers to a discourse entity, i.e., a 'student', that is the passive participant of some 'spotting' event. Since the relative clause *modifies* the noun phrase "the student", it could be argued that a *set* of possible discourse referents (i.e., a set of students) needs to be in discourse focus, from which the relative clause expression distinguishes a single entity (i.e., the particular student that was involved in a spotting event). Moreover, the verb "spotted" as a participial verb in a relative clause refers directly to an event already in the discourse. Thus, the participial verb in a relative clause has different discourse presuppositions than a past tense verb in a main clause. The verb "spotted" in a relative clause requires a spotting event in discourse to which the verb can refer, and places no restrictions on the temporal properties of the current discourse segment (see Trueswell & Tanenhaus, 1991, 1992).

If referential context can be used by the parser, then there are at least two classes of discourse constraint that could prevent syntactic misanalysis in "The student spotted by the proctor...". The contextual dependencies of the verb (e.g., "spotted") would support a relative clause over a main clause interpretation when the current discourse segment has a temporal relation that makes the introduction of past events infelicitous. The contextual dependencies of the noun phrase (e.g., "The student") would support a relative clause over a main clause interpretation when the current discourse segment has a set of students in focus.

Temporal Context

Trueswell and Tanenhaus (1991, 1992) explored whether temporal discourse constraints influence the processing of relative clauses in studies using contexts such as those in (6).

6. a. Several students were sitting together taking an exam in a large lecture hall earlier today. A proctor noticed one of the students cheating.

   b. Several students will be sitting together taking an exam in a large lecture hall

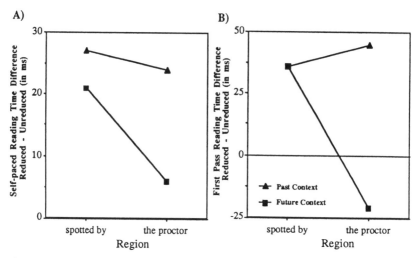

Fig. 1. (a) Two-word self-paced reading time differences (reduced minus unreduced) for past contexts and future contexts (from Trueswell & Tanenhaus, 1991). (b) First pass reading time differences (reduced minus unreduced) for past contexts and future contexts (from Trueswell & Tanenhaus, 1992).

later today. A proctor will notice one of the students cheating.

Target: The student (who was) spotted by the proctor will receive a warning.

A main clause interpretation of the fragment "The student spotted..." in the past context (6a) simply requires a new past event to be introduced into the current discourse segment. In contrast, a main clause interpretation in the future context (6b) requires considerable discourse modification, e.g., the establishment of a separate discourse segment with different temporal properties (see Trueswell & Tanenhaus, 1991, for examples). Therefore, a fragment like "The student spotted..." should be interpreted as part of a main clause in the past context and as part of a relative clause in the future context. This prediction was confirmed in a sentence completion study (Trueswell & Tanenhaus, 1992). Moreover, in two different two-word self-paced reading studies (Trueswell & Tanenhaus, 1991) and in a study monitoring eye movements (Trueswell & Tanenhaus, 1992), effects of relative clause reduction were decreased in the future contexts, suggesting that temporal context can influence structural commitments. Again, the results for self-paced reading with a two-word window and for eye-tracking were virtually identical, see Figure 1.

The only indication of difficulty with reduced relatives in future contexts came from small elevations found in the first half of the relative clause ("spotted by") in both self-paced reading and the first pass reading times of the eye movement study. In past contexts, longer reading times were observed at the verb + "by" region and at the noun phrase within the prepositional phrase. In sum, these results show that temporal context rapidly influences ambiguity resolution.

Referential Noun Phrase Contexts

Most other work examining referential effects in sentence comprehension has focussed on whether the presence of a set of possible noun phrase referents induces a preference for a modifier structure. For instance, Crain (1980) compared grammaticality judgements to sentences in which the ambiguous phrase, such as "that he was arresting", was either part of a sentential complement (7a) or a relative clause noun phrase modifier (7b). Introducing a context that should require noun phrase modification (e.g., two criminals, only one of which is being arrested by the policeman) resulted in subjects judging the relative clause sentences (7b) to be more acceptable than the sentential complement sentences (7a). The opposite preference was found when the context supported the simple noun phrase analysis (e.g., one criminal).

7. a. The policeman told the criminal that he was arresting everybody in the room.
   b. The policeman told the criminal that he was arresting to lie down on the floor.

Recently, and more crucially, Altmann, Garnham, and Denis (1992) have found that these off-line biases appear to influence initial parsing commitments. In a set of experiments in which readers' eye-movements were monitored while they read relative clause/sentential complement ambiguities, Altmann et al. (1992) showed that a context with two noun phrase referents biased the reader toward the relative clause interpretation, as indicated by slower first pass fixation times and more regressive eye-movements in the sentential complement sentences. With large scoring regions, however, it is difficult to determine whether the effect of context is indeed immediate. Using a one-word self-paced reading paradigm, and sentences which are disambiguated earlier (e.g., "The headmaster told the boy that (he) had...") Mitchell, Corley, and Garnham (1992) found only late effects of referential context.

Effects similar to those of Altmann et al. (1992) were also found in an earlier study (Altmann & Steedman, 1988), which examined self-paced reading times to sentences containing prepositional phrase attachment ambiguities, like those in (8):

8. a. The burglar blew open the safe with the dynamite and ran off with the loot.
   b. The burglar blew open the safe with the new lock and ran off with the loot.

The point of syntactic ambiguity in these sentences occurs at the preposition "with" and is not resolved until the noun "dynamite" or "new lock". The preposition can either attach to the verb as Instrument (8a) or it can attach to (and modify) the noun phrase "the safe" (8b). These constructions in isolation tend to be read with a preference for VP-attachment, thus causing a garden-path effect in the sentences that are more plausibly interpreted as NP-attached (Rayner et al., 1983; but cf. Taraban and McClelland, 1988). With contexts that contained two NP referents, (e.g., two safes, one with a new lock and one with an old lock), Altmann and Steedman (1988) reversed the result. Sentences which were more plausibly VP-attached elicited garden-paths (slowed reading of the PP).[2] This immediate effect of referential context on PP-attachment ambiguities has been replicated in self-paced reading experiments and in eye-tracking by Britt, Perfetti, Garrod and Rayner (1992); but see Ferreira and Clifton (1986).

In contrast, studies with reduced relative clauses have failed to find effects of referential context. Ferreira & Clifton (1986) tracked readers' eye-movements in reduced and unreduced relative clause sentences preceded by contexts containing one or two NP referents and found no immediate influence of context on the size of the reduction effect. Britt et al. (1992) also manipulated a form of focus/referential context with reduced relative clauses (i.e., the referent was backgrounded in discourse to make a complex NP reference more felicitous than a simple NP reference, and information was provided in the context that would support the content of a relative clause), and found that the biasing context did not decrease the reduction effect observed when the context did not support a relative clause. The only reading time study using reduced relatives that has found support for the traditional Referential Theory (e.g., Crain & Steedman, 1985) did not introduce a two NP referent context (Ni & Crain, 1990). Rather, the sentence was preceded by "Only" in order to bias the reader toward a complex NP interpretation because of the referential presupposition entailed by "only". Using word-by-word self-paced reading coupled with a grammaticality detection task, Ni and Crain (1990) found clear effects of "only" facilitating the reduced relative clause reading.

In sum, studies examining the effects of discourse constraints in on-line

---

2 In this conservative version of the Referential Theory, Altmann and Steedman (1988) may be drawing too narrow a picture of the context effect they observe. A close examination of their stimuli reveals that the contexts first set up the main character's plan, "He felt like smashing a window," and then provide two possible routes for completing that plan, "In front of him he saw a window made of stained glass and a window which had bars covering it." It is likely that such a context produces an expectation in the reader for discrimination between this minimal pair of windows: "Which window did he smash?" This expectation for resolution of a conceptual uncertainty, *regardless of referential considerations*, may cause the reader to prefer a complex NP analysis of "the window ..." in the target sentence (Spivey-Knowlton, 1992).

parsing have found somewhat mixed results. Although some studies have found clear discourse effects (Altmann & Steedman, 1988; Altmann et al., (1992); Britt et al., 1992; Ni & Crain, 1990; Trueswell & Tanenhaus, 1991, 1992), many others have failed to find such effects (Britt et al., 1992; Ferreira & Clifton, 1986; Mitchell et al., 1992). However, these differing results might be expected under a constraint-based perspective. Effects of discourse might only arise if (1) the contextual information is indeed highly constraining with respect to syntactic structure, and (2) local information makes sufficiently available the alternative forms of the ambiguity.

The present research examined the effects of noun phrase referential context on the processing of ambiguous reduced relative clauses. We explored whether referential contexts can influence parsing decisions under conditions in which: a) norms are used to establish that the contexts provide constraint at the point of ambiguity, and b) the mode of presentation (two-word format) facilitates the availability of the less frequent relative clause structure.

Experiment 1

This experiment examined reading times to relative clauses in contexts which either did or did not establish a unique referent for a noun phrase at the beginning of the reduced relative clause. Sentence (9a) begins with a definite noun phrase followed by a verb that is ambiguous between a simple past tense (main clause) or a participial form (reduced-relative clause):

9. a. The actress selected by the director believed that her performance was perfect.
   b. The actress who was selected by the director believed that her performance was perfect.

The definite NP, "the actress", presupposes a single actress in context. Interpreting "selected" as part of a main clause maintains this presupposition. However, interpreting "selected" as part of a relative clause makes it part of a complex NP ("the actress selected by..."). A complex definite NP, whether modified by a prepositional phrase or a relative clause, presupposes a *set of possible referents*, one of which is being referred to (cf. Heim, 1982). In a context that contains only one actress, the reader will not need a complex noun phrase to find a unique referent. Thus, upon encountering the ambiguous verb, the reader will opt for the main clause interpretation because it requires no revision of the mental model. However, in a context that contains two actresses, the reader should immediately opt for the reduced-relative interpretation because the *simple* NP interpretation of "the actress" does not have a unique referent.

Clifton and Ferreira (1989) have pointed out that relative clauses are frequently used for purposes other than selecting from an existing set of discourse entities. This is certainly true in the case of sentences outside of context. Consider the following sentence, "The husband angered by his wife walked out of the house." This sentence does not necessarily presuppose a set of husbands in discourse. (Although, it may be that the unrestrictive reading prefers commas around the relative clause more so than the restrictive reading does.) This would suggest that Referential Theory may not adequately explain parsing biases in isolated sentences (see Spivey-Knowlton & Sedivy, 1992). However, when appropriate discourse contexts are involved, such as those that contain two potential referents for the definite NP, it would seem that the purpose of discriminating between discourse entities is a particularly salient use of relative clauses.

METHOD
Subjects
Thirty-six undergraduates from the University of Rochester participated in this reading time experiment for course credit. All were native English speakers and were naive to the experimental manipulations.

Materials and Design
Twenty-four target sentences were constructed in which the first definite NP was both a plausible agent and a plausible patient of the subsequent syntactically ambiguous verb. Before conducting the reading time study, these 24 sentences (reduced versions only; embedded among 36 filler sentences) were normed in a sentence completion study performed by 24 undergraduates of the University of Rochester. Each sentence fragment ("The actress selected") was preceded either by a 2-NP-Referent context, a 1-NP-Referent context, or no context at all; thus three versions of each stimulus formed three stimulus lists. In eight of these sentences, there did not appear to be a substantial difference in reduced relative completions between the 1-NP-Referent and 2-NP-Referent contexts. The remaining sixteen stimuli were slightly revised in an attempt to increase their context-dependence. A similar completion study was then performed by another 24 undergraduates on these 16 improved stimuli (among 44 fillers). As in all of the statistical analyses we will present, stimulus list and item group (for subject and item analyses, respectively) were included in the analyses of variance as between-subject factors to better account for variance in the error term. The results revealed a main effect of Context; $F1(2,42) = 20.4$, $MS_e = .0514$, $p < .001$; $F2(2,26) = 103.69$, $MS_e = .0069$, $p < .001$. The sentence fragments were completed as reduced relatives 1% of the time in the Null Context, 25% of the time in the 1-NP-Referent Context, and 43% of the time in the 2-NP-Referent Context. Planned comparisons showed that all three means were significantly different from one another (all $ps < .02$).

Although the differences between the one and two NP referent contexts are reliable, they are, in fact, quite small. Several factors may contribute to this.

TABLE 1

Context
a. In the visiting room, two prisoners began yelling at each other. To prevent a fight, the guard removed one of the prisoners from the room but not the other.
b. In the visiting room, a prisoner and a visitor began yelling at each other. To prevent a fight, the guard removed the prisoner from the room but not the visitor.

Target
a. The prisoner removed by the guard fought violently to break free of the guard's grip.
b. The prisoner who was removed by the guard fought violently to break free of the guard's grip.

First of all, the relatively high proportion of relative clauses in one NP referent contexts (25%) may have been due to the fact that many of the fragments did not have natural main clause completions in the one NP referent context. Since all of the test sentences for the reading time study continued as relative clauses and because the oddity of a main clause would depend upon relating the fragment to the context, this was not a problem for the reading time study. However, in the completion study, subjects may have tried to complete the fragment as a main clause and then shifted to a relative clause because the main clause continuation that they generated was odd given the context. The percentage of relative clauses in the two NP referent contexts may have been reduced because the verb that ended the fragment was used in the past tense form in the preceding sentence. This would tend to make the participial form less available (Trueswell & Tanenhaus, 1991). In fact, seven of the 24 subjects did not generate any relative clause completions.

The percentages of reduced relative completion in the three context conditions for each of these sentences can be seen in the Appendix. These 16 sentences were then used in the reading time study. Table 1 displays two versions of a context and two versions of a target sentence.

As addressed in Trueswell and Tanenhaus's (1991) work, there may be some bias introduced by using the same verb in the context (in active form) as that in the target sentence (in passive form). Much like Bock's (1986) evidence for syntactic form priming in production, Trueswell and Tanenhaus (1991) found that when the context contains the same verb in the context (in active form) as in the target sentence (in passive form), there is a greater tendency toward interpreting the target sentence as an active main clause than when the context used a synonymous verb. Thus, in this study, the referential context must overcome not only the frequency bias toward a main clause, but also a possible syntactic form priming bias *against* a passive interpretation of the verb in the target sentence.

The reading time experiment had a 2 × 2 design with Context (1 NP Referent / 2 NP Referents) and Reduction (Reduced Relative / Unreduced Relative) as the independent variables. Four of the 16 target sentences were assigned to each of the four experimental conditions, which were rotated to create four versions of each stimulus. Each subject was exposed to only one of the four stimulus lists, and therefore to only one version of any one experimental item. The 16 experimental stimuli were randomly embedded within 32 filler stimuli, with at least one filler stimulus intervening every two experimental stimuli. Of the 32 filler items, 18 began with an NP-verb sequence, and were thus temporarily ambiguous between main clause and reduced relative readings. Fifteen of these sentences were resolved as main clauses. All of the experimental stimuli and half of the filler stimuli were followed by yes/no questions that (for the experimental stimuli) revealed what syntactic commitment the subject had finally made. Subjects pressed the 'yes' or 'no' buttons to give their answers.

Procedure

Stimuli were presented on an IBM clone with a Digitry board and button box installed. Subjects pressed one button to begin a trial, at which time a row of dashes appeared on the screen. (A dash replaced each character in the sentence; while spaces and the period remained unchanged.) Subjects then pressed a different button to present each sentence of the context, and then each segment of two words in the target sentence, in a non-cumulative fashion (Just, Carpenter, & Woolley, 1982). Reading times were recorded for the first four two-word segments of the reduced relative target sentence and the first five two-word segments of the unreduced relative. Recording regions of the target sentences totaled less than 80 characters long, and fit on a single line on the monitor.

Subjects were instructed to read the sentences at a comfortable pace that closely approximated their normal reading speed, and to read carefully enough to correctly answer the questions. Including a practice session of ten trials, the entire experiment lasted approximately 25 minutes.

RESULTS

The reading times and differences for each of the recorded regions are presented in Table 2. All subjects answered at least 80% of the comprehension questions accurately. An analysis of variance was computed for the reading times collapsed across all recorded regions. In this analysis, a main effect of Reduction showed that the recorded regions of unreduced relatives (461ms) were read faster overall than those of reduced relatives (491ms); $F1(1,32) = 6.61$, $MS_e = 20309$, $p < .02$; $F2(1,12) = 4.62$, $MS_e = 12911$, $p = .053$.

A main effect of Context was also observed. When the context contained two NP referents (460ms), the target sentences were read faster than when the

TABLE 2
Reading Time (ms) by Sentence Region

	Det + noun	Verb + "by"	Det + noun	Main verb region
1 NP referent				
Reduced	612	462	494	509
Unreduced	596	416	384	459
Reduction Effect	16	46	110	50
2 NP referents				
Reduced	547	410	422	472
Unreduced	572	403	410	443
Reduction Effect	−25	7	12	29

context contained only one NP referent (492ms); $F1(1,32) = 8.16, MS_e = 17594$, $p < .01$; $F2(1,12) = 13.76, MS_e = 4632, p < .005$. This felicity effect was also obtained by Altmann and Steedman (1988). It is accountable by the fact that modifying a noun phrase which has already achieved successful reference is less felicitous than modifying one which has not.

An interaction between Context and Reduction was also observed; $F1(1,32) = 7.63, MS_e = 11507, p < .01$; $F2(1,12) = 5.66, MS_e = 6355, p < .05$. In the 1-NP-referent context, reading times were slower to the reduced relatives (519ms) than to the unreduced relatives (464ms), whereas in the 2-NP-referent context, there was no difference (463ms vs. 457ms, respectively).

Focussing on the immediate points of ambiguity and disambiguation, an analysis of variance was computed separately for reading times in the verb + "by" region and for the following noun phrase region. Determining whether Context interacts with Reduction in either of these two regions, which together make up the relative clause, allowed us to identify the locus of the context effect. For the verb + "by" region, a main effect (significant by items only) of Reduction was observed (see Table 2); $F1(1,32) = 3.33, MS_e = 7472$, $p = .077$; $F2(1,12) = 8.44, MS_e = 1222, p < .02$. A marginal main effect of Context was also observed in this region (see Table 2); $F1(1,32) = 3.87$, $MS_e = 9792, p = .058$; $F2(1,12) = 3.65, MS_e = 4165, p = .08$. The interaction of Context × Reduction was not statistically significant for the verb + "by" region; $F1(1,32) = 2.12, MS_e = 6190$; $F2(,12) = 3.2, MS_e = 1610$. However, simple effects analyses revealed that the Reduction difference was significant (by items) in the 1-NP-Referent Context $[F1(1,32) = 3.25, MS_e = 11407$, $p = .08$; $F2(1,12) = 7.76, MS_e = 1935, p < .02]$, but not in the 2-NP-Referent Context $[F1$ and $F2 < 1.0]$.

In the next region, the Context × Reduction interaction was significant; $F1(1,32) = 8.05, MS_e = 10760, p < .01$; $F2(1,12) = 5.87, MS_e = 6277, p < .05$.

Within the 1-NP-referent context, the noun phrase region of a reduced relative clause was read more slowly than that of an unreduced relative clause, whereas in the 2-NP-referent context, there was no difference. Again, simple effects showed a significant effect of Reduction in the 1-NP-Referent Context $[F1(1,32) = 15.27, MS_e = 14303, p < .001; F2(1,12) = 10.6, MS_e = 8808, p < .01]$, but not in the 2-NP-Referent Context $[F1 < .5; F2 < .5]$. A main effect of Reduction, but not Context, persisted into this region also; $F1(1,32) = 13.62, MS_e = 9869, p < .005; F2(1,12) = 8.45, MS_e = 6831, p < .02$.

Table 2 shows, in the 2-NP-Referent Context, a slight rise in the Reduction difference as the sentence progresses. It is conceivable that statistically reliable slower processing at the fourth recorded region could be indicative of a delayed effect of Reduction, even in the 2-NP-Referent Context. To address this possibility, we analyzed reading times in this fourth region. However, both the analysis of variance and the simple effects analyses revealed no significant effects at this sentence region.

To analyze reading times for the relative clause as a whole, we collapsed across the verb + "by" and determiner + noun regions. Main effects of Context (by subjects only) $[F1(1,32) = 5.58, MS_e = 4860, p < .05; F2(1,12) = 3.22, MS_e = 3561, p < .1]$ and of Reduction $[F1(1,32) = 10.38, MS_e = 6622, p < .005, F2(1,12) = 10.07, MS_e = 2901, p < .01]$ were again observed. Most importantly, however, the interaction between Context and Reduction for the whole relative clause was robust; $F1(1,32) = 13.01, MS_e = 3210, p < .002; F2(1,12) = 9.44, MS_e = 1842, p < .02$. Once again, simple effects analyses revealed a reliable effect of Reduction (478ms vs. 400ms) in the 1-NP-Referent Context $[F1(1,32) = 15.15, MS_e = 7182, p < .001; F2(1,12) = 11.65, MS_e = 3933, p < .01]$, and none (416ms vs. 407ms) in the 2-NP-Referent Context $[F1 < 1; F2 < 1]$.

DISCUSSION

The results clearly demonstrated that referential context had immediate effects on ambiguity resolution for reduced relative clauses. Reduced relative clauses were more difficult than unreduced relatives in contexts that established a unique referent for a definite noun phrase at the beginning of the clause, whereas no reduction effect occurred when the context established two possible referents. Thus, the results confirm the predictions made by Referential Theory.

Nonetheless, there was a numerical difference between reduced and unreduced relative clauses that would be consistent with a small garden-path. However, there is another possible reason why unreduced relative clauses might be easier than reduced relative clauses. In an unreduced relative, the relative pronoun immediately establishes that the structure is a relative clause and allows the reader to begin to establish anaphoric links to the context. In a reduced relative clause, these processes cannot take place until the verb is encountered. Thus, reduced relatives may be more difficult than unreduced relatives for reasons unrelated to ambiguity resolution (Trueswell et al., 1992; Tanenhaus, Carlson & Trueswell, 1989). Moreover, Ferreira and Henderson (1993) present evidence that readers speed up as they proceed through a sentence, and therefore, comparing reading times from reduced and unreduced relative clause sentences may overestimate the overall reduction effect. One way to control for these problems is to compare reduced relative clauses with morphologically ambiguous verbs to reduced relative clauses with verbs that are morphologically unambiguous because they use different forms for the past tense and participial.

Experiment 2
This experiment used the same contexts as were used in Experiment 1 with a matched set of morphologically ambiguous (e.g., removed) and morphologically unambiguous verbs (e.g., taken). For example, "The prisoner removed..." can be the beginning of a main clause or the beginning of a reduced relative clause, whereas "The prisoner taken..." can only be the beginning of a reduced relative clause.

METHOD
Subjects
Thirty-two undergraduates from the University of Rochester participated in this experiment for course credit. All were native English speakers and were naive to the experimental manipulations.

Materials and Design
The 16 experimental items and 32 filler items from the reading time study of Experiment 1 were used in this experiment with small, but important, changes. Instead of the target sentences having reduced or unreduced relative clauses, they had ambiguous or unambiguous reduced relative clauses. The unambiguous participial verb that replaced the ambiguous participial verb (to create the baseline condition) did so in both the target sentence and in the context; see Table 3. When the target sentence is (b), then the context will have "took" instead of "removed". When the target sentence is (a), the context will have "removed" instead of "took". The experimental design was, analogous to Experiment 1, a 2 × 2 factorial manipulation of Context (1-NP-referent, 2-NP-referents) and Ambiguity (Ambiguous past participle, Unambiguous past participle).

Procedure
The procedure was identical to that in Experiment 1. A practice session of ten trials preceded the experimental session of 48 trials. The experiment lasted approximately 25 minutes.

TABLE 3

Context
a. In the visiting room, two prisoners began yelling at each other. To prevent a fight, the guard removed/took one of the prisoners from the room but not the other.
b. In the visiting room, a prisoner and a visitor began yelling at each other. To prevent a fight, the guard removed/took the prisoner from the room but not the visitor.

Target
a. The prisoner removed by the guard fought violently to break free of the guard's grip.
b. The prisoner taken by the guard fought violently to break free of the guard's grip.

RESULTS

Reading times and differences for each recorded region are presented in Table 4. All subjects answered at least 80% of the comprehension questions accurately. An analysis of variance was first computed for the reading times collapsed across all recorded regions. The main effect of Ambiguity did not reach significance ($F1(1,28) < 1$; $F2(1,12) = 2.10$, $MS_e = 4735$), although the ambiguous sentences (562ms per region) were read somewhat more slowly than the unambiguous sentences (549ms per region). A main effect of Context was observed, such that recorded regions of sentences that followed 2-NP-referent contexts (534ms) were read more quickly than regions of sentences that followed 1-NP-referent contexts (577ms); $F1(1,28) = 11.28$, $MS_e = 21221$, $p < .005$; $F2(1,12) = 12.87$, $MS_e = 9299$, $p < .005$. The interaction between these two factors did not approach significance in this global analysis; $F(1,28) = 1.5$, $MS_e = 15400$; $F(1,12) = .69$, $MS_e = 16699$.

Additional analyses of variance were computed for individual regions. At the verb + "by" region, there was a main effect of Context in which subjects read the verb + "by" faster when the context contained 2 NP referents than when it contained only 1 NP referent (see Table 4); $F1(1,28) = 6.44$, $MS_e = 5593$, $p < .02$; $F2(1,12) = 4.79$, $MS_e = 3764$, $p < .05$. Again, no main effect of Ambiguity was observed. The interaction between Context and Ambiguity at the verb + "by" region was significant by subjects but not by items; $F1(1,28) = 5.32$, $MS_e = 3233$, $p < .05$; $F2(1,12) = 2.28$, $MS_e = 3768$, $p = .15$. Simple effects analyses revealed a marginal effect of Ambiguity in the 1-NP-Referent Context [$F1(1,28) = 3.34$, $MS_e = 5720$, $p < .1$; $F2(1,12) = 3.25$, $MS_e = 2946$, $p < .1$] but none at all in the 2-NP-Referent Context [$F1$ and $F2 < 1.0$].

At the following determiner + noun region, a similar main effect of Context was also observed; $F1(1,28) = 4.54$, $MS_e = 15416$, $p < .05$; $F2(1,12) = 4.64$,

TABLE 4
Reading Time (ms) by Sentence Region

	Det + noun	Verb + "by"	Det + noun	Main verb region
1 np referent				
Ambiguous	691	532	543	594
Unambiguous	702	498	488	568
Ambiguity Effect	−11	34	55	26
2 NP referents				
Ambiguous	660	476	468	529
Unambiguous	635	487	470	545
Ambiguity Effect	25	−11	−2	−16

$MS_e = 7540, p = .05$. However, the interaction between Context and Ambiguity was not statistically significant. Again, simple effects analyses showed a reliable effect of Ambiguity in the 1-NP-Referent Context [$F1(1,28) = 4.80$, $MS_e = 10178$, $p < .05$; $F2(1,12) = 4.99$, $MS_e = 4893$, $p < .05$] but not in the 2-NP-Referent Context [$F1$ and $F2 < 1.0$].

Another analysis of variance was computed collapsing across the entire relative clause (i.e., "selected by the director"). In addition to the main effect of Context [$F1(1,28) = 7.4$, $MS_e = 6971$, $p < .02$; $F2(1,12) = 13.52$, $MS_e = 1908$, $p < .005$] and a marginal effect of Ambiguity [$F1(1,28) = 3.13$, $MS_e = 3764$, $p = .09$; $F2(1,12) = 3.38$, $MS_e = 1745$, $p = .09$], the analysis of variance revealed an interaction between Context and Ambiguity (significant by subjects only) [$F1(1,28) = 5.23$, $MS_e = 4047$, $p < .05$; $F2(1,12) = 1.92$, $MS_e = 5521$, $p = .19$], such that the 1-NP-Referent Context exhibited an Ambiguity effect (538ms vs. 493ms) and the 2-NP-Referent Context did not (472ms vs. 479ms). Simple effects analyses confirmed this result with a significant effect of Ambiguity in the 1-NP-Referent Context [$F1(1,28) = 8.41$, $MS_e = 3838, p < .01; F2(1,12) = 5.18, MS_e = 3116, p < .05$] and no such effect in the 2-NP-Referent Context [$F1$ and $F2 < 1.0$].

It could be argued that the difference in mean string length between the ambiguous verbs (8 characters) and the unambiguous verbs (5.69 characters) makes the unambiguous condition a less than perfect control. However, there is no reason to expect this difference in string length to affect reading times in one context but not the other. That is, the difference in string length cannot account for the interaction between ambiguity and context. Nevertheless, to eliminate this factor, we conducted a regression analysis of string length to reading time on each subject's data at the verb + "by" region, and computed corresponding residuals. This adjusts reading times for string length differences (cf. Ferreira & Clifton, 1986; Trueswell & Tanenhaus, 1991). We then conducted an analysis of variance on the residuals for that region. The results are similar to what was observed with unadjusted reading times at this region. The main effect of Context was present, but it is only marginal; $F1(1,28) = 3.54$, $MS_e = 6136$, $p = .07$; $F2(1,12) = 3.64$, $MS_e = 3365$, $p = .08$. There was no effect of Ambiguity at this region. The interaction between Context and Ambiguity, as with unadjusted reading times, was significant by subjects but not by items; $F1(1,28) = 8.30$, $MS_e = 3820$, $p < .01$; $F2(1,12) = 2.56$, $MS_e = 3196$, $p = .14$.

DISCUSSION

As in Experiment 1, referential context had clear effects on ambiguity resolution for reduced relative clauses that began with a definite noun phrase. When the context established a unique referent for the noun phrase, readers experienced difficulty processing an ambiguous reduced relative clause compared to an unambiguous reduced relative. However, when the context established two possible referents, no such difficulty was observed. In addition, the small, and non-significant, ambiguity effect that was seen in the two NP referent contexts of Experiment 1 was completely absent in this experiment. In sum, referential contexts have immediate on-line effects on ambiguity resolution under conditions where (1) the contexts have been demonstrated to establish constraint at the point of ambiguity and (2) a presentation mode is used that allows or imposes a segmentation of the stimuli that mimics that in normal reading and facilitates availability of syntactic alternatives.

Experiment 3

To further demonstrate the importance of the availability issue, the stimuli from Experiment 2 were used in a single-word-presentation self-paced reading format. When the ambiguous verb is presented *without* the short preposition following it, the relative availability of the two alternative verb forms (simple past tense and past participial) is highly skewed toward the far more common simple past tense. Under these conditions, the effects of context should be weaker and delayed.

METHOD
Subjects

Thirty-six undergraduates from the University of Rochester participated in this experiment for course credit. All were native English speakers and were naive to the experimental manipulations.

Materials and Design

The 16 experimental items and 32 filler items from Experiment 2 were used in this experiment. Instead of the target sentences being presented in two-word segments, they were presented in one-word segments. The rest of the display characteristics were unchanged from Experiment 2. The experimental design was identical to Experiment 2, a 2 × 2 factorial manipulation of Context (1-NP-referent, 2-NP-referents) and Ambiguity (Ambiguous past participle, Unambiguous past participle).

Procedure

Aside from the one-word presentation mode, the procedure was identical to that in Experiment 2. A practice session of ten trials preceded the experimental session of 48 trials. The experiment lasted approximately 25 minutes.

RESULTS

All subjects answered at least 80% of the comprehension questions accurately. The reading times and differences for the first noun through the main verb are presented in Table 5, and the differences for reduced and unreduced relative clauses at each of these word positions are plotted in Figure 2. The pattern of data was clearly different for this experiment than for either Experiment 1 or Experiment 2. At the verb and the "by", there were small ambiguity effects that were numerically larger in the two NP referent contexts, whereas in the following regions, the ambiguity effects were numerically larger for sentences in the one NP referent contexts. However, the only effects that were reliable are main effects. An analysis of variance was first computed for the reading times collapsed across all recorded word positions, as done in the previous experiments. A main effect of Context was observed, such that recorded word positions of sentences that followed 2-NP-referent contexts (319ms) were read more quickly than word positions of sentences that followed 1-NP-referent contexts (339ms); $F1(1,32) = 15.9$, $MS_e = 5267$, $p < .001$; $F2(1,12) = 10.61$, $MS_e = 3508$, $p < .01$. A main effect of Ambiguity was also observed in this analysis. Subjects read word positions of the sentences containing Unambiguous reduced relative clauses (323ms) faster than those in sentences containing Ambiguous reduced relatives (335ms); $F1(1,32) = 5.27$, $MS_e = 5636$, $p < .05$; $F2(1,12) = 5.37$, $MS_e = 2460$, $p < .05$. The interaction between Context and Ambiguity did not approach significance; $F1$ and $F2 < 1$.

More fine-grained analyses of variance were then computed for individual word positions. At the noun preceding the verb, a main effect of Context, in which 2 NP referents facilitated reading time, was robust by subjects but marginal by items; $F1(1,32) = 10.27$, $MS_e = 857$, $p < .005$; $F2(1,12) = 3.14$, $MS_e = 1245$, $p = .1$. This result suggests an early felicity effect, such that, when the context contained 2 NP referents, subjects had a greater expectation for one of those entities to be further discussed in the subsequent sentence. This interpretation fits well into Spivey-Knowlton's (1992) conceptual expectation proposal. He suggested that the referential theory's explanation of these context effects is conflated by the fact that the contexts may set up conceptual expectations for disambiguation of the critical NP (via

TABLE 5
Reading Time (ms) by Word Position

	Noun	Verb	"by"	Det	Noun	Verb
1 NP referent						
Ambiguous	338	351	347	334	331	371
Unambiguous	333	338	345	318	305	352
Ambiguity Effect	5	13	2	16	26	19
2 NP referents						
Ambiguous	322	332	335	297	316	341
Unambiguous	317	311	323	292	308	333
Ambiguity Effect	5	21	12	5	8	8

post-modification) whether it be definite or indefinite (see Footnote 1). Thus, independent of referential pragmatics, there is a potential role for conceptual expectations in the effects of these 2-NP-referent contexts.

As in the other experiments, an interaction between Context and Ambiguity anywhere from the verb to the following noun would suggest that context was having an immediate effect on the syntactic decisions of the language processor. At the verb, there was a main effect of Context (felicity effect) in which subjects read that word position faster when the context contained 2 NP referents than when it contained only 1 NP referent (see Table 5); $F1(1,32) = 6.37$, $MS_e = 3191$, $p < .02$; $F2(1,12) = 6.03$, $MS_e = 1500$, $p < .05$. The main effect of Ambiguity was not significant; $F1(1,32) = 2.00$, $MS_e = 5227$; $F2(1,12) = 4.69$, $MS_e = 989$. Moreover, the interaction between Context and Ambiguity at the verb did not approach significance; $F1$ and $F2 < 1$.

At the word position that follows, the preposition "by", no significant effects were observed. Then, at the determiner, a robust main effect of Context reveals another felicity effect in which this word position was read faster when the context contained 2 NP referents than when the context contained 1 NP referent (see Table 5); $F1(1,32) = 9.58$, $MS_e = 3748$, $p < .005$; $F2(1,12) = 10.83$, $MS_e = 1473$, $p < .01$. However, neither the main effect of Ambiguity ($F1 = 1.07$; $F2 = 1.09$) nor the interaction ($F1$ and $F2 < 1$) approached significance.

A turn-around was observed at the next word position, the noun. The main effect of Context was no longer present ($F1 < 1$; $F2 < 1$), but the main effect of Ambiguity, in which Ambiguous reduced relatives produced longer reading times than Unambiguous reduced relatives was reliable; $F1(1,32) = 4.98$, $MS_e = 2058$, $p < .05$; $F2(1,12) = 6.57$, $MS_e = 694$, $p < .05$. As with the other word positions, the interaction between Context and Ambiguity did not approach significance; $F1$ and $F2 < 1$. Finally, the main verb position showed only a main effect of Context again, reliable by subjects but marginal by items;

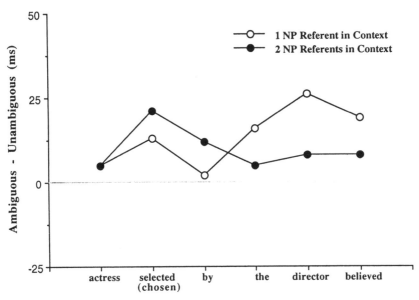

Fig. 2 Results of Experiment 3. Magnitude of the ambiguity effect in the two contexts as a function of word position.

$F1(1,32) = 5.86$, $MS_e = 3607$, $p < .05$; $F2(1,12) = 3.57$, $MS_e = 2630$, $p < .1$.

DISCUSSION

The only difference between this experiment and Experiment 2 was the mode of presentation. In Experiment 2, there was evidence for syntactic misanalysis in the one NP referent context but not in the two NP referent context. In contrast, the pattern of results was clearly different in the current experiment. Reading times were longer to ambiguous relative clauses in both contexts. Although context did not interact with ambiguity, the results across the word positions are suggestive. Early in the relative clause, the reduction effect was actually larger in the two NP referent context than in the one NP referent context, whereas the pattern reversed later in the clause. This pattern of results, which is similar to that reported by MacDonald (1992) and Pearlmutter and MacDonald (1992), is diagnostic of what happens when a contextual constraint supports the subordinate "reading" of an ambiguous word or phrase. These results are clearly parallel to the Burgess (1991) results with one-word presentation. As in the Burgess study, the present studies show that a contextual constraint that had clear and immediate effects with two-word presentation had weak and delayed effects with one-word presentation.

Clearly then, the effects of referential context depend upon the availability of the alternative readings of an ambiguity. Under conditions where both alternatives are likely to be available, context will have immediate effects, whereas context will have weak and/or delayed effects when it attempts to bias a reading that is not reasonably predictable from the local input. This generalization provides an explanation for why the literature on referential context effects is currently somewhat equivocal. It seems likely that the degree of bias among alternative readings differs for different structures. In addition, it seems likely that the contexts used across studies differ in how strongly constraining they are at the point of the ambiguity.

DISCUSSION OF EXPERIMENTS 1-3

Several important conclusions emerge from these experiments. First of all, referential contexts have immediate effects on ambiguity resolution for reduced relative clauses, under conditions where the participial form is likely to become available quickly. This result demonstrates that (a) readers consult their discourse model when they encounter a definite noun phrase and (b) referential information from the discourse can be an immediate source of constraint in syntactic ambiguity resolution. Thus, two of the basic assumptions of the referential theory receive strong support.

Two-word Presentation

One might argue that the two-word presentation mode is unnatural. However, for the sentences that we used, the two-word presentation format grouped short function words with content words, thus corresponding to the pattern of eye-movements usually observed in reading, in which short function words are frequently skipped (Rayner & McConkie, 1976). More convincingly, as we discussed, several experiments have directly compared eye-tracking to self-paced reading with a two-word window for relative clause "by"-phrase constructions and found nearly identical results. Those eye-tracking experiments that have failed to find influences from referential context on reduced relatives did not consistently have short potentially-agentive prepositions, such as "by"[3], immediately following the verb (Britt et al., 1992, Experiment 3; Ferreira & Clifton, 1986, Experiment 2). Instead, they tended to have locative prepositional phrases (i.e., "The boy stood in the corner..."), particles following the verb (i.e., "The animal curled up in the basket..."), or even potential direct objects following the verb (i.e., "The woman delivered the letter..."). Each of these continuations is consistent with a main clause construction.

---

3 Note that viewing "by" with the ambiguous verb does not at that point resolve the ambiguity in favour of a participial verb form in a relative clause. It simply increases the availability of that alternative by virtue of the fact that "by" is frequently used to introduce agents in passive constructions, i.e. "The woman hired *by Fred* quit." But "by" can also be used in a *locative* or a *manner* role in a main clause continuation with an optionally intransitive verb, i.e., "The boy stood *by the telephone pole*" and "The dragon killed *by breathing fire on his prey*" (cf. Tabossi et al., 1993).

Theoretical and Methodological Implications

The interaction of context effect and presentation mode has both theoretical and methodological implications. Experiments using single-word self-paced reading may underestimate context effects when they separate an ambiguous word from potentially disambiguating information which would normally be processed parafoveally. Under these conditions, weak and/or delayed effects of context may be mistakenly attributed to the system being unable to make use of the context, when in fact, bottom-up processing has not made the relevant alternatives available quickly enough. From a theoretical perspective, the results highlight the importance of understanding the local factors that control availability – factors which have received far too little attention in the parsing literature. The fact that context effects depend upon local availability also suggests that purely discourse-based theories of syntactic ambiguity resolution are by themselves inadequate.

Finally, we should note that our context effects were obtained with contexts that were only weakly constraining. However, unlike most context studies in the literature, we used off-line norms to establish that our contexts were constraining at the point of the ambiguity.

General Discussion

Our results demonstrate clear effects of both local semantic context and discourse context on ambiguity resolution for relative clauses. When context provides strong syntactically relevant constraints in favour of a relative clause, and the alternatives are available, then both local semantic context and discourse context rapidly affect ambiguity resolution.

Let's briefly consider the implications of these results for current approaches to ambiguity resolution. First of all, the results of the experiments offer strong support for two of the fundamental claims made by discourse-based approaches, in particular, the referential theory. The first is that readers try to immediately link contextually dependent expressions to discourse representations. Clear evidence comes from the effects we reported for temporal and noun phrase referential contexts. Secondly, the constraints made available by the discourse are used in syntactic ambiguity resolution. However, we also discussed results demonstrating that a contextual factor unrelated to discourse, namely local semantic context, had clear effects on syntactic ambiguity resolution. In addition, under certain circumstances, referential contexts will have only weak or delayed effects because there is a strong local bias in favour of a particular reading. Neither of these effects are accounted for in the referential theory. In short, discourse-based factors are clearly important constraints that are used in parsing, but a purely discourse-based approach is inadequate.

The results are nicely accommodated by recent versions of constraint-based approaches to parsing in which the bottom-up input determines the set of possible alternatives (e.g., MacDonald, 1992; Tabossi et al., 1993; Trueswell et al., 1992). For example, in MacDonald's model, alternatives will be partially activated depending on how likely they are given the input. Syntactically relevant contextual constraints can then provide evidence for or against competing alternatives. While these models need to be made more precise in order to generate quantitative predictions, they clearly predict an interaction between strength of contextual constraint and bottom-up availability of the alternatives. A brief scan of the literature supports this prediction. Where frequency of use is highly skewed toward one of the alternatives, as in reduced relatives (cf. Tabossi et al., 1993), on-line effects of context have been elusive (Britt et al., 1992; Ferreira & Clifton, 1986; Rayner et al., 1983; but see Ni & Crain, 1990). In contrast, for syntactic ambiguities in which the intrinsic availability of alternatives is less skewed, as in PP-attachment ambiguities (cf. Hindle & Rooth, 1990 and Spivey-Knowlton & Sedivy, 1992), on-line effects of context are more common (Altmann & Steedman, 1988; Britt et al., 1992; Spivey-Knowlton, 1992; but see Ferreira & Clifton, 1986 and Rayner et al., 1983).

We should note that this class of constraint-based approach does not predict that *all* of the information in a context will have immediate effects on parsing. First of all, local syntactic information will define the set of possible alternatives, much like the initial segments of a word will partially activate features of words belonging to a "cohort" (Marslen-Wilson, 1987; Norris, 1990). Secondly, the only information from the context that will have effects will be information that is both currently active and syntactically relevant. The two general types of contextual information that we explored in this article meet both of these conditions.

The constraint-based approach that we have outlined contrasts with the two-stage approach, adopted by restricted-domain models such as the garden-path theory, in which ambiguity resolution begins with a single analysis developed by a first-stage parser. Although the context effects just presented here are problematic for a two-stage approach, such an approach could accommodate these effects by treating them as part of the revision stage. This would require having a very small temporal window for the autonomous attachment stage, and it would require treating the revision process as constraint-based. However, the motivation for an autonomous first stage becomes less compelling as the temporal window shrinks and as the range of information that can have immediate, or nearly immediate, effects on ambiguity resolution increases (MacDonald, 1992; Trueswell, Tanenhaus, & Kello, in press). In the end, however, the issue will only be resolved when we have more detailed information about the time course of the resolution process and models (of both constraint-based and two-stage theories) that are precise enough to generate quantitative predictions.

This research was supported by an NSF Graduate Student Research Fellowship to the first author, and NIH grant #HD27206 to the third author. Chuck Clifton, Fernanda Ferreira, Murray Singer and an anonymous reviewer provided helpful comments. Send correspondence to Michael Spivey-Knowlton, Department of Psychology, Meliora Hall, University of Rochester, Rochester, NY 14627 E-mail: spivey@psych.rochester.edu

References

Altmann, G., & Steedman, M. (1988). Interaction with context during human sentence processing. *Cognition, 30*, 191-238.

Altmann, G., Garnham, A., & Denis, Y. (1992). Avoiding the garden-path: Eye movements in context. *Journal of Memory and Language, 31*, 685-712.

Bates, E. & MacWhinney, B. (1989). Functionalism and the competition model. In B. MacWhinney & E. Bates (Eds.), *The crosslinguistic study of sentence processing.* New York: Cambridge University Press.

Bever, T. G. (1970). The cognitive basis for linguistic structure. In J. R. Hayes (Ed.). *Cognitive development of language.* New York: Wiley.

Bock, J. K. (1986). Syntactic persistence in language production. *Cognitive Psychology, 18*, 355-387.

Britt, M. A., Perfetti, C. A., Garrod, S., & Rayner, K. (1992). Parsing and discourse: Context effects and their limits. *Journal of Memory and Language, 31*, 293-314.

Burgess, C. (1991). *The interaction of syntactic, semantic and visual factors in syntactic ambiguity resolution.* Unpublished Ph.D dissertation. University of Rochester, Rochester, NY.

Burgess, C. & Tanenhaus, M. (1992). *The interaction of semantic and parafoveal information in syntactic ambiguity resolution.* Manuscript in preparation.

Clifton, C. & Ferreira, F. (1989). Ambiguity in context. *Language and Cognitive Processes, 4*, SI, 77-104.

Crain, S. (1980). *Contextual constraints on sentence comprehension.* Unpublished Ph.D dissertation, University of California, Irvine.

Crain, S. & Steedman, M. (1985). On not being led up the garden path: The use of context by the psychological parser. In Dowty, Kartunnen, & Zwicky (Eds.), *Natural language parsing.* Cambridge: Cambridge University Press.

Ferreira, F., & Clifton, C. (1986). The independence of syntactic processing. *Journal of Memory and Language, 25*, 348-368.

Ferreira, F., & Henderson, J. (1993). Reading Processes During Syntactic Analysis and Reanalysis. *Canadian Journal of Experimental Psychology, 47*, 247-275.

Frazier, L. (1978). *On comprehending sentences: Syntactic parsing strategies.* Unpublished Ph.D dissertation, University of Connecticut.

Frazier, L., & Rayner, K. (1982). Making and correcting errors during sentence comprehension: Eye movements in the analysis of structurally ambiguous sentences. *Cognitive Psychology, 14*, 178-210.

Heim, I. (1982). *The semantics of definite and indefinite noun phrases*. Unpublished Ph.D dissertation, University of Massachusetts, Amherst.

Just, M., Carpenter, P., & Woolley, J. (1982). Paradigms and processes in reading comprehension. *Journal of Experimental Psychology: General, 111*, 228-238.

Marslen-Wilson, W. (1973). Linguistic structure and speech shadowing at very short latencies. *Nature, 244*, 522-523.

Marslen-Wilson, W. (1987). Functional parallelism in spoken word-recognition. *Cognition, 25*, 71-102.

Marslen-Wilson, W., & Tyler, K. (1987). Against modularity. In J. L. Garfield (Ed.), *Modularity in knowledge representation and natural language understanding*. Cambridge, MA: MIT Press.

Mitchell, D. C., Corley, M. M. B., & Garnham, A. (1992). Effects of context in human sentence parsing: Evidence against a discourse-based proposal mechanism. *Journal of Experimental Psychology: Learning, Memory and Cognition, 18*, 69-88.

MacDonald, M. (1992). Probabilistic constraints and syntactic ambiguity resolution. Manuscript submitted for publication.

McClelland, J. L., St. John, M., & Taraban, R. (1989). Sentence comprehension: A parallel distributed approach. *Language and Cognitive Processes, 4*, SI, 287-335.

Ni, W., & Crain, S. (1990). How to resolve structural ambiguities. *Proceedings of the 20th meeting of the North Eastern Linguistic Society*.

Norris, D. (1990). A dynamic net model of human speech recognition. In G. Altmann (Ed.), *Cognitive models of speech processing: Psycholinguistic and computational perspectives*. Cambridge, MA: MIT Press.

Pearlmutter, N., & MacDonald, M. (1992). Plausibility effects in syntactic ambiguity resolution. *Proceedings of the 14th Annual Meeting of the Cognitive Science Society*. Bloomington, IN.

Rayner, K., Carlson, M., & Frazier, L. (1983). The interaction of syntax and semantics during sentence processing: Eye movements in the analysis of semantically biased sentences. *Journal of Verbal Learning and Verbal Behavior, 22*, 358-374.

Rayner, K., & McConkie, G.W. (1976). What guides a reader's eye movements? *Vision Research, 16*, 829–837.

Spivey-Knowlton, M. (1992). Another context effect in sentence processing: Implications for the principle of referential support. *Proceedings of the 14th Annual Meeting of the Cognitive Science Society*. Bloomington, IN.

Spivey-Knowlton, M., & Sedivy, J. (1992). *On-line and Off-line effects of NP definiteness on parsing attachment ambiguities*. Manuscript submitted for publication.

Tabossi, P., Spivey-Knowlton, M., McRae, K., & Tanenhaus, M. (1993). Semantic effects on syntactic ambiguity resolution: Evidence for a constraint-based resolution process. In C. Umilta & M. Moscovitch (Eds.), *Attention and Per-

formance XV, Cambridge, MA: MIT Press.

Tanenhaus, M.K., Carlson, G., & Trueswell, J.C. (1989). The role of thematic structures in interpretation and parsing. *Language and Cognitive Processes, 4*, SI, 211-234.

Taraban, R., & McClelland, J. (1988). Constituent attachment and thematic role expectations, *Journal of Memory and Language, 27*, 597-632.

Trueswell, J., & Tanenhaus, M. (1991). Tense, temporal context and syntactic ambiguity resolution. *Language and Cognitive Processes, 6*, 303-338.

Trueswell, J., & Tanenhaus, M. (1992). Consulting temporal context in sentence comprehension: Evidence from the monitoring of eye movements in reading. *Proceedings of the 14th Annual Meeting of the Cognitive Science Society.* Bloomington, IN.

Trueswell, J., Tanenhaus, M., & Garnsey, S. (1992). *Semantic influences on parsing: Use of thematic role information in syntactic disambiguation.* Manuscript submitted for publication.

Trueswell, J., Tanenhaus, M., & Kello, C. (in press). Verb-specific constraints in sentence processing: Separating effects of lexical preference from garden-paths. *Journal of Experimental Psychology: Learning, Memory and Cognition.*

Appendix

The following are the contexts and target sentences used the experiments. For stimulus 1, the 2-NP-Referent Context is presented in brackets. For the remaining stimuli, only the 1-NP-Referent Context is shown. The 2-NP-Referent Contexts can be easily induced by analogy with stimulus 1. Following the segmented ("/") target sentence ("who was" is for Experiment 1 only), the percentage of reduced relative clause completions is given for the three context conditions in the norming study. Recall that Experiment 3 used one-word presentation format. Finally, the unambiguous participial verbs (from Experiments 2 and 3) are shown in parentheses with the ambiguous verb that they replace.

1. [Two patients were waiting for their doctor to introduce them to the team of specialists that would handle their case. The doctor presented one of the patients to them but not the other.] A patient and her son were waiting for their doctor to introduce them to the team of specialists that would handle their case. The doctor presented the patient to them but not the son. The patient / (who was) / presented by / the doctor / felt embarrassed / for getting / all the / attention. Null: 0, 1-NPR: .125, 2-NPR: .25 (presented/shown)

2. A knight and his squire were attacking a dragon. With its breath of fire, the dragon killed the knight but not the squire. The knight / (who was) / killed by / the dragon / fell to / the ground / with a / thud. Null: 0, 1-NPR: .375, 2-NPR: .125 (killed/slain)

3. A woman and a man wearing overcoats walked into a bank. The bank guard watched the woman but not the man. The woman / (who was) / watched by / the

guard / realized that / she was / no longer / inconspicuous. Null: 0, 1-NPR: 0, 2-NPR: .125 (watched/seen)

4. A mother took her son and daughter shopping with her at the market. When she left, she abandoned her son who was still in the toy aisle but not her daughter. The son / (who was) / abandoned by / his mother / continued to / play with / the toys. Null: .125, 1-NPR: .5, 2-NPR: .375 (abandoned/forgotten)

5. In the visiting room, a prisoner and a visitor began yelling at each other. To prevent a fight, the guard removed the prisoner from the room but not the visitor. The prisoner / (who was) / removed by / the guard / fought violently / to break / free of / the guard's / grip. Null: 0, 1-NPR: .375, 2-NPR: .375 (removed/taken)

6. The old lady was very abusive to certain members of her family. She constantly battered her daughter but not her son. The daughter / (who was) / battered by / her mother / thought that / she deserved / the punishment. Null: 0, 1-NPR: .125, 2-NPR: .25 (battered/beaten)

7. The likely suspect and his accomplice in the crime were placed in a line-up of several other men. The victim identified the suspect but not the accomplice. The suspect / (who was) / identified by / the victim / claimed that / he was / innocent. Null: .125, 1-NPR: .375, 2-NPR: .75 (identified/chosen)

8. One night a thief was checking out the neighboring homes of a family and a bachelor. He robbed the family but not the bachelor. The family / (who was) / robbed by / the thief / called the / police as / soon as / they realized / what had / happened. Null: 0, 1-NPR: .375, 2-NPR: .75 (robbed/woken)

9. A college admissions council was considering the applications of a student and a blue collar worker. They admitted the student but not the blue collar worker. The student / (who was) / admitted by / the council / suggested to / his friends / that they / apply to / the same / college. Null: 0, 1-NPR: .375, 2-NPR: .625 (admitted/taken)

10. A boy and a girl were fighting in their bedroom when their father walked in. He punished the boy but not the girl. The boy / (who was) / punished by / his father / began to / cry and / ran to / his mother. Null: 0, 1-NPR: .375, 2-NPR: .625 (punished/beaten)

11. An actress and the producer's niece were auditioning for a play. The director selected the actress but the not the niece. The actress / (who was) / selected by / the director / believed that / her performance / was perfect. Null: 0, 1-NPR: .375, 2-NPR: .625 (selected/chosen)

12. An actor and an actress were rehearsing on stage with the curtain half-closed. The curtain covered the actor but not the actress. The actor / (who was) / covered by / the curtain / complained about / the incident / for weeks. Null: 0, 1-NPR: .375, 2-NPR: .625 (covered/hidden)

13. A senator and a lawyer were debating on TV about international law. The next day, a news reporter criticized the senator but not the lawyer. The senator / (who was) / criticized by / the reporter / called the / TV station / and complained / about the / injustice. Null: 0, 1-NPR: .125, 2-NPR: .5 (criticized/shown)

14. A guide and a cameraman got stuck in a narrow crevice while traveling with a research team in the Arctic. The team had to abandon the guide but not the cameraman. The guide / (who was) / abandoned by / the team / died before / they could / contact help. Null: 0, 1-NPR: .25, 2-NPR: .25 (abandoned/forsaken)

15. A boy and a girl were smoking behind the school gym when the principal came walking toward them. He recognized the boy but not the girl. The boy / (who was) / recognized by / the principal / received a / two-day suspension. Null: 0, 1-NPR: 0, 2-NPR: .25 (recognized/known)

16. A boy was conducting an experiment on a rabbit and a hamster. He raised the rabbit himself but not the hamster. The rabbit / (that was) / raised by / the boy / responded to / him with / affection. Null: 0, 1-NPR: .125, 2-NPR: .5 (raised/grown)

9 The Intensity Dimension of Thought: Pupillometric Indices of Sentence Processing

MARCEL ADAM JUST and PATRICIA A. CARPENTER
Carnegie Mellon University

Abstract   This article explores the intensity of processing during sentence comprehension by measuring pupillary response during reading. Two experiments contrast the processing of simpler versus more complex sentences. The two more complex sentence types, object-relative center-embedded sentences and filler-gap sentences, not only take longer to process than their simpler counterparts, but they also produce a larger change in pupil diameter. We propose that the pupillary response is an indicator of how intensely the processing system is operating. The more complex sentences evoke some intense processing at the point in the sentence where a syntactic complexity is first encountered. The gaze durations at these points are elevated, indicating the immediate response to the demand of the syntactic processing. The pupil then starts to dilate, reaching a maximal diameter approximately 1.3 s later. The results from these various performance measures are integrated within a resource-limited computational model of comprehension. The paper develops a model of comprehension that includes an intensity dimension of thought, drawing a correspondence between the computational model's consumption of resources and the human pupillary response.

Résumé   Nous avons mené des recherches sur l'intensité du traitement nécessaire à la compréhension des phrases, en mesurant les réponses pupillaires durant la lecture. Deux expériences ont fait ressortir le contraste entre le traitement des phrases simples et celui des phrases complexes. Les phrases complexes, soit celles qui sont entrecoupées d'une proposition relative et les phrases bouche-trous, sont plus longues à traiter que les phrases simples, et leur traitement provoque un changement plus important dans le diamètre de la pupille. Nous croyons que la réponse pupillaire est un indicateur de l'intensité avec laquelle le système de traitement est activé. Les phrases plus complexes mettent en oeuvre un certain processus de traitement intense lorsque surgit une complexité syntaxique dans la phrase. Les durées des fixations oculaires sont alors élevées et témoignent de la réponse immédiate à la demande du traitement syntaxique. En pareil cas, la pupille commence à se dilater et atteint un diamètre maximal après environ 1,3 s. Les résultats de ces différentes mesures de la performance sont intégrés dans un modèle computationnel de compréhension faisant appel à des ressources limitées. Nous exposons un modèle de compréhension qui tient compte de l'intensité de la pensée et qui établit une correspondance entre la dépense de ressources faite par le modèle computationnel et les réponses pupillaires chez l'humain.

Reading can be hard work. For an unskilled reader, the effort is obvious. But even for a skilled reader, some sentences and texts are harder than others, and sometimes readers feel that they have put in more effort than at other times. In this article, we explore the nature of difficulty and effort in sentence comprehension. It is already well known that more complex sentence structures take longer to process and are more susceptible to a comprehension error. We claim that there exists another, often neglected facet of difficulty, related to how hard the processing system has to work to understand a sentence. The analogy between mental and physical work provides an insight into the dimension of thinking that corresponds to effortfulness or intensity. A task might not just take longer, but might require more cognitive effort. The intensity dimension in other realms of human activity suggests some parallel questions about the intensity dimension in thought. In physiology, for example, intensity corresponds to metabolic rate, the rate at which biochemical resources are generated and consumed. This measure has modulations; it frequently varies from moment to moment, but it can also have long-term plateaus (roughly corresponding to resting metabolic rate). Analogously, it makes sense to ask whether there are corresponding modulations of the intensity of thought.

This article examines the modulation of cognitive intensity during the processing of complex sentences, and examines a methodology for assessing intensity and relating it to a model of capacity constraints on comprehension. In the current article, intensity is construed as rate of mental resource consumption to support processing or to maintain information in active storage. This definition is later made more precise in terms of a computer simulation model of comprehension.

The concept of intensity arises from a capacity theory that traces part of its roots to research on attention and, in particular, to Kahneman's (1973) capacity theory of attention, which laid a foundation for most of its successors in that domain. Capacity theories of attention account for performance decrements that occur when the resource demands of the task exceed the available supply (Navon & Gopher, 1979; Wickens, 1984). Attention theories often refer to some underlying commodity that enables performance, usually labeling it "capacity", or "resources". More capacity is required for more difficult tasks (e.g., Hirst, Spelke, Reaves, Caharack, & Neisser, 1980; Norman & Bobrow, 1975; Shallice, 1982; Shiffrin & Schneider, 1977). The current research extends these empirical results by showing that there are transient demands on capacity within the left-to-right processes of compre-hending a sentence. More importantly, the current research proposes to sharpen the concept of resources, by defining it as the amount of activation available for information storage and processing. This definition builds on the proposal of Baddeley and Hitch (1974; Baddeley, 1986), arising from their research on the articulatory loop.

In most sciences, but quite obviously in psychology, the usefulness of a construct is influenced by the ease of its measurement. Intensity has proven much less easily measured than the duration of mental processes or error patterns in performance. Intensity is a characteristic of an internal process that does not necessarily leave a trace on the final output. Interestingly, some of the intensity-probing methodologies that have been explored have a physio-logical component; such methodologies include physiological studies of cerebral glucose metabolism (PET) (Haier et al., 1988). A more widely available technique is pupillometry, the measurement of changes in pupil size, as espoused by Kahneman (1973). Previous studies suggest that the greater the demand on capacity, the more the pupil dilates (Ahern & Beatty, 1979; Beatty, 1982). For example, pupil dilation is greater during more difficult mental multiplication (e.g., $14 \times 19 = ?$) than simpler multiplication (e.g., $6 \times 12 = ?$). The neurophysiological basis for the relation between pupil dilation and the consumption of cognitive resources, according to Beatty (1982), may be the cortical modulation of the reticular formation which may also modulate some peripheral systems, such as the pupillary control system. The implication is that the pupillary response is only a correlate of cognitive intensity, hence the marker is indirect and not causally linked. In addition, there is a temporal lag between the resource consumption and the pupillary response.

Several earlier studies indicated that pupillary response may be sensitive to resource demands in language processing. One study assessed pupillary responses during a reasoning task in which an auditorily presented sentence, either active/passive or affirmative/negative, was verified against a subsequent display, for example, "A doesn't precede B" followed by the display "B-A." The averaged pupillary waveforms showed reliable differences in dilation between the affirmative and negative sentences, with the most dilation for the more complex negative-passive construction, particularly during the verifica-tion process (Ahern, 1978, reported in Beatty, 1982). In another study, in which subjects had to listen to and repeat back six-word sentences, larger dilations were associated with greater deviation from standard English, specifically, more dilation for randomly scrambled sentences than for syntactically anomalous sentences, and the least for normal sentences (Beatty & Schluroff, reported in Beatty, 1982; Schluroff, 1982). In both cases, the pupillary responses were largest in the period after the sentence was presented, either the repetition phase or the verification phase. Task effects were also found in a study involving the oral presentation of sentences with lexical ambiguities, in which choosing one of two interpretations of the ambiguity was associated with greater dilation than the task of explaining the meaning (Ben-Nun, 1986). In a study involving syntactic ambiguity, sentences whose meanings were more uncertain (as indicated by a lack of agreement among an independent group of subjects) elicited slightly larger dilation than those that were less uncertain, although the differences as analyzed by a principal components analysis were not reliable (Schluroff et al., 1986). Cumulatively, the research suggests that there are small, but potentially consistent effects of linguistic processing demands on pupillary response during comprehension, although most of the studies have involved demanding post-sentential tasks, such as verbal report or sentence transformation.

In addition to its sensitivity to task demands, pupillary response may indicate systematic individual differences. The most systematic report of such effects occurred in a study of mental multiplication by two groups; a group of 17 college students with average verbal and quantitative combined SAT scores of 877 showed more dilation than another group with average scores of 1407 (Ahern & Beatty, 1979). Ahern and Beatty argued that pupillometric measures were sensitive to the relative demands placed on individuals by a task, as well as sensitive to differences in task demands themselves.

The research by Beatty (1982) suggests that the most relevant characteristic of the pupillary response is the peak amplitude of the dilation, which tends to occur approximately 1200 ms after the first encounter with the demand (Ahern & Beatty, 1979; Janisse, 1977). Following Beatty, the studies reported below compare peak amplitudes in contrasting pairs of sentence types. However, the research to be reported below brings some methodological innovations to the pupillometry paradigm. First, we will examine the variation in pupil diameter within a trial, in response to the fluctuating demands imposed in various parts of the sentence, as opposed to processing that may arise as a consequence of preparing or outputting a subsequent response. In addition, we will measure pupil diameter as subjects are reading and in conjunction with measures of their gaze location and gaze duration, as indices of comprehension processing. The pupillometric results will also provide a converging measure that can be combined with the reading time and error data that we and others have used to construct models of comprehension.

Experiment 1: Object-relative and Subject-relative sentences
The classic example of a syntactic structure that makes large demands on working memory capacity is a center-embedded relative clause, such as the one in sentence (1):

(1) The reporter that the senator attacked admitted the error.

It is also called an *object relative* for brevity, a name that reflects the role that the head noun *reporter* plays as the object of *attacked* in the relative clause. One index of the difficulty of such sentences is that when subjects try to paraphrase such sentences, they incorrectly match the agents with their verbs approximately 15% of the time (Larkin & Burns, 1977). The error rate rises to 30% for college students with a small working memory capacity for language (King & Just, 1991). The difficulty of such sentences arises from at least three kinds of demands that they make on the comprehender's working memory. First, the interruption of the main clause by the embedded clause imposes a storage or retrieval demand. The representation of the main clause segment that precedes the interruption must either be retained in working memory during the processing of the embedded clause, or be re-activated at the conclusion of the embedded clause (Miller & Chomsky, 1963; Wanner & Maratsos, 1978). Second, some difficulty is imposed by the assigning of the proper thematic roles to the two noun phrases. In particular, deciding whether the head of the relative clause is the agent or the patient of the relative clause verb causes comprehension of the relative clause to be less accurate than comprehension of the main clause in this kind of sentence (e.g., Holmes & O'Regan, 1981; King & Just, 1991). The nouns of the relative clause are not in the canonical order (subject-verb-object), whereas the nouns of the main clause are. Third, the assignment of two different roles to a single syntactic constituent also taxes working memory capacity. In the example above, *reporter* is the agent in one clause and the recipient of the action in the other. Associating a single concept with two different roles simultaneously seems to be a source of difficulty in language comprehension (Bever, 1970) and the switching of perspective in the construction of such a concept can also tax cognitive resources (MacWhinney & Pleh, 1988).

The difficulty of processing an object relative sentence contrasts with the comparative ease of processing a related construction, called a *subject relative*, like (2):

(2) The reporter that attacked the senator admitted the error.

In a subject relative sentence, the main clause is interrupted, but role assignments can be made one at a time, and the constituents have parallel roles in the two clauses. Moreover, the nouns in the relative clause of a subject relative sentence are in the canonical NVN order, whereas in the object relative sentence, they are not in the canonical order. Correspondingly, subject relative sentences are comprehended more quickly and more accurately than comparable object relative sentences like (1) (Holmes & O'Regan, 1981; King & Just, 1991). The three aspects that make the processing of an object relative sentence demanding of working memory are all mitigated in a subject relative sentence. In a subject relative, the head of the relative clause needs to be maintained over only a short distance, thus there is only a single thematic role to assign when *the senator* is reached; furthermore, the agent in the relative clause is also the agent of the main clause, thus requiring no assignment of conflicting roles and necessitating no perspective shift.

The distribution of processing load during comprehension is reflected in the word-by-word reading times for object relative and subject relative sentences like (1) and (2) (King & Just, 1991). We assume that readers try to interpret each word as soon as they encounter it, in accord with the Immediacy of Interpretation Principle (Just & Carpenter, 1980, 1987). In the case of the object relative sentence such as (1), the increased processing demands first manifest themselves when the reader reaches the first verb *(attacked)*. At that point, the head noun *(reporter)* must be assigned to the thematic role of patient and *senator* must be assigned to the thematic role of agent. Judging by the types of comprehension errors readers make, there is sometimes difficulty in correctly assigning the two nouns to two roles (King & Just, 1991). Next, the reader encounters the verb *admitted* and must find an agent for this verb, but this agent is *not* the same as the agent of *attacked*. Thus the two adjacent verbs should be the locus of the extra processing load. This result was found by Ford (1983) with a continuous lexical decision task in which readers judged each successive word of a sentence to determine whether it was a real word or a non-word. Subjects took 25 ms longer to make a lexical decision on the verbs *attacked* and *admitted* in an object relative sentence like (1) than in a subject relative sentence like (2). Similar results were obtained by Holmes and O'Regan (1981) in a reading task which measured the duration of subjects' eye fixations using sentences in French, which has a similar subject/object relative clause distinction. More recently, it was found that word-by-word reading times for the two sentence types were also sensitive to differences in working memory capacity in a college-age population (King & Just, 1991). Not only did the reading times for the object relative sentence show the expected increase at the verbs, but the increases were systematically greater for readers who had less working memory capacity for language, as assessed by the Reading Span Test (Daneman & Carpenter, 1980).

The contrast between these two sentence types provides a context in which to examine pupillary responses during comprehension. Experiment 1 examines the differences in pupillary response in the reading of sentences with embedded subject relative or object relative clauses: For both sentence types, pupil diameter should increase from a baseline level to some higher level after the main clause verb is encountered, given that this is the area that makes the largest demands. In particular, the increase should be greater for the more demanding sentence, the object relative sentence, than for the less demanding subject relative sentence.

METHOD

Materials and Design

Subjects read sentences while their eye fixations and pupil diameters were recorded. Following 6 practice trials, there were 60 trials, consisting of 36 experimental trials randomly intermixed with 24 filler trials of similar superficial appearance. The experimental and filler trials were presented in a different random order for each subject.

Each trial consisted of a context-setting sentence (that did not focus on any of the noun phrases in an experimental test sentence) followed by the experimental sentence, followed by a comprehension question that interrogated the experimental sentence, as shown in the sample object-relative trial below:

The news media like to cover political events extensively.
The reporter that the senator attacked admitted the error publicly after the hearing.
The reporter attacked the senator. (False)

Half of the experimental trials contained object relative sentences, while the other half contained subject relative sentences. All the experimental sentences, which were between 12 and 17 words long, were reversible, such that both the correct and incorrect noun-verb pairing were equally plausible in the context of the sentence. Eighteen familiar transitive verbs that take animate subjects and objects were each used twice (with different grammatical subjects and objects) in the embedded clauses of the experimental sentences. The direct object of the main verb was followed by an extra prepositional or adverbial phrase, so that the reading time on the direct object was not contaminated by end-of-sentence effects (Just & Carpenter, 1980). The true-false comprehension test probe that followed an experimental sentence was constructed by combining one of the two verbs in the sentence with two of the three nouns. Subjects pressed the button marked "TRUE" or the button marked "FALSE" to indicate their answer to the probe. After they answered, the screen was cleared and the next trial began when they pushed a "START" button.

Subjects' working memory capacity for language was measured using the Reading Span Test (Daneman & Carpenter, 1980), which assesses simultaneous storage and processing capacity. The subjects were classified according to their performance as having either *High, Medium,* or *Low* Span. High Span subjects were those whose reading spans were 4.0 or higher, whereas Low Span subjects were those whose reading spans were 2.5 or lower. All subjects whose reading spans were either 3.0 or 3.5 were classified as Medium Span subjects.

Subjects

There were 40 students from either Carnegie Mellon University or the University of Pittsburgh who participated for $5.00 payment or for course credit. The data considered below exclude five subjects (four low-span and one mid) whose error rate (38%) in answering the comprehension probes was substantially higher than that of other subjects.

Data analysis: Pupillometry

Eyetracking and pupillometry were done with an Iscan Model RK-426 eyetracker (accurate to about 1 degree of visual angle) and a DEC VAXstation 3200 for stimulus presentation and data acquisition, which acquired both types of data at a sampling rate of 60 Hz. The eyetracker measured pupil diameter in terms of video scan lines. To relate this measure to absolute pupil size, the tracker's measure was calibrated to an artificial pupil positioned at the same distance as the average subject's pupil. The average pupil diameter measurement during the reading of the neutral context-setting sentence was about 4.5 mm. The luminance of the display did not systematically differ between the conditions to be compared, because subject and object-relative sentences differ only in word order.

The object and subject relative sentences, respectively, were divided into regions to be used for scoring, as indicated by the square brackets.

The [reporter that the senator] [attacked] [admitted] [the error] [publicly after] the hearing.
The [reporter that attacked the] [senator] [admitted] [the error] [publicly after] the hearing.
             1   2   3   4   5

It is important to note that a line break occurred at or within one word of the end of Region 5. The main dependent measure, in broad terms, was the amount of change in pupil diameter between a baseline and a maximum obtained after encountering Region 3. More precisely, the baseline was the minimum pupil diameter during the reading of the neutral, context-setting sentence (which occupied no more than one line of print), excluding both the sentence-initial and sentence-final words. The interval on which the pupil diameter maximum was based started when the reader first fixated Region 3, and ended at the return sweep at the end of the line, which coincided with the end of Region 5. If this interval turned out to be longer than 3000 ms, then only the first 3000 ms were used in the analysis. Thus, the pupil data excluded any return sweep, which could cause a change in pupil size. The measurement of pupil size started at the first fixation of the main clause verb (Region 3) rather than at the relative clause verb because the latter occurs at different serial positions in the object and subject relative sentences. Moreover, starting the measurement at the main clause verb (which is briefly after the first encounter with the extra processing load associated with an object relative) would not miss the pupil change response, which has a long latency of over 1000 ms. The interval over which the pupil data were acquired averaged 1847 ms for object relatives and 1677 ms for subject relative sentences (even though the two sentence types are identical from the point at which pupillometric measurements were started; we will describe in more detail below how the readers distributed their gaze duration). Both of these intervals are adequately long, given the 1200 ms latency for the peak amplitude reported by Beatty (1982). The pupil diameter data were digitally filtered to eliminate spikes and artifacts due to blinks.

Data analysis: Gaze duration
In each of the experimental conditions, the first-pass and total gaze duration per word were calculated for Regions 1, 2, 3, 4, and the combination of Regions 2 through 5. The two regions of primary interest were the relative clause ending (Region 2) and the main verb (Region 3). These two regions are expected to be the loci of difficulty, relative to the regions that precede and follow. The gaze duration and pupillometric results reported below include those trials in which the comprehension question interrogating the target sentence was answered incorrectly; however, the results are not substantially changed when such trials are excluded.

RESULTS AND DISCUSSION
Of central interest in this study are the pupillometric results, specifically, the effects of sentence difficulty on changes in pupil diameter. The reading of the more difficult object-relative sentences elicited a greater change in the pupil diameter (0.249 mm) than subject-relative sentences (0.203 mm), $F(1,32) = 5.11$, $MS_e = 20.0$, $p < .05$. Table 1 shows the mean change in pupil diameter for the two types of experimental sentences and the three groups. The difficulty effect was very consistent across subjects, although there was considerable variation in the size of the effect among subjects, even within a reading span group. On average, the low span group showed more change in pupil diameter (i.e., a larger pupillary response) (0.24 mm) than did either the medium (0.21 mm) or high span groups (0.22 mm), but the between-group differences in pupillary response were not reliable, nor was there any interaction with span and sentence type, both F's < 1. The difference between the two sentence types suggests that pupillary responses vary with the processing demands during reading comprehension, reflecting the greater resource requirements of the object-relative clause construction. The contribution of this study is the evidence that the pupillary response is sensitive to variation in demand during language comprehension.

A graphical presentation of some of the data indicates in another way that the pupil size is affected differently by the two sentence types. The waveforms presented in Figure 1 depict the mean pupil size during the

TABLE 1
Mean Pupillary Response (mm) to Subject and Object
Relative Sentences

	Sentence Type	
	Subject Relative	Object Relative
Span Group		
Low	.214	.268
Medium	.190	.235
High	.205	.243
Average:	.203	.249

sampled interval. They were obtained by averaging over only a subset (45%) of all the trials, obtained by excluding those trials (19%) in which the maximum occurred within 113 ms (7 data samples) after the beginning of the interval and those in which (36%) it occurred within 113 ms of the end of the interval. The averages were obtained by aligning the pupil size measurements at the point where the maximum occurred, and including 1 s of data before the occurrence of the maximum and 500 ms after the maximum. An average waveform was computed for each subject in this way, and then an average of the subject averages was taken, and this grand average was smoothed, producing the curves in Figure 1. These curves show that the maximum pupil size was larger during the reading of the object relative sentences than for the subject relative sentences. This graphic analysis of the pupil maximum on a subset of the trials complements the analysis of the *change* in pupil size reported above that included all of the trials.

The time at which the pupil diameter reached its maximum diameter, measured from the first encounter with the main clause verb, was 1074 ms for object relative sentences and significantly shorter, 958 ms, for subject relative sentences, a difference that was reliable, $F(1,32) = 5.91$, $MS_e = 37,349$, $p < .05$. These are slightly shorter latencies than those in Beatty's work in mental arithmetic, in which the peak response occurred about 1200 ms after the onset of the difficult computation. But the actual beginning of the increased demand in our study occurs on the word preceding the main clause verb, so the latency of the maximum pupil diameter might also include the first-pass reading time on that word. The mean first-pass reading time on the word preceding the main clause verb was approximately 300 ms in the case of the subject relative sentence, and 400 ms for the object relatives. If we add these durations to the latencies above, we obtain latencies of 1250 ms (subject relative) and 1475 ms (object relative) for the maximum pupil diameter, which are more similar to the latencies of the waveform peaks that Ahern and Beatty (1979) reported.

The pupil diameter maxima in the current studies are calculated using a

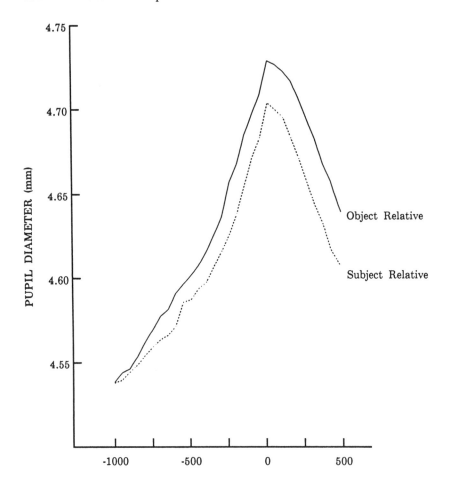

DISTANCE IN TIME FROM MAXIMUM AMPLITUDE (msec)

Fig. 1 Maximum pupil diameter during the reading of object relative and subject relative
sentences, for selected trials.

simple maximum measure, rather than a waveform peak, as in Beatty's work.
One of the reasons for basing the pupillary response on a simple maximum
rather than a waveform peak was that on approximately 40% of the trials the
pupil diameter measure did not constitute a conventionally modulated
waveform. Some of the trials (approximately 17%) had more than one mode,
and some trials (approximately 23%) had no mode. As a result, much of the
data could not be analyzed in terms of waveform characteristics, such as the
peak to trough distance or the latency of the waveform peak. Instead, the
measurements were treated as a simple data stream.

The lack of reliable individual differences in the pupillary response suggests that this measure is less sensitive to such differences than error rates in comprehension, as noted below. The mean pupillary effects were generally larger for lower-span readers than for higher-span readers, but the between-groups difference was not reliable, which reflected the large range of pupil diameter changes for readers of a given span. The lack of reliable group differences contrasts with the reliable individual differences in pupillary responses during mental multiplication reported by Ahern and Beatty (1979). The difference in the sensitivity of the pupillometric measure to individual differences may be attributable to some combination of differences between the studies. One difference is that the Ahern and Beatty study compared the performance of two groups that differed more extremely, with mean SAT scores of 1407 and 877. Although the reading span correlates with SAT (between .5 and .6), the differences among the three groups we studied are smaller. Another difference concerns the range of task difficulty in the two studies. In the Ahern and Beatty experiment, the simpler multiplication problems ($6 \times 12 = ?$) were fairly routine, compared to the most difficult problems ($14 \times 18 = ?$). In the current experiment, the lower-span subjects may have found all of the structures relatively challenging, so that the difference in the demand imposed between the simple (subject relative) and difficult (object relative) may have been smaller and more difficult to measure pupillometrically. Third, our application of pupillometric analysis to changes in demand within the reading task may have attenuated the size of the effects; certainly the changes in pupil size in the current study were relatively small. One reason may be that the baseline was taken during reading, rather than a non-processing period. By contrast, Ahern and Beatty obtained their baseline measure while no stimulus was being presented and no task demand was being made. The inclusion of easier baseline sentences in future pupillometric studies might reveal more sensitivity to individual differences.

Errors

As expected, the error rates, shown in Table 2 were greater for the more difficult object relative (21%) than subject relative sentences (11%), $F(1,32) = 24.23$, $MS_e = 66.3$, $p < .01$, and greater for the low-span subjects (23%), than medium (14%) and high span (12%) subjects, $F(2,32) = 5.98$, $MS_e = 118.9$, $p < .01$; this result was obtained in spite of having excluded the five subjects (4 low span and 1 mid span) who exceeded the pre-set cut-off error rate of 38%. There was a tendency for lower-span subjects to have a greater error rate on the more difficult sentences, although the interaction was not significant, $F(2,32) = 2.29$, $p = .11$.

Gaze duration

The gaze duration data supported the hypothesis that the object relative

TABLE 2
Mean Comprehension Error Rate (%)

	Sentence Type	
	Subject Relative	Object Relative
Span Group		
Low	15.2	30.3
Medium	11.1	16.3
High	8.1	16.7
Average:	11.4	20.8

sentence is more difficult to process than the subject relative, as other reading time studies have also found. The total gaze durations for Regions 1, 2, 3, and 4 are shown in Figure 2. Readers took more time in total on the object relative (328 ms/word) from the beginning of the difficult region (Region 2) to the end of the sentence than for the subject relative sentence (310 ms/word), $F(1,32) = 8.02$, $MS_e = 117,760$, $p < .05$. The difference was particularly large in Region 2, where subjects had longer forward and total gaze durations in the object relative than the subject relative case, $F(1,32) = 25.96$, $MS_e = 5368$, $p < .01$, for forward durations, and $F(1,32) = 38.61$, $MS_e = 13,979$, $p < .01$, for total duration). The total time per word was much longer on the two critical words, Regions 2 and 3, (averaging 634 ms and 528 ms for the object and subject relative constructions, respectively) than on the words that preceded them, namely those of Region 1 (averaging 332 ms and 325 ms, respectively), $F(1,32) = 23.58$, $p < .01$. Moreover, this "extra" time in Regions 2 and 3 was reliably greater in the case of object relative sentences than in subject relative sentences, $F(1,32) = 22.79$, $p < .01$. So, gazes are longer in the sentence on the words that trigger more demanding computations, and particularly longer for the more demanding syntactic structures.

Although as expected, the low span group typically spent more time on the more difficult constructions, and the high span group spent the least time, but contrary to expectation, the mid-span subjects had longer gazes than the low spans, and none of these differences among groups was reliable, nor did the span differences interact reliably with the sentence type. This study involved less than half as many subjects per condition as the word-by-word reading study that obtained reliable between-group differences (King & Just, 1991).

In summary, this study indicates that pupillary changes are sensitive to variation in the processing demands during sentence processing. The differential effects of sentence complexity on pupil diameter during sentence reading provide more than a converging measure of sentence difficulty. Error rates and reading times already provide convergence indicating that object relative sentences are more difficult than subject relatives. The error rates

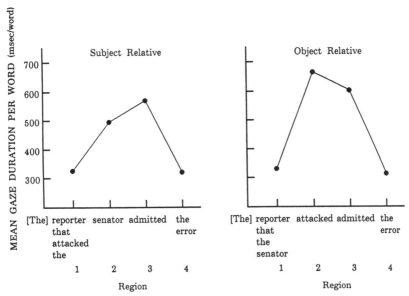

Fig. 2 Total gaze duration on Regions 1-4 of the sentences in Experiment 1.

simply measure the higher probability of an error occurring in the computations associated with object relatives. The reading times indicate that extra processing time is consumed in the case of object relatives. But this extra processing time could be "extra" in the same sense that adding five single-digit numbers takes longer than adding four single-digit numbers. The pupillometric results provide additional new information, relating to the nature of the difficulty imposed by object relative sentences. The pupillometric results indicate that the computations for object relatives are not just more time consuming and error prone, but also that the processing is making greater demands on mental resources.

Experiment 2: Wh-phrase vs. Whether-clause Sentences

To examine the generality of the pupillary response to complexity during on-line processing, it is useful to examine other constructions as well as other tasks. Experiment 2 examines the processing of sentences with *unbounded dependencies*, such as:

(3) The confused police didn't know which leader the rioters followed noisily down the street after the meeting.

Such constructions have been analyzed from the vantage of linguistic theory as examples of *filler-gap* constructions (e.g., Fodor, 1978; Stowe, 1986). The name reflects the claim that comprehension involves "gap-filling," specifically, that there is an intermediate level of representation in which the wh-phrase (the *filler*) is associated with the empty category where its constituent would occur in the canonical version of the sentence (in this type of construction, immediately after the verb). Whether or not such a linguistic analysis is illuminating of the processing of sentences with a *wh-* phrase, sentences such as (3) are complex because of the non-canonical ordering of their constituents. Consequently, such sentences are more complex than similar structures in which the constituents appear in a canonical order, such as:

(4) The confused police didn't know whether the rioters followed the leader noisily down the street after the meeting.

In the *whether* clause, the constituents occur in canonical order and hence should evoke less of a pupillary response. In terms of searching for intensity effects in sentence processing, the useful property of *wh-phrase* sentences is that they place an extra demand on a reader when he/she encounters the verb and attempts to determine the roles of its constituents, a demand that should be reflected in a greater pupillary response.

Experiment 2 also manipulated processing difficulty a second way, namely, by asking subjects to evaluate the plausibility of the sentence. Sentence plausibility was varied by substituting nouns in half of the conditions to make implausible direct objects of the subordinate clause verb. For example, in implausible versions of sentences (3) and (4), the word *leader* was replaced by *blanket* as the direct object of *followed*, as in sentences (5) and (6).

(5) The confused police didn't know which blanket the rioters followed noisily down the street after the meeting.

(6) The confused police didn't know whether the rioters followed the blanket noisily down the street after the meeting.

The hypothesis was that encountering and evaluating an implausible direct object should contribute to processing demands over that caused by encountering a plausible constituent. Consequently, the implausible condition should result in a greater pupillary response. In addition, the plausibility manipulation may provide evidence about when in the left-to-right processing of the sentence, a reader computes the syntactic or thematic role of a constituent.

The readers' gaze durations during the comprehension of these constructions should provide evidence about the on-line comprehension processes. Specifically, if the assignment of roles for the wh-phrase in the *wh-construction* occurs at the first encounter with the verb that imposes the subcategorization constraints (as *followed* does in sentences (3) and (5)), there should be longer gaze durations when the reader initially fixates that verb if the direct object is implausible. Evidence that the role assignment can be initiated by processing the verb in such sentences comes from a study that used evoked potentials as a processing index (Garnsey, Tanenhaus, & Chapman, 1989). That experiment examined the N400, a waveform component of the evoked potential that occurs approximately 400 ms after the onset of a word that is implausible or incongruous in the context (Kutas & Hillyard, 1980). Garnsey et al. examined the evoked potentials for *wh-* phrase sentences that had plausible and implausible direct objects, similar to sentences (3) and (5) above. The N400 did occur for the implausible condition, like sentence (5), triggered by the verb *followed*, compared to the plausible condition. This suggests that readers were at least considering the possible role of the earlier constituent when they processed the verb. The reading process was unusually slow, however, because the evoked potential methodology required that the words of the sentence be presented one at a time at a rate (500 ms/word) that is considerably slower than normal reading. Nevertheless, these data are consistent with an immediacy strategy of attempting to interpret each word on the constituent that first enables the computation of its possible role.

The gaze duration should also indicate when readers detect the implausibility of the relation between a constituent and the verb for the *whether clause* construction, as in sentences (4) and (6). For those sentences, the verb of the subordinate clause precedes the crucial noun, and so when the noun is fixated, readers have sufficient information to calculate its relation to the verb. This predicts that an implausible direct object, such as *blanket* in sentence (6), will elicit longer gaze durations than a plausible direct object, such as *leader* in sen-tence (4), because readers will detect its implausibility when fixating the noun.

Design and Materials

There were four conditions, formed by crossing two factors: (1) *wh-phrase* versus *whether-clause* and (2) plausible or implausible object of the verb in the subordinate clause. Sentences (3), (4), (5) and (6) are examples of the four conditions. The stimulus sentences were slightly modified versions of the materials used by Garnsey et al. (1989). The plausible and implausible nouns were approximately matched in frequency and length. There was a total of 32 sentence frames that were used to generate stimuli of each of the four types. Four different lists of 32 experimental sentences were created, with eight sentences in each of the four conditions. Subjects were randomly assigned to one of the four lists.

The experimental sentences were presented in random order along with 32 other sentences that served as filler material. Sixteen of the filler sentences were related to the plausibility manipulation. In eight of these, the implausible constituent was something other than a direct object, whereas the other eight were similar in construction but had no implausible constituent. The remaining sixteen fillers were all plausible, and equally divided between sentences with *wh*-phrases that were not direct objects and other types of *whether*-clause constructions.

Subjects

There were 36 subjects who were classified as 12 high span, 14 mid span, and 10 low span readers according to their scores on the Reading Span Test.

Procedure

Subjects were asked to read each sentence and judge its plausibility, which they indicated by pressing one of two buttons on a response box. The rest of the procedure was identical to that used in Experiment 1.

The data analysis of the change in pupil size during reading was similar to that in Experiment 1. The *wh*-phrase and *whether* clause sentences, respectively, were divided into two regions to be used for scoring, as indicated by the square brackets in the following examples:

The [confused police didn't know which leader the rioters] [followed noisily down the street after the meeting.]

The [confused police didn't know whether the rioters] [followed the leader noisily down the street after the meeting.]

The baseline interval, over which the minimum diameter was obtained, was during the reading of the first portion of the sentence, beginning with the reading of the second word of the sentence and ending with the word preceding the subordinate clause verb. The experimental pupil diameter data (i.e., the interval over which the maximum value was obtained) were collected starting from the time at which the reader first fixated the verb of the subordinate clause and ending either after 3 s or when the subject reached the end of the sentence, whichever occurred first. (Note that the number of words to be read during this interval differed by two words in the *wh*- and *whether* cases, but for both types of sentences, the plausibility of the direct object could only be computed based on information in the second region.)

RESULTS AND DISCUSSION

The experimental hypothesis predicted a larger pupillary response when a constituent has to be maintained and assigned at the verb (exemplified by the *wh-phrase* sentence), than when the verb and its object are presented in canonical order (exemplified by the sentences in which the embedded clause is introduced with *whether*). Consistent with this hypothesis, the changes in pupil size were greater for the *wh-phrase* sentences, 0.322 mm, compared to the *whether* clause sentences, 0.296 mm, $F(1,33) = 21.52$, $MS_e = .004$, $p < .01$,

TABLE 3
Mean Pupillary Response (mm) to *Wh-phrase* and *Whether* Clause Sentences

| | Experimental Condition | | | |
| | Wh-phrase | | Whether-clause | |
	plausible	implausible	plausible	implausible
Span Group				
Low	.347	.368	.285	.312
Medium	.298	.335	.265	.279
High	.307	.349	.275	.291
Average:	.315	.349	.274	.292

as shown in Table 3. [Note that this result was obtained despite the fact that the *whether* sentences were slightly longer, and pupil size may increase as subjects process more and more of a sentence (Stanners, Headley, & Clark, 1972)]. The results support the hypothesis that comprehending the non-canonical order of the direct object and verb in the *wh*-phrase sentences required more processing resources than comprehending constituents in the canonical order, as in the *whether*-clause sentences. In addition, implausibility added to the processing demand. Sentences with implausible direct objects were associated with greater changes in pupil size (0.321 mm) than those with plausible ones (0.297 mm), $F(1,33) = 5.69$, $MS_e = .004$, $p < .05$. As shown in Table 3, the increase due to implausibility occurred for both the *wh-phrase* and the *whether* clause constructions, with no interaction between plausibility and sentence type, $F(1,33) < 1$. Although the low span subjects showed slightly greater pupil increases (0.327 mm) than either the medium (0.293 mm) or high span (0.306 mm) subjects, there was no significant main effect of span nor any interaction with either sentence type or plausibility, all F's < 1. In sum, these data suggest that pupillary responses vary with the processing demands during reading comprehension, reflecting the greater difficulty of relating an implausible implied direct object.

The mean latency of the pupil diameter maximum (measured from the first encounter with the subordinate clause verb) was 1416 ms for the plausible *wh*-phrase constructions and 1427 ms for the implausible. For the *whether* clause construction, the average latency of the maximum pupil diameter was 1401 ms for the plausible condition and 1235 ms for the implausible condition. The total reading time from the point at which the reader first fixated the verb of the subordinate clause was 2651 ms for the *wh*-phrase construction and 2872 ms for the *whether* subordinate clause construction, indicating that readers typically took less than 3 s to complete their reading of the sentence. Hence, the duration during which the pupillary response was assessed (operationalized as 3 s after the verb or until the end of the sentence,

TABLE 4
Errors in Plausibility Judgments (%)

| | Sentence type | | | |
| | Wh-phrase | | Whether-clause | |
	plausible	implausible	plausible	implausible
Span Group				
Low	23	28	20	27
Medium	14	17	13	15
High	3	18	16	15
Average:	13	20	16	18

whichever came first) typically included most of the reading of the rest of the sentence.

In sum, the modulation of the pupillary response during sentence processing was sensitive both to the difficulties caused by processing the *wh-phrase* and by encountering and judging an implausibility.

Errors

The two constructions, the *wh-phrase* construction and the *whether* clause construction, produced similar error rates of approximately 16%. As expected, the error rates decreased with increasing span, from 25% for the low span group, to 17% for the medium, and 13% for the high span group, as shown in Table 4. When the errors made on the *wh-phrase* construction were analyzed separately, the rate was higher for the implausible than the plausible version, $F(1,33) = 4.22$, $MS_e = 213$, $p <.05$. Moreover, the error rate varied with span in the predicted direction, $F(2,32) = 5.02$, $MS_e = 237$, $p <.05$, although the interaction between span and plausibility was not significant, $F(2,33) =1.31$.

Gaze duration

According to the immediacy principle, readers should attempt to compute the syntactic or thematic role of the previously encountered *wh-phrase* on the verb, rather than waiting until later in the sentence to evaluate if there were another possible role for the filler. The initial (first-pass) gaze durations on the verb of the subordinate clause (e.g., *followed* in sentence (5)) were longer for the implausible condition (344 ms) than the plausible condition (295 ms), $F(1,33) = 5.01$, $MS_e = 8459$, $p < .05$, indicating its implausibility in that role was immediately detected. The gaze duration was slightly (30 ms) but not reliably longer on the next word, an adverbial modifier (e.g., *noisily* in sentence (5)), in the implausible condition, $F(1,33) = 2.34$, $MS_e = 13,424$, $p = .14$. The longer processing times on the verb in the implausible condition were found for all three span groups, so that there was no interaction with span, $F(2,33) < 1$. Although the low span group spent more time on the initial reading of the verb or its modifier (351 and 417 ms) than did either the medium (299 ms and 350 ms) or high span groups (308 and 337 ms), the differences among span groups were not significant when the time on either word was considered alone. Analogous results were found for the total time, which includes not only the initial gaze, but any subsequent regressions to the two words, except that the span effect was marginally significant, $F(2,33) = 2.80$, $MS_e = 20,392$, $p = .07$. In sum, readers showed immediate effects of the filler's implausibility on the verb and also spent more total time on the verb and its modifier.

The effect of detecting an implausibility was also apparent in the initial gaze durations in the *whether*-clause sentences. In that construction, the implausible (or plausible) noun occurred after the verb, e.g., [...*whether the rioters followed the leader/blanket noisily...*]. Consistent with the immediacy strategy, readers seemed to detect the constituent's implausibility on the noun phrase, as reflected in longer reading times on it and the subsequent modifier, $F(1,33) = 20.04$, $p < .01$, ($MS_e = 2839$). Although low span readers spent more time than medium or high span readers, the differences among span groups were not reliable, $F(2,33) = 1.74$, nor was there any interaction between span and plausibility. The same pattern was found for the total gaze durations. Thus, the analysis of first-pass gaze durations suggest that in both constructions readers attempted to interrelate constituents and assign their semantic roles as they encountered each constituent in their left-to-right processing of the sentence.

Filler-gap processing

The *wh*-phrase sentence is an example of a "filler-gap" construction, a type of sentence containing an implicit anaphoric reference, and that has been the object of recent linguistic and psychological interest. For the current study, the main concern is that these constructions present some complexity to the comprehender because the constituents are not in canonical order. Of less central concern are the linguistic claims about the specific internal representation constructed during their processing. One proposal is that transitive verbs are associated with certain thematic or syntactic roles (for example, an agent and recipient with the verb *told*), which gives rise to "gaps" that occur at the canonical position of those roles in some intermediate-level representation (Fodor, 1979). The claim is that during comprehension, the *wh*-phrase is represented as a filler that is "assigned" to the gap. This type of linguistic analysis has been applied to a variety of constructions, including the representation of relative clause constructions such as those in Experiment 1, where the relative pronoun is postulated to be a filler. A more recent linguistic analysis argues for an alternative view of these constructions, suggesting that constituents may be assigned to the verb directly, without postulating an empty category in an intermediate-level representation (Pickering & Barry, 1991). Behavioral data do not discriminate between the two proposals for the current construction; both proposals are consistent with the reports of increased response time to probe words that are related to the filler after the verb but not before the verb (Nicol & Swinney, 1989), and to the current results showing increased reading times on the verb in the implausible object condition, as in the current study (also, Tanenhaus, Boland, Garnsey, & Carlson, 1989).

General Discussion

Sentences that are deemed more complex on grounds of their linguistic properties and the psychological processes that they evoke produce larger pupillary responses than sentences that are simpler. The pupillary response we observed was relative to a baseline obtained in the reading of a preceding portion of the same sentence or text. Thus the encounter with a syntactic complexity while a person is reading is a sufficient condition to evoke a change in pupil diameter. We treat the pupillary response as an indirect measure of the intensity dimension of thought.

Our experiments have manipulated the intensity of processing by varying sentence complexity and thereby affecting the demand on cognitive resources. It should be possible in principle to affect the intensity of processing in other, converging ways. One possible direction is to vary the amount of "concentration" by directly instructing the subjects. Readers sometimes report different degrees of concentrating on a particular task. For example, speedreaders often report the need for intense concentration during speedreading, so much so that they also report that speedreading is too difficult to sustain over a long period. At the other end of the intensity continuum are the situations in which individuals seem to glide on the surface of the comprehension task. For example, readers sometimes report finding themselves at the end of a paragraph with no clue as to its content because they started to think about something else during the reading.

The results of the pupillometric experiments and these informal observations concerning concentration during reading suggest a need for a formal theory within which "intensity of processing" can be precisely defined and related to other concepts. We propose that the intensity dimension of thought might be clarified by considering it in the context of a computational model of comprehension that we have developed. We will now briefly describe this model, and consider how the model suggests that intensity might be construed.

The model

Central to the model is the idea that a common resource, namely activation, mediates both information maintenance and computation, and that working-memory constraints exist in the amount of activation available or its allocation between storage and computation. The account is instantiated in a simulation model called CC READER; its initials reflect the assumption that comprehension processes are (C)apacity (C)onstrained (Just & Carpenter, 1992). Like the original READER model (Thibadeau, Just, & Carpenter, 1982), CC READER is a hybrid of a production system and an activation-based connectionist model. It can parse a limited number of sentence constructions from left to right, constructing a syntactic and semantic representation as fully as possible as it goes (Carpenter & Just, 1983; Just & Carpenter, 1980). The number of processing cycles that CC READER expends on the successive words of the sentence is correlated with the time human readers spend reading those words. As is the case with conventional production systems, the procedural knowledge in CC READER consists of a set of units called productions, each of which is a condition-action contingency that specifies what symbolic manipulation should be made when a given information condition arises in working memory. For example, a typical condition is that "if the current word is a determiner (e.g., the)" then the action is to "expect that one is processing a noun phrase." The execution of the manipulation can change the contents of working memory, thereby enabling another production. CC READER, however, deviates in many important ways from conventional production systems by incorporating mechanisms that are common to activation-based parallel connectionist models (Cottrell, 1989; Waltz & Pollack, 1985; St. John & McClelland, 1990).

First, each element, which can represent a word, phrase, grammatical structure, or thematic structure, has an associated activation level, such that the element can have varying degrees of activation. The condition part of a production, thus, specifies not just the presence of an element but also the minimum activation level, the threshold, at which the element satisfies the condition. Only if the activation level of an element is above the threshold is it effectively "in" working memory and, consequently, available to initiate other computational processes. Second, productions change the activation level of an element by propagating activation from a source element to that output element. Third, productions can fire re-iteratively over successive cycles so that the activation levels of the output elements become gradually incremented until they reach some threshold. In other words, the symbolic manipulation occurs as a repeated action with cumulative effects. Finally, CC READER allows multiple productions to fire in parallel on a given cycle, as long as their conditions are met. The processor, hence, can work on different levels of language comprehension, such as syntactic, semantic, and referential, at the same time and generate new partial computational products simultaneously from different levels. Hence, processing is done in a single pass (Wanner, 1987), rather than in two passes, as in parsers that have a first-pass syntactic analysis followed by a second-pass semantic and pragmatic analysis (Berwick

& Weinberg, 1985; Frazier & Fodor, 1978; McRoy & Hirst, 1990).

Within this framework, activation underlies all the activities that take place in working memory. Consider the processing of an object-relative sentence, such as:

The reporter that the senator attacked admitted the error.

To comprehend the relative clause of this sentence, the reader must first retain the noun *reporter* in working memory until the occurrence of the verb *attacked*, and only then associate that noun with its thematic role. In CC READER, maintaining the element *reporter* in working memory means keeping its activation level above a threshold. Similarly, the assignment of a thematic role to a noun (in this case, the assignment of the patient role to *reporter*), involves propagating activation to a new element (i.e., a proposition that *reporter* plays the patient role) and incrementing its activation level above the threshold. Thus, the storage and computations that constitute comprehension are expressed in terms of the maintenance and manipulation of activation.

The constraint on capacity is imposed by limiting the amount of activation that can be consumed on each cycle. If the total demand for activation (for both storage and processing) exceeds the allowable maximum (some number of units of activation, called the Cap), then both the storage and processing are scaled back (de-allocated). Our initial de-allocation scheme limits both functions proportionately, akin to an across-the-board cut. This scaling-back of activation has important consequences for both the time course and the content of language processing. First, the de-allocation of the activation to computation can slow down processing by increasing the number of cycles required for an element to reach the threshold. Second, the de-allocation of activation to the maintenance of earlier elements produces forgetting because the activation levels of some of the elements are continuously decremented with each new cycle of processing that exceeds the activation quota. An allocation parameter determines the relative extent to which computation or information maintenance suffers when the demands for storage and processing exceed the activation quota.

The CC READER model simulates the processing time profile of readers in Experiment 1 reasonably well. Figure 3 shows CC READER's processing time profile (in terms of the number of production-system cycles) in processing such sentences. The lower panel of the figure shows the corresponding total gaze durations observed in Experiment 1. Like college readers, CC READER spends relatively more cycles on the verbs of the object-relative sentence than in the other regions, because more computations were needed on the verbs to allow different constituents in the sentence (such as subjects and direct objects) to coalesce. Like the human readers, the model takes longer on

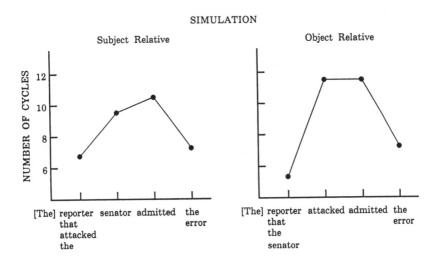

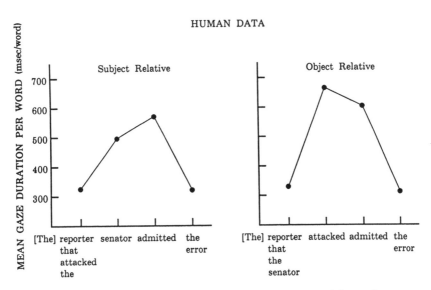

Fig. 3 The upper panel of the figure presents the number of cycles expended on various parts of the subject relative sentences (on the left) and object relative sentences (on the right) by the simulation. The lower panel presents the human gaze duration data from Experiment 1.

object-relative than on subject-relative sentences. Individual differences in working memory capacity (high-span vs. low-span readers) can also be implemented in CC READER by varying the maximum amount of activation available to the system.

Resource Allocation Policy

In a system with resource limitations, the deployment of the limited resources can have a large effect on performance, especially when the resource demands greatly outstrip the supply. One immediate consequence of an allocation policy is that it can be the mechanism that brings about the trading relation between speed and accuracy of comprehension processing, where accuracy refers to maintaining and later using partial products appropriately. The current across-the-board percentage de-allocation policy produces processing that is both slower and more errorful when the resource demands outstrip the supply. This is also the performance exhibited by most subjects.

High demand could have a different effect on performance if allocation policy were different. By differentially de-allocating activation to either maintenance or processing, the comprehension process can maintain its speed and sacrifice accuracy or sacrifice its speed and maintain its accuracy. Some subjects (low-capacity subjects on high demand sentences) maintain or even increase speed on high demand sentences, at the cost of failing to comprehend the sentences (King & Just, 1991). The model provides a mechanism to account for these different "strategies" or allocation policies.

There are other allocation policies that seem plausible and merit future investigation. One alternative is to have different allocations *among* processes. Specifically, the allocation policy might favor more automatic processes, which presumably consume fewer resources anyway. But in the event of a resource shortfall, the automatic processes might receive a larger proportion of their demand than the higher level, controlled processes. In addition, the allocation policy might be sensitive to the nature of the task or even subject to strategic control. For example, the more costly the loss of a partial product, the greater the relative allocation of storage might be. More generally, the allocation policy elicited by tasks with different characteristics is an important research issue that is highlighted by the model (see Haarmann & Kolk, 1992, for a related discussion).

Intensity in CC READER

There are several aspects of CC READER that might plausibly correspond to the intensity of processing that is reflected in the pupillary responses. It seems sensible to relate the intensity of processing to the consumption of resources, the common pool of activation. In the simulation runs we have done, each sentence is treated as text-initial, as though working memory were previously unused. Thus, the processing begins with some total amount of available activation. The quota is presumed to differ for the simulations of low, medium and high capacity subjects. As each successive word is read, some of the total activation is consumed by the partial and final products that are generated in processing that word. These products are part of the orthographic, lexical, semantic, and syntactic representation of the word and sentence. (A more complete model would also generate a referential level of representation). Words that initiate more processes, such as a verb that initiates the calculation of various role assignments, result in greater consumption of activation than words that initiate few processes. In general, the total amount of activation that is consumed increases as the successive words of the sentence are processed, up to the point where the maximum activation is reached. The higher the maximum capacity, the later in the sentence is the maximum consumption reached. In the current model, once the consumption reaches the maximum level (the quota), the consumption generally remains at the maximum throughout the rest of the sentence. One implication of the current scheme is that any sentence that is long enough or complex enough can bring any person to their maximum consumption. Second, the partial products from a completed sentence must be purged if the processing of an ensuing sentence (or clause) is to start out at a consumption level far below the maximum. Presumably, any such purging would spare the highest levels of representation.

This model provides a framework for considering possible operationalizations of the intensity dimension. One possible measure of the intensity of processing that is related to resource consumption is the number of units of activation that are in use on each cycle, or the average number over a set of cycles (such as the set during which a sentence is processed). This might be analogous to measuring individual's annual consumption of economic resources by measuring that individual's average monthly expenditures. In more demanding years (for example, when illness produces additional medical expenses), the consumption would increase, all other things being equal. This simple index of consumption seems inadequate for measuring intensity because it fails to take into account the resource availability. This measure would be equal for two individuals with equal expenditures, regardless of their income. Yet it would be desirable to differentiate the consumption of individuals whose expenditures are one-half their income from individuals who are spending the same amount, but the amount is twice their income. So an alternative measure that expresses this distinction might be a ratio of expenditures to resources. In CC READER, this might be a measure of the average number of units of activation consumed per cycle, relative to the maximum number of units available. As this ratio increases, we might expect the pupillary response to increase.

Another possible measure might relate not just expenditure of resources relative to the supply, but the demand relative to the supply. In terms of the financial analogy, we would not measure the amount spent, but the total amount of bills that are due, relative to the income. As the ratio of demand to supply increases, we might expect the pupillary response to increase.

Other possible variations in the measurement of CC READER's intensity could take into account the temporal distribution of the resource consumption. For example, we can observe the value of each of the possible measures above at the completion of each word of a sentence, or at the end of a sentence. Or we can observe the length of time for which that measure stays at a high level. The pupillary response could correspond to any one of these measures.

The data are currently not detailed enough to permit these fine-grain discriminations concerning the measurement of cognitive intensity. Furthermore, the nature of the consumption would vary depending on the kind of resource allocation policy that was in effect. But the very existence of the formal model makes the questions concrete and the possible answers plausible. Such questions define a new set of issues about the intensity of processing to be explored in sentence comprehension and in other thought processes.

This work was supported in part by grant MH 29617 and Research Scientist Development Awards MH-00661 and MH-00662 from NIMH, as well as a grant from the Andrew W. Mellon Foundation. We thank Susan Garnsey for providing the stimulus sentences used in Experiment 2. We also thank Stuart Steinhauer for his insights and advice concerning pupillometric analysis, and Akira Miyake for comments on the manuscript. Correspondence should be addressed to: Marcel Adam Just, Department of Psychology, Carnegie Mellon University, Pittsburgh, PA 15213.

References

Ahern, S.K. (1978). *Activation and intelligence: Pupillometric correlates of individual differences in cognitive abilities.* Unpublished doctoral dissertation, University of California, Los Angeles, CA.

Ahern, S.K., & Beatty, J. (1979). Pupillary responses during information processing vary with Scholastic Aptitude Test scores. *Science, 205,* 1289-1292.

Baddeley, A.D. (1986). *Working memory.* New York: Oxford University Press.

Baddeley, A.D., & Hitch, G. (1974). Working memory. In G.H. Bower (Ed.), *The psychology of learning and motivation* (Vol. 8). (pp. 47-89). New York: Academic Press.

Beatty, J. (1982). Task-evoked pupillary responses, processing load, and the structure of processing resources. *Psychological Bulletin, 91,* 276-292.

Beatty, J., & Schluroff, M. (1980). *Pupillometric signs of brain activation reflect both syntactic and semantic factors in language processing.* Paper presented at the meeting of the Society for Psychophysiological Research, October, Vancouver, B. C., Canada.

Ben-Nun, Y. (1986). The use of pupillometry in the study of on-line verbal processing: Evidence for depths of processing. *Brain and Language, 28,* 1-11.

Berwick, R.C., & Weinberg, A. (1985). Deterministic parsing and linguistic explanation. *Language and Cognitive Processes, 1,* 109-134.

Bever, T.G. (1970). The cognitive basis for linguistic structures. In J.R. Hayes (Ed.), *Cognition and the development of language* (pp.279-362). New York: Wiley.

Carpenter, P.A., & Just, M.A. (1983). What your eyes do while your mind is reading. In K. Rayner (Ed.), *Eye movements in reading: Perceptual and language processes.* (pp. 275-307). New York: Academic Press.

Cottrell, G.W. (1989). *A connectionist approach to word sense disambiguation.* San Mateo, CA: Morgan Kaufmann.

Daneman, M., & Carpenter, P.A. (1980). Individual differences in working memory and reading. *Journal of Verbal Learning and Verbal Behavior, 19*, 450-466.

Fodor, J.D. (1978). Parsing strategies and constraints on transformation. *Linguistic Inquiry, 9*, 427-473.

Fodor, J.D. (1979). Superstrategy. In W.E. Cooper & E.C.T. Walker (Eds.), *Sentence processing: Psycholinguistic studies presented to Merrill Garrett.* Hillsdale, NJ: Erlbaum.

Ford, M. (1983). A method for obtaining measures of local parsing complexity throughout sentences. *Journal of Verbal Learning and Verbal Behavior, 22*, 203-218.

Frazier, L., & Fodor, J.D. (1978). The sausage machine: A new two-stage parsing model. *Cognition, 6*, 291-325.

Garnsey, S.M., Tanenhaus, M.K., & Chapman, R.M. (1989). Evoked potentials and the study of sentence comprehension. *Journal of Psycholinguistic Research, 18*, 51-60.

Haarmann, H.J., & Kolk, H.H.J. (1992). *On-line sensitivity to subject-verb agreement violations in Broca's aphasics: The role of syntactic complexity and time.* Manuscript submitted for publication.

Haier, R.J., Siegel, B.V., Nuechterlein, K.H., Hazlett, E., Wu, J. C., Paek, J., Browning, H. L., & Buchsbaum, M.S. (1988). Cortical glucose metabolic rate correlates of abstract reasoning and attention studied with positron emission tomography. *Intelligence, 12*, 199-217.

Hirst, W., Spelke, E.S., Reaves, C.C., Caharack, G., & Neisser, R. (1980). Dividing attention without alternation or automaticity. *Journal of Experimental Psychology: General, 109*, 98-117.

Holmes, V.M., & O'Regan, J.K. (1981). Eye fixation patterns during the reading of relative clause sentences. *Journal of Verbal Learning and Verbal Behavior, 20*, 417-430.

Janisse, M.P. (1977). *Pupillometry: The psychology of the pupillary response.* Washington D.C.: Hemisphere.

Just, M.A., & Carpenter, P.A. (1980). A theory of reading: From eye fixations to comprehension. *Psychological Review, 87*, 329-354.

Just, M.A., & Carpenter, P.A. (1987). *The psychology of reading and language comprehension.* Newton, MA: Allyn and Bacon.

Just, M.A., & Carpenter, P.A. (1992). A capacity theory of comprehension: Individual differences in working memory. *Psychological Review, 99*, 122-149.

Kahneman, D. (1973). *Attention and effort.* Englewood Cliffs, NJ: Prentice-Hall, Inc.

King, J., & Just, M.A. (1991). Individual differences in syntactic processing: The role of working memory. *Journal of Memory and Language, 30*, 580-602.

Kutas, M., & Hillyard, S.A. (1980). Reading senseless sentences: Brain potentials reflect semantic incongruity. *Science, 207*, 204-206.

Larkin, W., & Burns, D. (1977). Sentence comprehension and memory for embedded structure. *Memory & Cognition, 5*, 17-22.

MacWhinney, B., & Pleh, C. (1988). The processing of restrictive relative clauses in Hungarian. *Cognition, 29*, 95-141.

McRoy, S.W., & Hirst, G. (1990). Race-based parsing and syntactic disambiguation. *Cognitive Science, 14*, 313-353.

Miller, G.A., & Chomsky, N. (1963). Finitary models of language users. In R.D. Luce, R. Bush, & E. Galanter (Eds.), *Handbook of mathematical psychology,* Vol. 2. (pp. 419-491). New York: Wiley.

Navon, D., & Gopher, D. (1979). On the economy of the human processing system. *Psychological Review, 86*, 214-255.

Nicol, J., & Swinney, D. (1989). The role of structure in coreference assignment during sentence comprehension. *Journal of Psycholinguistic Research, 18*, 5-19.

Norman, D.A., & Bobrow, D.G. (1975). On data-limited and resource-limited processes. *Cognitive Psychology, 7*, 44-64.

Pickering, M., & Barry, G. (1991). Sentence processing without empty categories. *Language and Cognitive Processes, 6*, 229-259.

Schluroff, M. (1982). Pupil responses to grammatical complexity of sentences. *Brain and Language, 17*, 133-145.

Schluroff, M., Zimmermann, T.E., Freeman, R.B., Jr., Hofmeister, K., Lorscheid, T., & Weber, A. (1986). Pupillary responses to syntactic ambiguity of sentences. *Brain and Language, 27*, 322-344.

Shallice, T. (1982). Specific impairments of planning. *Philosophical Transactions of the Royal Society of London B, 298*, 199-209.

Shiffrin, R.M., & Schneider, W. (1977). Controlled and automatic human information processing: II. Perceptual learning, automatic attending, and a general theory. *Psychological Review, 84*, 127-190.

St. John, M.F., & McClelland, J.L. (1990). Learning and applying contextual constraints in sentence comprehension. *Artificial Intelligence, 46*, 217-257.

Stanners, R.F., Headley, D.B., & Clark, W.R. (1972). The pupillary response to sentences: Influences of listening set and deep structure. *Journal of Verbal Learning and Verbal Behavior, 11*, 257-263.

Stowe, L.A. (1986). Parsing WH-constructions: Evidence for on-line gap location. *Language and Cognitive Processes, 3*, 227-245.

Tanenhaus, M.K., Boland, J., Garnsey, S.M., & Carlson, G. (1989). Lexical structure in parsing long-distance dependencies. *Journal of Psycholinguistic Research, 18*, 37-50.

Thibadeau, R., Just, M.A., & Carpenter, P.A. (1982). A model of the time course and content of reading. *Cognitive Science, 6*, 157-203.

Waltz, D.L., & Pollack, J.B. (1985). Massively parallel parsing: A strongly interactive model of natural language interpretation. *Cognitive Science, 9,* 51-74.

Wanner, E. (1987). The parser's architecture. In F. Kessel (Ed.), *The development of language and language researchers: Essays in honor of Roger Brown* (pp. 79-96). London: Lawrence Erlbaum.

Wanner, E., & Maratsos, M. (1978). An ATN approach to comprehension. In M.J. Halle, J. Bresnan, & G.A. Miller (Eds.), *Linguistic theory and psychological reality.* (pp. 119-161). Cambridge, MA: MIT Press.

Wickens, C.D. (1984). Processing resources in attention. In R. Parasuraman & D.R. Davies (Eds.), *Varieties of attention.* (pp. 63-102). New York: Academic Press.

10 Causal Bridging Inferences: Validating Consistent and Inconsistent Sequences

MURRAY SINGER *University of Manitoba*

Abstract   It is proposed that causal bridging inferences must be validated against pertinent knowledge before being accepted by the reader. According to this analysis, understanding each of the consistent sequence, *Dorothy poured the water on the bonfire, so the bonfire went out*, and the inconsistent, *Dorothy poured the water on the bonfire, but the bonfire grew hotter*, invokes the pertinent knowledge, "water extinguishes fire." In agreement with this prediction, subjects answered *Does water extinguish fire?* more quickly after reading both consistent and inconsistent sequences than after the control temporal sequence, *Dorothy PLACED the water BY the bonfire, The bonfire grew hotter*. However, removing the appropriate conjunction, "but," from the inconsistent sequence abolishes its answer time facilitation (Experiment 3). It is proposed that, in the latter case, text ideas feed back to and so qualify pertinent knowledge.

Résumé   Il est proposé que les inférences de relations causales doivent être validées en fonction de connaissances pertinentes avant d'être acceptées par le lecteur. Selon cette analyse, la compréhension de la séquence logique «*Dorothy poured the water on the bonfire, so the bonfire went out*» et de la séquence illogique «*Dorothy poured the water on the bonfire, but the bonfire grew hotter*» met en oeuvre la connaissance pertinente: «l'eau éteint le feu». Conformément à cette prédiction, les sujets ont répondu à la question «*Does water extinguish fire?*» plus rapidement après avoir lu les séquences logique et illogique qu'après avoir lu la séquence de contrôle temporelle «*Dorothy PLACED the water BY the bonfire. The bonfire grew hotter.*» Toutefois la suppression de la conjonction «but», de la séquence illogique, a eu pour effet d'allonger les temps de réponse (expérience 3). Dans ce cas-ci, il est donc proposé que les idées exprimées dans le texte renvoient à la connaissance pertinente et viennent la modifier.

Inference processing has been a central issue in the psychology of language during the past twenty years. One type of inference that has received extensive consideration during this period is the bridging inference (Haviland

& Clark, 1974). Bridging inferences serve to establish connections between the current clause and preceding discourse, and accomplish this in one of two closely related ways. First, the bridging inference may simply identify the relationship between two discourse ideas, or "propositions." In this regard, the propositional content of *Ken stepped on the banana peel, He fell down* might be shown as P1 (STEP-ON, TOM, BANANA-PEEL), P2 (FALL-DOWN, TOM) (Kintsch, 1974). However, if the reader detects that the first event caused the second event, then the resulting representation also includes the linking proposition, P3 (CAUSE, P1, P2).

Second, a bridging inference may also involve unstated ideas that mediate the explicit ones. That is, to properly understand *The spy quickly threw his report in the fire, The ashes floated up the chimney*, one must infer a new idea, such as "The report burned to ashes" (Singer & Ferreira, 1983).

Evidence stemming from the use of both on-line and memory measures has converged on the conclusion that bridging inferences frequently accompany comprehension. On-line measurements have revealed that reading time varies systematically with the semantic distance between a sentence and the antecedent ideas to which it must be bridged (Bloom, Fletcher, van den Broek, Reitz, & Shapiro, 1990; Keenan, Baillet, & Brown, 1984; Myers, Shinjo, & Duffy, 1987; Singer, 1979; see McKoon & Ratcliff, 1980b, for a critique). This result indicates that the reader strives to bridge text ideas during understanding.

Memory measures have yielded findings consistent with those stemming from the on-line indices. For example, judgement times for ideas expressing the bridging inferences suggested by a message are similar to the judgement times for explicitly stated ideas. In contrast, judgement times are longer for plausible inferences that elaborate but do not bridge discourse ideas (Potts, Keenan, & Golding, 1988; Singer & Ferreira, 1983). It is concluded that if understanders failed to compute bridging inferences during comprehension, then discourse coherence would be disrupted (Haviland & Clark, 1974; Kintsch & van Dijk, 1978; Singer, 1980).

Recently, the mental processes of bridging inference have been studied in the framework of a "validation model" (Halldorson & Singer, 1992; Singer, Halldorson, Lear, & Andrusiak, 1992; Singer, Revlin, & Halldorson, 1990). Consider the sequence, *Dorothy poured the water on the bonfire, The bonfire went out*. To completely understand this sequence, one ought to detect that the first event caused the second. The validation model states that, before this event bridge is accepted, the reader must identify an idea which, when coupled with the fact that water was poured on the fire, accounts for the fire going out. It is as though the antecedent event and outcome event respectively play the roles of minor premise and conclusion in an incomplete mental syllogism (called an "enthymeme"). For the present example, the syllogism is readily solved with an idea such as "water extinguishes fire." Comparing this "validating idea" with general knowledge reveals that it is true. This determination validates the tentative bridging inference.

In view of the central contribution of causal relations to narrative and expository text, the evaluation of the validation model has predominantly proceeded with reference to causal bridging inferences (but see Singer et al., 1990). Set (1) is typical of the experimental materials that have been used:

(1) a. Dorothy poured the bucket of water on the fire. The fire went out.
     b. Dorothy placed the bucket of water by the fire. The fire went out.
     c. Does water extinguish fire?

Each experimental subject views either the causal sequence (1a) or the control temporal sequence, (1b). (Throughout this treatment, "antecedent" and "outcome" will refer to the first and second sentences of such sequences, respectively). After reading, the subject answers question (1c), which probes the knowledge pertinent to the hypothetically validating fact. According to the validation analysis, the reader strives to bridge both sequences. However, only the causal sequence invokes the knowledge underlying (1c). Therefore, it has been predicted that answer time for (1c) will be faster in the causal condition than the temporal condition.

This prediction has been supported in a variety of circumstances. First, answer time is faster in the causal condition than the temporal condition when people read two-sentence sequences, such as (1a) or (1b). Second, the same effect has been measured when those sequences are embedded in longer passages (Singer et al., 1992, Experiment 2). Third, the outcome is observed even when effect precedes cause, as in *Dorothy's bonfire went out, She poured the bucket of water on it* (Singer et al., 1992, Experiment 4). Therefore, even chronological reversal does not obscure the causal relation.

These causal answer time advantages could be due to the integration of the validating facts with the new text information, or to the heightened activation of those facts in conceptual memory. To distinguish these alternatives, Halldorson and Singer (1992) embedded Singer et al.'s (1992) materials in a priming paradigm. The subjects encountered sets of sequences, such as (1), in the causal condition or the temporal condition. In a subsequent series of questions, outcome questions from those sequences (e.g., *Did the fire go out?*) immediately preceded validating questions (e.g., *Does water extinguish fire?*). Answer time was faster in the causal than the temporal condition. Following the logic of the priming procedure (e.g., McKoon & Ratcliff, 1980a), it was concluded that the validating facts had been integrated with the text representation (see also Kintsch & Welsch, in press; McKoon & Ratcliff, 1988).

Other findings have helped to refute some competing explanations of these effects. First, temporal answer times for (1c) might be slow because processing has spilled over from the reading phase to the answering phase of the trial (e.g., Ehrlich & Rayner, 1983). However, spillover cannot account for the answer time difference that is observed when the sequences are embedded in brief texts and followed by a random sequence of questions (Singer et al., 1992, Experiment 2).

Second, although the causal and temporal antecedent sentences used similar content words (McKoon & Ratcliff, 1986; Potts et al., 1988), it is conceivable that the questions were primed more by the causal antecedents than the temporal ones. To address this possibility, Singer et al. (1992) conducted a control experiment in which the outcome portions of the causal and temporal sequences, *The fire went out*, were omitted. According to the priming view, the causal answer time advantage ought to be preserved in this condition. The validation analysis, in contrast, predicts that the causal advantage should be abolished, because the causal antecedent sentence alone does not require validation. Consistent with the validation analysis, no causal advantage was detected in the control experiment.

Third, a "context checking" interpretation states that, even if readers did not engage in inference validation during encoding, a causal answer time advantage might result from greater compatibility of the test question with the causal sequence than with the temporal sequence (McKoon & Ratcliff, 1986; Potts et al., 1988). For the present findings, context checking is refuted by the result that the causal answer time advantage was detected using a priming paradigm (Halldorson & Singer, 1992). As discussed earlier, priming effects of this sort are typically attributed to the processes of text encoding (McKoon & Ratcliff, 1980a, 1988).

The answer time prediction of the validation model has been evaluated against the backdrop of another familiar effect. As discussed earlier, the time needed to read a sentence expressing a causal outcome increases systematically with its semantic distance from its text antecedent (Keenan et al., 1984; Myers et al., 1987). For the present materials, temporal sequences, such as (1b), are comparable to the far causal sequences of Myers et al. Therefore, it was predicted that it would take longer to read the outcome sentence, *The fire went out*, in the temporal condition than the causal condition. This prediction was consistently supported (Halldorson & Singer, 1992; Singer et al., 1992).

Until now, the evaluation of the validation model has focussed on consistent causal sequences, such as *Dorothy poured the water on the bonfire*, *The bonfire went out*. However, events do not always have expected consequences, either as we observe them or read about them. In this regard, sequence (2) conveys an unexpected but by no means impossible chain of events.

(2)   Dorothy poured the water on the bonfire. The bonfire grew hotter.

The goal of the present study was to examine the contribution of validation processes to the comprehension of such sequences.

It seems clear that validation processes must be applicable to sequence (2). First, if (2) were not subjected to validation, then the reader could not notice that its outcome is less usual than the "fire went out" outcome. Second, the validation concept would make no sense if the process could detect only plausible causal sequences.

In fact, the validation analysis of understanding inconsistent sequences is proposed to be similar to that for consistent sequences. Understanding sequence (2) requires the computation of an idea that, combined with the fact that water was poured on the fire, accounts for it growing hotter. This idea might take the form "water feeds fire" or "water is combustible." Of course, the comparison of this idea with one's general knowledge yields the ready determination that it is false, because water is known to extinguish fire. As a result, sequence (2) may be judged to be inconsistent.

It is interesting that, according to this account, validating both the consistent sequence, "went out," and the inconsistent sequence, "grew hotter," ultimately invokes the same familiar fact: namely, "water extinguishes fire." This suggests the possibly counterintuitive prediction of similarly fast answer times for *Does water extinguish fire?* after reading the consistent sequence and the inconsistent sequence. In contrast, answer time after a corresponding temporal sequence should, as before, be longer. Several experiments tested this new corollary of the validation model.

Experiment 1

In Experiment 1, the basic hypothesis was evaluated with reference to materials such as set (3).

(3)   a. Dorothy poured the bucket of water on the bonfire. The bonfire went out. (consistent)
     b. Dorothy placed the bucket of water by the bonfire. The bonfire burned hotter. (temporal)
     c. Dorothy poured the bucket of water on the bonfire. The bonfire burned hotter. (inconsistent)
     d. Does water extinguish fire?

On each trial, the subject viewed either (3a), (3b), or (3c), the consistent, temporal, and inconsistent sequences, respectively. The first sentence was read in a self-paced fashion. Then, the subject read the second sentence and judged whether or not it was consistent with the first. Finally, the subject answered question (3d). It was predicted that answer time would be longer in the temporal condition than in the other conditions.

In part, the consistency judgement task was designed to create a reading context in which some inconsistencies could be expected. This was intended to avoid simply confusing the subjects with the inconsistencies. However, the consistency instructions equipped the subjects with a special set of reading goals, the impact of which will be considered later.

The outcome sentences of the consistent and inconsistent sequences were necessarily different. It was decided that the temporal and inconsistent conditions should use the identical second sentence, *The bonfire grew hotter*, because the comparison of these two conditions was paramount. One reason for this was that the causal and temporal conditions had already been frequently compared. Second, the validation model predicts equal answer times in the consistent and inconsistent conditions, which, in the experiment, would be represented by a null result. It was more important that the newly predicted *difference* in answer times, namely that between the temporal and inconsistent conditions, be based on identical outcome sentences.

METHOD
Subjects
The subjects were 46 introductory psychology students at the University of Manitoba. They participated to earn credit toward a course requirement. All subjects were native speakers of English.

Materials
Three counterbalanced lists were derived from 21 sentence frames such as (3), considered earlier. They were adapted from the 24 frames used by Singer et al. (1992, Appendix B). For the remaining three frames, there was no convenient inconsistent version. Each frame included three versions of a two-sentence sequence, corresponding to the consistent, temporal, and inconsistent conditions. In addition, a question queried the knowledge that was posited to validate both the consistent and the inconsistent sequence.

In the first list, seven frames were randomly assigned to each experimental condition. The frames were also randomly assigned to list position, subject to the restriction that either three or four items in each condition appear in each half of the list. For the second and third lists, the items were cycled across experimental condition in such a way that, across lists, each item appeared once in each condition.

Each list also included 39 randomly ordered filler items, of three types, illustrated by set (4):

(4)   a. Beverley ate a lot of candy. The dentist found that she had five cavities.
      b. Does sugar prevent tooth decay?
      c. Did Beverley eat a lot of candy?
      d. Did Beverley eat a lot of fruit?

After sequence (4a), question (4b) asks a pertinent general knowledge question with the answer, "no." Questions (4c) and (4d) are respectively "yes" and "no" items that query the details of (4a). There were 15 general knowledge "no" fillers, and 12 each of the detail-yes and detail-no filler categories. The fillers were intended to approximately equate the number of correct "yes" and "no" answers, and to require the subjects to attend to the details of the sequences. Approximately half the exemplars of each type of filler appeared in each half of the list. The sentence sequences of the filler items used the consistent, temporal, and inconsistent forms one-third of the time, each. No more than three consecutive items, whether experimental or filler, could be from the same condition.

Each list was preceded by eight practice items that represented a cross-section of the different item types. In total, there were 68 items per list.

Procedure

The subjects were tested at separate subject stations in groups of one to four. Each subject was randomly assigned to view one of the lists. The experimental materials were presented on the screen of computer-controlled monochrome video monitors at a distance of 22 cm from the subject. The Yes and No keys ("z" or "/" on the keyboard) were randomly assigned to be pressed with the left and right index fingers, and the ready button (space bar) was pressed with the preferred thumb.

The experimental instructions were presented in written form. They included several sample items, to which the subjects wrote their outcome (second) sentence consistency judgements and their final question answers. This practice was intended to minimize the error rates.

On each experimental trial, the signal "READY" appeared on the screen. When the subject pressed the ready bar, a fixation point appeared for 500 ms. Then, the first sentence of the two-sentence sequence was presented. It remained on the screen either until the subject pressed the ready button to indicate that the sentence had been understood, or until an 8-s time limit was exceeded.

Next, the second sentence appeared. The subject had 5 s to judge its consistency with its antecedent, using the "yes" and "no" keys. When the subject responded, the sentence was removed from the screen. After an interval of 3 s, a fixation point was again presented for 500 ms, followed by the question. The subject had a 5-s time limit to answer "yes" or "no." Then, after a 3-s intertrial interval, the ready signal initiated the next trial.

Error feedback in the form of a 500 ms tone was presented if the subject responded incorrectly or exceeded the time limit both for the consistency judgement of the outcome sentence, and for the final answer.

All responses and response times were automatically recorded. Answer time was measured as the interval between the appearance of the question and the press of the response button. Practice was not explicitly distinguished for the subjects. There was a 30-s rest period after trial 38, that is, after practice plus half of the experimental list proper.

RESULTS

Analysis of variance was applied to the data, alternately treating subjects (F_1) and items (F_2) as the random variable. A statistical criterion of $\alpha = .05$ is used throughout unless otherwise indicated.

All subjects met a criterion of less than 33% errors on the experimental final questions. Data were obtained for 15, 16, and 15 subjects for lists 1, 2, and 3, respectively.

The results are shown in Table 1. On the measure of mean correct answer times for questions probing the validating knowledge (second row of the table), there was a significant effect of relation, $F_1(2,86) = 9.17$, $MS_e = 45,824$, $F_2(2,40) = 7.22$, $MS_e = 37,598$. This reflects answer times that were very similar in the consistent and inconsistent conditions, and about 200 ms slower in the temporal condition.

The relation effect was likewise significant for correct consistency judgement times for the outcome sentence, $F_1(2,86) = 44.2$, $MS_e = 98,055$, $F_2(2,40) = 9.86$, $MS_e = 182,083$. Judgement time was faster in the consistent than the inconsistent condition, $F_1(1,43) = 24.5$, $MS_e = 56,583$, $F_2(1,20) = 10.5$, $MS_e = 73,673$, which in turn was faster than the temporal condition, $F_1(1,43) = 26.1$, $MS_e = 116,928$, $F_2(1,20) = 4.04$, $MS_e = 254,970$, $p = .06$.

The error rates of Experiment 1 are also shown in Table 1. Errors in *answering* the validating questions did not vary significantly as a function of condition. However, the relation effect in consistency judgement errors was significant, $F_1(2,86) = 111.4$, $MS_e = .017$, $F_2(2,40) = 16.8$, $MS_e = .050$. Consistency judgement errors were lowest in the consistent condition and highest in the temporal condition.

DISCUSSION

In agreement with the main hypothesis, answer time was similar in the consistent and inconsistent conditions, and slower in the temporal condition. This supports the analysis that understanding the consistent and inconsistent sequences invokes the same pertinent knowledge. The positive correlation between the mean answer times and error rates (Table 1) indicates that the data do not reflect a speed-accuracy trade-off.

This conclusion is tempered by the 44% error rate of the temporal condition consistency judgements, and by the long latencies of those judgements. These two results are considered in turn. The high error rate defied one goal of Experiment 1: namely, to diminish the consistency judgement error rate from that observed in an otherwise identical unpublished experiment. The changes implemented in Experiment 1 included the written practice integrated with the instructions, and the error feedback that accompanied the experimental task.

TABLE 1
Correct Answer Latencies (in milliseconds) as a Function of Relation in
Experiment 1

	Relation		
Measure	Consistent	Temporal	Inconsistent
Consistency judgement time	2007 (.05)	2590 (.44)	2278 (.19)
Answer time	1958 (.05)	2168 (.07)	1988 (.04)

Note – Error rates in parentheses.

Like the unpublished experiment, the present instructions clearly indicated that
The bonfire burned hotter was not interpreted as contradicting its antecedent,
Dorothy placed the bucket of water by the bonfire. These features did not alter
the results, however. In the unpublished experiment, answer times of 2154 ms,
2419 ms, and 2082 ms were observed in the consistent, temporal, and
inconsistent conditions, respectively. The temporal condition consistency
judgement error rate was 47%.

Second, whereas one might have expected correct consistency judgement
time to be slower for inconsistent outcomes than temporal outcomes, the
opposite was true. Therefore, the processing of the temporal outcome may
have spilled over into the answer phase, thus contributing to long temporal
answer times. To evaluate the possibility that the present *answer time* pattern
reflected uncertainty about the consistency of temporal outcomes, the answer
time analysis was repeated for the subset of trials on which a correct
consistency judgement was registered. This yielded data patterns highly
similar to those of the overall analysis. The relation effect was significant,
$F_1(2,66) = 21.6$, $MS_e = 67,069$, $F_2(2,38) = 6.60$, $MS_e = 54,244$. This reflected
mean answer times of 1938 ms, 2165 ms, and 1928 ms in the consistent,
temporal, and inconsistent conditions, respectively. This outcome discourages
the conclusion that difficulty with the consistency judgements was the main
basis of the answer time pattern.

In summary, consistent with the validation model, answer times for
questions about hypothetically pertinent knowledge were highly similar in the
consistent and inconsistent conditions; temporal answer times were slower.
However, support for the validation model was qualified by the error prone
and slow consistency judgements observed in the temporal condition.

Experiment 2 therefore implemented two modifications, designed to lend
stronger support to the present proposals. First, the subjects read the
two-sentence sequences in a self-paced fashion, and then answered a pertinent
question. As a result, the subject did not have to make a consistency
evaluation of the outcome sentence of the sequence. Second, the consistent
and inconsistent sequences of Experiment 2 were rewritten to include an
appropriate conjunction. This is illustrated in set (5).

(5) a. Dorothy poured the bucket of water on the bonfire, so the bonfire went out. (consistent)

  b. Dorothy placed the bucket of water by the bonfire. The bonfire burned hotter. (temporal)

  c. Dorothy poured the bucket of water on the bonfire, but the bonfire burned hotter. (inconsistent)

  d. Does water extinguish fire?

The conjunctions signaled the appropriateness of the discourse outcome. They were added to preclude confusion on the part of the readers, particularly for the inconsistent sequences. However, their inclusion does not alter the necessity of validating the sequences. Although causal and adversative conjunctions provide useful cues to the reader, it is assumed that the assessment of the congruence of a causal outcome should still have to be made.

As before, it was predicted that temporal answer times would be slower than those of the other conditions. It was further predicted, however, that outcome sentence reading time would be at least as slow in the inconsistent condition as in the temporal condition. This is because the detection of inconsistency might cause the subject to try to reconcile antecedent and outcome in some fashion.

Experiment 2

METHOD

Subjects

The subjects were 41 individuals from the same pool that was used in Experiment 1.

Materials

The experimental materials of Experiment 1 were modified by the addition of appropriate conjunctions in the consistent and inconsistent sequences, as discussed with reference to example (5), above. The conjunction was always part of the outcome display. No conjunction was added to the temporal sequence because there is no conjunction that unambiguously signifies a temporal relation. For example, the ostensively neutral "and" takes on a causal sense in the sequence, *Dorothy placed the bucket of water by the bonfire, AND the bonfire burned hotter*. The consistent and inconsistent filler sequences were likewise modified to include appropriate conjunctions.

Procedure

The procedure was identical to that of Experiment 1 except in the following respects: First, the antecedent and outcome portions of the experimental sequences were separated by either a period or a comma, as shown in set (5) above. Second, the subjects read the outcome display in a self-paced fashion, rather than judging its consistency. Third, no written practice accompanied the reading of the instructions, and no feedback was provided concerning erroneous answers to the questions.

RESULTS

All of the subjects met the error criterion. As a result, answer times were obtained from 13, 14, and 14 subjects for lists 1, 2, and 3, respectively. However, due to experimenter error, the reading times were lost for six subjects. The reading time analyses were based on the scores of the remaining 35 subjects.

The results are presented in Table 2. The analysis of answer times revealed an effect of relation, $F_1(2,76) = 12.2$, $MS_e = 35,662$, $F_2(2,40) = 4.91$, $MS_e = 51,644$. As in Experiment 1, temporal answer time was longer than that of the other conditions, which were approximately equal. ANOVA applied to the corresponding error rates revealed no significant effects.

There was also a main effect of relation among the outcome sentence reading times, $F_1(2,76) = 12.2$, $MS_e = 35,662$, $F_2(2,40) = 7.92$, $MS_e = 121,541$. Reading time was 227 ms faster in the consistent condition than the temporal condition, $F_1(1,32) = 9.69$, $MS_e = 67,641$, $F_2(1,20) = 3.39$, $MS_e = 158,625$, $p = .08$, which in turn was 201 ms faster than the inconsistent condition, $F_1(1,32) = 10.5$, $MS_e = 85,470$, $F_2(1,20) = 3.33$, $MS_e = 128,113$, $p = .08$.

Finally, the subjects-random analysis also revealed a list X relation interaction, $F_1(4,64) = 6.73$, $MS_e = 72,675$. Because sentence frames are randomly assigned to condition in the lists, there is no guarantee that the frames in the different conditions within a list will be comparable on extraneous dimensions such as the length of the outcome sentence. This may result in interactions of this sort. However, this has no bearing on the main hypothesis.

DISCUSSION

The results conformed closely with the predictions. As in Experiment 1, answer times in the consistent and inconsistent conditions were very similar, and their average was faster than the temporal answer times. However, outcome sentence reading time was slower in the inconsistent than the temporal condition, just the reverse of the pattern detected among the Experiment 1 consistency judgements.

The reading time disadvantage of the inconsistent condition, relative to the temporal condition, may have been partly due to its extra conjunction, "but." However, the reading time measure reversed the temporal-inconsistent consistency judgement time difference of Experiments 1 by 513 ms. Table 2 provides estimate of the impact of the conjunction on reading time. In particular, the reading time advantage of the *consistent* condition over the temporal condition was 116 ms greater in *Experiment 3*, in which neither

TABLE 2
Results of Experiments 2 and 3 (in milliseconds) as a Function of Relation

	Relation		
Measure	Consistent	Temporal	Inconsistent
Experiment 2			
Reading time	1905	2132	2333
Answer time	2131	2331	2153
Error rate	.04	.06	.06
Experiment 3			
Reading time	2097	2440	2476
Answer time	2139	2342	2274
Error rate	.05	.07	.12

condition presented a conjunction, than in Experiment 2, in which only the consistent condition used the conjunction, "so." The 116 ms difference could not have been the sole basis of the 513 ms reversal.

These data support the proposal that understanding causal sequences, whether consistent or inconsistent, requires the validation of a tentative bridging inference. By virtue of the construction of the present materials, validation in both of these conditions was posited to invoke the same or similar knowledge. The outcome sentence reading times suggest that it is relatively difficult to reconcile an inconsistent outcome with its antecedent. This is evidenced particularly by the comparison of the inconsistent and consistent reading times; the outcome sentences in both of these conditions included appropriate conjunctions, but the inconsistent outcome reading times were longer. In spite of this, understanding the inconsistent sequence ultimately provided the same degree of answering facilitation as in the consistent condition.

Thus, two concerns about Experiment 1 were addressed. First, because the reading times of Experiment 2 were longer in the inconsistent condition than the temporal condition, the answer time pattern cannot be attributed to processing spillover. Second, because the subjects made few errors in Experiment 2, the answer times can likewise not be ascribed to confusion on the subjects' part.

Finally, it is useful to note that the self-paced reading plus answering procedure of Experiment 2 was identical to that used throughout by Singer et al. (1992). In fact, the present consistent and temporal conditions replicated the results that were measured by Singer et al. in the corresponding causal and temporal conditions.

In Experiment 1, subjects encountered inconsistent sequences without the conjunction "but," such as (6):

(6) Dorothy poured the bucket of water on the bonfire. The bonfire burned hotter.

Despite the absence of the conjunction, this sequence should not have unduly puzzled the subject; after all, it was presented in the context of a consistency judgement task. Suppose, in contrast, sequence (6) were presented in the self-paced reading task of Experiment 2. Two things might happen. First, comprehension might proceed just as it does when the conjunction "but" is present. That is, the reader might simply view the sequence as unusual. Alternatively, understanding this sequence might prompt the reader to reevaluate the knowledge pertinent to the validating fact. That is, the comparison of the validating fact, "water feeds fire," and the pertinent knowledge, "water extinguishes fire," might result in an altered estimate of the latter.

It is not proposed that understanding sequence (6) will result in serious doubts concerning the well-established fact that water extinguishes fire. However, new discourse information must be able to affect one's assessment of pertinent knowledge. People frequently encounter sequences such as *The solution was acidic but it did not turn the litmus paper red.* The absence of any pertinent knowledge about chemistry is not likely to completely stymie comprehension. Rather, to the extent the writer is trusted, the reader might form a new belief that acid, in general, turns litmus paper red (Noordman, Vonk, & Kempff, 1992). Likewise, sequence (6) might result in faint doubts or qualifications about the general impact of water on fire.

Experiment 3 was designed to evaluate these alternative hypotheses about the effects of reading a sequence such as (6), above. The experiment inspected the comprehension of the materials of Experiment 2 in the absence of the causal conjunctions. If the conjunctions, particularly the adversative "but," provide only marginally useful information, then the answer time pattern in Experiment 3 ought to replicate that of Experiment 2. However, if the absence of the conjunction affects the reader's evaluation of the pertinent knowledge, the answer times in the inconsistent condition might no longer be faster than the temporal answer times.

Experiment 3

METHOD

The method was identical to that of Experiment 2 except for the following details. The subjects were 43 individuals selected from the same pool that was used in the previous experiments. The materials of Experiment 2 were altered so that the conjunctions were eliminated from the consistent and inconsistent sequences, both experimental and filler. As a result, for example, consistent sequences reverted to their Experiment 1 form, such as *Dorothy poured the bucket of water on the bonfire, The bonfire went out.*

In Experiment 3, the intertrial interval and the interval preceding the test questions were each 2.5 s rather than 3.0 s. Finally, response panels replaced the computer keyboards as the response devices.

RESULTS

The data of one subject, whose error rate on experimental items exceeded the 33% criterion, were discarded. ANOVA was applied to the data of 13, 14, and 15 individuals who read lists 1, 2, and 3, respectively. The results appear in Table 2.

As before, there was a main effect of relation among the answer times, $F_1(2,76) = 8.09$, $MS_e = 57,326$, $F_2(2,40) = 7.45$, $MS_e = 29,963$. However, the inconsistent mean was 135 ms slower than the consistent mean, $F_1(1,39) = 7.16$, $MS_e = 57,551$, $F_2(1,20) = 5.71$, $MS_e = 24,102$. The 68 ms answer time advantage of the inconsistent condition over the temporal condition did not reach significance, $Fs < 2.03$. The inconsistent error rate was 12%, in contrast with the 6% average for the other conditions, $F_1(2,76) = 4.71$, $MS_e = .005$, $F_2(2,40) = 3.40$, $MS_e = .611$.

Analysis of the outcome sentence reading times likewise revealed a main effect of relation, $F_1(2,76) = 15.0$, $MS_e = 130,999$, $F_2(2,40) = 8.92$, $MS_e = 103,250$. Reading time was faster in the consistent condition than the other two conditions, which were about equal. The subjects-random analysis also revealed a list X relation interaction, $F_1(4,76) = 6.96$, $MS_e = 130,999$.

DISCUSSION

The results of Experiment 3 differed from those of the previous experiments, particularly in their bearing on the main hypothesis. Unlike Experiments 1 and 2, the inconsistent condition answer times were slower than consistent ones, and were statistically indistinguishable from the temporal answer times. In the specific context of Experiment 3, this outcome suggests that inconsistent sequences that are not accompanied by an explicit signal, such as the adversative *but*, may either weaken the reader's confidence about the pertinent knowledge or otherwise slightly confuse the reader about the appropriate answer. This proposal is supported by the doubling of the inconsistent condition error rates in Experiment 3, as compared with Experiment 2.

An alternative explanation is that the absence of *but* in an inconsistent sequence precludes the integration of the validating fact in the text representation. Then, no benefit would accrue from either a serial or a parallel memory search that included the text representation. The simplest interpretation of this proposal is that causal (or adversative) conjunctions are needed to instigate causal processing. However, this interpretation is inconsistent with the detection of validation effects for causal and temporal sequences that include no conjunctions (Singer et al., 1992). Because the reader does not know the status of the current sequence until validation is performed, it seems inevitable that the relevant knowledge will be engaged, and so integrated with the text representation.

The results of Experiment 3 highlight a facet of the validation hypothesis, one which I have not yet carefully inspected. In particular, there is a continuum of familiarity of the knowledge that needs to be invoked to validate a bridging inference. For sequences based on familiar knowledge, such as *Ted put ice in his drink, It cooled off*, validation proceeds as described at the outset. At the other extreme, readers may encounter a causal sequence based on unfamiliar knowledge, such as *Julie dipped the litmus paper in the acid, The paper turned red*. The validating fact, "acid turns litmus paper red," is computed as usual. However, if the reader lacks any knowledge that may be used to evaluate this fact, a variety of things may occur. First, the reader may simply assume that the validating fact is true. Second, the reader may fail to bridge causal sequences of complex, unfamiliar facts (Noordman et al., 1992). Third, if too many sequences of this sort are encountered, the reader may sense that the text is not being understood, and give up.

In this framework, consider an inconsistent sequence of Experiment 3, *Walt drank the milk that was left for a week by the kitchen stove, The milk tasted good*. The reader may react to this sequence in a variety of ways. First, it may be recognized as a clear exception to the rule, in our culture, that milk needs to be refrigerated. Experiment 2 suggests that this would be more readily achieved if the sentences were linked by an adversative conjunction. Second, the sequence might be interpreted to qualify the reader's knowledge about refrigerating milk. The reader might decide that, though milk eventually spoils, it takes a long time to do so. Alternatively, the reader might deduce that, in certain circumstances, milk does not need to be refrigerated. In this regard, the sentence might remind the reader of having seen unrefrigerated milk cartons in European stores.

General Discussion
VALIDATING CAUSAL SEQUENCES
This study was designed to evaluate a new prediction derived from the validation model of bridging inferences. According to the validation model, before a causal bridging inference is accepted by the understander, it must be validated with reference to existing knowledge. In the context of causal bridges, the reader first computes a validating fact that, when coupled with the cause, would account for the appearance of the outcome. Then, the truth of the validating fact is assessed on the basis of existing knowledge.

For these steps of validation to make sense, they must be applicable both to consistent and inconsistent causal sequences. If validation processing could not detect an inconsistency, it would serve no function. The present experiments provided evidence that the validation of both consistent and inconsistent causal sequences facilitates the hypothetically pertinent general knowledge.

Indeed, it is important to emphasize that the present analysis posits the validation of temporal, consistent, and inconsistent sequences, both in the absence and presence of causal conjunctions. This raises the questions of what initiates causal validation and of how the impact of validation varies with sequence type. First, causal analysis in text comprehension was proposed to be initiated by the appearance of causal conjunctions, of verbs with a causal sense (e.g., *solidify*), and particularly of changes of state (Singer et al., 1992). In the latter regard, the change of state conveyed by *The fire went out* prompts a search for the cause of this outcome (e.g., Cheng & Holyoak, 1985).

Second, every type of sequence included the outcome *The fire went out* or the *fire grew hotter*, but the impact of comprehension varied with condition. In consistent sequences, the validating fact was activated. For temporal sequences, such as *Dorothy placed the bucket of water by the bonfire, The fire grew hotter*, the reader is presumed to search for the cause of the fire intensifying. This search may either fail, or else identify a perhaps speculative cause, such as that the wind picked up. If a potential cause is identified, validation processing will ensue, and perhaps activate a different relevant fact. In neither case, however, will "water extinguishes fire" be reliably activated.

For inconsistent sequences, the present results indicate that validation results in the activation of the hypothetically relevant fact, as long as the task instructions or the appropriate conjunctions "signal" a reasonable context for the anomalies (Experiments 1 and 2). The slower inconsistent answer times in Experiment 3 might suggest that validation processes were simply not executed. However, this would require that the reader be able to divine the current causal condition. Rather, I propose that the reader of an unsignaled inconsistent sequence still strives to identify a cause, and then to validate the cause. Answer times to questions about the "validating fact" would then be slow because of the conflict between text information and conceptual knowledge, as outlined in the discussion of Experiment 3.

In summary, the present results provide additional support for the validation model of bridging inference. The validation model expands on former assumptions of the role of general knowledge in inference processing, by beginning to specify the mental processes of bridging inference.

Although the primary motivation of this study was to test a corollary of the validation model, the particulars of these experiments have focussed attention on the reader's ability to make assessments of discourse consistency. Consistency detection and the reader's awareness of it have been inspected in the framework of studies of comprehension monitoring. Whereas readers are surprisingly deficient in their comprehension monitoring, the present experiments identify an instance in which text consistency is successfully monitored. Therefore, the relationship between inference validation and comprehension monitoring will be considered next.

INFERENCE VALIDATION AND COMPREHENSION MONITORING

To understand a message, one must subject it to constant evaluation, a process known as "comprehension monitoring" (Markman, 1979). Without such scrutiny, it should be impossible for the understander to construct coherent message representations. In spite of this, people's comprehension monitoring is seriously flawed. In fact, there is evidence that children (Markman, 1979), young adults (Glenberg, Wilkinson, & Epstein, 1982), and older adults (Cohen, 1979) frequently fail to detect even glaring discourse inconsistencies.

The puzzle of comprehension monitoring has resisted easy solution. First, discourse representation must be monitored at numerous levels of analysis, including the syntactic, semantic, and pragmatic (Markman, 1979). This raises the possibility that monitoring is more efficient at some of these levels than others. However, people's misapprehension of text, coupled with their lack of awareness of this difficulty, encompasses the surface, text base, and situation representations derived from the text (Glenberg, Sanocki, Epstein, & Morris, 1987).

A second hypothesis states that, for factual inconsistencies to be detected, those facts must co-occur in working memory. Consistent with this view, factors that reduce the likelihood of co-occurrence, such as the text distance between facts, increase the failure to detect inconsistencies (Epstein, Glenberg, & Bradley, 1984). However, Markman (1979) reported that asking children to repeat the pairs of sentences bearing the inconsistencies, a manipulation intended to promote coactivation, did not eliminate detection failure. In fact, co-occurrence in working memory is viewed as a necessary but not sufficient condition for the detection of text inconsistencies (Epstein et al., 1984; Markman, 1979).

Third, comprehension monitoring may be influenced by the understander's purpose in examining a message. The reader's orienting task may determine the level of representation at which coherence will be preserved (Glenberg et al., 1982, p. 601). Consistent with this analysis, there is evidence that superficial tasks, such as proofreading, promote local discourse processing, whereas tasks requiring the extraction of meaning favour global processing (e.g., Cirilo, 1981; Mayer & Cook, 1981). However, the orienting task hypothesis has not been directly tested in the context of the detection of inconsistencies.

It is noteworthy, therefore, that the present results provide a counterexample to demonstrations of ineffective comprehension monitoring. At its essence, the validation of causal bridging inferences is a process of monitoring a message for sense. Without this process, the sequences *Ted put ice in his drink, It COOLED OFF*, and *Ted put ice in his drink, It GREW WARMER* would seem equally agreeable.

The experiments of this project may therefore provide some useful clues about the conditions that promote comprehension monitoring. The participants were instructed to read for comprehension, a basic orienting task. The crucial antecedent and outcome ideas are likely to have co-occurred in working memory, because they always appeared in adjacent text sentences. Therefore, the materials fulfilled an important necessary condition for effective comprehension monitoring.

Perhaps most importantly, whereas the text inconsistencies in some other studies have hinged upon simple or complex deductions or upon the text details (Cohen, 1979; Glenberg et al., 1982), the present materials focussed on the causal consistency of the text. The causal network of a discourse forms a fundamental part of its situation model (Trabasso & Sperry, 1985; van den Broek, 1990). Accordingly, the present findings suggest that one way in which the reader maintains global coherence is by monitoring comprehension with reference to the causal network underlying a discourse. Further research will be needed to directly test this proposal.

This research was supported by grant OGP9800 from the Natural Sciences and Engineering Research Council of Canada. I am grateful to Peter Andrusiak and Susan Larson, who collected the data for these experiments. I would also like to thank Fernanda Ferreira and Paul van den Broek for their thoughtful comments about a previous draft of this manuscript. Experiments 1 and 2 were presented at the meeting of the Psychonomic Society, San Francisco, November, 1991. Requests for reprints should be addressed to Murray Singer, Department of Psychology, University of Manitoba, Winnipeg, Canada R3T 2N2.

References

Bloom, C. P., Fletcher, C. R., van den Broek, P., Reitz, L., & Shapiro, B. P. (1990). An on-line assessment of causal reasoning during comprehension. *Memory & Cognition, 18*, 65-71.

Cheng, P. W., & Holyoak, K. J. (1985). Pragmatic reasoning schemas. *Cognitive Psychology, 17*, 391-416.

Cirilo, R. K. (1981). Referential coherence and text structure in story comprehension. *Journal of Verbal Learning and Verbal Behavior, 20*, 358-367.

Cohen, G. (1979). Language comprehension in old age. *Cognitive Psychology, 11*, 412-429.

Ehrlich, K., & Rayner, K. (1983). Pronoun assignment and semantic integration during reading: Eye movements and immediacy of processing. *Journal of Verbal Learning and Verbal Behavior, 22*, 75-87.

Epstein, W., Glenberg, A. M., & Bradley, M. M. (1984). Coactivation and comprehension: Contribution of text variables to the illusion of knowing. *Memory & Cognition, 12*, 355-360.

Glenberg, A. M., Sanocki, T., Epstein, W., & Morris, C. (1987). Enhancing calibration of comprehension. *Journal of Experimental Psychology: General, 116*, 119-136.

Glenberg, A. M., Wilkinson, A. C., & Epstein, W. (1982). The illusion of knowing: Failure in the self-assessment of comprehension. *Memory & Cognition, 10*, 597-602.

Halldorson, M., & Singer, M. (1992). *Integration of general knowledge and text information in the validation of causal bridging inferences.* University of Manitoba: Unpublished manuscript.

Haviland, S. E., & Clark, H. H. (1974). What's new? Acquiring new information as a process in comprehension. *Journal of Verbal Learning and Verbal Behavior, 13*, 512-521.

Keenan, J. M., Baillet, S. D., & Brown, P. (1984). The effects of causal cohesion on comprehension and memory. *Journal of Verbal Learning and Verbal Behavior, 23*, 115-126.

Kintsch, W. (1974). *The representation of meaning in memory.* Hillsdale, NJ: Erlbaum.

Kintsch, W., & van Dijk, T. A. (1978). Toward a model of text comprehension and production. *Psychological Review, 85*, 363-394.

Kintsch, W., & Welsch, D. M. (in press). The construction-integration model: A framework for studying memory for text. In W. Hockley & S. Lewandowsky (Eds.), *Relating theory and data: Essays on human memory.* Hillsdale, NJ: Erlbaum.

Markman, E. M. (1979). Realizing that you don't understand: Elementary school children's awareness of inconsistencies. *Child Development, 50*, 643-655.

Mayer, R. E., & Cook, L. K. (1981). Effects of shadowing on prose comprehension. *Memory & Cognition, 9*, 101-109.

McKoon, G., & Ratcliff, R. (1980a). Priming in item recognition: The organization of propositions in memory for text. *Journal of Verbal Learning and Verbal Behavior, 19*, 369-386.

McKoon, G., & Ratcliff, R. (1980b). The comprehension processes and memory structures involved in anaphoric reference. *Journal of Verbal Learning and Verbal Behavior, 19*, 668-682.

McKoon, G., & Ratcliff, R. (1986). Inferences about predictable events. *Journal of Experimental Psychology: Learning, Memory, and Cognition, 12*, 82-91.

McKoon, G., & Ratcliff, R. (1988). Contextually relevant aspects of meaning. *Journal of Experimental Psychology: Learning, Memory, and Cognition, 14*, 331-343.

Myers, J. L., Shinjo, M., & Duffy, S. A. (1987). Degree of causal relatedness and memory. *Journal of Verbal Learning and Verbal Behavior, 26*, 453-465.

Noordman, L. G. M., Vonk, W., & Kempff, H. J. (1992). Causal inferences during the reading of expository texts. *Journal of Memory and Language, 31*, 573-590.

Potts, G. R., Keenan, J. M., & Golding, J. M. (1988). Assessing the occurrence of elaborative inferences: Lexical decision versus naming. *Journal of Memory and Language, 27*, 399-415.

Singer, M. (1979). Processes of inference in sentence encoding. *Memory & Cognition, 7*, 192-200.

Singer, M. (1980). The role of case-filling inferences in the coherence of brief passages. *Discourse Processes, 3*, 185-201.

Singer, M., & Ferreira, F. (1983). Inferring consequences in story comprehension. *Journal of Verbal Learning and Verbal Behavior, 22*, 437-448.

Singer, M., Halldorson, M., Lear, J. C., & Andrusiak, P. (1992). Validation of causal bridging inferences. *Journal of Memory and Language, 31*, 507-524.

Singer, M., Revlin, R., & Halldorson, M. (1990). Bridging-inferences and enthymeme. In A. Graesser & G. Bower (Eds.), *Inferences and text comprehension: The psychology of learning and motivation*, Vol. 25 (pp. 35-51). New York: Academic Press.

Trabasso, T., & Sperry, L. L. (1985). Causal relatedness and importance of story events. *Journal of Memory and Language, 24*, 595-611.

van den Broek, P. (1990). Causal inferences and the comprehension of narrative texts. In A. Graesser and G. Bower (Eds.), *The psychology of learning and motivation*, Vol. 25 (pp. 175-196). New York: Academic Press.

11 Writing Quality, Reading Skills, and Domain Knowledge as Factors in Text Comprehension

JULIA E. MORAVCSIK and WALTER KINTSCH
University of Colorado

Abstract Subjects listened to and recalled three passages. Each subject was also given a general reading comprehension test. The passages were presented either in such a way that subjects could use their general knowledge to help understand them, or in such a way that no specific world knowledge seemed applicable. This was achieved by giving the passages a helpful title, versus no title or an unhelpful title. The passages were written in two different versions, preserving their content but varying their style. In one version, the language was as helpful as we could make it in signalling to the listener discourse importance, while in the other version the language was as unhelpful as we could make it while still writing an English text. All three factors – domain knowledge, writing style, and skill – significantly affected reproductive recall, and there were no interactions between these factors. However, while good writing was sufficient to improve the reproduction of the texts, an analysis of the recall elaborations subjects made revealed that the correctness of their elaborations depended strongly on the availability of appropriate domain knowledge. Thus, good writing and domain knowledge are not simply substitutable, but affect comprehension in somewhat different ways.

Résumé Les sujets devaient écouter et rappeler trois passages et chacun d'eux a été soumis à un test général de compréhension de textes. Les passages étaient présentés de façon que les sujets pouvaient utiliser leurs connaissances générales pour les comprendre ou de façon qu'aucune connaissance précise du monde ne semblait applicable. Les passages avaient un titre significatif, n'avaient pas de titre ou avaient un titre non significatif. Ils étaient rédigés en deux versions qui avaient le même contenu, mais un style différent. L'une des versions était rédigée de manière à éclairer le plus possible le lecteur en lui signalant l'importance du discours, tandis que l'autre était rédigée de manière à l'éclairer le moins qui puisse se faire en utilisant quand même l'anglais. Trois facteurs – connaissance du domaine, qualité de l'écriture et compétence du lecteur – ont influé considérablement sur le rappel de reproduction, et il n'y avait aucune interaction entre ces facteurs. Toutefois, bien que la qualité de l'écriture suffisait à améliorer la reproduction des textes, l'analyse des élaborations de rappel des sujets montrait que l'exactitude de celles-ci était largement fonction de la connaissance du domaine en question. La qualité de l'écriture et la connaissance du domaine ne sont donc pas simplement substituables, mais elles influencent la compréhension quelque peu différemment.

Domain knowledge, or background knowledge, almost always facilitates text comprehension (for recent reviews, see Schneider, Körkel, & Weinert, 1990, and Voss, Fincher-Kiefer, Greene, & Post, 1986). However, there are some exceptions which seem to depend on the nature of the text and task. One occurs when texts do not provide occasions for experts to use their superior knowledge, as in Voss, Vesonder, and Spilich (1980). In this study, baseball experts recalled baseball stories better than novices when the stories were generated by other experts, but there was no difference when the stories were generated by novices. Moreover, Kintsch & Franzke (in press) found that even uninformed readers were able to reproduce news stories that did not require special knowledge quite well on the basis of their superficial understanding. Knowledge differences were apparent, however, for those sections of the stories that required deeper understanding. Knowledge effects also are not found when the memory test is too easy; typically these effects are reduced on a cloze test and not found at all with a recognition test (Schneider et al., 1990). On the whole, however, knowledge effects in text comprehension and memory are pervasive.

Understanding stories requires a particular kind of domain knowledge, consisting of knowledge about people's motivations, goals, and actions, and how they are related to events in the world. It consists of causal knowledge about what happens and why. The importance of this knowledge to story understanding has repeatedly been demonstrated (e.g., Trabasso & van den Broek, 1985). A good account of story comprehension and recall can be obtained by assuming that these causal links play a major role in how the reader constructs a mental representation of the story. According to this view, if these relationships are not explicit in the text, they are inferred on the basis of domain knowledge. Domain knowledge is therefore a necessary condition for understanding. However, computer simulations with a model of human text comprehension have revealed some interesting alternatives (Kintsch, 1992). In the simulations at least, it is not necessary to assume that causal links are inferred and hence that domain knowledge must be used in story understanding. Mental representations which are structurally almost identical are obtained if, instead, syntactic signals in the text are attended to that indicate discourse relevance. Linguists have noted that syntactic cues[1] play a complex role in comprehension. Their effect is by no means restricted to

1 The term "syntactic" is used here in a broad sense to include any kind of change in the surface form of a text, including rhetorical or stylistic devices, in addition to syntax proper.

indicating to the reader the intended parsing of a sentence into its semantic structure, i.e., a propositional representation. In addition, syntax is used extensively to signal discourse relevance (Givón, 1989). For instance, there is a reason why a particular proposition is selected to be the subject and predicate of a sentence, whereas another one is hidden in a modifier or relegated to a dependent clause. Numerous other syntactic constructions are used to foreground certain kinds of information and background other kinds, and to indicate what is important and what is less important in a discourse. Kintsch (1992) has shown that if a simulated story comprehender uses these syntactic signals of discourse relevance in a text, a mental representation is constructed that is indistinguishable from the one obtained by attending to the causal structure of the story. This is perhaps not a surprising result; if causal links are important in a story, then the writer or speaker would indicate this importance by using syntactic cues to highlight them.

Stories thus contain redundant information; the syntactic cues point in the same direction as the domain knowledge. This raises the question of whether good writing, which has clear syntactic cues, can compensate for a reader's lack of domain knowledge. Presumably, in normal story understanding, readers use their domain knowledge as well as their syntactic knowledge, for in a normal text the two are redundant. If these factors are experimentally unconfounded by writing texts in which the syntactic cues are uncorrelated or even negatively correlated with discourse importance, how will comprehension be affected? The computer simulations of Kintsch (1992) imply that either source of information – domain knowledge or syntactic cues – should suffice, though a combination should lead to best results.

If syntactic cues, indeed, play a role in discourse comprehension, as suggested by the computer simulations, the skill with which readers use these cues might very well be an additional factor to consider. It has been recognized for some time now that general intellectual ability, when assessed by means of the usual psychometric intelligence tests, plays a minor role compared to specific domain knowledge. This is true both in problem solving in general (Ericsson & Crutcher, 1989) and in reading comprehension in particular (Schneider et al., 1990). However, that does not mean that more specific ability differences in skills directly related to text comprehension are irrelevant. Indeed, Schneider et al. report that metacognitive skills of their subjects pertaining to recall – both general knowledge about it and ability to predict their own performance – were strongly correlated with performance. Similarly, it may be that differences in reading skill, over and above knowledge differences, may be an important factor in comprehension. Reading skill may indeed be a cognitive ability, independent of domain knowledge, as Perfetti (1989) has claimed, because readers with high skills are better able to use the general syntactic signals in a discourse for the construction of mental representations.

While there are good reasons to believe that domain knowledge, writing style, and reading skill all affect comprehension, there remains the question of how these factors interact. Can good writing compensate for lack of domain knowledge in the sense that comprehension could be achieved either through high domain knowledge or good writing, thus yielding an interaction between these factors, or are both factors helpful, but in different ways, thus producing additive effects? How does reading skill interact with these factors? Are skillful people simply better at using whatever knowledge they have or exploiting whatever cues the language offers to them, or is skill particularly important when there is no knowledge, or when the language of the text is not helpful? Furthermore, do these factors affect all components of comprehension similarly, or do knowledge, writing style, and skill affect different components of the comprehension process?

Comprehension is not a unitary process. One cannot simply ask what the effects of domain knowledge, writing style, and reading skills on comprehension are, as the title of this paper suggests. Comprehension and understanding are vague, common sense terms that may be used in different ways, as in superficial comprehension or deep comprehension. A theory of comprehension is needed to explicate just what is meant by comprehension and what various different ways of comprehending involve. The theory of van Dijk and Kintsch (1983) specifies the notion of comprehension in terms of the level of the mental representation that is being produced. Of greatest relevance here are the levels of the textbase and the situation model. The textbase represents the meaning and structure of the text as a network of propositions. It enables the reader to reproduce the text, i.e., to recall it or to summarize it. The situation model represents the content of the text as it is integrated with the reader's domain knowledge. It enables the reader to use the information acquired from the text in novel ways, e.g., to make inferences, elaborate on the text, or solve problems. Factors that facilitate the construction of a good textbase do not necessarily facilitate the construction of a good situation model, and vice versa (e.g., Mannes & Kintsch, 1987). It is therefore an important question whether domain knowledge, writing style, and reading skill affect textbase and situation model in the same way or not. Experimentally, this means that we shall have to employ experimental indicators that are sensitive to these different aspects of comprehension, such as reproductive recall for the textbase, and reconstructive, elaborative recall for the situation model. If knowledge, writing style, and reading skill have differential effects upon reproductive recall and reconstructive recall, this would mean that one of these factors are more important for the formation of the textbase, while another is more important for the construction of a situation model. We shall also include a recognition test to evaluate surface memory, solely with respect to the question of whether subjects remember if they have heard a sentence in its good form or in its poor form.

In the present study subjects listened to texts with or without specific domain knowledge. In one case, following Bransford and Johnson (1972), a complex, unidentified procedure was described for which no specific domain knowledge was available. However, when the same procedure was identified by its title, – "Washing Clothes," readers could use their domain knowledge about washing clothes to help understand the text. Similarly, following Sulin and Dooling (1974), subjects were also given brief biographies to read which were either identified as descriptions of fictitious characters or familiar famous persons. Only in the latter case could readers apply their special domain knowledge about the lives of the famous people to help them understand and remember the texts. In both studies it was observed that readers performed much better when they could use their domain knowledge than when that was not possible. Furthermore, two additional factors were introduced. The texts were rewritten so that the language signalled discourse importance either very coherently or very confusingly. This was done to see whether, or to what extent, good writing could compensate for lack of domain knowledge. Finally, the subjects' reading skills were introduced as a third factor to see whether their use of the linguistic cues in the texts depended on their reading skill.

METHOD
Subjects
One hundred three students from the University of Colorado participated in the experiment for class credit. Six subjects were excluded for various reasons. The subjects were randomly assigned to groups according to a 2×2 factorial design with the factors title and no-title, and good and poor writing varied between subjects as explained below. Seventeen subjects in the no-title group who guessed the title of the "Washing Clothes" passage were replaced, so that in the end there were 20 subjects in each group. The data from the subjects who guessed the title were not excluded from the analyses, however, and will also be reported.

Materials
Three texts were used, each in a good and a poor version. The first text was the "Washing Clothes" text of Bransford and Johnson (1972). It described a procedure which was either identified by a title as "Washing Clothes" or which remained unidentified. In constructing the good version of this passage, the original text was somewhat modified to make it even clearer and more comprehensible. A poorly written version was then constructed by using run-on sentences, sequences of very short sentences, using pronouns with ambiguous referents, sentences with two unrelated clauses, by switching clauses to make passive sentences, and by rearranging the order of the sentences. However, all sentences were grammatical, and the content of both

versions remained the same. That is, no facts were mentioned in one version which were not also mentioned in the other version.

The other two texts were taken from Sulin and Dooling (1974). They were short biographical sketches of people which were either identified as well-known, famous characters (Adolf Hitler and Helen Keller, respectively) or as anonymous characters (Gerald Martin, or Carol Harris). For the good versions the original texts were used, while poor versions were constructed in the same way as described above for the Washing Clothes text.

Thus, knowledge use was manipulated by giving subjects a (helpful) title or not; their knowledge was the same in either case, but with the good title they could apply this knowledge and without the title they could not.

Both versions of the experimental texts are shown in Appendix A. All passages were recorded for oral presentation. The good and poor versions of each passage lasted approximately the same time.

Test statements for a recognition test were constructed by selecting six sentences from each well-written passage and the six corresponding sentences from the poorly written passages.

Procedure

Subjects participated in the experiment in groups ranging from one to six participants. All subjects in a group were assigned to the same condition. The subjects were given a stapled package of materials. The front page consisted of overall instructions for the experiment, explaining to the subjects that they would be listening to three texts, taking a general reading comprehension test, and then taking tests on their comprehension of the experimental passages that they had heard at the beginning of the experiment. After reading these general instructions, the subjects then listened to the three experimental passages. The Washing Clothes text was always presented first, followed by the Helen Keller and Adolf Hitler passages. The latter two texts were always presented in a form opposite to the first one on both factors, so that if the first text was given a title, the other two did not have a title, and if the first text was presented in the poor version, the others were in the good version.

After listening to the texts, the subjects were given the Nelson-Denny Reading Test (Brown, Bennett, & Hanna, 1981), which lasted 15 minutes. The vocabulary section of the test was excluded. Only the comprehension section was used, which consisted of eight passages with comprehension questions following each passage.

After the subjects finished the reading test, they were instructed to recall the experimental passages. They were asked to reproduce the exact wording if they could, or otherwise to simply write down what they remembered from each passage. A separate page of the booklet was used for each passage, with a statement like "Please write down everything that you can remember about the Gerald Martin passage" as a cue. At the bottom of the untitled Washing Clothes passage there was a question asking them to guess what the procedure was.

For the recognition test, subjects were given a list of the 12 test sentences, six from each version of the text. They were asked "Place a check next to each of the following sentences if you think that you heard that exact same sentence in one of the passages. Do not worry about whether these sentences are true or not. Instead, indicate whether you think these are the sentences you actually heard verbatim."

RESULTS

The results for the Washing Clothes text and the two biographical passages will be described separately. The former was considerably longer and quite different in character than the two biographies. The biographies were understandable even when they were attributed to unknown characters, whereas the Washing Clothes passage without a title was quite puzzling. Thus, the difference between the high- and low-knowledge versions was much more extreme for the Washing Clothes passage.

The Washing Clothes Text

When the passage was presented without a title, 14 subjects correctly guessed that the text was about washing clothes when it was well-written, but there were only three correct guesses when it was poorly written, $x^2(1)=7.12$, $p < .01$. This difference is a direct indication that good writing can facilitate comprehension, independent of domain knowledge. Indeed, good writing allowed subjects to use their domain knowledge, to recognize that the text actually referred to a procedure with which they were quite familiar.

The recall protocols were scored both for reproductive and reconstructive recall. For reproductive recall, the number of idea units each subject reproduced from the text was noted. Two ANOVAs with the between subjects factors Knowledge (Title and No-Title), Writing (Good and Poor), and Reading Skill (High and Low, determined by a median split) were conducted, with and without the data from the subjects who were able to guess the title of the passage. Since the two analyses yielded comparable results, only the statistics from the complete data set will be reported here.

Table 1 shows the significant main effects due to the presence or absence of a title ($F(1,95)=19.38, p < .001$), good or bad writing style ($F(1,95)=27.15$, $p < .001$), and reading skill ($F(1,95)=4.08, p < .05$). The table also shows that there were no significant interactions between these factors, nor was there a significant triple interaction.

The fact that subjects recalled the Washing Clothes passage much better when they were given a title than when they were not given a title replicates the original results of Bransford and Johnson (1972). However, regardless of whether or not the appropriate domain knowledge was available, subjects recalled much more when the passage was well written than when it was

TABLE 1

Reproductive Recall: Mean Number of Units Recalled in
the Washing Clothes Text as a Function of Knowledge,
Writing Quality, and Reading Skill

	Knowledge	
Writing	High	Low
Good	6.75	4.65
Poor	4.35	2.09
	5.55	3.62

	Writing	
Skill	Good	Poor
High	5.74	3.48
Low	4.90	2.82
	5.43	3.14

	Skill	
Knowledge	High	Low
High	5.96	4.94
Low	4.03	3.12
	4.87	3.81

written in a disorganized, misleading style. Furthermore, skilled readers performed better than less skilled readers, regardless of the presence or absence of background knowledge.

Reconstructions in recall were measured in terms of the number of non-text statements included in a protocol. These elaborations were either situationally correct inferences or incorrect ones. An example of a correct elaboration from the "Washing Clothes" passage would be "Do not do more than you can handle", while "Then go through each pile and rearrange them" is a false elaboration, indicating that the subject did not understand the role served by making separate piles. The data are shown in Table 2. The total number of elaborations is roughly the same in all groups. However, if we look at the correctness of these elaborations, there is a big difference; the likelihood that an elaboration is erroneous is more than four times greater in the low-knowledge condition than in the high-knowledge condition, whereas it is close to equal in the good- and poor-writing conditions, $x^2(1) = 8.24, p < 01$. There were no significant differences due to the skill factor.

Thus, subjects generated about the same number of elaborations, whether or not they understood the text. However, when they did understand what was going on, their elaborations were primarily correct ones, whereas when they did not, they were almost always wrong. But elaborate they did, whether they had something to say or not.

For the analysis of the recognition data the hit- and false-alarm-rates from each subject were combined into d' values. These scores were analyzed as a

TABLE 2
Reconstructive Recall: Total Number of Elaborations and Percent Correct Elaborations

Washing Clothes Text	Knowledge		Writing	
	High	Low	Good	Poor
Total Number of Elaborations	96	80	81	95
Percent Erroneous Elaborations	21%	94%	46%	55%

Biographical Texts	Knowledge		Writing	
	High	Low	Good	Poor
Total Number of Elaborations	100	93	112	81
Percent Erroneous Elaborations	41%	81%	54%	69%

three-factor (Knowledge, Writing, and Skill) ANOVA. None of the interaction effects were significant. There was no significant main effect of knowledge, $F < 1$. Readers with high knowledge recognized the test sentences about as well (or rather, as poorly) as subjects with low knowledge. There were no skill effects either, $F < 1$. However, the quality of writing had a pronounced effect on recognition performance, $F(1,95)=76.21$, $p < .001$. The average d' was 1.01 for well-written sentences and −1.44 for poorly written sentences. Subjects saw both the good and the poorly written version of each test sentence on the recognition test, but they failed to recognize the poorly written version, even when they had actually seen it. The fact that the d' for the poorly written texts is negative indicates that subjects thought they had seen the well-written version even when that was not the case. Presumably, this is explained by the fact that their memory representations were mostly at the propositional or situational level, rather than at the surface level, and they chose the more adequate linguistic expressions of what they remembered, irrespective of what they actually had heard.

The Biographical Texts

The results from the two short biographical texts are in over-all agreement with those from the Washing Clothes text, as is shown by Table 3. The main effects of knowledge (famous name vs. unknown character) was significant, $F(1,95)=5.91$, $p < .05$, as were the main effects for writing style and reading skill, $F(1,95)=7.94$, $p < .01$, and $F(1,95)=4.87$, $p < .05$, respectively. None of the interactions between these factors and the two different texts (Keller & Hitler) were statistically significant.

The total number of elaborations as well as the percent erroneous elaborations is shown in Table 2. Whether the biographies were attributed to famous people or not, the total number of elaborations was roughly the same.

TABLE 3
Reproductive Recall: Mean Number of Units Recalled
in the Biographical Texts as a Function of Knowledge,
Writing Quality, and Reading Skill

	Knowledge	
Writing	High	Low
Good	2.41	1.93
Poor	2.06	1.43
	2.25	1.74

	Writing	
Skill	Good	Poor
High	2.02	1.50
Low	2.36	2.01
	2.19	1.82

	Skill	
Knowledge	High	Low
High	1.98	2.39
Low	1.44	1.83
	1.77	2.15

However, the likelihood that an elaboration was erroneous was twice as high when subjects could not use their knowledge about famous persons than when they could, whereas differences due to writing quality were less pronounced. This interaction was statistically significant, $x^2(1) = 9.28$, $p < .01$.

The recognition results parallel those obtained with the Washing Clothes passage. There were no significant differences either due to knowledge or skill, but there was a highly significant writing effect, $F(1,95)=38.23$, $p < .001$. The average d' for well-written sentences was .85 and, once again, the d' value for the badly written sentences was actually negative, $-.66$, indicating a preference for the well written text, irrespective of what was actually presented.

DISCUSSION

High-knowledge subjects recalled the experimental passages better than low-knowledge subjects, replicating the general findings in the literature, as well as earlier results with these passages. However, by looking at both reproductive recall and at elaborative recall and its correctness, we were able to distinguish between superficial and deeper levels of understanding. Only domain knowledge appeared to help subjects achieve a deeper level of understanding, in the sense that it made possible the construction of an appropriate situation model that enabled them to correctly elaborate on the textual materials.

The main results of the present study, however, concern the effects of writing style. A well-written passage (at least for texts whose main function is information transmission) is one in which the language supports the message. That is, the language is redundant with the content, in the sense that what is known to be important information is also emphasized by the language itself. Domain structure and the linguistic discourse structure are highly correlated. The language signals what is important in the situation. High-knowledge comprehenders, confronted with a well written text, can use both their domain knowledge as well as the domain independent general linguistic cues offered by the text for the construction of the mental representation of the text. When comprehenders are not allowed to use their domain knowledge, they can still build adequate mental representations based only upon the general linguistic information. The performance decrement caused by a lack of domain knowledge was about the same as that caused by poor writing. When the passages were written in a misleading way, that is, when what was signalled as important by the language was not in fact important in terms of the content of the passage, recall was reduced, even when comprehenders could still apply their knowledge. The worst performance was obtained when comprehenders could neither rely on the linguistic signals they received, nor had any specific expertise in the subject domain.

There was no indication of a statistical interaction between these factors. Their effects were strikingly additive, presumably because they affected different components of the comprehension process – subjects constructed better situation models when they could use their domain knowledge, and they could form more coherent, better organized textbases when the texts were well written.

Domain knowledge is still crucially involved in the formation of the situation model, however. When it is absent, the kind of mental representation that is constructed is a different one, even when syntactic help is still available. In this case, syntax alone allows the comprehender to construct an adequate, appropriately structured textbase so that reproductive recall is well supported. However, even though syntactic discourse cues inform the comprehender about what is significant in the text and what is not, they cannot replace the missing domain knowledge which one needs to form an appropriate situation model. The situation model remains ill-structured and undeveloped. It fails, therefore, to support reconstructive recall, leading to the many erroneous elaborations and inferences such comprehenders make.

As we hypothesized in the introduction, there are two ways to comprehend a text – via domain knowledge or in a domain independent way, via the general syntactic signals the language provides. However, comprehension is not the same in the two cases. When a situation model is constructed, we observe deep, or real comprehension, in the sense that the subject not only reproduces the text, but is able to use it further to make inferences. Inferences and elaboration require knowledge. The second, syntax-based path to comprehension, resulting in a textbase without an adequate situation model, is more superficial. It suffices for recall (or even summarization), but correct inferencing is not possible in this case. "Comprehension" is, after all, merely a common-sense term, which needs to be further specified within a theoretical framework for scientific purposes. It is of crucial importance whether comprehension involves the construction of a situation model or merely processes at the level of the textbase.

For this reason, good writing cannot entirely compensate for a comprehender's lack of domain knowledge. It has strong positive effects, just as domain knowledge does, but the effects are not quite the same in the two cases. Good writing helps comprehenders form a coherent textbase which enables them to reproduce the text. But by itself it is not sufficient for the formation of an adequate situation model which is necessary to support reconstructive recall processes, inferencing, and problem solving (Mannes & Kintsch, 1987). Domain knowledge, on the other hand, enables comprehenders both to reproduce the text and to use it constructively. It allows the textbase representation to be embedded in a well elaborated and accurate representation of the situation depicted by the text. This kind of a representation is capable of supporting richer behaviour than a textual representation alone does.

The recognition results indicate a lack of surface memory. The form in which subjects had heard the sentences did not matter; they tended to think that they had been given the well-written version. Knowledge plays no role in this (see also Schneider et al., 1990). The fact that there is little surface memory when subjects read artificial, confusing texts has long been established (e.g., Bransford, Barclay, & Franks, 1972).

Just as there are two ways for readers to comprehend texts, the texts themselves are often specifically written to be primarily understood either via domain knowledge or via explicit linguistic cues. For example, technical science texts rely strongly on the reader's domain knowledge. They guide the reader in modifying an already existing situation knowledge in certain ways; they are formulaic and conventionalized, and readers who do not have the domain knowledge (which includes an important sociological component) simply cannot understand these texts. Popular science texts, on the other hand, are written to allow readers without specialized competence to understand scientific problems through the use of explicit linguistic signals that indicate the cohesive relations in a text, or permit them to be inferred (Myers, 1991).

In the present study we have consistently observed that more skilled readers performed better in recall than less skilled readers. Indeed, skill effects are probably underestimated in this study, since only a very brief test was used to discriminate between high- and low-skill readers. These findings are not surprising; even though general intelligence appears to be unrelated to text recall (Schneider et al., 1990), reading skill, as measured here, clearly is a factor in text recall since it was determined by means of a closely related task – answering comprehension questions after reading a variety of brief texts. What is informative about the skill results in the present study, however, is the absence of interactions of the skill factor with either knowledge or writing quality.

Far from diminishing the importance of domain knowledge in text comprehension, the results reported here allow us to understand its role in the context of other factors, specifically the way texts are written. However, there still is much to be learned about how writing affects text comprehension. We manipulated writing style in a global, indeed crude way – by comparing texts which were as well written as we could make them with texts which were as poorly written as we could make them, while still being English texts. More analytic studies in which the role of particular linguistic constructions are investigated are obviously needed next.

This research was supported by Grant MH 15972 from the National Institute of Mental Health. The paper was written while the second author enjoyed the hospitality of the Max Planck Institut für Psychologische Forschung in Munich.

References

Bransford, J.D., Barcley, J.R., & Franks, J.J. (1972). Sentence memory: A constructive versus interpretive approach. *Cognitive Psychology, 3,* 193-209.

Bransford, J.D., & Johnson, M.K. (1972). Contextual prerequisites for understanding: Some investigations of comprehension and recall. *Journal of Verbal Learning and Verbal Behavior, 11,* 717-726.

Brown, J.L., Bennett, J.M., & Hanna, G. (1981) *The Nelson-Denny reading test.* Chicago: Riverside Publishing Co.

Ericsson, K.A., & Crutcher, R.J. (1989). The nature of exceptional performance. In P.B. Baltes, D.L. Featherman, & R.M. Lerner (Eds.), *Life-span development and behavior.* Hillsdale. NJ: Erlbaum.

Givón, T. (1989). *Mind, code and context: Essays in pragmatics.* Hillsdale, NJ: Erlbaum.

Kintsch, W. (1992). How readers construct situation models for stories: The role of syntactic cues and causal inferences. In A.F. Healy, S.M. Kosslyn, & R.M. Shiffrin (Eds.), *From learning processes to cognitive processes: Essays in honor of William K. Estes.* (pp. 261-278). Hillsdale, NJ: Erlbaum.

Kintsch, W. & Franzke, M. (in press). The role of background knowledge in the recall of a new story. In R. Lorch & E. O'Brien (Eds.). *Sources of coherence in text comprehension.* Hillsdale, NJ: Erlbaum.

Mannes, S.M., & Kintsch, W. (1987). Knowledge organization and text organization. *Cognition and Instruction, 4,* 91-115.

Myers, G. (1991). Lexical cohesion and specialized knowledge in science and popular science texts. *Discourse Processes, 14,* 1-26.

Perfetti, C.A. (1989). There are generalized abilities and one of them is reading. In L. B. Resnick (Ed.), *Knowing, learning, and instruction.* (pp. 307-336).

Hillsdale, NJ: Erlbaum.

Schneider, W., Körkel, J., & Weinert, F.E. (1990). Expert knowledge, general abilities, and text processing. In W. Schneider & F.E. Weinert (Eds.), *Interactions among aptitudes, strategies, and knowledge in cognitive performance.* (pp. 235-251). New York: Springer Verlag.

Sulin, R.A., & Dooling, D.J. (1974). Intrusion of a thematic idea in retention of prose. *Journal of Experimental Psychology, 103*, 255-262.

Trabasso, T., & van den Broek, P. (1985). Causal thinking and the representation of narrative events. *Journal of Memory and Language, 24*, 612-630.

van Dijk, T.A. & Kintsch, W. (1983). *Strategies of discourse comprehension.* New York: Academic Press.

Voss, J.F., Fincher-Kiefer, R.H., Greene, T.R., & Post, T.A. (1986). Individual differences in performance: The contrastive approach to knowledge. In R. J. Sternberg (Ed.), *Advances in the psychology of human intelligence.* (pp. 297-334). Hillsdale, NJ: Erlbaum.

Voss, J.F., Vesonder, G.T., & Spilich, G.J. (1980). Text generation and recall by high-knowledge and low-knowledge individuals. *Journal of Verbal Learning and Verbal Behavior, 19*, 651-667.

Appendix

PROCEDURE PASSAGE – POORLY WRITTEN VERSION

The procedure is actually quite simple. Things are arranged by you into different groups first. Depending upon how much there is to do, it may be that one pile will be sufficient, of course. There are certain preparations which need to be made. If you have to go somewhere else due to lack of the facilities that is the next step. You are pretty well set otherwise. It is important not to overdo things and doing too few is better than too many at once. Using color to separate them is the best thing. In the short run it may not seem important. What can easily arise are complications which can occur if facilities are overloaded. A mistake can be expensive as well because damage might occur to the materials. It will at first seem that the whole procedure is complicated. Soon it will become just another facet of life. It is difficult to foresee an end in the immediate future to the necessity for it. One can never tell. One arranges them into these different groups again after the procedure is completed and they can be put into their appropriate places and eventually they will be used once more but the whole cycle will have to be repeated and in one's lifetime the whole procedure will thus be performed many times.

PROCEDURE PASSAGE – WELL-WRITTEN VERSION

The procedure is actually quite simple.

There are certain preparations which need to be made. First you arrange the materials into different piles. It is best to separate them by color. Of course one pile may be sufficient depending upon how much there is to do. If the facilities you need for the procedure are not available in your home, you have to go somewhere else next.

Otherwise you are pretty well set.

When it comes to the actual procedure, it is important not to overdo things. That is, it is better to do too few materials at once rather than too many. In the short run this may not seem important, but complications can easily arise if the facilities are overloaded. A mistake can be expensive as well because materials might be damaged.

After the procedure is completed one arranges the materials into different piles again. Then they can be put into their appropriate places. Eventually they will be used once more and the whole cycle will have to be repeated.

In one's lifetime, the whole procedure will thus be performed many times. At first it will seem complicated. Soon, however, it will become just another facet of life. It is difficult to foresee an end to the necessity for this task in the immediate future, but then one can never tell.

CAROL HARRIS (HELEN KELLER) PASSAGE – POORLY WRITTEN VERSION

From birth a problem child was what Carol was and Carol Harris was wild and stubborn and Carol was violent. Still unmanageable, Carol turned eight. A private teacher was hired by them for her. The mental health of Carol was something her parents were very concerned about and her parents took action finally. No good institution existed in her state for her problem.

CAROL HARRIS (HELEN KELLER) PASSAGE – WELL-WRITTEN VERSION

Carol Harris was a problem child from birth. She was wild, stubborn, and violent. By the time Carol Harris turned eight, she was still unmanageable. Her parents were very concerned about her mental health. Unfortunately, there was no good institution for her problem in her state. Her parents finally decided to take some action anyway. They hired a private teacher for Carol Harris.

GERALD MARTIN (ADOLF HITLER) PASSAGE – POORLY WRITTEN VERSION

The government in existence was what Martin was striving to undermine to satisfy these political ambitions. His country had a downfall which was his rule's ultimate effect. Taking over was relatively easy because of current problems that were political and the old government had groups remaining loyal to it causing problems. They were silenced by his confronting groups directly and this ruthless dictator who was uncontrollable was what he became. Support was given for his efforts by many people of his country.

GERALD MARTIN (ADOLF HITLER) PASSAGE – WELL-WRITTEN VERSION

Gerald Martin strove to undermine the existing government to satisfy his political ambitions. Many of the people of his country supported his efforts. Furthermore, current political problems also made it relatively easy for Martin to take over. However, certain groups still remained loyal to the old government and hence caused Martin some trouble. So, he confronted these groups directly and thereby silenced them. He became a ruthless, uncontrollable dictator. The ultimate effect of his rule was the downfall of his own country.

12 Effects of Sentence Form on the Construction of Mental Plans from Procedural Discourse

PETER DIXON, KAREN HARRISON, and DEAN TAYLOR
University of Alberta

Abstract   Memory for procedural discourse was examined in two experiments. In Experiment 1, memory was assessed using recall; in Experiment 2, a recognition test was used. In both experiments, the memorability of three types of action statements were compared: a transitive verb form, in which the action was described by a main clause; a verbal adjective form, in which the action was indicated by an adjective derived from a verb; and an implicit action form, in which the action was only implied. Information associated with transitive verbs and verbal adjectives was more likely to be recalled than information associated with implicit actions. Although a manipulation of prior knowledge affected overall recall performance, it did not interact with sentence form. In addition, recognition accuracy was affected by neither sentence form nor prior knowledge. To account for these results, it was proposed that transitive verbs and verbal adjectives generate a semantic representation that includes features of the action, whereas implicit actions do not. This difference in semantic representation leads to structural differences in a mental plan for the task. The obtained effects on recall reflect these differences in plan structure.

Résumé   Deux expériences ont porté sur la mémoire du discours procédural. Nous avons évalué la mémoire à l'aide d'une épreuve de rappel (expérience 1) et d'une épreuve de reconnaissance (expérience 2). Dans les deux expériences, nous avons comparé la mémorabilité de trois genres d'instructions: un énoncé reposant sur un verbe transitif, dans lequel une proposition principale décrit l'action; un énoncé axé sur un adjectif verbal, où l'action est indiquée par un adjectif issu d'un verbe, et un énoncé indiquant implicitement une action. L'information transmise par les verbes transitifs et par les adjectifs verbaux était plus susceptible d'être retenue que l'information reliée aux actions implicites. Bien que la manipulation des connaissances antérieures ait influé sur la performance globale de rappel, il n'y a pas eu d'interaction entre cette manipulation et les énoncés. De plus, ni les énoncés ni les connaissances antérieures n'ont eu d'effets sur l'exactitude de la reconnaissance. Pour rendre compte des résultats, nous croyons que les verbes transitifs et les adjectifs verbaux produisent une représentation sémantique qui comprend des éléments de l'action, alors que les énoncés décrivant une action implicite n'en produisent pas. Cette distinction mène à des différences structurelles du plan mental de la tâche. Les effets obtenus dans le cas du rappel témoignent de ces différences dans la structure du plan.

In recent years, a consensus has emerged among text-processing researchers that at least three kinds of representations are involved in understanding text (e.g., Just & Carpenter, 1987; van Dijk & Kintsch, 1983). The first level of representation provides information about the sequence of words encountered in the text. We refer to this representation as a word-level representation; it might also be described as a surface-level or verbatim representation. We refer to the second level as a semantic representation; it describes to some level of detail the meaning and interrelationship of sentences in the text. We identify this level of representation with the propositional text base of Kintsch (1974; Kintsch & van Dijk, 1978). Finally, a number of researchers have noted that there must also be some type of referential representation (e.g., Johnson-Laird, 1983; Just & Carpenter, 1987; van Dijk & Kintsch, 1983). The defining characteristic of this level of representation is that it is a representation not of the text, but of that to which the text refers. In the present research, we investigated the process of constructing a type of referential representation, mental plans, from procedural discourse. Our results indicate how particular features of the word-level representation determine the characteristics of the semantic representation, which, in turn, affect the organization of information in mental plans.

The initial work on referential representation in discourse processing was concerned primarily with demonstrating the necessity of this type mental representation. Logical arguments for some type of referential representation were made by Johnson-Laird (1983) and van Dijk and Kintsch (1983) among others, and compelling empirical demonstrations of referential representation were provided, for example, by the work of Bransford and his colleagues (e.g., Bransford & Franks, 1972; Bransford & Johnson, 1972). Building on these ideas, further research focussed on the properties of spatial mental models, which can be thought of as referential representations based on spatial descriptions (e.g., Morrow, Greenspan, & Bower, 1987; Morrow, Bower, & Greenspan, 1989; Franklin & Tversky, 1990; Perrig & Kintsch, 1985). This research shows that readers of spatial descriptions can construct a referential representation that is inherently spatial, that supports spatial inferences that go beyond information provided by the text, and that is organized around a particular point of view. However, the notion of referential representation must of necessity be much more general than that of spatial mental models, and relatively little progress has been made at characterizing referential representations and their construction in general.

We suspect that this relative lack of progress reflects the heterogeneity of referential representations; different types of referential representations may be used in different reading situations and by different types of readers. For example, in reading a concrete description of a spatial configuration, readers may construct a spatial mental model of the type discussed by Morrow and others. On the other hand, when reading action-based narrative, one might construct a referential representation consisting of a sequence of events and actions, or perhaps some type of goal-subgoal hierarchy (cf. Mandler, 1984; Schank & Abelson, 1977). It has been argued in earlier work that in the course of processing directions for a task, readers construct a representation of how to carry out the task, that is, a mental plan (e.g., Dixon, 1982, 1987a). Much of this work supports the view that the content and structure of the mental plan is determined by the nature of the task and the reader's knowledge of how to perform similar tasks; it generally is not determined in essential respects by the way in which the task is described. In this sense, a mental plan is a type of referential representation. However, our working assumption is that the process of constructing mental plans is not necessarily the same as that for other types of referential representations.

THE HIERARCHICAL PLANNING FRAMEWORK

Our approach to the construction of mental plans from procedural discourse is the *hierarchical planning framework* described by Dixon (1987a, b). The central assumption in this approach is that mental plans have a hierarchical structure, in which the task is described in general terms at the top of the hierarchy and specified more precisely at lower levels (cf. Miller, Galanter, & Pribraum, 1960; Sacerdoti, 1977). This view is consistent with a variety of evidence. For example, directions are followed more accurately when they are preceded by a high-level description of the task organization (Smith & Goodman, 1984; Dixon, 1987c), directions are read more quickly when the overall goal of the task is encountered first (Dixon, 1987b, c), and manuals are more effective when they are organized hierarchically by functional categories (Dixon & Egan, 1988). These results support the view that high-level, general, or functional information is needed first in constructing mental plans. In our terms, we argue that mental plans are hierarchical structures that are constructed from the top down. That is, the task is first represented at a general, abstract level, and more detailed component steps are added piece by piece.

We hypothesize that the actions in a plan hierarchy are represented by action schemas (Dixon, 1987a). For the present purposes, an action schema can be thought of as a mental structure containing (at least) an action descriptor, a list of component steps, and a result descriptor, as shown in Figure 1, Panel a. The action descriptor refers to long-term memory information about the action; in many cases it may be simply a verbal label

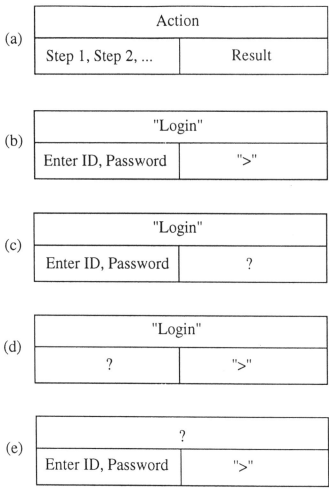

Fig. 1 Structure of schemas in the hierarchical planning framework; see text for explanation.

for the action. The component-step list indicates, in chronological order, other action schemas that must be executed in the course of carrying out the action and generates the embedding hierarchy that marks the organization of mental plans. The result descriptor describes conditions that should be produced by the action; in effect, the result descriptor indicates the intended goal of the action. For example, Panel b in Figure 1 illustrates a schema that might be generated from the direction, "Logging in to the system entails entering your login ID and your password; the system will respond with the prompt '>'." The schema includes a label for the overall action ("login"), a series of component steps to be performed (entering an ID and entering a password), and the result that should ensue (the prompt ">"). Note that the component steps may in themselves be action schemas with their own component steps and results.

Any of the elements of an action schema may be left unspecified. For example, if the direction were simply, "Logging in to the system entails entering your login ID and your password," the schema might be instantiated without any particular result, such as the schema illustrated in Panel c. Alternatively, a schema may have no component steps. For example, the schema illustrated in Panel d might result from the direction, "After logging in, the system will respond with the prompt '>'." A special case is an action schema that has no action descriptor. Such a schema might serve to group a number of component steps together to form an (unlabelled) subprocedure or to indicate that some unspecified action is needed to produce a given result. For example, the direction "To start with, enter your login ID and your password; the system will respond with the prompt '>'" might result in the schema illustrated in Panel e.

According to the hierarchical planning framework, readers must evaluate how each piece of information encountered in the text fits with their evolving plan representation and incorporate it accordingly. For example, when an action is encountered in the text, a new action schema generally will be instantiated and added to the plan at an appropriate level. Similarly, when new condition information is encountered, the action schema that produces that condition must be found in the plan and elaborated to reflect the new information. However, the process of incorporating condition information in the mental plan must also allow for the possibility that the action that produces the condition may not be present in the representation. Under such circumstances, the reader may need to infer an appropriate action schema and add it to the mental plan first. For example, consider the direction, "Insert your bank card with the magnetic stripe down." The phrase "with the magnetic stripe down" describes a condition that results from some unspecified action, presumably grasping the card and orienting it in a particular manner. In other words, the phrase suggests that there is an unmentioned step, "Grasp the card so that the stripe faces down," that one must carry out. Thus, in formulating a mental plan based on this direction, the user must instantiate an action schema for grasping the card, add the orientation information as a result descriptor in the new schema, and then add the schema to the mental plan. In this way, adding information to the mental plan may require the creation of steps in the plan that are not explicitly mentioned in the text.

The hierarchical planning framework we have outlined admits a wide range of plan organizations for any given task. The organization adopted in a particular situation is likely to depend on the idiosyncrasies of the task, the way in which actions are described, and the knowledge and experience of the user. The aim of the present experiments was to investigate how the features of the text and the prior knowledge of the reader interact to determine the structure and content of mental plans.

EFFECTS OF SENTENCE FORM

Dixon, Faries, and Gabrys (1988) proposed that the distinction between implicit and explicit actions in the text provides an important cue for how to incorporate information in mental plans. In one experiment, explicit action statements in recipes were recalled more often than the same information provided implicitly. For example, "Wrap in wax paper and refrigerate 1 hour" lead to better recall than an instruction to "Refrigerate in wax paper 1 hour." The step of wrapping in wax paper is implied by the latter description, but it was more likely to be omitted from recall of the procedure than if it were described explicitly. Dixon et al. hypothesized that this effect was mediated by the organization of mental plans, and that explicit actions were represented higher in the mental plan hierarchy than implicit actions. In turn, the difference in memorability occurred because information near the top of the hierarchy was more likely to be recalled than information lower in the hierarchy (cf. Meyer, 1975; Kintsch, Kozminsky, Streby, McKoon, & Keenan, 1975). The hypothesis developed in this article is that the difference in hierarchical structure is due to the semantic information implied by explicit and implicit actions and the way in which this information is used during the process of constructing mental plans.

In the present experiments, we investigated this effect of sentence form more carefully. Explicit actions in the earlier experiments were generally transitive verbs, but implicit actions were conveyed in a variety of different ways. Some implicit actions described the position or state that resulted from an action (e.g., "in wax paper" in the previous example), other implicit actions used adjectives derived from action verbs (e.g., "1 cup grated cheddar cheese" instead of "grate 1 cup of cheddar cheese"), while still other implicit actions used nouns derived from action verbs (e.g., "arrange the dough slices" instead of "slice the dough and arrange"). In addition, the relationship of the implicit action to the following and preceding steps in the recipe varied considerably across the materials in the experiment. Consequently, it is difficult to ascertain which features of the text produced the obtained effect on recall.

In order to delineate precisely those sentence forms that led to more better recall, we began by selecting a procedural domain, scuba diving, with which our subjects were unlikely to have had much direct experience. We then devised three types of action descriptions that could be closely replicated in a range of different scuba diving procedures. The first type of action description was a transitive verb. Target actions in this condition typically consisted of a verb of movement or spatial arrangement, such as "position," "centre," or "hold," followed by a prepositional phrase indicating the spatial arrangement or configuration more precisely. For example, a direction might be stated as, "Centre the tank in front of you." The second type of description used a "with" prepositional-phrase containing an adjective derived from the transitive verb. For example, "Centre the tank in front of you" would become "With the tank centred in front of you...". We refer to this as a verbal adjective form. Finally, in an implicit action description, the verbal element was dropped altogether, leaving just the embedded prepositional phrase to carry the information, as in "With the tank in front of you...". This relationship among the three types of descriptions held across all of the items used in the experiment.

These three types of action descriptions vary in terms of the information provided about the action and its surrounding circumstances. The transitive verb form is the most specific. For example, a direction such "Place the tank in front of you" explicitly identifies the agent of the action (*you*), the precise manner of the action (the tank should be *placed*), and the intended goal of the action (the tank should be *in front of you*). The verbal adjective form of this direction, "With the tank placed in front of you...", is similar except that the agent of the action is unspecified; although it seems likely that the reader is responsible for positioning the tank, it is at least conceivable given this form that some other agent is involved (e.g., your diving buddy or an instructor). Finally, the implicit action form is the least specific with respect to the nature of the action. Although the phrase "With the tank in front of you..." may invite the inference that some form of movement or positioning is necessary to get the tank to its desired configuration, it leaves the nature of this action open. For example, the tank could be dragged, dropped, or rolled instead of placed.

Based on the results of Dixon et al. (1988), we anticipated that the transitive verb form of the direction would be recalled best; this form corresponds closely to the explicit actions used in the previous research. Similarly, sentence forms such as "With the tank in front of you" should be recalled poorly because the action is not mentioned at all but is entirely implicit. However, the previous results do not provide clear expectations regarding verbal adjectives. On one hand, the required action is precisely specified by the verbal form "placed," and this might be sufficient to make it accessible during later recall. On the other hand, there is no surface-level verb in phrases such as these and the agent of the action is left unspecified by the syntax. If the essential feature of explicit actions is that the reader is explicitly marked as the agent, recall of these descriptions may be poor. Thus, recall of verbal adjectives may provide crucial evidence about the nature of the textual cues that determine mental plan organization and later recall.

EFFECTS OF PRIOR KNOWLEDGE

We also investigated effects of domain knowledge on the process of constructing mental plans. Dixon et al. (1988) found that effects of sentence form were not obtained among readers with extensive prior knowledge of the domain. It was argued that domain experts did not need to use textual cues to organize their mental plan because they could use their prior knowledge of the content of the procedure to organize their plan appropriately. In other words, sentence-form cues to plan organization were used only when readers had insufficient knowledge to devise a mental plan organization on their own. This result fits with other research indicating that the nature of referential representations is strongly dependent on the knowledge and experience of the reader. For example, the work of Bransford and Johnson (1972) indicates that prior information concerning the spatial layout of a situation dramatically changes the structure and sense of the representation. The work of Voss (e.g., Voss, Vesonder, & Spilich, 1980) indicates that extensive domain knowledge improves the quality and structure of the referential representation of narratives. We view this type of work as supporting the general position that the construction of a referential representation depends on the reader's knowledge and background.

Despite these results, the specific nature of the prior knowledge that determines plan organization remains an open question. Because the high-knowledge subjects in Dixon et al. (1988) were simply selected from the population of readers, it is difficult to tell what aspect of their knowledge or experience was related to their recall performance. For example, high-knowledge subjects may have been able to retrieve procedures from memory that were similar to the target task, they may have been more adept at reasoning about the task goals and subgoals, they may have been better able to understand the meaning or effect of particular actions, or they simply may have been more motivated to think carefully about the procedure. In the present experiment, we attempted to find more precise information about the effect of prior knowledge by experimentally manipulating readers' domain knowledge rather than simply sampling subjects with different levels of experience.

Our manipulation of prior knowledge was intended to provide subjects with some background concerning the principles and mechanisms that underlie the procedures used in scuba diving. The logic was that such knowledge might allow the subjects to reason about the steps in the procedure and to decide which of the steps were crucial and which were less important. In turn, this assessment would allow subjects to organize their mental plan in an appropriate manner, irrespective of the cues in the text. Most of the information in the background material was attuned to particular procedures that would be used in the memory task. For example, one of the procedures (shown in Table 1) concerned the process of attaching the regulator to the tank; thus, background material was provided about the components and operation of regulators and tanks and their relationship to one another. An uninformed control group was given background material about scuba diving that was deemed to be unrelated to the procedures being tested.

In sum, the present research examined memory for procedural steps described with transitive verbs, verbal adjectives, and implicit actions. Two groups of subjects were examined: an informed group who were given prior exposure to the domain of the procedures, and an uninformed group who were given no such prior exposure. In Experiment 1, subjects' recall of the manipulated target actions was assessed. The entire design was replicated in Experiment 2 using a recognition test.

Experiment 1
METHOD
Materials

The materials for this experiment were drawn from common procedures used in scuba diving. Five test procedures were constructed, containing on average 21 discrete steps run together in paragraph format. The average length of the procedures was 304 words. Each procedure contained six target actions that could be described equally well with transitive verbs, verbal adjectives, or implicit actions. An example is shown in Table 1. Prior to reading these procedures, subjects studied one of two background readings of about 4700 words. The informed group were given material containing a discussion of the theory and operation of various pieces of scuba diving equipment used in the test procedures, as well as a description of principles that motivated aspects of the procedures. Substantive information about the content of the procedures was carefully omitted from this material; an excerpt is shown in Table 2. The uninformed group was given material describing scuba diving instruction, scuba diving as a recreational sport, and equipment unrelated to the test procedures.

Conditions

Each subject in the informed and uninformed groups read the five test procedures and then recalled them. Within each procedure, two of the six of the target actions were stated as transitive verbs, two were described using verbal adjective, and two were described implicitly. Thus, there were a total of 30 target actions consisting of 10 transitive verbs, 10 verbal adjective, and 10 implicit actions. The assignment of target actions to sentence form was done randomly for each subject. This procedure intentionally confounded variance due to subjects with variance due to materials and allowed one to generalize to both populations simultaneously.

Procedure

The experiment consisted of five phases. During the first phase, subjects studied the background material they were given. In this phase, subjects were first were asked to read the material; then they were given ten study questions

TABLE 1
Example of Test Procedure and Target Actions[1]

ASSEMBLING the TANK and REGULATOR

Attaching the first stage of the regulator to the tank is a critical operation since these two apparatus together are what allow you to breathe underwater. Spread the buoyancy compensator (B.C.) on the ground with the backpack facing up at you. *Centre the tank on the backpack and /With the tank centred on the backpack, / With the tank on the backpack,* fasten the tank band securely around the tank. Lifting the backpack by the handle at the top, give it a gentle shake to see if the strap is tight enough and refasten if necessary. Then, *position the tank upright in front of you and / with the tank positioned upright in front of you, / with the tank upright in front of you,* momentarily open the tank valve to blow out any dust or moisture which may have accumulated. Check the 'o'-ring in the valve as well – if it is nicked or broken, replace it. *Hold the first stage of the regulator in your right hand and / With the first stage of the regulator held in your right hand, / With the first stage of the regulator in your right hand,* put the yoke over the tank valve. *Tighten the regulator yoke screw finger tight and / With the regulator yoke screw tightened finger tight, / With the regulator yoke screw finger tight,* check the exhaust valve by attempting to inhale through the regulator. If you cannot inhale, the valve is functioning properly. *Turn the valve knob to the open position, / With the valve knob turned to the open position, / With the valve knob in the open position,* hold the pressure gauge down and away from your face (in case it ruptures) and listen carefully for leaks. If you hear one, turn the valve off and locate the source of the leak. Press the purge valve, *place the mouthpiece in your mouth and / and with the mouthpiece placed in your mouth, / and with the mouthpiece in your mouth,* inhale and exhale to make sure it is working. If the exhaust is stuck shut, place the second stage in water for a few moments, then blow hard into the mouthpiece. Now that you have assembled the regulator to the tank, you are ready to put the tank and B.C. assembly on for a dive.

---

[1] In this table, the transitive verb, verbal adjective, and implicit action forms of the target actions are printed in italics separated by slashes. The actual versions given to subjects contained only one form of each target action printed in normal text.

and were asked to reread the material, underlining the answers to the questions. The five test procedures were read during the second phase. Each procedure was printed on a separate page with a descriptive title. Subjects were asked to read each procedure and then rate it on how long the procedure would take, how much training it would require, how physically taxing the procedure was likely to be, and how difficult it would be to perform from memory. The intent of this rating task was to encourage subjects to think about the procedures as if they were going to perform them (cf. Dixon, 1987a). The order of the procedures was randomly chosen for each subject. The third phase consisted of a retention interval. During this phase, subjects were tested on their knowledge of the background material. The background test consisted of twenty multiple choice questions, half of which were taken from the informative material and half of which were taken from the uninformative material. The difference in performance on the two halves of the test was expected to be related to the type of material each subject

TABLE 2
Excerpt from Informative Background Reading

The two-stage regulator is a finely adjusted, precise piece of equipment designed for reliability and durability. It is made up of a hose with two ends. On one end is the regulator yoke which attaches to the tank valve and allows air to pass through the "first stage". The first stage adjusts air to a close to breathable pressure level, which then travels down the hose to the actual regulating device. This "second stage" device controls for the air demanded by the diver. It is a circular rubber and metal contraption (the mouthpiece) that the diver both breathes from and exhales into. The inside edges fit in the space between the gums and mouth. The first time it is tried, it feels very odd, but with experience, it becomes barely noticeable. On the side of the mouthpiece, opposite the part that goes in the mouth, is a purge valve. When this is pressed, the force of the air from the tank will expel any water that might have entered it if, for example, the regulator was taken out of the mouth while underwater.

---

studied. This phase took 7.5 m on average. The fourth phase of the experiment consisted of a recall test for the procedures. Subjects were given five pages on which the titles of the test procedures were printed and were asked to try to recall as much of the procedures as they could. The order of recall for each subject matched the order in which the procedures were originally encountered. During the final phase, subjects completed a short questionnaire designed to assess their prior exposure to scuba diving.

Subjects were run in groups ranging from 4 to 18. All of the materials were presented to subjects in a notebook, and subjects moved through the five phases at their own pace. The time needed to accomplish each portion of the experiment was measured by asking subjects to record in their booklet at specific points the elapsed time in centiminutes showing on a large digital clock. The entire task took approximately 60 to 90 minutes.

Subjects
Subjects were students recruited through undergraduate psychology classes at the University of Alberta.

Analysis
Recall protocols were scored independently by two judges for the presence of each of the target actions; disagreements were resolved by consultation. The judges were blind to the form of the initial presentation. Recall of a target action was scored as correct as long as it included a clear reference to the result or goal of the target action; an explicit mention of the action itself was not required. Generally, the result of the action was specified by the same embedded prepositional phrase in all three sentence forms. For example, the transitive verb form, "Place the tank in front of you," was changed to "With the tank placed in front of you..." in the verbal adjective form and to "With the tank in front of you..." in the implicit action form. Recall was scored as correct as long as the tank was described as in front.

TABLE 3
Proportion Recall (and Standard Errors) for Target Actions in Experiment 1

Background Reading Group	Sentence Form		
	Transitive Verb	Verbal Adjective	Implicit Action
Informative	.154 (.018)	.126 (.029)	.095 (.022)
Uninformative	.067 (.019)	.078 (.022)	.033 (.013)

Recall of the target actions was quite low overall (less than 10%) and varied considerably over the 30 target actions. That is, some actions were recalled by a large number of people regardless of condition, while other actions were recalled by no one. In order to correct for this variability, the average effect of the identity of target actions was partialled from the recall scores statistically prior to further analyses.

RESULTS

As shown in Table 3, there was an overall effect of type of action (F (2,76) = 4.30, MS_e = 0.006, $p < .05$); a priori contrasts indicated that the verbal forms (i.e., transitive verbs and verbal adjectives) produced significantly better recall than the implicit target actions (F (1, 76) = 8.38, $p < .05$, MS_e = 0.006). There was no difference between transitive verbs and verbal adjectives (F (1,76) < 1, MS_e = 0.006). However, there was no statistical evidence of an interaction between the effect of action type and background reading (F (2,76) < 1, MS_e = 0.006). In fact, the difference between recall of verbal forms and implicit actions was significant for both the informed group (F (1,40) = 4.06, MS_e = 0.007, $p < .06$) and the uninformed group (F (1,36) = 4.73, MS_e = 0.004, $p < .05$). Background reading did, however, affect overall recall performance; on average, the informed group recalled more than twice as much as the uninformed group (.125 vs. .059; F (1,38) = 7.72, $p < .01$, MS_e = 0.017).

Although the present manipulation of background knowledge failed to interact with sentence form, there was some indication that real expertise in scuba diving would have produced the pattern of results observed by Dixon et al. Although none of the subjects in our sample reported substantial experience in scuba diving, seven of our subjects reported some exposure to scuba diving procedures (e.g., an hour-long high school course). These subjects showed virtually no effect of action type (F (2,12) < 1, MS_e = 0.008), while subjects who reported no experience whatsoever showed strong effects (F (2, 64) = 6.06, MS_e = 0.005, $p < .005$; see Table 4). This pattern suggests that a more systematic sampling of scuba diving experience would have replicated the interaction with expertise obtained previously.

A further analysis was conducted to verify that subjects learned from the background material they were given. The two groups of subjects were tested

TABLE 4
Proportion Recall (and Standard Errors) for Target Actions in Experiment 1 as a
Function of Prior Experience

	Sentence Form		
Prior Experience	Transitive Verb	Verbal Adjective	Implicit Action
Some Experience	.158 (.047)	.137 (.058)	.156 (.039)
No Experience	.100 (.015)	.094 (.019)	.044 (.013)

on questions derived from both the informative and uninformative background materials; their performance is presented in Table 5. If subjects learned from the materials they were given, their performance should be better with those questions that were specific to the materials they read. An analysis of variance confirmed this expectation (78% vs. 47%; $F (1, 38) = 79.32$, $MS_e = 241.6$, $p < .001$). In addition, performance by the uninformed group was somewhat better overall than that by the informed group (66% vs. 58%; $F (1, 38) = 6.76$, $MS_e = 187.0$, $p < .05$). This effect may have occurred because the two background readings were not entirely independent; subjects in the uninformed group may have learned some information that was helpful in the answering the questions designed for the informative background material.

On average, it took subjects 11.9 m to read and evaluate the procedures; there was no difference between the informed and uninformed groups. In contrast, the informed group took 16.0 m to complete the recall test, while the uninformed group took 11.5 m ($t(37) = 2.88$, $p < .01$). Presumably, the informed group took longer to complete the test because they had more information to recall.

DISCUSSION

The major result from Experiment 1 was that verbal adjectives produced recall that was similar to that produced by transitive verbs, and that both produced better recall than implicit actions. This result replicates the effect of sentence form obtained by Dixon et al. (1988), and further indicates that it is the verbal component of the action that provides the crucial cue for plan organization. As described above, the verbal forms differ from the implicit action forms in that they contain specific information about the manner in which the action should be performed. We hypothesize that this difference in specificity is reflected in the semantic representation constructed for these sentence forms, and that the more specific action representation arising from the verbal forms is incorporated higher in the mental plan hierarchy than the representations generated from implicit actions. In turn, this difference in hierarchical height leads to the obtained differences in recall performance. A concrete proposal for how this process might work is described in the General Discussion.

The effects of sentence form found in the present study is particularly striking given that the manipulation left the critical target information

TABLE 5
Proportion Correct (and Standard Errors) on Background Reading
Tests in Experiment 1

| | Background Reading Group | |
Type of Test	Informative	Uninformative
Informative	.762 (.035)	.532 (.041)
Uninformative	.400 (.027)	.790 (.027)

untouched. For example, consider the three forms, "Place the tank in front of you," "With the tank placed in front of you...", and "With the tank in front of you..." This target action was scored as correctly recalled whenever subjects indicated that the tank was to be in front, regardless of whether they indicated how the tank came to occupy that position. This was precisely the information that was common to all three forms of the description. In other words, the lack of a verbal component in the implicit action form caused some other part of the sentence – the embedded prepositional phrase – to be recalled less often. In one sense, it would not be surprising if our results showed simply that implicit actions were unlikely to be recalled; they were, after all, only implicit in the text. However, our results go beyond such a finding and show that the circumstances surrounding an implicit action are unlikely to be recalled as well. To be precise, we have found that the results of implicit actions are less likely to be recalled than the results of actions conveyed by verbal forms, even though the results themselves are equally explicit in all cases.

The similar levels of recall for transitive verbs and verbal adjectives suggests that the type of syntactic constituent used to convey an action is of little importance. A priori, one might have hypothesized that an important cue to an action's importance is the use of a full clause to describe the action; actions described with adjective or adverb phrases might be interpreted as less important. However, the results for the verbal adjective forms provide a strong argument against this view. The target action in these sentences were recalled as well as those from the transitive verb forms, even though the information about the action was embedded in a prepositional phrase. On the assumption that recall performance reflects the structure of the mental plan, the present results suggest that the nature of the syntactic constituent has little effect on plan organization (cf. Dixon, 1987a).

Experiment 1 also suggests that familiarity with the principles and mechanisms involved in a procedure has little bearing on the effects of sentence form. Specifically, both the informed and the uninformed subjects relied on the sentence form equally in organizing their mental plans. A different type of knowledge might have been more effective in reducing subjects' reliance on textual cues. Although relevant to the test procedures, the information we provided subjects in the informed condition was relatively abstract, and its relationship to the circumstances and contingencies involved in carrying out the procedures was not spelled out. A variety of research suggests that people often have difficulty in applying abstract principles if they are not given specific practice at doing so (Anderson, Farrell, & Sauers, 1984; Gick & Holyoak, 1980; LeFevre & Dixon, 1986). Thus, it is perhaps not surprising that subjects failed to apply their abstract knowledge in the present context. An alternative manipulation that might have worked better may have been to provide concrete and specific experience with the equipment and procedures involved in scuba diving. Such information might help subjects visualize the contingencies and interrelationships among steps that would allow one to select an appropriate plan organization. In this regard, it is suggestive that the few subjects with a small amount of concrete experience with scuba diving were unaffected by sentence form.

Another explanation of the failure to find an interaction with prior knowledge is that our informed subjects simply did not learn enough from the material they were given. Although this possibility cannot be discounted entirely, several aspects of the data suggest it is not the whole story. First, the results of the background reading exam indicated that the informed group did indeed know more about the principles and mechanisms involved in scuba diving than the uninformed group. Second, there were substantial effects of background reading on overall recall, as might be expected based on other studies of expertise and text processing (e.g., Voss et al., 1980). Finally, there was no evidence that subjects who learned more from the background material showed less of an effect of explicit actions: The correlation between the size of the sentence form effect and the score on the background reading exam was small and not significant ($r = .08$). Thus, we suspect that the failure to find the anticipated interaction was due to the use of an inappropriate type of background knowledge; we doubt that more extensive knowledge similar to that provided here would have changed the pattern of results.

Experiment 2

In Experiment 2, we replicated the design and manipulations used in Experiment 1, but tested memory with a recognition test rather than a recall test. This manipulation may provide more precise information about how sentence form affects the process of constructing mental plans. Broadly speaking, the poor recall of implicit actions could have two different kinds of causes. On one hand, information concerning implicit actions may simply be left out of the mental plan. If this were the case, poor recognition of these actions may be found as well as poor recall. On the other hand, implicit actions may be included in the mental plan, but marked as minor or unimportant. For example, Dixon et al. (1988) argued that implicit actions were represented lower in the plan hierarchy than explicit actions. In this case, it is possible that the recognition of different sentence forms could be quite similar. For example, a correct recognition response might be produced if the recognition probe matches an action found anywhere in the mental plan. On this reasoning, the recognition test may provide evidence about how information conveyed by implicit actions is incorporated in mental plans.

METHOD

The method was generally identical to that described in Experiment 1. The only difference was the substitution of a recognition test for the recall test used in Experiment 1. A recognition test was constructed for each procedure from paraphrases of the six target actions together with six distracter actions that plausibly could have been included in the procedures. All of the actions were described using transitive verbs (although not the verbs found in the original test procedures). Subjects marked each of the action statements as either new or old. Performance was analyzed in terms of a′, a nonparametric measure of sensitivity that incorporates both hit and false alarm rates (Pollack & Norman, 1964); a′ can be interpreted as the proportion correct that would result were a two-alternative forced-choice task to be used.

RESULTS

In contrast to the recall results, recognition performance did not vary as a function of sentence form (F (2,74) < 1, MS_e = 0.004; see Table 6). If anything, performance was slightly better with implicit actions than with transitive verbs, a trend that is opposite what was observed in Experiment 1. As might be expected, recognition performance was slightly better in the informed group. However, this tendency did not approach significance (F (1,37) < 1, MS_e = 0.025).

As in Experiment 1, we tested whether subjects acquired information from the informative and uninformative background reading. Subjects performed better with the questions appropriate to their reading than with the other questions (80% vs. 50%; F (1,35) = 81.65, MS_e = 221.4, $p < .001$). As before, the uninformed grouped performed somewhat better overall (71% vs. 60%; F (1,35) = 8.58, MS_e = 256.6, $p < .01$). These data are shown in Table 7.

On average, subjects took 12.1 m to read and evaluate the procedures; there was no difference between the informed and uninformed groups. There was a tendency for informed subjects to take longer to complete the recognition test, but this difference was not statistically significant (10.2 vs. 8.8 m; $t(36) = 1.87$, $p < .10$).

DISCUSSION

The results of Experiment 2 stand in clear contrast to those obtained in Experiment 1 and to the results from the earlier studies of the recall of directions. Previously, we had found that actions described with verbal forms were more likely to be recalled as part of the procedure than actions that were

TABLE 6
Recognition a' (and Standard Errors) in Experiment 2

Background Reading Group	Sentence Form		
	Transitive Verb	Verbal Adjective	Implicit Action
Informative	.847 (.018)	.838 (.020)	.856 (.025)
Uninformative	.821 (.028)	.839 (.023)	.828 (.025)

only implicit in the text. However, the recognition results obtained here suggest little distinction among sentence forms; transitive verbs, verbal adjectives, and implicit actions were recognized equally well. This result suggests that recall and recognition are differentially sensitive to aspects of the mental plan representation. Specifically, we assume that in producing a recall protocol, subjects intentionally concentrate on the major steps of the procedure (i.e., the top levels of the mental plan hierarchy) and omit less important details even when it might be possible to retrieve information about them. Thus, on the view that verbal forms are likely to be incorporated near the top of the hierarchy, these actions are likely to be recalled. In contrast, implicit actions may be assigned to lower levels of the plan and consequently are relatively less likely to be produced during recall. Recognition, on the other hand, may be a sensitive measure of the content of mental plans, regardless of where that information lies within the representation. In particular, subjects may recognize an action as belonging to a procedure even if the action were represented as an unimportant detail.

An alternative account of the results of Experiments 1 and 2 might be based on the idea that implicit actions are unlikely to be included in the mental plan, and that recognition taps other levels of representation in addition to mental plans. For example, a step may be recognized correctly if information pertaining to it can be found in the semantic representation of the text. The present results then would imply simply that information from all three sentence forms is equally available in the semantic representation and that information pertaining to implicit actions is relatively unlikely to be available in the mental plan. On this view, similar recognition of verbal sentence forms and implicit actions might obtain, even though implicit actions were not included in the mental plan.

Two arguments might be raised against this account. First, even if recognition does not depend exclusively on the mental plan representation, the mental plan is likely to be used to some extent. Thus, one might expect to see at least some decrement for implicit actions if they were not included in the mental plan: Verbal forms could be recognized if they were found in either the mental plan or the semantic representation, while implicit actions could only be recognized from the semantic representation. The second argument concerns the representation of implicit actions in the semantic representation.

TABLE 7
Proportion Correct on Background Reading Tests in Experiment 2

Type of Test	Background Reading Group	
	Informative	Uninformative
Informative	.761 (.041)	.560 (.034)
Uninformative	.433 (.032)	.850 (.034)

The semantic representation of an implicit action cannot include information about the manner in which an action is to be performed because such information was never presented. Thus, the representation of these actions should not match the representation of the corresponding recognition probes as well as transitive verbs or verbal adjectives. By this reasoning, one might expect implicit actions to be recognized less well even if only the semantic representation of the text were consulted. Although these arguments are not definitive, they lead us to prefer the view that all of the target actions are equally likely to be included in one's mental plan regardless of sentence form, but that only the top levels of the mental plan are likely to be retrieved during recall. A model of plan construction incorporating this view is described in the General Discussion.

Regardless of which account is correct, the results of Experiment 2 make it clear that the effect of sentence form lies in the structure of mental plans rather than in the initial decoding of the text. For example, it might be hypothesized that verbal forms are more likely to be recalled because implicit actions are simply not noticed when the text is read initially. According to this view, the effect of sentence form would have little to do with the mental representation of procedures, but would be due to some more general feature of the language comprehension process. However, this view would also predict that implicit actions would be omitted from the semantic representation as well as the mental plan, and consequently should be poorly recognized. The failure to find such an effect suggests that all three types of action statements used in this study are decoded and parsed equally well, and that the subsequent recall effects are due to the organization and content of the mental plan.

General Discussion

The central result of the present research is that actions conveyed with transitive verbs and verbal adjectives are more likely to be recalled than actions conveyed implicitly. According to our view of the comprehension process, three different kinds of representations intervene between the text and recall performance: the word-level representation, the semantic representation, and the mental plan representation. Consequently, an adequate account of how features of the text determine recall must specify how each level of representation is affected by properties of other levels at each stage of processing. The following sketch of mental plan construction is offered in order to illustrate how the difference between specifying an action with a verbal form and specifying it implicitly might affect the three levels of representation and lead to the pattern of effects obtained here. We hasten to add that the present results do not provide unique support for the details of this particular view; a variety of quite different accounts may also be possible. However, we regard this proposal as a tentative step towards a detailed and explicit model of the process of understanding procedural discourse.

THE WORD-LEVEL AND SEMANTIC REPRESENTATIONS

We assume that the word-level representation generally is constructed on a word-by-word basis (e.g., Just & Carpenter, 1980), and produces a representation of the identity of each of the words in the text and the sequence in which they appear. The information in this representation is parsed and used to construct a semantic representation. A formal treatment of the nature and content of the semantic representation is beyond the scope of this paper; however, we assume that it can be thought of as a collection of predicates describing relationships among entities encountered in the text. We distinguish two broad classes of predicates that might be found in this representation: *transitional* predicates describe how entities or relations change during the task, while *relational* predicates refer to states or conditions that ensue in the course of the procedure. This distinction between types of predicates in the semantic representation underlies our ability to account for the present results.

Crucially, information conveyed by transitive verbs and verbal adjectives would be represented by transitional predicates, while information conveyed by implicit actions would be represented by relational predicates. Whatever formal definition is used for transitional predicates, it is clear that the label should apply to the transitive verb forms used in the present research. These sentences always describe how some action on the part of the user changes the configuration or conditions that exist in the task. Although it is perhaps more debatable, we claim that information conveyed by verbal adjectives is also represented as transitional predicates. Although verbal adjective forms do not describe the action with a main verb, the wording seems to require some description of a change in order to capture the full sense of the meaning. Finally, we claim that implicit adjectives are represented as relational predicates. The argument here is that the semantic representation seldom contains information that is neither immediately implied by the words in the sentence nor required for coherent interpretation (Singer, 1988). Thus, the semantic representation of implicit actions would not describe a change or action because the sentence contains no reference to change or action. The result is that the semantic representation would describe the implicit action forms simply in terms of the condition or state indicated by the embedded prepositional phrase.

Support for this difference in semantic representation can be found in the types of adverbial modifiers that can be added to these forms. Both verbal forms allow the addition of modifiers that describe the action more precisely, but implicit actions do not. For example, the transitive verb form, "Place the tank in front of you," can be changed to "Place the tank carefully in front of you," and the verbal adjective form, "With the tank placed in front of you...", can be changed to "With the tank placed carefully in front of you.... However, it is ungrammatical to change the implicit action form, "With the tank in front of you..., to "With the tank carefully in front of you.... It seems unparsimonious to account for this difference simply in terms of the syntactic structure. For example, all three forms admit superficially similar modifiers that specify the *result* of the action more precisely. For example, one can say "Place the tank directly in front of you," "With the tank placed directly in front of you..., and "With the tank directly in front of you.... Our interpretation is that the semantic representation of all three forms express the result of the action; thus, it is appropriate to add more details to this result. On the other hand, the semantic representation of only transitive verbs and verbal adjectives express the action itself; the semantic representation of implicit actions does not. As a consequence, there is no predicate in the semantic representation that can be elaborated to encompass the meaning of a word like "carefully." In sum, it seems reasonable to suppose that the verbal forms used here are represented as transitional predicates while the implicit action forms are represented as relational predicates.

CONSTRUCTING MENTAL PLANS

The first step in incorporating information in the mental plan is to identify the action schemas that need to be added. We assume that at the conclusion of each clause in the text, the semantic representation is searched for transitional predicates that describe actions by the user. In conjunction with prior knowledge from long-term memory, these predicates are used to select and instantiate new schemas to be appended to the mental plan. After these schemas have been added, the semantic representation is searched for relational predicates that should be incorporated in the plan, typically as result descriptors in existing action schemas. The assumption that information from transitional predicates is added first seems reasonable given that the mental plan is designed to indicate what the user is supposed to do in the course of carrying out the task, and is of necessity focussed on actions. However, the effect of this assumption is to dictate that the information from implicit actions (which we argue is represented by relational predicates) will be incorporated in the mental only after actions from the balance of the clause have been processed.

Although transitional predicates are the main source of actions to be added to the plan, action schemas are sometimes generated on the basis of relational predicates. If the information conveyed by such a predicate clearly belongs in the plan, and if it does not make sense as a result of an action that is already in the plan, a new schema will be generated and added to the plan with the relevant information. The implicit actions in the present research typically would be treated in this way: Although implicit actions are likely to be interpreted as relevant to the task, they are generally inappropriate as a description of the result of some action mentioned elsewhere in the text. For example, in the direction, "With the tank on the backpack, fasten the tank band securely around the tank," the phrase "on the backpack" clearly describes information that belongs in the mental plan, but just as clearly the phrase does not describe the result of fastening the tank band. The solution is to construct a schema that indicates that some unspecified action produces the result of having the tank on the backpack. This new schema can then be added to the plan so that the information about the location of the tank is not lost. The net result is that implicit actions will generally produce action schemas in the mental plan, but that these schemas will be added later than the schemas generated from transitional predicates. As elaborated below, this difference in timing can have an effect on the structure of the resulting mental plan.

The crucial issue in adding information to a mental plan is where in the action hierarchy to add a new schema. We assume that by default readers will attempt to build downwards from existing nodes in the action hierarchy. This assumption is motivated by a variety of empirical results indicating that directions are easier to understand when high-level information is encountered prior to lower-level information (e.g., Dixon, 1987a, c). In the present context, the assumption means that subjects will first attempt to add the new action as a component step of the most recently added action schema. Adding the schema at this level would mean interpreting the new action as an elaboration or component of the last mentioned step. If that position in the hierarchy is inappropriate for the new schema, we assume that readers will move to the embedding schema at the next level up, and try adding the new step as a component there; in effect, this would mean interpreting the new action as the next step in sequence, following from the action schema just added. Finally, if the action does not fit as the next step in sequence, they would add the step at a higher level, in effect creating a new subprocedure or subtask. In sum, the assumption that new action schemas are appended to the lowest branch possible means that readers will focus on the last step previously added to the plan and first attempt to interpret the new action as a component of the step added earlier. If that fails, readers will attempt to interpret the new action as the next step in sequence. Finally, if that fails as well, the new action will be interpreted as a new subprocedure in the task.

EFFECTS OF SENTENCE FORM

These assumptions concerning the way in which mental plans are constructed produce different plan organizations for the sentence forms used in the present research. When an action is specified by a transitive verb or a verbal adjective, the corresponding action schema generally will be represented in the plan at the same hierarchical level as the action that follows in the procedure. For example, consider the direction, "Centre the tank on the backpack and fasten the tank band securely around the tank." The semantic representation of this sentence will contain two transitional predicates, one corresponding to "centre" and one corresponding to "fasten". Both will generate action schemas that will be added to the plan as component steps in the more general process of attaching the regulator to the tank. If the direction uses the verbal adjective form, "With the tank centered on the backpack, fasten the tank band securely around the tank," a similar semantic representation would result. In particular, the representation would include a transitional predicate corresponding to "centred". Consequently, the "centre" action and the "fasten" action again would be represented at the same hierarchical level.

The situation changes with the implicit action forms because there is no transitional predicate corresponding to the implied action. Although we assume an action schema usually will be inferred, it will be added to the mental plan only after the actions from the balance of the sentence have been included. This means that readers will first attempt to add the new action as a component step subordinate to the action that follows in the sentence. For example, the semantic representation of the implicit action form, "With the tank on the backpack, fasten the tank band securely around the tank" would contain one transitional predicate ("fasten") as well as a relational predicate corresponding to "on the backpack." By hypothesis, readers first will add the action schema for "fasten" to the plan. Subsequently, the reader will generate an action schema for the inferred action of positioning the tank on the backpack and attempt to add it to the lowest level of the action hierarchy. In this case, the new "position" schema would be incorporated as a component step that needs to carried out in the course of the "fasten" action. Roughly speaking, getting the tank on the backpack becomes a minor precondition to fastening the strap instead of a separate step in its own right. Consequently, the operation of positioning the tank is represented one level lower in the hierarchy than it would be were it expressed as a transitive verb or verbal adjective.

We hypothesize that this difference in hierarchical height produces the effects of recall observed in Experiment 1, as well as the failure to find those effects in the recognition task of Experiment 2. The crucial assumption is that during recall, subjects tend to produce just the top few levels of the action hierarchy, even if some information from other levels is available to them. In a sense, subjects generate a recall protocol by finding the information in the plan that is the most important or general. This might serve to provide the intended audience with a general overview of the task. Depending on number of actions produced in the recall protocol and the depth and breadth of the mental plan hierarchy, a difference of a single level in the hierarchy could have a substantial impact on recall probability. For example, if the fan at each level of the hierarchy were approximately three on average and the top twenty actions in the hierarchy were typically recalled, actions at the third level in the hierarchy would almost always be recalled, actions at the fourth level of the hierarchy would sometimes be recalled, and actions at the fifth level would almost never be recalled. By this logic, a difference of one level in the hierarchy could easily produce the modest-sized recall differences observed between implicit actions and transitive verbs in Experiment 1. Recognition performance, on the other hand, is likely to be determined primarily by factors other than hierarchical height. For example, information that is distinctive or unexpected might be easier to distinguish from the recognition foils. In any event, effects of height in the action hierarchy would not occur because no explicit search of the plan representation is needed to decide on a response. In other words, only recall shows effects of sentence form because only recall depends directly on the organization of the mental plan.

EFFECTS OF PRIOR KNOWLEDGE

The predicted interaction between prior knowledge and sentence form was not obtained in the present experiments, yet a clear interaction between expertise and sentence form was observed by Dixon et al. (1988). In order to understand this difference in outcomes, it is necessary to consider in some detail how prior knowledge might be used in understanding written direction. In the present approach, we can identify three possible loci for the interaction between knowledge and form. One locus is the construction of the semantic representation. If users know from previous experience that a particular condition or relationship is tightly linked with a particular action, a transitional predicate might be used to describe the relation even though no verbal form occurs in the text. According to the present analysis, this would lead implicit actions to be represented at the same level as transitive verbs and verbal adjectives, and no difference in recall would be expected.

A second locus for interactions with prior knowledge lies in the process of evaluating action schemas while constructing mental plans. We assume that there is some process by which readers can decide whether a schema is appropriate at a given level, and this process is likely to depend heavily on prior knowledge. For example, readers need to be able to evaluate whether an action makes sense as a component step, as a step following in sequence, or as a description of a more general subprocedure. Presumably, the knowledge that is used in this evaluation can overrule the default tendency to add new schemas at the lowest possible level of the plan. Thus, potentially, the right kind of background information could negate any inclination to represent implicit actions at a subordinate level.

Finally, a third locus of prior knowledge lies in the nature of the action schemas used in the mental plan. If a user has little knowledge of the domain, each action schema to be added must be generated afresh and filled with relevant information garnered from the text. However, if a user knows a great deal about the domain, he or she may have a variety of action schemas stored in long-term memory that are similar to the procedure being described (e.g., LeFevre, 1987). Consequently, the process of constructing a mental plan may consist mostly of locating a relevant action schema learned from previous experience and modifying it to perform the task at hand. Under some circumstances, most of the transitional predicates found in the semantic representation may simply be matched against actions that are already present in the retrieved action schema, and few new action schemas would need to be generated. Effects of sentence form on the organization of the mental plan in this case would be minimal because most of the plan's structure would be determined by information in long-term memory.

The manipulation of prior knowledge used in the present research was intended to affect the second locus, the evaluation of action schemas. Our reasoning was that some knowledge of the mechanisms and principles involved in the domain might serve subjects in deciding when an action should be interpreted as subordinate component step, and that this knowledge might overrule the tendencies based on sentence form and semantic representation. The failure to find any interaction between the prior knowledge manipulation and the effect of sentence form suggests either that readers typically do not use abstract knowledge in evaluating action schemas, or that the tendencies based on sentence form were difficult to override in this instance.

Dixon et al. (1988) found that sentence form only affected recall performance of novices, and no effects of sentence form were found with domain experts. It is possible that this effect of expertise was produced at the third locus, the structure of action schemas. The procedural discourse in this case consisted of recipes, and the experts were students who were relatively experienced cooks. Our intuition is that many recipes fall into well-known categories with stereotyped structures. Thus, an expert cook may be able to retrieve an overall schema for any given recipe that would include many of the actions and steps described in the text. In this context, the expert's task is to simply modify the default procedure to suit the particular recipe being read. Such a process is unlikely to be affected by sentence form.

Concluding Comments

In sum, the present results provide a crucial constraint on the process of constructing mental plans from procedural discourse: Information conveyed with implicit actions is less likely to be recalled than information conveyed by verbal forms. We have suggested that this effect of sentence form arises because information from the semantic representation is ordered with respect to type of predicate, and that new actions typically are added to mental plans at the lowest possible level. Related principles may underlie the construction of other types of referential representations. For example, the organization of spatial mental models may depend on the order in which spatial predicates are encountered in the semantic representation and the principles that determine how information is added to spatial mental models. We anticipate that an accurate account of how procedural discourse is understood will advance our understanding of the process of constructing referential representations generally.

This research was supported by a Natural Sciences and Engineering Research Council of Canada grant to the first author. The authors wish to thank Robert Gordon for help in running subjects and scoring data. Correspondence should be sent to Peter Dixon, Department of Psychology, University of Alberta, Edmonton, Alberta, Canada T6G 2E9, or via electronic mail to Pete_Dixon@bsp4.psych.ualberta.ca

References

Anderson, J.R., Farrell, R., & Sauers, R. (1984). Learning to program in LISP. *Cognitive Science, 8*, 87-129.

Bransford, J.D., & Franks, J.J. (1972). The abstraction of linguistic ideas. *Cognitive Psychology, 2*, 331-350.

Bransford, J.D., & Johnson, M.K. (1972). Contextual prerequisites for understanding: Some investigations of comprehension and recall. *Journal of Verbal Learning and Verbal Behavior, 11*, 717-726.

van Dijk, T.A., & Kintsch, W. (1983). *Strategies of discourse comprehension*. New York: Academic.

Dixon, P. (1982). Plans and written directions for complex tasks. *Journal of Verbal Learning and Verbal Behavior, 21*, 70-84.

Dixon, P. (1987a). The structure of mental plans for following directions. *Journal of Experimental Psychology: Learning, Memory, and Cognition, 13*, 18-26.

Dixon, P. (1987b). Actions and procedural directions. In R.S. Tomlin (Ed.), *Coherence and grounding in discourse* (pp. 70-89). Amsterdam: Benjamins.

Dixon, P. (1987c). The processing of organization and component step information in written directions. *Journal of Memory and Language, 26*, 24-35.

Dixon, P., & Egan, D.E. (November, 1988). *Structural and conditional information in directions for computer systems*. Paper presented at the Psychonomic Society Meeting, Chicago.

Dixon, P., Faries, J., & Gabrys, G. (1988). The role of explicit action statements in understanding and using written directions. *Journal of Memory and Language, 27*, 649-667.

Franklin, N., & Tversky, B. (1990). Searching imagined environments. *Journal of Experimental Psychology: General, 119*, 63-76.

Gick, M.L., & Holyoak, K.J. (1980). Schema induction and analogical transfer.

Cognitive Psychology, 15, 1-38.

Johnson-Laird, P.N. (1983). Mental Models. Cambridge, MA: Harvard University Press.

Just, M.A., & Carpenter, P.A. (1987). *The psychology of reading and language comprehension.* Boston: Allyn and Bacon.

Just, M.D., & Carpenter, P.A. (1980). A theory of reading: From eye fixations to comprehension. *Psychological Review, 87*, 329-354.

Kintsch, W. (1974). *The representation of meaning in memory.* Erlbaum: Hillsdale, NJ.

Kintsch, W., & van Dijk, T.A. (1978). Toward a model of text comprehension and production. *Psychological Review, 85*, 363-394.

Kintsch, W., Kozminsky, E., Streby, W.J., McKoon, G., & Keenan, J. M. (1975). Comprehension and recall of text as a function of content variables. *Journal of Verbal Learning and Verbal Behavior, 14*, 196-214.

LeFevre, J.A. (1987). Processing instructional texts and examples. *Canadian Journal of Psychology, 41*, 351-364.

LeFevre, J.A., & Dixon, P. (1986). Do written instructions need examples? *Cognition and Instruction, 3*, 1-30.

Mandler, J.M. (1984). *Stories, scripts, and scenes: Aspects of schema theory.* Hillsdale, NJ: Erlbaum.

Meyer, B.J.F. (1975). *The organization of information in prose and its effects on memory.* Amsterdam: North-Holland.

Miller, G.A., Galanter, E., & Pribraum, K.H. (1960). *Plans and the structure of behavior.* New York: Henry Holt.

Morrow, D.G., Bower, G.H., & Greenspan, S.L. (1989). Updating situation models during narrative comprehension. *Journal of Memory and Language, 28*, 292-312.

Morrow, D.G., Greenspan, S.L., & Bower, G.H. (1987). Accessibility and situation models in narrative comprehension. *Journal of Memory and Language, 26*, 165-187.

Perrig, W., & Kintsch, W. (1985). Propositional and situational representation of text. *Journal of Memory and Language, 24*, 503-518.

Pollack, I., & Norman, D.A. (1964). A nonparametric analysis of recognition experiments. *Psychonomic Science, 1*, 125-126.

Sacerdoti, E.D. (1977). *A structure for plans and behavior.* New York: Elsevier North-Holland.

Schank, R.C., & Abelson, R. (1977). *Scripts, plans, goals, and understanding.* Hillsdale, NJ: Erlbaum.

Singer, M. (1988). Inferences in reading comprehension. In M. Daneman, T. Waller, & G. MacKinnon (Eds.), *Reading research: Advances in theory and practice*, Vol. VI. New York: Academic.

Smith, E.E., & Goodman, L. (1984). Understanding instructions: The role of explanatory material. *Cognition and Instruction, 1*, 359-396.

Voss, J.F., Vesonder, G.T., & Spilich, G.J. (1980). Text generation and recall by high-knowledge and low-knowledge individuals. *Journal of Verbal Learning and Verbal Behavior, 19*, 651-667.

13 Transfer of Fluency Across Repetitions and Across Texts

BETTY ANN LEVY, LAUREN BARNES, and
LISA MARTIN *McMaster University*

Abstract   Three experiments examined transfer of reading fluency across repeated readings of the same text and across related but different texts. In Experiment 1, we demonstrated that a paraphrase that altered the syntactic structure of sentences, but not the lexical identity of main concepts or the unfolding of the message, was reprocessed as an unchanged repetition. However, when the paraphrase altered the lexical identity of main concepts, even though the message unfolded in the same manner, there was a loss in the repetition benefit. In Experiments 2 and 3, we demonstrated that there is transfer from a representation of one text to the reading of a second text only if the messages are continuous, not if the passages simply share a large number of overlapping words. The experiments are discussed in terms of the influence of 'episodic' text representations on reading fluency.

Résumé   Trois expériences ont porté sur le transfert de la facilité de lecture au cours de lectures répétées d'un même texte et de textes connexes mais différents. Dans l'expérience 1, nous avons démontré qu'une paraphrase modifiant la structure syntaxique de la phrase, mais non pas l'identité lexicale des principaux concepts ou la formulation du message, était traitée de nouveau comme une répétition inchangée. Par contre, quand la paraphrase modifiait l'identité lexicale des principaux concepts, même si le message était formulé de la même façon, la répétition perdait de son utilité. Dans les expériences 2 et 3, nous avons démontré qu'il y a transfert de la représentation d'un premier texte à la lecture d'un second seulement si les messages sont continus; il n'y a pas de transfert si les textes ont simplement en commun bon nombre de mots. Il est question de l'influence des représentations de textes «épisodiques» sur la facilité de lecture.

The experiments to be described examined transfer of reading fluency across rereadings of the same text and across readings of different texts. Transfer across readings provides a model of how experience influences the development of reading fluency. What is left in memory following the reading of one text that allows a subsequent text to be read more fluently? By fluently, we mean that the text is read more rapidly, *but with comprehension*, as a function of the prior reading experience. To ensure that reading was focused on meaning, subjects were not only instructed to read for meaning but this instruction was reinforced by the use of some form of comprehension testing following reading. This meaning focus reflects our interest in understanding the representations formed during 'real' reading for the purpose of understanding a message. Our main interests were, a) in the representation that remains in memory after reading a text that facilitates reprocessing of that *same* text on subsequent encounters, and b) in whether a text representation in memory can be used to more fluently process a subsequent text that *differs* from the first. We used variations between the two texts to determine the characteristics that must be shared by the memorial representation and the subsequent passage before transfer of reading fluency will be observed.

In Experiment 1, we explored characteristics that must be shared for the second text to be processed as a *repetition* of the first text. In Experiments 2 and 3, we examined conditions that might produce transfer *across* texts. The notion we will develop is that in both cases the memorial representation is of the text 'episode' and transfer depends on the ability of the second text to recruit that episodic representation. To do that, there must be message overlap. There is now a considerable literature studying transfer, for skilled adult readers, across repeated readings of the same text, but there is a dearth of evidence on transfer across different texts, except for studies of children with reading problems. We will first discuss the text repetition effects and present Experiment 1 before we discuss the across-text research with children and the final two experiments.

The study of text repetition effects stems from Kolers' seminal work on reading skill for transformed typographies. Kolers (1975) asked subjects to read aloud sentences typed in normal or in inverted typography. They then reread those sentences in the inverted typography. Kolers found that rereading was faster when the prior reading had been in the inverted rather than the normal typescript. He argued that the improved skill in processing the 'strange' graphemic arrays indicated that representations of these unusual visual patterns existed in memory and could be used to facilitate rereading. The surprising point at that time was that visual characteristics of words read in text influenced reprocessing over intervals of up to a year (Kolers, 1976). Kolers and his colleagues went on to argue that the skill in rereading transformed typographies was related to the formation of pattern recognition processes for combinations of letters. Changes between readings, in the spacing of letters or in the typefont, were sufficient to decrease the reprocessing effect (Kolers & Magee, 1978; Kolers, Palef, & Stelmach, 1980). The important point was that the surface characteristics played a long-term role in determining reading fluency.

Although there has been considerable controversy about the explanation of the transformed typography effect (see Levy, 1993, for a recent review), Kolers' use of transfer as a way to explore text representations has been well received. He also demonstrated the power of reading and rereading times as implicit measures of memorial representations. Like other implicit memory measures, reading times reflect effects of prior experience when the subject's attention is directed to the current reading event, with no explicit reference to the prior experience. Thus the measures reflect a more 'automatic' influence of a prior experience during current processing. When rereading is faster than original reading, one can infer that representations from the earlier experience are being recruited and used to facilitate reading of the current passage. The debate lies in the *nature* of the representation that mediates the rereading fluency. Within the text processing domain, two major positions have been articulated. In both cases, the research has focused on the reprocessing of texts typed in normal, rather than transformed, typographies. The issue is the representation following 'normal' reading, unencumbered by strategies used to deal with unusual visual configurations.

One position suggests that rereading fluency results from the use of 'primed' abstract word representations. Carr, Brown, and Charalambous (1989) had subjects read aloud short paragraphs that were either coherent or were 'word salads' produced by scrambling the paragraph's words. They then reread either the coherent or the scrambled form. Carr et al. found that rereading was faster than original reading for both the coherent and scrambled forms, indicating that the first reading had made a usable 'impression' on memory that could be recruited to aid in subsequent reading. Importantly, there was no *differential* benefit in rereading when the form of the passage read on the two occasions matched rather than mismatched. That is, rereading the coherent text was facilitated as much by a prior reading of just the words of the text as by a prior reading of the text itself. Similarly, rereading of the 'word salad' was benefited equally from a prior reading of the scrambled words or of the coherent text. Based on this insensitivity to semantic context, Carr et al. concluded that transfer was mediated by individual word representations. Further, because transfer in this task also proved to be insensitive to changes in visual configuration (typescript versus handwriting), Carr et al. concluded that the word representations were abstract linguistic units that did not maintain characteristics of the individual presentations. Thus, by this view, rereading transfer is mediated by *abstract word* representations.

A different position was offered by Levy and Kirsner (1989). They too examined transfer at the single word and text levels, but in a different manner. They first asked subjects to process either single words or those words embedded in texts. This was followed by a perceptual identification test, where subjects identified words flashed rapidly on a computer scope. Half of these perceptual identification items were 'old' words that had been previously processed in the word or text task. Levy and Kirsner also varied the typescript and modality between the two tasks. The words in the perceptual identification task were always typed in a 'standard' font. However, during the original task the 'old' words may have been read in the 'standard' font, in a dissimilar font, or they may have been presented auditorily. These font and modality manipulations were varied orthogonally with the context in which the words were first processed (word array or text). The 'old' words were better recognized than the 'new' words in the perceptual identification task, but only if they had first been processed in the word array. If they had first been read or heard in a text, there was *no* benefit to reprocessing those words in the perceptual identification task. The word to word repetition benefit was larger for words that were read, rather than heard, during the first task, indicating that visual processes were involved in mediating the reprocessing benefit. However, this word reprocessing effect appeared to be lost when the words were originally processed in a text context (see also MacLeod, 1989; Oliphant, 1983).

These results were inconsistent with the Carr et al. suggestion that rereading effects were mediated by abstract single word units. This explanation did not handle the modality effect for word to word transfer, nor did it address the disappearance of word to word transfer when the words were first read in a text. In two subsequent experiments, Levy and Kirsner offered a solution. They used the same texts as in their first experiment, but the second task was rereading those texts, rather than the perceptual identification of words taken from the texts. The script and modality variations between the first and second tasks were also used. Rereading was faster than original reading, indicating that a memorial representation was used to aid in reprocessing the text. Importantly, the modality specificity found for word to word transfer was also found for text reading to rereading transfer. This modality specificity suggested that text reprocessing maintains specific data-driven information about each reading experience. Levy and Kirsner argued that in text processing, the memorial representation is a holistic record of that processing episode. The modality effect suggests that perceptual information is part of the record. However, the failure to see facilitation in perceptual identification in Experiment 1 suggests that the perceptual information cannot be recruited unless the entire representation is 'called up' by the second processing task. We argued that individual words do not recruit text representations, not because those words are not represented in the episode, but because the words are contextually bound in an episodic representation of the text. They are not abstract, independent units.

In a series of subsequent studies, we explored further the boundary conditions of episodic text representations, as these are reflected in rereading transfer measures. Levy and Burns (1990) reported three experiments that varied the similarity of the versions read on two readings of texts. Of importance here are comparisons where the subjects always read a normal, well-structured text on the *second* reading. This reading could be preceded by reading that same text, that text with the paragraphs re-ordered, that text with the sentences scrambled, or that text with the words scrambled into a 'word salad'. The *first* reading passage systematically loses more of the text and linguistic structure over these four conditions. When the paragraphs are re-ordered the text's macro-structure is lost; with sentence scrambling all idea development is disrupted; finally, with word scrambling all linguistic information is lost. If rereading transfer is mediated by abstract single word representations, then there should be no difference in transfer for the four conditions, because the word units are processed in all cases. However, if text and linguistic structure are 'boundary' conditions in determining when the new event will be processed as a repetition of the first occurrence, then a loss in transfer should occur across the conditions. Levy and Burns found no loss in transfer when the paragraphs were re-ordered, but there was some, but not complete loss, when the sentences were re-ordered. These findings suggested that the texts must have a similar unfolding of semantic propositions to be viewed as the same event. There was complete loss of transfer when the 'word salad' was read as the first text. Thus, unlike Carr et al. (1989), Levy and Burns found no transfer at the single word level when those words were not reprocessed in their original context.

Carr and Brown (1990) and Carlson, Alejano, and Carr (1991) suggested that the difference in results found by Carr et al. (1989) and Levy and Burns (1990) was due to the 'focus of attention' during reading. The Carr et al. subjects were reading aloud and perhaps with a more word-by-word focus, while the Levy and Burns subjects were told to read for meaning even when the text was scrambled. Carlson et al. asked readers either to read texts word by word with sanctions against relating any two words, or to read them for meaning. The former orientation produced transfer at the single word level, like that found in the Carr et al. study, whereas the orientation to meaning produced the Levy and Burns 'episodic' transfer. Although this may explain the discrepancy, Levy, Masson, and Zoubeck (1991) were unable to produce the word-level transfer when subjects focused on the print while reading to detect Greek letters randomly distributed across the page. Thus the focus that produces abstract word-level transfer must be toward *no* relational processing while reading, not just a data-driven focus to analyze the print carefully (see Levy, 1993, for a more detailed review). A data-driven focus to text reading produces text-specific transfer, but no abstract word transfer. Levy et al. (1991) argued that when the fluent reader is engaged in *normal* text processing then the reprocessing advantage is mediated by 'episodic' text representations that act as holistic records of the text processing event. Although different task orientations may change the absolute reading rates, we know of no evidence that task requirements alter the *nature* of the repetition effects, as long as the passage is processed as discourse and not as unrelated words.

Experiment 1 attempted to explore another aspect of text similarity to determine its importance in mediating transfer of fluency across repetitions. We know from earlier studies that even subtle disruptions of meaning can cause loss of reprocessing fluency (Levy & Burns, 1990; Levy, Di Persio, & Hollingshead, 1992). The question addressed here was whether reprocessing fluency would be disrupted if the text's ideas unfolded in a consistent fashion for the two text versions, but the linguistic medium that expressed the ideas was altered across readings. In Experiment 1, we explored transfer across *paraphrases* of a text, when the paraphrases varied syntactic structure but altered few content words, versus when the paraphrase expressed the same ideas in as many new words as possible. The contrast, then, explores the role of syntactic structure and lexical identity in rereading transfer.

Experiments 1a and 1b

Experiments 1a and 1b were identical in design; subjects read each of five passages twice in succession, as rapidly and accurately as possible. Following each reading, they wrote a brief summary of the main ideas of the passage. The summarization requirement was to ensure that readers focused on the text's meaning, while still reading as rapidly as possible. The important data were the reading times on the first versus second readings of a text. This comparison indicates the transfer of reading fluency across reading encounters.

In both experiments, the versions of a passage read on the two encounters were either identical or different. When they were different, the second text was a sentence-by-sentence paraphrase of the first text. Experiments 1a and 1b differed only in how the paraphrases were created. In Experiment 1a, the paraphrases were created by changing the syntactic structure of each sentence in a passage, but making as *few* word substitutions as possible. If the 'episodic' representation is limited by the syntactic structure used to express the ideas, then rereading transfer should suffer if syntactically different, rather than identical, versions are read on the two encounters. In Experiment 1b, the paraphrases were created by rewriting each sentence using as *many* new words as possible, while still expressing the same ideas. Although these paraphrases also contained some syntactic changes, their main contrast with the paraphrases used in Experiment 1a was in the wording alterations. If lexical identity is a defining characteristic of episodic representations, then transfer across rereadings should suffer when the main ideas are expressed with different rather the same words across the two readings. In both experiments, then, the paraphrased versions maintained the sentence-by-sentence unfolding of the text's message, but in Experiment 1a mainly syntactic structure varied, while in Experiment 1b the passage wording was also substantially changed. Our interest was in how similar two texts must be to be processed as repetitions of the same 'text episode'. Experiment 1a queried the role of syntactic structure in defining a text repetition; Experiment 1b examined the importance of maintaining the lexical identity of main concepts across the reading encounters.

METHOD

Subjects

Thirty different undergraduate volunteers, from an introductory psychology class at McMaster University, participated in each of Experiments 1a and 1b. All were native English speakers under the age of 35. They received course credit for their participation.

Materials and design

The experiments used five 525-word passages that were originally used by Levy and Kirsner (1989). Each passage discussed a social problem: drug abuse, overpopulation, overweight children, pollution, and famine in Ethiopia. Each text was typed on two pages, with 10 paragraphs per text. These ten paragraphs conformed to a particular text structure; the first two paragraphs introduced the problem, followed by two paragraphs each on its causes, its effects, possible solutions and then some conclusions. For each original passage (A versions), two paraphrases were written. For the syntactic paraphrases (B versions), the syntactic structure of each sentence in the original passages was changed, with a minimal number of word changes, particularly content word changes. The final texts were 525 words in length. Thus the syntactic paraphrases were sentence-by-sentence paraphrases that maintained meaning and most of the wording, but where the syntactic structure of each sentence was changed. For the lexical paraphrases (C versions), each sentence of the A versions was rewritten to express the same idea but using as many different words as possible. Each text was again 525 words in length. These paraphrases had little overlap in surface form with the original passages, but they conveyed the same messages. Appendix A contains the first two paragraphs of the passage on drug abuse, in the A (original), B (syntactic), and C (lexical) versions.

In Experiment 1a, subjects read two passages with identical versions on the two encounters (AA, BB), two with different versions on each encounter (AB, BA), and one passage (A for half subjects, B for the other half) was read only once at the end of the experiment. This *new* passage was used to assess the amount of general practice benefit that accrued over the experimental session. In Experiment 1b, the identical repetitions were AA and CC, the different repetitions were AC and CA, and the *new* passage was A for half the subjects, and C for the remainder. In both experiments, the five conditions (2 identical, 2 different, and new) were tested equally often using each of the 5 passages, across subjects. This counterbalancing ensured that there were no differences in materials for the critical comparisons. The order of encountering identical and different repetition conditions was also counterbalanced across subjects, but the new passage was always read last.

Procedure

Subjects were tested individually in sessions lasting approximately two hours, with short breaks between passages as required. They were first given written instructions indicating that they were to read each passage as rapidly and accurately as possible, while attending to the message to summarize the main ideas after each reading. The instructions stressed that each passage was to be read only once, silently, and with no backtracking. A short practice passage, one page in length, was given to familiarize subjects with the procedure. A trial began with a passage placed face-down in front of subjects. The experimenter started a stop watch when subjects turned over the pages in front of them, and stopped the watch when they turned the pages face-down again. After each reading, a lined page was provided for writing summaries. Each experimental passage was read twice in succession, following this procedure.

RESULTS
Experiment 1a

Table 1 shows the mean reading times for the first and second readings in all conditions. For *first* readings, t-test comparisons indicated that there were no differences among any of the four conditions. Similarly, for *second* readings, t-test contrasts among the repetition conditions indicated that transfer was equivalent in all conditions. However, there was significant transfer from the prior experience. Comparisons of the first reading times for all conditions combined, with the mean of AA and BB on the second reading, indicated that identical texts were *reread* faster, $t(29) = 7.81$, $p < .001$. Similarly, this comparison of first reading times, with the mean of AB and BA on the second encounter, indicated that rereading was faster than original reading, even when the versions differed on the two encounters, $t(29) = 10.36$, $p < .001$. Thus reading fluency improved across encounters, but this benefit was insensitive to differences in the syntactic structure of sentences in the text. This finding suggests that the memorial representation that mediates rereading fluency either does not encode, or does not use, information about syntactic structure.

One final point to note is that the benefit observed for repeated readings cannot be explained by any general practice benefits accrued across the experimental session. Reading time for the *new* condition, that was always tested last in the experiment, did not differ from the original reading time ($t < 1.0$). However, the *new* condition was slower than both the identical repetitions (AA + BB) and the different repetitions (AB + BA), $ts(29) = 7.04$, 8.25, respectively, $ps < .001$. Thus rereading fluency was quite specific to the

TABLE 1
Mean Reading Times (in seconds) and Standard Deviations for Experiment 1a.

	Conditions	AA	BB	AB	BA	New
First Reading	M	151.47	157.21	152.71	156.11	
	SD	35.42	34.31	38.89	40.10	
Second Reading	M	122.97	128.56	128.49	123.41	156.43
	SD	30.73	35.41	34.65	32.48	37.63

practiced texts, suggesting that the representation that mediated the practice effect was episodic in nature.

Experiment 1b

Results of Experiment 1a, indicating insensitivity to syntactic differences between repeated texts, can be contrasted with those of Experiment 1b where the paraphrases altered lexical identity of main concepts. Table 2 shows the first and second reading times for these conditions. T-test comparisons of *first* reading times again indicated that there were no reliable differences among conditions. Comparison of *second* readings for the two identical repetition conditions (AA, CC) indicated that they were equivalent. Consequently a mean for identical repetitions was taken. This was contrasted with second reading times for each of the different conditions (AC, CA). Both comparisons indicated that the different versions were reread more slowly than the identical versions, $ts(29) = 2.84$, 2.17, $ps < .01$, $.04$, respectively. Thus a change in wording, even when the message was unchanged, led to a loss in the reprocessing benefit. However, all repetition conditions showed significant transfer. Comparisons of the first reading time (mean of all conditions) with the second reading times for identical repetitions (AA + CC), for AC, and for CA, all indicated that rereading was faster than original reading, $ts(29) = 6.64$, 4.27, 3.77, respectively, $ps < .001$. Thus compared with the identical repetitions, there was a loss in reprocessing facilitation when wording was altered between encounters, but even then there was significant benefit from the prior reading.

This transfer observed for repetitions was specific to the repeated texts, and was not a general practice benefit. Reading time for the *new* passage, at the end of the experiment, did not differ from the original reading time. It was reliably slower than identical repetitions, $t(29) = 4.31$, $p < .001$, and than AC and CA repetitions, $ts(29) = 2.52$, 3.63, $ps < .02$, $.001$, respectively. Thus, the transfer benefit for repetitions was specific to the practiced reading episodes.

Taking Experiments 1a and 1b together, it is clear that use of prior text representations to aid in rereading is sensitive to some text properties, but not to others. Evidence reported here indicates that variations in the syntactic structure of sentences that maintain meaning and lexical identity of main concepts do not affect the magnitude of the reprocessing benefit. However,

TABLE 2
Mean Reading Times (in seconds) and Standard Deviations for Experiment 1b.

	Conditions	AA	CC	AC	CA	New
First Reading	M	144.65	147.92	146.43	152.63	
	SD	33.48	33.45	38.60	37.39	
Second Reading	M	123.33	124.87	132.22	133.51	149.09
	SD	31.19	33.53	38.84	34.29	35.36

rewording of the ideas leads to some, but not a complete, loss in rereading transfer. Levy and Burns (1990) found no loss in rereading transfer when paragraphs were re-ordered, but some loss when sentence order was scrambled, and complete loss when wording was scrambled on the first reading. Recruitment or use of the text representation during rereading appears to be related to the similarity between texts read on the two encounters.

While both data-driven and conceptually-driven processes are involved in the fluent reprocessing of texts, they appear to be of differential importance. If the variations between repetitions are 'signal' based, such as differences in typescript, modality, or wording, then there is some, but not complete, loss of the reprocessing benefit (Levy, Di Persio, & Hollingshead, 1992; Levy & Kirsner, 1989; Experiment 1b). This suggests that the representation that mediates the fluency gains is sensitive to 'signal' variations and is slowed down when this occurs. Higher-order variations in the macrostructure of the text (caused by reordering paragraphs) did not influence reprocessing for the type of texts we have studied. This level of processing may be critical when processing more causally connected texts, such as fairy tales, but for the expository texts we have studied macrostructure did not influence reprocessing fluency (Levy et al., 1990). However, processes connecting ideas within a paragraph are important, because scrambling sentences within a paragraph led to some, but not complete, loss in fluency (Levy et al., 1990). The organization of ideas seems to be critical here, not the linguistic structures that express these ideas, because changes in syntactic structure that allow the ideas to unfold in the same sequence (Experiment 1a) did not affect the reprocessing gains.

It is message similarity, however, that appears to be of prime importance. If even small variations in meaning occur in the rereading text, reprocessing benefits essentially disappear (Levy & Begin, 1984; Levy et al., 1992). Further, there is *on-line* sensitivity to semantic discrepancies in familiar texts, in that rereading time losses are centered at the point when the discrepancy is encountered during reading (Levy et al., 1992). Thus, rereading fluency is 'driven' by representations that encode and rely on a range of text attributes. Although meaning consistency is critical to maintaining the reprocessing fluency, even signal variations influence the magnitude of the gains observed across experiences. Transfer across rereadings provides a good picture of text characteristics that 'define' the limits of a repetition. All of the experiments described above examined repetitions with no lag between readings. Future studies with spaced repetitions across longer time intervals may indicate that the 'signal' effects of episodic representations are less durable than the semantic ones, but Kolers' (1976) work with typescript variations suggests that even early signal analyses may have long-lasting effects.

Experiment 2

Experiment 1, combined with earlier studies, indicates that only limited variations in a text will be accepted as a repetition of the prior event. Thus, transfer of reading fluency gained across repetitions appears to be fairly narrow. However, the scope of transfer from a text representation may be broader if one examines transfer, not to variations of the *same* text, but rather to new related texts. Here the prior episode may facilitate integration of a new message with the prior message, rather than being reprocessed as a repetition. That is, the prior context sets up a representation that will accept and aid the processing of subsequent messages. In the next two studies, we questioned the dimensions of similarity that would support transfer across different texts.

The only studies on across-text transfer have focused on the use of repeated readings as a remedial treatment for children with reading problems. We know of no repetition studies with adult readers that focused on across-text transfer, so our studies have been guided by the developmental research. Dahl (1979) selected poor readers in second grade for training with the repeated readings method. Children were asked to read a short passage repeatedly, until a criterion speed of 100 wpm was reached. After that the child selected another passage to read repeatedly to criterion, and this procedure continued in 20-minute daily sessions. After 8 months of training, Dahl found that trained readers outperformed control subjects, given 'regular' reading instruction, on a number of rapid word identification tasks and on a cloze test of comprehension. She argued that, " Repeated readings training provides the missing practice necessary for early development of fluent reading. Using repeated practice in meaningful context gives the child the opportunity to integrate the subskills" (p. 62). Her conclusion that the training effect was related to integration of subskills during text reading stemmed from a failure to see any benefits for a separate group of children who received 8 months of training on rapid single word identification. She reasoned that text reading must do more than 'automate' single word decoding skills to produce the training benefit.

Samuels (1979) made similar claims for poor readers. He reported a decrease in reading errors and an increase in reading speed with repeated readings. He also found across-text transfer of training, in that the first reading of later training texts was faster than the first reading of texts read early in training. Further, it took fewer readings to reach criterion speed as training advanced, suggesting some generalized training gains. Because the consecutive texts were not selected according to any relational criteria, it is impossible to assess the basis of transfer across texts. Samuels appears to credit the improvement to 'automating' word recognition skills, thus freeing attention for higher-order processing.

An interesting alternative stems from studies of 'talking books' and of paired aural reading. Prior or simultaneous listening to the story also aids in later reading of that story (eg. Carbo, 1978; Chomsky, 1978; Morgan & Lyons, 1979). Clearly, the listening effect cannot be related to development of visual decoding skills, although it might aid in developing sight vocabulary. However, auditory familiarity may aid in 'adding' speech-based information to printed text. For example, benefits to sentence parsing and prosodic reading may result from a prior reading or from hearing the print correctly parsed into meaningful phrases. Herman (1985) trained 8 elementary school children with poor reading skills, over a 3 month period, using the repeated readings technique. She found improvements in speed and accuracy both across repetitions of the same text and across texts. Later texts were read faster and more accurately than earlier texts, on the initial readings. Thus, like Samuels, Herman found a generalized benefit due to extensive rereading practice. However, Herman also measured the number of pauses made while reading. She took pausing to be an indication of reading disruption. While pausing decreased across repetitions of the *same* story, there was no decrease in pausing *across* texts. This failure to see generalization of improved pausing led Herman to conclude that the generalized skill across texts was mediated by improved single word recognition, not by improved semantic parsing.

Rashotte and Torgeson (1985) also argued that rereading benefits across texts were mediated at the single word level. They tested 12 nonfluent elementary school children in three repeated readings conditions. In one condition they read a different text four times on each of seven days (28 readings). The 7 texts (1/day) had little word overlap, with repeated words being function rather than content words. The 7 texts were also semantically unrelated. They compared this *low word overlap* condition with one where the 7 semantically unrelated texts, read one per day, four times each, had a *high* degree of *word overlap*. These two conditions were compared to the nonrepetitive reading of 4 different texts per day for 7 days, each text being read once only. They found transfer of reading fluency across different texts only when the texts shared many words. The low word overlap condition did not differ from the nonrepetitive condition. There was no difference among conditions in comprehension as measured by question answering. Rashotte and Torgeson concluded that any transfer of reading skill across texts was mediated entirely by the more rapid identification of shared individual words.

The notion that there is no higher-order involvement in across text-transfer has been questioned, however (Dowhower, 1987; Schreiber, 1980). Dowhower trained second graders using a read-along and a repeated reading procedure. She found transfer to unpracticed similar passages for both methods when the measures were reading speed, accuracy, and comprehension. For the read-along procedure she also found facilitation in prosodic reading, suggesting that auditory repetition may facilitate parsing and provide cues such as intonation. These findings suggest that factors other than words may support across-text transfer, but there have been no systematic investigations of possible factors.

In the next two studies, we questioned how similar two different texts must be in order to observe transfer across texts, and what text attributes could mediate transfer between different texts. To examine these issues, we studied *pairs* of texts that were either related or unrelated. In one condition the texts in a pair were consecutive passages from a novel. Thus they had overlapping characters and theme, and a large number of shared words. In a second condition the passages of a pair were unrelated in characters and theme, but the texts shared as many words as the text pairs in the first condition. If transfer across texts is mediated by context-free word representations, then these two conditions should yield equivalent transfer. If, however, message overlap is critical in determining transfer across texts, as it is for within-text repetitions, then the first condition should show transfer, but not the second. Both of these conditions are compared to 'baseline' transfer across two unrelated texts that share only a few function words. To maximize the chances of seeing across-text transfer, we first made the subjects very familiar with the initial passage. The first passage was read five times to build up reading fluency and then transfer was measured to the second text of the pair. These studies, then, explored a broader domain of possible influences of episodic text representations, in that they looked at transfer to the processing of related, but not identical, messages.

METHOD
Subjects
Twenty-four undergraduate volunteers from an introductory psychology course at McMaster University took part in the study. All subjects were native English speakers under the age of 35. They received course credit for their participation.

Materials and design
Subjects read six pairs of passages, two pairs in each of three experimental conditions. The first passage of a pair was read 5 times in succession to build up reading fluency, followed by a set of 4 comprehension questions to be answered orally. Then the second passage of the pair was read 5 times in succession, followed by 4 comprehension questions. The question was whether

the fluency gains for the first passage would transfer to reading the second passage, either by decreasing initial reading times for the second passage, or through faster decreases in reading time slopes over the five readings of the second text. The comprehension questions were used only to influence the subjects to read for meaning. We expected that most questions would be answered after five readings of a passage. Each pair of texts was tested following this procedure.

The three experimental conditions were defined by the relationship between the two texts of a pair. In the *related* condition, the two texts were successive sections of a novel. They therefore were related in theme and characters and they had many overlapping words. Transfer between these texts could be related to overlap in content or in wording. In the *word overlap* condition, the two texts in a pair were unrelated in theme and characters, but the two texts had as many overlapping words as the texts in the related condition. Thus transfer between these texts could only be mediated by abstract word representations. Contrasts between the related and the word overlap condition indicate the amount of context free word-level transfer observed across texts. In the *unrelated* condition, the two texts were dissimilar in theme and characters, and they had few overlapping words. Any overlap was in function, rather than content words. This condition provided the baseline to assess transfer in the other two conditions.

To meet the constraints of these experimental conditions, six texts were selected to become the transfer or *second* reading passages. Then 3 *first* reading passages were selected or written for each transfer text, that would meet the requirements of the three experimental conditions. With this design, each transfer passage could be tested equally often in each experimental condition across subjects, by selection of one of the three first stories from that set. This ensured that the same materials were involved in all comparisons on the transfer test. All passages used in the experiment were 350 words in length and each was typed on a single page.

The six transfer passages were modified selections from six different Harlequin Romances. For each of these transfer passages, three first texts were created. For the related texts, the first passage was taken from the previous page of the novel. Relatedness was then emphasized by modifying transfer texts so that they began with a paragraph that 'reminded' the reader of the episode in the first text. These modifications in the transfer text strongly connected the two episodes for the related condition, but did nothing to relate the texts in the two other conditions. Besides the content overlap, the related and transfer texts had an average of 224 overlapping words (range of 206-247), most of which were content words. These overlapping words consisted of repetitions of 80 to 85 different individual words, many of which occurred several times in each text. Thus, the texts in the related condition were thematically connected and shared considerable vocabulary.

In the word overlap condition, new stories were written in the Harlequin Romance genre, that used the same number of overlapping words as the related texts. They shared 80-85 individual words, most of which were content words; with repetitions of these words, there was an average of 202 shared words (range of 189-210) between the word overlap and transfer texts. These texts, then, shared vocabulary but they were on different themes and they had different characters, so they were conceptually unrelated. Finally, texts for the unrelated condition were selections from other Harlequin Romances that differed in theme and characters, and that shared few words. They had 30-35 individual words in common with the transfer texts, but almost all of these were function words and adverbs (the, of, as, before, etc.). These texts had little conceptual and little content-word overlap with the transfer text. They provided a baseline for exploring transfer in the two other conditions. Appendix B provides excerpts of the texts used in the three experimental conditions.

Each subject read two story pairs in each of the three conditions. Counterbalancing ensured that each transfer story was tested equally often with each of its three first passages (related, word overlap, unrelated) across subjects. The order of encountering the three experimental conditions across the session was also counterbalanced across subjects. After the 5 readings of each text (first and transfer), subjects orally answered 4 comprehension questions about that passage. Each question probed a main idea or fact that was stated in the text. These questions were used to force readers to attend to the passage's message while reading. There were two sets of 4 questions for each story and half of the subjects received each set.

Procedure

The subjects participated in individual testing sessions lasting approximately 2 hours. They were given instructions and a practice passage to familiarize them with the experimental task. Instructions indicated that the subjects should read quickly but accurately because their reading times were being recorded, also encouraged them to read for meaning in order to answer the comprehension questions. At the beginning of each trial, a passage was placed upside down in front of the subject. The experimenter started a millisecond stopwatch when the subject turned the page over to begin reading and stopped the watch when the subject turned the page face down again to indicate completion of the reading task. Subjects read silently. Following the five reading trials of each passage, subjects were asked four comprehension questions and they responded orally.

RESULTS AND DISCUSSION
Reading times: First passage

Table 3 shows the mean reading times for the first passages read in each experimental condition. A 3×5 analysis of variance on these first reading times, where the variables were conditions (related, word-overlap, unrelated) and repetitions (1 to 5), indicated that the conditions main effect was marginal, $F(2,46) = 2.85$, $MS_e = 64.41$, $p = .07$. However, there was a significant effect of repetitions, $F(4,92) = 36.34$, $MS_e = 225.83$, $p < .001$, and a conditions by repetitions interaction, $F(8,184) = 3.38$, $MS_e = 22.50$, $p < .01$. Examination of the interaction showed that the conditions differed on the first two repetitions, but the differences were unreliable as readers became familiar with the passages on the final three readings. The word-overlap passages were read faster than both the related and unrelated passages on the first, $ts(23) = 3.03$, 3.05, $ps < .01$, and the second repetitions, $ts(23) = 4.79$, 3.40, $ps < .01$. These initial reading time differences probably indicate that the word-overlap passages that we wrote were somewhat easier than the other texts. However, reading times for all three conditions decreased over the five reading repetitions and after the second reading any differential difficulty effects disappeared. The question of interest, then, is whether there was differential transfer from these initial reading experiences to reading the transfer passages.

Reading times: Transfer passage

Table 3 also shows the mean reading times for the transfer passages, following reading of the three different types of prior passages. The same 3×5 analysis of variance on these data indicated that there was differential transfer from the three prior experience conditions, $F(2,46) = 8.83$, $MS_e = 111.40$, $p < .001$. There was also a significant effect of repetitions, $F(4,92) = 35.85$, $MS_e = 216.84$, $p < .001$, but no conditions by repetitions interaction $(F = 1.19)$. In all three conditions, reading times decreased systematically over the five reading repetitions, indicating gains in rereading fluency for the same passage. Newman-Keuls comparisons of the three experimental conditions revealed that the transfer passage was read faster when it was preceded by a related passage (58.31 s) than when it was preceded by either the word-overlap (63.71 s, $p < .01$) or the unrelated texts (62.64 s, $p < .01$). The word-overlap and unrelated conditions did not differ. These data indicate that there was a processing benefit across texts when the two passages were conceptually related and shared many words, but not when many words were shared but the passages were conceptually unrelated. Further, this difference in influence lasted over the 5 readings of the transfer passage. Thus, as with transfer across readings of the same text, facilitation across different texts appears to require that the episodes are semantically linked. Again, we would suggest that the second text episode must be conceptually similar to the first episode before its processing will retrieve and use the prior representation.

TABLE 3
Mean Reading Time (in seconds) and Standard Deviations for Experiment 2.

First Passage		Trial				
		1	2	3	4	5
Related	M	80.14	70.93	60.95	54.16	52.11
	SD	21.06	17.96	16.33	15.09	14.11
Word-Overlap	M	77.05	65.70	59.26	55.10	50.20
	SD	21.68	15.55	15.29	18.51	14.72
Unrelated	M	76.24	71.94	60.49	54.91	54.12
	SD	20.27	19.55	16.21	17.55	17.06
Transfer Passage		1	2	3	4	5
Related	M	74.14	63.83	54.38	49.52	49.65
	SD	21.05	17.14	14.08	14.42	14.79
Word-Overlap	M	79.86	70.52	59.50	55.49	53.19
	SD	22.23	17.98	16.05	16.32	17.05
Unrelated	M	76.03	68.54	59.30	55.30	54.03
	SD	19.25	18.26	13.56	14.97	14.55

Comprehension

The 4 comprehension questions for each passage were scored 0, 1 or 2, where 0 was given for incorrect answers, 2 for correct answers, and 1 for partially correct answers. There were no differences among the three conditions in comprehension for the transfer passage, and the only difference for the first reading text was that questions for the word overlap text were answered better (.92) than those for the related (.83) and unrelated (.85) texts. This difference again suggests that the texts that we wrote were easier, but the important point was that they did not facilitate processing or comprehension of the transfer text. Because the comprehension questions were asked only after five readings of each text, they did not provide a sensitive index of transfer of knowledge during the initial stages of reading the second passage.

Experiment 3

Experiment 2 indicated that there was facilitation in reading a transfer passage when it was preceded by a passage that was contextually related to it and shared considerable vocabulary, but not when only words overlapped or when the texts were unrelated. In Experiment 3, we attempted to replicate this effect using slightly different learning conditions, and a modified transfer test that might better reflect effects in comprehension. In Experiment 2, each text was read five times in succession, providing a form of massed practice. But, studies of verbal learning indicated that better learning occurs under conditions of distributed practice (Underwood, 1961). Perhaps more facilitation would result, particularly for the word overlap condition, when the first passage was learned with distributed rather than massed practice. This might better 'burn in' the word representations, thus providing better representations to mediate transfer to the new text. Therefore in Experiment 3, the three first passages (one in each of the three experimental conditions) were each read five times, but the repetitions of an individual passage were not successive. Rather, readings of other passages were interspersed between passage repetitions. Thus each first passage received the same practice as in Experiment 2, but the fluency was built up over distributed rather than massed repetitions. The question was whether this change would lead to faster learning or more across-text transfer. The second difference was that the transfer texts were read only twice rather than five times, followed by the comprehension questions. After two readings a difference in comprehension of the transfer text might become apparent.

METHOD

Subjects

Forty-eight undergraduate volunteers from an introductory psychology course at McMaster University took part in the study. All subjects were native English speakers under the age of 35. They received course credit for their participation.

Materials and design

The 6 passage sets used in Experiment 2 were randomly divided into two sets of materials with 3 passages per set. Half of the subjects were tested on each set of materials in Experiment 3. Each subject received one *first* passage representing each of the related, word overlap and unrelated conditions. Again, across subjects, counterbalancing ensured that each transfer story was tested equally often in each experimental condition, so that no differences in materials existed for the critical contrasts. In the first phase of the study, the three *first* passages were read 5 times each, with repetitions of the 3 passages being randomly distributed with the restriction that at least one different passage intervened between readings of the same text. After these 15 reading trials, the three transfer texts were read twice each, with each text being read once before any repetitions occurred. The order in which the 3 transfer texts occurred was counterbalanced across subjects to ensure that each experimental condition was tested equally often as the first, second, and third transfer text. This phase was followed by a set of comprehension questions. Two questions were asked about each text, one about an idea from the first half and one from the second half of the story. Questions about the 3 first passages preceded questions about the transfer stories.

TABLE 4
Mean Reading Times (in seconds) and Standard Deviations for Experiment 3.

First Passage				Trials		
		1	2	3	4	5
Related	M	80.40	67.65	62.76	58.83	55.75
	SD	21.91	21.60	19.66	20.77	19.71
Word-Overlap	M	82.44	68.04	63.75	58.45	56.65
	SD	21.76	19.16	20.19	18.93	18.65
Unrelated	M	81.56	70.34	61.60	59.78	55.61
	SD	22.86	20.69	19.51	18.95	18.27
Transfer Passage		1	2	3	4	5
Related	M	74.62	65.80			
	SD	19.86	17.60			
Word-Overlap	M	81.02	72.89			
	SD	23.24	19.63			
Unrelated	M	79.67	68.45			
	SD	21.86	20.95			

Procedure

The subjects participated in individual testing sessions lasting approximately one hour, with a five-minute break between first and transfer phases. The procedure was the same as in Experiment 2, except for the changes noted above. The data of interest were the reading times and answers to the comprehension questions.

RESULTS

Reading times: First passage

Table 4 shows the mean reading times for the three *first* passage conditions over the five repetitions. A 3 × 5 analysis of variance, where the variables were conditions (related, word overlap, unrelated) and repetitions (1 to 5), found no effect of conditions ($F < 1$), suggesting that these readers found the first passages to be of approximately equal difficulty. There was a significant effect of repetitions, $F(4,188) = 102.45$, $MS_e = 142.33$, $p < .001$, that did not interact with conditions. Comparison of the reading time slopes for the first passages in Experiments 2 and 3 suggests that there were no differences in speed of learning for massed versus distributed practice regimes (see Tables 3 & 4).

Reading times: Transfer passage

Table 4 shows the mean reading times for the transfer passage, for the three prior exposure conditions, over the two repetitions during transfer. A 3 × 2 analysis of variance revealed a significant effect of condition, $F(2,94) = 15.28$, $MS_e = 71.97$, $p < .001$, and of repetitions, $F(1,47) = 41.95$, $MS_e = 151.38$, $p < .001$, but with no interaction between these factors ($F = 1.35$). In all three conditions, reading time decreased over the two repetitions. Newman-Keuls comparisons indicated that reading times for the transfer passage after reading the related passage (70.21 s) were significantly shorter than those for the transfer passage following reading of the word overlap (76.96 s, $p < .01$), and unrelated texts (74.06 s, $p < .01$). Times in the unrelated condition were also reliably shorter than those in the word overlap condition ($p < .05$).

Experiment 3 thus replicated the facilitation effect in Experiment 2, where there was more facilitation in reading the second text when the first passage overlapped both conceptually and in vocabulary with the transfer text. Unlike Experiment 2, where the word-overlap and unrelated conditions did not differ, here there was actually *negative* transfer between texts that shared a large number of words read in different contexts in the two stories. Although massed versus distributed repetitions (Experiments 2 versus 3) did not appear to affect reading time slopes for the related and unrelated conditions, for the word overlap condition times were slower under distributed conditions. One possibility is that the distributed readings during the first phase led to the word representations becoming more bound to their processing context, so that a change in context for repeated words then had a negative effect on transfer. The critical point from these studies, however, is that although there was facilitation across different texts when they were conceptually related, there was no benefit due to word overlap per se. Again, the text representations appear to be conceptual 'wholes' with their wording bound to those episodic contexts.

Comprehension

Questions were scored as in Experiment 2. An analysis of variance examining differences among conditions for the *first passage* indicated a significant effect of condition, $F(2,94) = 6.65$, $MS_e = .58$, $p < .01$. Newman-Keuls tests revealed that comprehension for the word overlap passage (.93) was better than comprehension for the related (.85, $p < .05$), and unrelated conditions (.79, $p < .01$). There was no difference between related and unrelated conditions. Thus, while reading times did not differ for the first passages, as they had in Experiment 2, subjects did seem to find the word overlap passages easier to understand. Again, the passages we wrote appear to have been a bit easier, but the important question was whether this led to better transfer.

Analysis of variance of comprehension scores for the *transfer passages* indicated a significant effect of conditions, $F(2,94) = 4.08$, $MS_e = .80, p < .05$. Newman-Keuls tests showed that comprehension of the transfer text when it was preceded by the related text (.79) was better than when it was preceded by the word overlap (.66, $p < .05$) or the unrelated texts (.69, $p < .05$). The unrelated and word overlap conditions did not differ. Thus, when subjects were given only two repetitions of the transfer passages, reading a related passage first was beneficial to comprehension of the transfer passage. No benefit accrued from words read in a different semantic context.

Thus, taken together, Experiments 2 and 3 show that a reading time benefit was conferred upon a subsequent passage when the prior text was conceptually related to that text and shared vocabulary with it. Experiment 3 shows that comprehension of the second text also benefited from the prior experience. However, when the prior text shared only wording that was embedded in unrelated messages, then transfer did not occur. In fact, in Experiment 3 there was actually negative transfer under these conditions. Thus the representation of one text can facilitate the processing of a subsequent text, but only when the two events are conceptually related. One point to note is that transfer, even in the related condition, was not complete. The transfer text was not read at a rate equal to that for the first text on its fifth reading (see Tables 3 & 4). However, the transfer text was read faster than the first text had been when it was initially encountered. That is, the fluency obtained after five readings was not transferred from the first to the transfer text. We cannot be sure that the five repetitions were necessary to obtain transfer here. Perhaps one reading of each text would have been sufficient to see the relatedness effect. The important point, though, is that the representation of one reading event mediates processing of a second reading event, and this mediation seems to rely on a semantically-based record of the episode, not on priming individual context-free word representations. Transfer across texts in this sense resembles transfer of fluency across readings of the same text.

General Discussion

The experiments described here provide further evidence that the representation of texts that have just been read are 'episodic' records that maintain information about the perceptual, lexical and message aspects of that reading encounter. That record will be retrieved, and will act to facilitate the reading of a subsequent passage, only when the later text repeats or continues the previous message. Repetition of words in a different context is insufficient to allow retrieval of a prior text representation. Variations in perceptual, lexical and linguistic structure will lead to some loss of facilitation in processing subsequent texts, suggesting that once an episodic representation has been retrieved, perhaps through some content-addressable retrieval route, then the linguistic details of the specific episode will determine the magnitude of the fluency benefit.

Experiment 1 demonstrates further limits on variations that will be processed as the repetition of a prior episode. In earlier research we have shown that variations in typescript and modality can cause loss in rereading transfer (Jacoby, Levy, & Steinbach, 1992; Levy & Kirsner, 1989; Levy et al., 1992), indicating that the episodic representation retains information about the perceptual processes involved in reading. However, it is still unclear why this information fails to influence rereading transfer under some circumstances (see Levy, 1993, for further discussion). Levy and Burns (1991) reported that rereading transfer was insensitive to changes in text macrostructure, as measured by changes in paragraph ordering, but was sensitive to sentence scrambling, suggesting that the proper unfolding of the message was important in maintaining transfer. Experiment 1a indicates that there can be variation in the linguistic structures that transmit the message, but Experiment 1b suggests that the lexical identity of main concepts must be maintained. The null effect of the large syntactic changes in Experiment 1a suggest that the loss in transfer in Experiment 1b cannot be attributed to the small syntactic variations in the paraphrases in Experiment 1b. When the ideas were re-worded, even though the message was very similar, some but not complete loss of transfer was observed. Lexical changes lead to loss in the rereading benefit. Thus the representation of a text, when that text was read for meaning (see Carlson et al. for other circumstances), appears to be an episodic record that retains fairly specific information about that reading encounter. Although this record can still be recruited when there are variations in the perceptual, lexical, and syntactic aspects of the texts across repetitions, these variations lead to some loss in the rereading fluency. However, alterations at the message level can cause failure of retrieval during reprocessing, particularly when the message is scrambled and only wording is repeated. Together these studies suggest that repetition fluency is limited to fairly small variations between texts.

However, Experiments 2 and 3 demonstrate a broader influence of episodic text representations. These experiments explored the effect of reading a text on the subsequent reading of a different text. The results show clearly that, as with text repetition, across-text transfer is also reliant on reinstatement of the message context. When the two passages were semantically continuous, there was a reading time and a comprehension advantage in processing the second text. This advantage was not due to repetition of words alone, which naturally occurs when texts are continuous developments of a theme, because there was no transfer across semantically unrelated texts that had equivalent word overlap. Again, the message appears to be the 'core' of episodic transfer between different texts. This is *not* to say that lexical units fail to be recorded in the episodic representation. We would argue that the word units are an important part of the record that mediates across-text transfer, but those units are 'bonded' to that episodic context, and message overlap is critical to retrieving the episodic record. Once it has been retrieved, then alterations in perceptual and lexical features may limit the amount of transfer observed. These notions need testing with across-text transfer, because they have so far been demonstrated only in text repetition. The main point, though, is that episodic text representations may have a broader base of influence on reading fluency than is obvious from studies of repetition effects. In past literature these effects may have been treated as 'prior knowledge' or 'schema' effects. The main difference between the episodic view described here and a 'schema' view is that the representations we have studied are very specific to particular passages. They are not based on 'generic' or 'abstract' knowledge about situations, with default values to cover failures in retention. Rather, the episodic representation is a specific contextual 'trace' that is integrated into the later processing event to allow that processing to be more fluent. The memory representation is text specific, not 'generic'.

The data reported here are consistent with previous studies of text transfer for fluent adult readers (see Levy, 1993, for a review). They are not consistent with studies of across-text transfer for reading-delayed children. In that domain, there is evidence of transfer across texts that may be based on abstract word units per se (eg. Dowhower, 1987; Rashotte & Torgeson, 1985). These studies suggested that prior to the time that word recognition processes become 'automated', children may gain from simply reprocessing the words. In some recent studies in our laboratory (Faulkner & Levy, 1993), that used paradigms to measure repetition and across-text transfer like those described here, we have found that poor, but not good, readers in primary school show a benefit from prior experience in reading just the words of a text in a different context. Thus the effects of 'episodic bonding' of words to their context that we have described here may be related to reading skill and reading development. Much is left to explore in the use of episodic representations in mediating reading fluency.

This research was supported by an operating grant to the first author from the Natural Science and Engineering Research Council of Canada. Preparation of the paper was aided by a Senior Research Fellowship to the first author from the Ontario Mental Health Foundation. Address correspondence to: Dr. B.A. Levy, Department of Psychology, McMaster University, Hamilton, Ontario Canada L8S 4K1. Electronic mail address: LEVY@MACMASTER.CA.

References

Carbo, M. (1978). Teaching reading with talking books. *The Reading Teacher, 32*, 267-273.

Carlson, L., Alejano, A., & Carr, T.H. (1991). The level of focal attention hypothesis in oral reading: Influences of strategies on the context specificity of lexical repetition effects. *Journal of Experimental Psychology: Learning, Memory, and Cognition, 17*, 924-931.

Carr, T.H., & Brown, J.S. (1990). Perceptual abstraction and interactivity in repeated oral reading: Where do things stand? *Journal of Experimental Psychology: Learning, Memory, and Cognition, 16*, 731-738.

Carr, T.H., Brown, J.S., & Charalambous, A. (1989). Repetition and reading: Perceptual encoding mechanisms are very abstract but not very interactive. *Journal of Experimental Psychology: Learning, Memory, and Cognition, 15*, 763-778.

Chomsky, C. (1978). After decoding: What? *Language Arts, 53*, 288-296.

Dahl, P.R. (1979). An experimental program for teaching high speed word recognition and comprehension skills. In J.E. Button, T.C. Lovitt, & T.D. Rowland (Eds.), *Communications research in learning disabilities and mental retardation* (pp. 33-65). Baltimore, MD: University Park Press.

Dowhower, S.L. (1987). Effects of repeated reading on second-grade transitional readers' fluency and comprehension. *Reading Research Quarterly, 22*, 389-406.

Faulkner, H. & Levy, B.A. (1993). *Good and poor reader differences in rereading transfer: Words and their context.* Manuscript in preparation.

Herman, P.A. (1985). The effect of repeated readings on reading rate, speech pauses, and word recognition accuracy. *Reading Research Quarterly, 20*, 553-565.

Jacoby, L.L., Levy, B.A., & Steinbach, K. (1992). Episodic transfer and automaticity: The integration of data-driven and conceptually-driven processing in rereading. *Journal of Experimental Psychology: Learning, Memory , and Cognition, 18*, 15-24.

Kolers, P.A. (1975). Specificity of operations in sentence recognition. *Cognitive Psychology, 7*, 283-306.

Kolers, P.A. (1976). Reading a year later. *Journal of Experimental Psychology: Human Learning and Memory, 2*, 554-565.

Kolers, P.A., & Magee, L.E. (1978). Specificity of pattern-analyzing skills in reading. *Canadian Journal of Psychology, 32*, 43-51.

Kolers, P.A., Palef, S.R., & Stelmach, L.B. (1980). Graphemic analysis underlying literacy. *Memory & Cognition, 8*, 322-328.

Levy, B.A. (1993). Fluent rereading: An implicit indicator of reading skill development. In P. Graf & M. Masson (Eds.), *Implicit Memory: New directions in cognition, development, and neuropsychology.* Hillsdale, NJ: Erlbaum (in press).

Levy, B.A., & Begin, J. (1984). Proofreading familiar text: Allocating resources to perceptual and conceptual processing. *Memory & Cognition, 12*, 621-632.

Levy, B.A., & Burns, K.I. (1990). Reprocessing text: Contributions from conceptually driven processes. *Canadian Journal of Psychology, 44*, 465-482.

Levy, B.A., Di Persio, R., & Hollingshead, A. (1992). Fluent rereading: Repetition, automaticity and discrepancy. *Journal of Experimental Psychology: Learning, Memory, and Cognition, 18*, 957-971.

Levy, B.A., & Kirsner, K. (1989). Reprocessing text: Indirect measures of word and message level processes. *Journal of Experimental Psychology: Learning, Memory, and Cognition, 15*, 407-417.

Levy, B.A., Masson, M.E.J., & Zoubek, M.A. (1991). Rereading text: Words and their context. *Canadian Journal of Psychology, 45*, 492-506.

MacLeod, C.M. (1989). Word context during initial exposure influences degree of priming in word fragment completion. *Journal of Experimental Psychology: Learning, Memory, and Cognition, 15*, 398-406.

Morgan, R., & Lyon, E. (1979). "Paired Reading" – A preliminary report on a technique for parental tuition of reading-retarded children. *Journal of Child Psychology & Psychiatry, 20*, 151-160.

Oliphant, G.W. (1983). Repetition and recency effects in word recognition. *Australian Journal of Psychology, 35*, 393-403.

Rashotte, C.A., & Torgeson, J.K. (1985). Repeated reading and reading fluency in learning disabled children. *Reading Research Quarterly, 20*, 180-202.

Samuels, S.J. (1979). The method of repeated readings. *The Reading Teacher, 32*, 403-408.

Schreiber, P.A. (1980). On the acquisition of reading fluency. *Journal of Reading Behavior, 12*, 177-186.

Underwood, B.J. (1961). Ten years of massed practice on distributed practice. *Psychological Review, 68*, 229-247.

Appendix A

The first two paragraphs of a text in the A (original), B (syntactic), and C (lexical) versions.

(A) DRUG ABUSE

Currently there is a national concern over the illegal use of drugs. Any drug, legal or not, is a chemical substance used with the intention of affecting the physical and emotional functioning of the body. The abuse of drugs can produce physical illness and is detrimental to an individual's economic and social adjustment.

Among young people the first contact with drugs is often due to curiosity. The illegal nature of some drugs provides added excitement. In their search for social identity, young people might feel obliged to conform to group behaviour. To avoid alienation, they prefer to submit to peer pressure.

(B) DRUG ABUSE

The illegal use of drugs is currently a national concern. Legal or not, any drug is a chemical substance affecting the body's emotional and physical functioning when used. Physical illness and detriments to an individual's social and economic adjustment are produced by drug abuse.

Often, the first contact with drugs among young people is due to curiosity. Added excitement is provided by some drugs because of their illegal nature. Young people might feel an obligation to conform to group behaviour in their search for social identity. Submitting to peer pressure is preferred by young people to avoid alienation.

(C) DRUG ABUSE

At present, there is public concern regarding drug abuse. All drugs are chemically-based products, and are taken to alter the body's physical and emotional operations. Sickness, and financial and social problems can result from substance abuse.

With youth, it is often inquisitiveness that leads to initial experimentation with drugs. The fact that certain drugs are illicit adds to their attraction. Youth may feel that they have to follow the crowd in order to develop social affinity with their peers. Rather than be left out, they succumb to peer pressure.

Appendix B

Excerpts From A Story Set Used In Experiments 2 and 3.

TRANSFER STORY

Mary had just left the consulting room to return to her desk in the waiting room. She worked for her uncle, Dr. Thomas, and had just attended to one of his patients, a Mrs. Fullerton, for whom she had re-bandaged a sprained ankle.

The people in the waiting room all knew this pretty woman with the chestnut hair and large brown eyes. She had lived in the village since she was a child, and they all thought she had turned out to be a fine young lady. Mary smiled at them all, sifted through the patients' cards and counted heads. If Mr. Stokes, the old man with chronic bronchitis who was currently in Dr. Thomas's office, didn't finish his grumbling soon, the morning schedule was going to get behind.

RELATED FIRST STORY

The waiting room was full and smelled of wet raincoats and old Mr. Stoke's menthol cough lozenges; he had chronic bronchitis and treated himself with a variety of cures from the chemist until he finally gave in and went to the doctor. He sat glowering at the people around him, his eyes on the green light over the consulting room door; he was next in.

But when the light changed it flickered on and off, a signal for the girl sitting behind the desk to go into the consulting room. Mary got up without haste to obey the summons, aware that her uncle, Dr. Thomas, wanted her to see to Mrs. Fullerton's sprained ankle. She smiled at her uncle as she went in; smiled, also, at his patient and urged that lady to the curtained-off cubicle behind his desk. Mrs. Fullerton eased her stout person on to the chair and extended her leg on to the stool provided for her.

WORD OVERLAP FIRST STORY

The village of St. Mary was bustling with activity. Everyone was waiting for the Fullerton-Stokes Equestrian Show, being held at Fullerton Farms today. This was a very prestigious horse-jumping competition and people from all around always travelled to St. Mary to watch.

On a ranch one mile from Fullerton Farms, a young woman was in the tack room, running through last minute preparations with her horse and equipment. This was her third show with her horse, "Lady of the Morning", and they had placed second in the other two competitions. This year, there was a strong chance they'd win. The girl stroked Lady's chestnut brown hair, running her fingers gently through the long mane.

"We can do it, Lady," she whispered. "We can out-jump them all."

While the young woman was busy with Lady, Thomas, the stable boy, was consulting with his employers, Mr. and Mrs. Grayling.

UNRELATED FIRST STORY

Their play was going to close. Somehow Kirsty felt it; she could taste the bitter flavour of defeat, had sensed from the audience response that all was not going well. Her meagre savings were nearly exhausted and unless she found a temporary job to tide her over she would have to go, tail between her legs, back to her parents.

Much as she loved her parents, her mother was inclined to fuss, and indeed had never wanted her to become an actress. Her aunt, though, understood. An actress, Kirsty grimaced wryly, slipping out of the theatre without bothering to join the others in the lounge. If it hadn't been for theatre critic Drew Chalmers' biting review of her in her last play she might still have been appearing in it; might indeed have gone with it to New York with the rest of the cast.

14 Episodically Enhanced Comprehension Fluency

MICHAEL E.J. MASSON *University of Victoria*

Abstract   Fluent reading comprehension was explored in a series of experiments involving sentences presented in normal and inverted typography. Sentences read in a test phase had been read earlier in exactly the same form, or in versions that were created by (a) altering the word order within sentences to create randomly ordered word strings or (b) exchanging causally related clauses to form new meaningful sentences. Variation from exact repetition of word order or clause combination increased the time taken to read the test sentences and these effects were evident over retention intervals ranging from one day to four months. Varying word order across repeated presentations of a sentence was also shown to reduce reporting accuracy in a rapid serial reading task. These results support an episodic view of the basis for rereading fluency in which comprehension processes responsible for constructing and integrating propositions are automatically recruited and reapplied when a sentence is reread.

Résumé   La facilité de compréhension de textes a fait l'objet d'une série d'expériences dans lesquelles les sujets devaient lire des phrases dont la typographie était tantôt normale, tantôt inversée. Les phrases présentées à l'étape d'essai avaient été lues auparavant soit sous une forme identique, soit sous une nouvelle forme où a) l'ordre des mots dans les phrases était modifié de manière à créer des suites de mots agencés au hasard ou b) les propositions causales étaient combinées autrement pour créer de nouvelles phrases sensées. Lorsque l'ordre des mots ou l'agencement des propositions était modifié par rapport à celui qui était répété fidèlement, le temps de lecture des phrases présentées à l'essai était plus long, et cet effet se manifestait de façon évidente après les intervalles de rétention allant d'un jour à quatre mois. La présentation répétée d'une même phrase dans laquelle l'ordre des mots était modifié avait également pour effet de réduire l'exactitude des réponses données pendant une tâche de lecture rapide en série. Les résultats obtenus témoignent des bases épisodiques de la facilité de relecture où les processus de compréhension responsables de la construction et de l'intégration des propositions sont automatiquement sélectionnés et réactivés lors de la relecture d'une phrase.

Literacy skills have been cultivated and prized in part for their artistic merits, but their primary function remains that of communicating meaningful messages. Much of the value of written and spoken messages lies in the lasting impact they have on the receiver. A central issue regarding the communicative function of language, therefore, is how the persistent influence of a message is maintained in memory across time and how it is called forward to guide behavior when appropriate. One very fruitful approach to this issue has been the exploration of text structure and its influence on the ability to remember intentionally the content of a text (e.g., Moravcsik & Kintsch, 1993; Trabasso & van den Broek, 1985). A second approach, pursued further in this article, has emphasized the idea that memory for a comprehension episode is captured procedurally and is revealed through the fluent reapplication of these procedures when a previously comprehended message (or critical components of it) is encountered at a later time (e.g., Kolers & Roediger, 1984).

The view that memory for text comprehension episodes is captured in a set of processing operations was advanced by Kolers (1975) as a contrast to the prevailing emphasis on memory for the meaning of text. The procedural nature of memory was demonstrated by showing that the analysis of the surface features of a sentence was an integral part of memory for the sentence. The time taken to reread typographically transformed (e.g., upside down) sentences varied depending on whether sentences were read initially in that form. Sentences read in normal typography on the first occasion (or heard, rather than read) were not read as fluently when re-presented for reading in transformed typography. In a particularly striking demonstration of the long-lasting influence of memory for processing operations, Kolers (1976) showed that typographically transformed texts read one year earlier were reread faster than new texts.

The procedural view of memory for reading episodes has been encouraged by work with certain types of memory-impaired subjects using both normal and typographically transformed materials. Despite impairment in their ability consciously to remember previously read texts, sentences, or words, these subjects nonetheless show normal levels of fluency when rereading these materials (Cohen & Squire, 1980; Moscovitch, Winocur, & McLachlan, 1986; Musen, Shimamura, & Squire, 1990; Musen & Squire, 1991). These results suggest that reapplication of processing operations can go forward without support from consciously recollected aspects of the original reading experience.

Although Kolers emphasized the components of processing operations responsible for analyzing the graphemic aspects of text, there is ample evidence of the important role played by conceptually driven operations in generating rereading fluency. In earlier work, I have found that memory for normal but not typographically transformed sentences can be enhanced by requiring subjects to perform an elaborative encoding task during initial reading (Masson, 1984; Masson & Sala, 1978). This finding suggests that the task of deciphering typographically transformed sentences recruits an analysis of the meaning of the sentence to provide contextual information. The importance of conceptually driven processes in fluent rereading of typographically transformed texts has been pushed further by Graf and Levy (1984), Horton (1985), and Tardif and Craik (1989), who argued that although subjects developed a general improvement in pattern analyzing skill, the specific influence of prior reading episodes was due entirely to semantic processing operations (e.g., gist and lexical information). In their experiments two different typographical transformations were used and there was no reliable difference in rereading fluency when the original or the alternative transformation was used on the second reading of a text.

More recently, however, Craik and Gemar (cited in Craik, 1991) found that using different transformed typographies on the two readings of a text does produce a small but reliable reduction in rereading fluency. In addition, Jacoby, Levy, and Steinbach (1992) showed that subjects were sensitive to changes in normal type font (e.g., script and elite) across two reading occasions, but only when the task was to read and answer questions. Reading aloud the same questions failed to produce sensitivity to changed font. Jacoby et al. concluded that integrated episodic representations of initial reading experiences are effectively recruited only when reading is carried out in service of some other primary goal, not when the act of reading is the focus of attention, as in reading aloud.

The pattern of results that has followed in the wake of Kolers' original demonstrations is consistent with the major theme he advocated, namely that a variety of processing operations (including analysis of surface features) are integrally represented in memory as a consequence of a reading experience. Although it is clear that conceptually driven operations make a contribution to rereading fluency, we know relatively little about the comprehension processes that contribute to this fluency. A series of proofreading studies with normally typed texts by Levy and her colleagues (Levy & Begin, 1984; Levy, Newell, Snyder, & Timmins, 1986), however, has established a number of important facts. First, proofreading is done more quickly and without loss of accuracy if a text has been read previously, even when errors consist of words that violate semantic or syntactic constraints. This result implies that rereading fluency is attained without attenuating the analysis of the text's meaning. Second, rereading fluency depends on preserving the semantic message in a text. When texts were tested in normal word order following an initial reading, reading time was lower when the initial reading also involved normal rather than scrambled word order. The reverse was true when texts were tested in scrambled word order.

Sensitivity to changes produced by scrambling word order has been explored using other reading tasks, such as reading in preparation for a memory test (Levy & Burns, 1990; Levy & Kirsner, 1989). For example, Levy and Burns obtained varying degrees of reduction of rereading time on normal texts by applying a range of text scrambling procedures to texts on their first reading. Rereading fluency was not affected by scrambling the order of paragraphs within a text, but was reduced by reordering the sentences, and was eliminated when words were randomly reordered. In contrast to the sensitivity to text meaning indicated by these studies, Carr, Brown, and Charalambous (1989) and Carlson, Alejano, and Carr (1991) obtained inconsistent effects of scrambling on rereading fluency when texts were read aloud. Carr et al. failed to find an effect of scrambling on rereading fluency, but Carlson et al. did find an effect when subjects were directed to focus on the meaning of the texts. Requiring subjects to read texts in a word by word manner with instruction to ignore the meaning of the texts, however, eliminated the scrambling effect. Carlson et al. proposed that attentional focus determines whether scrambling will have an effect on rereading coherent texts. When attention is focused at the level of text meaning, rereading fluency is based in part on text comprehension processes, but when attention is focused at the lexical level, fluency is driven by lexical processes.

An alternative proposal was put forward by Levy, Masson, and Zoubek (1991) on the basis of evidence from their experiments and the Levy and Burns (1990) study. These experiments indicate that for texts tested in normal word order, sensitivity to scrambling of word order during initial reading is obtained across a variety of reading tasks, ranging from oral reading and detecting Greek letters to reading in preparation for recall or summarization tasks. Levy et al. argued that processing the meaning of text and using that experience to enhance later rereading fluency has a Stroop-like quality that is impervious to all but the most extreme task demands. In contrast, when rereading involves scrambled text, the effect of initially reading the text in scrambled or normal form varies with reading task. A reliable advantage for initially normal texts was found with tasks that required processing the meaning of the texts. With superficial reading tasks such as oral reading there was no effect of initial text format. These results suggest that rereading scrambled texts is more susceptible to instructional influences than rereading normal texts.

The line of research involving normal and scrambled texts provides us with the best clue so far concerning the role of comprehension processes in rereading fluency. The Levy and Burns (1990) experiments in which sentence and word order were manipulated offer the most detailed information with respect to specific comprehension processes. The experiments described here were designed to examine sentence-level comprehension processes that contribute to fluent rereading. The general paradigm used in all of the reported experiments involved having subjects read sentences in a training phase, then reread these sentences (sometimes after undergoing a reordering of units) in a subsequent test phase. Unrelated sentences rather than entire texts were studied because reordering of units applied at one level of a text (e.g., changing sentence order or word order) is bound to influence not only operations that are specific to that level, but also all other higher level operations (e.g., construction of a situation model).

In Experiments 1-4, contributions of conceptually driven processes to fluent rereading of typographically transformed sentences were examined. Transformed typography was used for two reasons: (1) to enhance the role of conceptually driven processes (e.g., Horton, 1985; Masson & Sala, 1978; Tardif & Craik, 1989), thereby increasing the sensitivity of the experiments to manipulations that affect these processes, and (2) to make contact with the rich body of earlier work on reading fluency involving transformed typography. In Experiment 1 three different methods of rearranging words within and across sentences were used to determine the relative importance of lexical, syntactical, and propositional processing for the conceptually driven operations that are invoked when reading typographically transformed sentences.[1] Only propositional operations were found to make a significant contribution to the conceptually driven processes used to decode typographically transformed sentences. Experiments 2 and 3 provide evidence that these operations play a crucial role in fluent rereading of such sentences after delays of up to four months. These results run counter to the conclusion drawn by Kolers (1976) that fluent rereading of typographically transformed texts should be attributed to memory for graphemic pattern analyzing operations. Evidence from Experiment 4 rules out the possibility that rereading fluency is based on sensitivity to repeated word order, independent of any higher order linguistic processing.

In two additional experiments, fluent rereading of sentences in normal typography is examined. The results of Experiment 5 demonstrate that conceptually driven processes operate and form re-useable memory representations even under severely constrained reading conditions. Processes involved in the integration of causally related clauses are shown in Experiment 6 to contribute to the fluent rereading of sentences, extending the range of conceptual processes implicated in fluency effects.

Experiment 1

In Experiment 1 the objective was to determine which of several sentence-level comprehension processes are involved in reading typographically transformed sentences. The experiment was patterned after classic studies by Miller and his colleagues (Marks & Miller, 1964; Miller & Isard, 1963) involving perception and recall of aurally presented sentences. They

---

1 I use the term *proposition* to refer to a unit of meaning similar to that developed by Kintsch (1974).

used sentences created by varying word order within normal, meaningful sentences (to create scrambled sentences) and by exchanging words across sentences to create grammatically correct but meaningless (anomalous) sentences. Performance on normal sentences was better than on scrambled or anomalous sentences, which yielded similar levels of accuracy. Performance was worst on sentences created by scrambling the word order of anomalous sentences (scrambled-anomalous). The advantage of normal sentences over all other sentence types indicates that construction of meaningful propositions made an important contribution to the perception of word strings. The advantage of the scrambled and anomalous sentences over the scrambled-anomalous items suggests that semantic relatedness of words and syntactical processing, respectively, also served to enhance language perception.

These four sentence types were used in Experiment 1. Sentences were presented visually in transformed typography and the task was to read aloud each sentence. In the training phase of the experiment, one set of sentences of each type was read, then in the test phase these sentences were reread along with one set of new sentences of each type. Repeated sentences were always tested in the same format as that used during training. It was expected that if construction of meaningful propositions was an important component in reading typographically transformed sentences, reading time would be lower in the normal sentence condition than in any other condition. Contributions from semantic relatedness between words and syntactical processes would be reflected in a reading time advantage for scrambled and anomalous conditions over the scrambled-anomalous condition. A subset of the sentences were presented in both phases to determine whether the component processes that contribute to fluent reading change across two readings of the same sentence. If the components remain stable, it would be expected that new and old sentences in the test phase would show the same pattern of reading times across the four sentence types.

METHOD

Subjects

The subjects were 16 undergraduate students at the University of Victoria who volunteered to participate in the experiment. All subjects who served in the experiments reported here were drawn from this population and each subject took part in only one experiment.

Materials and design

A set of 60 sentences was constructed and randomly divided into four lists of 15 sentences each. A sentence occupied about one to one and a half lines on a computer monitor capable of displaying 80 characters on each line (e.g., Water purification techniques will be drastically changed following the commission meeting). Three additional versions of each list of 15 sentences were created. The scrambled version was created by randomly reordering the words within each sentence (e.g., the drastically following changed techniques will Water purification be meeting commission). The words from each list of 15 sentences were rearranged to form a list of 15 anomalous sentences that were grammatically correct but that constituted meaningless phrases (e.g., Distances in the literary cars can be described as commission following the objective city). For the last version, the words within each of the anomalous sentences were randomly reordered to produce scrambled-anomalous sentences (e.g., Objective be described the can as cars commission literary distances following the in city). An additional set of four sentences, one of each type, was constructed for use as practice items at the start of the experiment.

Subjects read 15 unique sentences in each version. The assignment of lists to subjects was counterbalanced so that each list of 15 sentences was read equally often in each version.

Procedure

Instructions and sentences were presented to subjects using an Apple II+ microcomputer equipped with two green monochrome monitors and a timing card that provided millisecond timing accuracy. One monitor was viewed by the subject and the other was visible only to the experimenter. The second monitor was used to present sentences in normal type font so the experimenter could check the accuracy of the subjects' reading. This set-up was used in all the experiments reported here.

Subjects were tested individually in two phases. In the training phase of the experiment, subjects were told that they were to read aloud a series of sentences, some of which would not make sense. They were also informed that to make the task more challenging each sentence would be presented upside down. Subjects were encouraged to read the sentences as quickly as possible. At the beginning of a trial the word READY appeared in normal font at the right side of the middle line of the subject's monitor to indicate the position of the first word in the sentence. The subject pressed a key on a computer keypad, causing the monitor to be cleared and a sentence to be presented 500 ms later. The sentences were presented in a geometrically transformed typography equivalent to the view provided when reading a printed page that has been turned upside down, requiring subjects to read from right to left. The computer clock was started as soon as the sentence appeared on the monitor and stopped as soon as the experimenter pressed a key on the keyboard to indicate that the subject had read the final word of the sentence. The experimenter ensured that the subject correctly read each word. When a word was misread the subject was told immediately to try it again and continued until it was correctly identified. The subject then moved on to the next word. No record was kept of reading errors and time to reread words was included in the reading time measure. The four practice sentences were

TABLE 1
Mean Reading Time (in seconds) in Experiment 1

Phase	Sentence			
	Normal	Scrambled	Anomalous	Scrambled-anomalous
Training	17.31	22.89	25.05	22.60
Test				
Old	11.27	15.27	15.23	15.30
New	14.57	19.79	20.44	22.82

Note. The estimated standard deviations of subjects' mean reading times, pooled across all four sentence conditions, were 11.82, 5.91, and 9.08 in the training, test-old, and test-new conditions, respectively.

presented first, followed by eight randomly selected sentences from each list of 15 sentences assigned to the subject. These 32 critical sentences were presented in a randomly determined order. At the beginning of the test phase subjects were told that they would read another set of sentences, some of which would be the same as the ones they had just read. Subjects then read the entire set of 60 critical sentences presented in a random order.

RESULTS

Reading times greater than 120 s were excluded from the analysis, resulting in a loss of 0.1% of the trials. Three reading time means for each type of sentence were computed for each subject. One mean was based on the eight sentences read in the training phase, another on the same sentences when they were reread in the test phase, and one was based on the seven new sentences of each type that were presented in the test phase. The mean reading time for each of these conditions, computed over subjects, is shown in Table 1.

The mean reading times for the training phase were included in an analysis of variance (ANOVA) with sentence type as a within subjects factor, and type I error rate set at .05 (as in all experiments reported here). There was a reliable effect of sentence type, $F(3, 45) = 9.56$, $MS_e = 18.14$. As can be seen in Table 1, only in the normal condition was the mean reading time less than that in the scrambled-anomalous condition. Test phase reading times were analyzed in an ANOVA with prior presentation (old, new) and version as factors. Old sentences took less time to read than new ones (14.27 s vs 19.40 s), $F(1, 15) = 27.28$, $MS_e = 30.98$, and the difference among versions was significant as well, $F(3, 45) = 24.66$, $MS_e = 9.42$. The interaction between prior presentation and version was not significant, $F(3, 45) = 2.11$, $MS_e = 11.92$.

Although the interaction was not significant in the analysis of test phase data, the pattern of means suggests that among the new but not the old sentences there was an advantage for scrambled and for anomalous over scrambled-anomalous sentences. This possibility was tested in two additional ANOVAs. In one, scrambled and scrambled-anomalous versions of old and new sentences were compared. Once again, old sentences were read faster than new ones (15.28 s vs 21.30 s), $F(1, 15) = 21.92$, $MS_e = 26.43$. Scrambled sentences were read faster than scrambled-anomalous sentences (17.53 s vs 19.06 s), $F(1, 15) = 7.17$, $MS_e = 5.24$, and the interaction between prior presentation and version was significant, $F(1, 15) = 5.54$, $MS_e = 6.51$. The reliable interaction indicates that subjects made use of semantic relatedness among words in the scrambled sentences to reduce reading time, but only if the sentences had not been read previously. In the other ANOVA, anomalous and scrambled-anomalous versions of old and new sentences were compared, but only the effect of prior exposure was significant (15.26 s and 21.63 s for old and new sentences, respectively), $F(1, 15) = 23.09$, $MS_e = 28.08$. These results fail to support the proposition that subjects reliably made use of syntactic regularity, independently of semantic content, in reading inverted sentences.

DISCUSSION

Normal sentences were read in less time than any of the other three sentence types, indicating that the the advantage associated with these sentences is not due entirely to either the semantic relatedness between words or to syntactic regularity. The most reasonable conclusion is that constraints associated with the construction of meaningful propositions enabled subjects to more quickly read the normal sentences. Moreover, the fact that the normal sentence advantage appeared on both readings of repeated sentences indicates that proposition-construction processes contributed to fluent reading on both reading occasions. This result is important because it supports conclusions drawn from the remaining experiments in this series regarding the basis for rereading fluency.

In contrast to the strong contribution made by proposition construction, there was no evidence that syntactical processing in the absence of meaningful propositions enhanced reading fluency. Evidence regarding the role of semantic relatedness between words, as measured by performance on scrambled sentences, was somewhat ambiguous. Only among new sentences in the test phase was there any evidence that scrambled sentences were read more fluently than scrambled-anomalous sentences. Repeated sentences and sentences in the training phase did not show this effect. A possible account of this difference is that when sentences are reread the reapplication of procedures used during the first reading can inhibit the use of an emerging strategy that involves additional procedures. This notion is rather speculative, given the post hoc nature of the analyses involving scrambled sentences, but it is suggestive of the powerful nature of memory for processing episodes.

Experiment 2

The question addressed in Experiment 2 was whether proposition-building processes applied on the first reading of a sentence are remembered and reapplied to promote fluent rereading. Although the results of Experiment 1 showed that these conceptually driven processes operate when a sentence is reread, that experiment was not designed to detect a contribution of memory for processes executed during the first reading of a sentence. The reapplication of reading operations can be demonstrated, however, by manipulating the word order of sentences across their two readings. When a meaningful sentence maintains its word order across both readings, proposition-building operations can be reapplied on the second reading and should increase fluency. When a sentence initially is read in scrambled word order, then reread with the words arranged in a meaningful order, the subject would not have had prior experience at constructing the appropriate propositions. In this case, fluency should suffer relative to the case in which meaningful word order is maintained across both readings.

In Experiment 2, which was similar to experiments involving normal and scrambled texts (e.g., Carr et al., 1989; Levy & Burns, 1990), subjects first read a set of normal and scrambled sentences in transformed typography, then reread these and new sentences in either normal or scrambled form. If comprehension processes that contribute to the reading of meaningful sentences also contribute to later rereading fluency, rereading time for normal sentences should be less when the original reading involved normal rather than scrambled word order. A transfer-appropriate processing view (e.g., Morris, Bransford, & Franks, 1977; Roediger, Weldon, & Challis, 1989) leads to the prediction that rereading sentences in scrambled word order might be expected to benefit more from an initial reading in scrambled form. Experiments with texts have produced conflicting results regarding this comparison (e.g., Carr et al., 1989; Levy & Begin, 1984; Levy & Burns, 1990; Levy et al., 1991), suggesting that the reading of scrambled texts may be affected by strategies that vary with the reading task set by the experimenter (e.g., read aloud or provide a summary). It was expected that the task of reading individual sentences would not be strongly affected by such strategies and that a more clear test of the transfer-appropriate processing view would be possible. To help discourage the use of strategies that might be motivated by the initial reading of sentences, a delay interval of seven days was inserted between training and test phases for one group of subjects.

METHOD

Subjects

A sample of 36 subjects was randomly assigned to two groups of 18. One group received the training and test phases with no delay interval and the other was tested after a delay interval of seven days.

Materials and design

A set of 90 sentences similar to the normal sentences used in Experiment 1 was constructed and randomly divided into six lists of 15 sentences each. A scrambled version of each sentence was also created by randomly reordering the words within each sentence. One list of sentences was assigned to each of six conditions produced by a factorial combination of sentence version presented during the training phase (normal, scrambled, new – meaning that the sentences were presented only in the test phase) and version presented during the test phase (normal, scrambled). This assignment was counterbalanced across subjects so that each sentence appeared in each condition equally often. Two practice sentences, one normal and one scrambled, were constructed for use in the training phase.

Procedure

Instructions to subjects and the procedure were the same as in Experiment 1, and all sentences were presented in the same inverted typography as that used in Experiment 1. In the training phase subjects read aloud the two practice sentences followed by four sets of 15 sentences presented in a random order. Two of the sets consisted of sentences with normal word order and the other two sets were scrambled sentences. After the training phase, subjects in the immediate-test group then read aloud all 90 critical sentences. There were 15 sentences in each of the six conditions and they were presented in a random order. Subjects in the delayed-test group were dismissed and reminded to return one week later, at which time the test phase was administered.

RESULTS

Reading times longer than 120 s were not included in the analyses, resulting in the exclusion of 0.1% of the trials. Training and test phase reading time means for each sentence condition were computed for each subject. The mean training phase reading time was not reliably different for the two groups of subjects, but across both groups normal sentences were read in less time than scrambled sentences (19.13 s vs 27.23 s), $F(1, 34) = 93.99$, $MS_e = 13.31$. The mean reading times for the test phase are shown in Figure 1.

The test-phase reading times were submitted to an ANOVA with test delay (immediate, seven days), training version (normal, scrambled, new), and test version (normal, scrambled) as factors. There was a reliable effect of test version, $F(1, 34) = 120.13$, $MS_e = 15.71$, indicating that normal sentences were read more quickly than scrambled sentences (21.01 s vs 29.35 s). The main effect of training version was significant, $F(2, 68) = 43.88$, $MS_e = 7.61$, as normal (15.76 s) and scrambled sentences (16.35 s) were read more quickly than new sentences (19.75 s). There also was a reliable training by test version interaction, $F(2, 68) = 5.05$, $MS_e = 4.06$. None of the effects involving delay were significant.

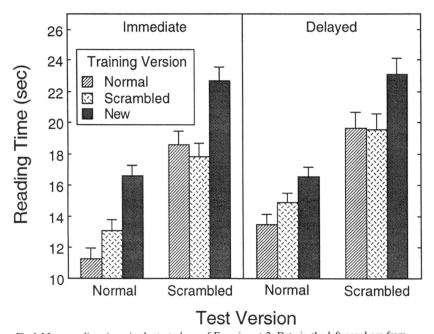

Fig.1 Mean reading times in the test phase of Experiment 2. Data in the left panel are from the immediate-test group; data in the right panel are from the 7-day delayed-test group. Error bars indicate one standard error of the difference between means, computed separately for each cluster of three training version conditions.

The training by test version interaction was explored by examining separately the effect of training version on sentences tested in normal and scrambled versions, including delay group as a factor. For normal test sentences, one ANOVA was used to compare originally normal and scrambled sentences. Sentences trained in normal form were reread in less time than sentences trained in scrambled form (12.40 s vs 14.00 s), $F(1, 34) = 22.24$, $MS_e = 2.08$, and there was no effect of delay.[2] A second ANOVA compared originally scrambled and new sentences that were tested in normal form. Originally scrambled sentences were read more quickly than new ones (14.00 s vs 16.59 s), $F(1, 34) = 39.65$, $MS_e = 3.05$, but this effect interacted with delay, $F(1, 34) = 5.10$, $MS_e = 3.05$, indicating that the advantage of the specific

2 An additional experiment, not reported in detail, was conducted as a replication of Experiment 2. In this study delay interval was manipulated within subjects, so that half of the critical sentences were tested immediately and half after a delay of seven days. Only normal word order was used in the two test phases. The pattern of means for each of the three training versions (normal, scrambled, and new) was the same as in Experiment 2, with a robust advantage of normal over scrambled training versions. Moreover, the interaction between delay and training version did not approach significance, indicating no decrease in the potency of memory for comprehension processes over the one-week interval.

reading experience with scrambled sentences was reduced over the seven-day retention interval (an advantage of 3.52 s in the immediate group and 1.66 s in the delayed group). Two similar ANOVAs were applied to data taken from sentences tested in scrambled form. In the analysis comparing originally normal and scrambled sentences (mean reading times of 19.12 s and 18.70 s, respectively), there were no reliable effects ($Fs < 1$). The other analysis compared normal and new test sentences, and indicated that there was a reliable advantage for sentences that had been read in normal form (19.12 s vs 22.91 s), $F(1, 34) = 24.55$, $MS_e = 10.54$. No other effects were significant ($Fs < 1$).

DISCUSSION

The results of Experiment 2 indicate that sentence comprehension processes applied during the first reading of a meaningful sentence are invoked when that sentence is later reread. Rereading fluency among normal test sentences was also produced by first reading scrambled versions of those sentences. Experience with scrambled sentences either enabled subjects to construct and reuse an impoverished version of a sentence's meaning or provided subjects with word-specific experience that could be reapplied when those words were later encountered in a meaningful sentence.

Reading normal sentences was as beneficial as reading scrambled sentences when scrambled test sentences were assessed, contrary to what would be expected from the transfer-appropriate processing view. This result is in agreement with the results of earlier text reading experiments (e.g., Levy & Burns, 1990, Exp. 4; Levy et al., 1991, Exp. 1), but is inconsistent with the finding that reading words in the context of a text or meaningful sentence produces little or no facilitation on a subsequent word identification task (e.g., Levy & Kirsner, 1989; MacLeod, 1989). The current result involving rereading scrambled sentences, as well as previous studies with scrambled texts, may reflect a strategic use of memory for the message of the earlier reading to construct a meaningful interpretation of the scrambled version of the sentence.

Experiment 3 was conducted to reduce the feasibility of this strategy by imposing a very long retention interval between training and test phases. With such a delay in effect, subjects should be less likely to make intentional use of memory for the message constructed during the first reading of a sentence. It was not expected that this would alter the pattern of results found with normal test sentences inasmuch as rereading fluency is viewed as resulting from automatic reapplication of comprehension processes. In the case of scrambled test sentences, however, the delay might differentially reduce the rereading fluency that arises from first reading the sentences in normal versus scrambled word order. If subjects in Experiment 2 intentionally used memory for a sentence's meaning when rereading it in scrambled form, they should have drawn more benefit in doing so from initially normal sentences. Reduction of this benefit brought on by a sufficiently long retention interval could produce a rereading advantage for sentences initially read in scrambled as compared with normal form. This result should occur if prior reading of scrambled sentences can sustain rereading fluency across a long retention interval by enhancing the identification of individual words, independently of the surrounding context.

Experiment 3

METHOD

A sample of 24 subjects was tested. A set of 90 sentences of less than 80 characters in length was constructed and randomly divided into six lists of 15 sentences each (e.g., He had no choice but to sell the house and dismiss all the servants). A scrambled version of each sentence was created as in the earlier experiments. The design and procedure were identical to those of Experiment 2, with the following exceptions. First, only one group of subjects was tested, with a four-month delay interval between training and test phases. Second, at the conclusion of the training phase, subjects were led to believe that the experiment was at an end. They were not told that they would be contacted four months later for a test phase. Third, at the beginning of the test phase, subjects were not told that they would be rereading sentences from the first phase of the experiment.

RESULTS

One subject did not return for the test phase so the data reported here are based on 23 subjects. Reading times greater than 120 s were excluded from the analyses, resulting in the loss of 0.4% of the trials. Because of the shorter sentences, reading times generally were lower than in Experiments 1 and 2. In the training phase normal sentences were read in less time than scrambled sentences (10.10 s vs 15.40 s), $t(22) = 7.69$, $SE_{dm} = 0.69$. The mean reading time for each condition in the test phase is shown in Figure 2. The pattern of means was similar to that of Experiment 2, except that the specificity of transfer effects was stronger in Experiment 3.

An ANOVA applied to test phase reading times with training and test version as factors revealed a significant effect of test version, with normal sentences read in less time than scrambled sentences (8.18 s vs 11.80 s), $F(1, 22) = 61.65$, $MS_e = 7.35$. The effect of training version was also reliable, with normal (9.78 s) and scrambled (9.81 s) sentences read more quickly than new sentences (10.38 s), $F(2, 44) = 6.88$, $MS_e = 0.75$. The interaction between training and test version was significant as well, $F(2, 44) = 5.16$, $MS_e = 1.16$. A series of t-tests were used to examine specificity of transfer in each of the test versions. For normal test sentences, reading times were shorter if sentences originally were read in normal rather than scrambled form (7.68 s

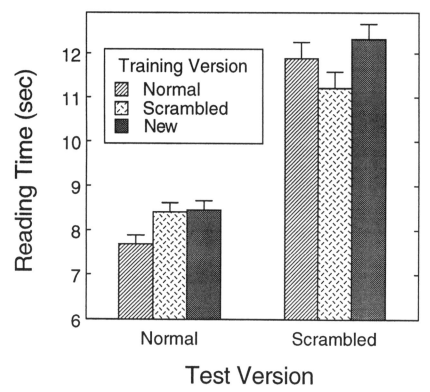

Fig. 2 Mean reading times in the test phase of Experiment 3. Error bars indicate one standard error of the difference between means, computed separately for each cluster of three training version conditions.

vs 8.40 s), $t(22) = 3.51$, $SE_{dm} = 0.21$, and there was no significant benefit of prior reading in scrambled form over reading new normal sentences (8.45 s), $t < 1$. For scrambled test sentences, the advantage for previously reading a scrambled rather than a normal version was significant by a directional test (11.22 s vs 11.88 s), $t(22) = 1.82$, $SE_{dm} = 0.36$, and the difference between originally normal and new sentences (12.30 s) was not significant, $t(22) = 1.54$, $SE_{dm} = 0.27$.

DISCUSSION

With an extended delay imposed between readings, the specificity of the effects of initial reading were more pronounced than in Experiment 2. In the task of reading normal test sentences, no benefit was derived from an earlier reading of a scrambled version. This result is particularly interesting in light of Kolers' (1976) demonstration of fluent rereading of text after a delay of one year. The fluency with previously read texts demonstrated in that study typically has been attributed to memory for pattern analyzing operations of a perceptual nature. The present results suggest that a more accurate explanation of Kolers' result is that subjects were reapplying comprehension processes that were carried out during the initial reading of the texts. Exposure to component words is not adequate to produce long-lasting fluency effects when meaningful sentences are read.

The pattern of results regarding sentences tested in scrambled form is consistent with the transfer-appropriate view, although the data show a certain reluctance to escape the influence of initially reading a meaningful sentence. There was a trend favoring sentences that first were read in scrambled form. By the transfer-appropriate processing view, this trend is the result of using similar processes on both readings to encode words with little or no contextual assistance when sentences were trained and tested in scrambled form. Contextual support provided by normal training sentences was not available at the time of test, leaving subjects less prepared for the more difficult word identification task engendered by reading scrambled sentences.

Experiment 4

Before accepting the conclusions drawn from Experiment 3, an alternative explanation needs to be addressed. The advantage of presenting a sentence in the same version in both the training and test phases might arise not from processing specific to comprehension of sentence meaning or to identification of individual words, but from repetition of the order in which a string of words is presented. This suggestion is plausible, given that Whittlesea (1990) has shown that the second reading of a scrambled text is faster when the same rather than a different random ordering of words is used on the two readings. Whittlesea's account, however, was not one of word order per se, but rather that subjects were able to construct a meaningful message from the scrambled text and that this constructed message was more stable when a fixed random word order was used. Moreover, there is a large amount of variability among texts with respect to whether maintaining the random word order matters (Carr & Brown, 1990). In any case, this view of word order effects is compatible with the present emphasis on the role of comprehension processes in rereading fluency.

A more important concern is whether word order effects might arise from perceptual or lexical processes unrelated to construction of a meaningful message. To test this possibility, Experiment 4 was conducted using randomly ordered lists of unrelated nouns or nonwords. Each list read in the training phase was later presented in the same or a different random ordering. A delay of seven days was imposed between training and test sessions, as in Experiment 2. If lexical or perceptual benefits of maintaining word order across both readings were the critical factor in producing the results of Experiments 2 and 3, rereading lists of unrelated words or nonwords should be more fluent when the order of items is consistent across training and test readings.

METHOD

Subjects

A sample of 18 subjects was tested.

Materials and design

A set of 45 eight-word lists was constructed using unrelated nouns that were five or more characters in length (e.g., curtain sandwich parent octopus mattress pilot empress meteor). A set of 45 lists of eight pronounceable nonwords also was constructed (e.g., misk nin hort cron fum cluve shog hent). The nonwords were only three to five characters in length so that initial reading times for the lists of words and nonwords would be similar. Items in each list were randomly ordered. A second version of each list was constructed by randomly reordering items within the list. The word and nonword lists were treated as three sets of 15 lists each for purposes of counterbalancing. One list of each type was assigned to each of the three conditions in the experiment: trained and tested in the same order, trained and tested in different orders, and not trained. Assignment of lists to conditions was counterbalanced across subjects so that each version of the word and nonword lists appeared equally often in each condition.

Procedure

Subjects were tested using the same procedure and inverted typography as in the earlier experiments. In the training phase they read aloud four practice lists, two of words and two of nonwords, followed by 30 lists of words and 30 lists of nonwords. These 60 critical lists were presented one at a time in a randomly determined order. At the conclusion of the training session subjects were reminded to return seven days later for a second session. At the start of the test session subjects were not told that some of the lists they would read were the same as lists that had been presented in the training session. They read aloud four practice lists followed by 45 lists of words and 45 lists of nonwords, presented in random order. Within each list type, 15 lists had not been read in the training phase, 15 had been read in the same order as they appeared during the test, and 15 lists had been read but the items within a list had been in a different order in the training session.

RESULTS

Reading times longer than 30 s were not included in the analyses, resulting in the exclusion of 3.1% of the trials. Using shorter nonwords was sufficient to produce very similar reading times for the word and nonword lists in the training phase (12.29 s vs 12.43 s), $t < 1$. The mean reading time for each condition in the test phase is shown in Table 2. The test phase data were analyzed in an ANOVA with list type and training version as factors. There was a reliable effect of training version (9.11 s, 9.18 s, and 10.17 s for same,

TABLE 2
Mean Reading Time (in seconds) in the Test Phase of Experiment 4

List	Training version		
	Same order	Different order	New
Words	8.70	8.82	10.31
Nonwords	9.52	9.53	10.03

Note. The estimated standard deviations of subjects' mean reading times, pooled across all three training versions, were 4.30 and 2.92, for the word and nonword lists, respectively.

different, and new, respectively), $F(2, 34) = 22.82$, $MS_e = 0.56$, and an interaction between list and training version, $F(2, 34) = 6.92$, $MS_e = 0.47$. The list main effect was not significant ($F < 1$). The significant interaction indicates that the effect of prior reading was greater for the lists of words than for the lists of nonwords. Of particular interest was whether changing the order of items within lists influenced the effect of training on rereading time. The same- and different-order conditions were compared for each type of list. Neither comparison resulted in a significant effect, $ts < 1$. Finally, the average reading time across the same and different conditions was compared with the reading time in the new condition for each list type (8.76 s vs 10.31 s for words and 9.52 s vs 10.03 s for nonwords). Both comparisons were significant, $t(17) = 4.95$, $SE_{dm} = 0.31$, and $t(18) = 2.96$, $SE_{dm} = 0.17$, for the word and nonword lists, respectively.

DISCUSSION

The results of Experiment 4 clearly indicate that although lists of words and nonwords both produce a reliable rereading effect, changing the order of items across training and test phases had no influence on this effect. The lack of an order effect suggests that the results of Experiments 2 and 3 were not due to a sensitivity to word order that is independent of the semantic message conveyed by the word string. It appears safe to conclude that in the case of normal test sentences, the effect of training phase version is due to the fluent reapplication of comprehension processes. For scrambled test sentences, memory for specific lexical items and possibly memory for a message constructed from the randomly ordered words are the strongest candidates as sources of rereading fluency that are specific to the original reading episode.

Another feature of Experiment 4 is that its main result, the lack of an item-order effect, is not consistent with the finding reported by Whittlesea (1990). In that study, changing the word order across two scrambled versions of a text reduced rereading fluency relative to the case in which the same scrambled word order was used on both readings. As noted earlier, the sensitivity of rereading fluency in that situation varies considerably across different texts (Carr & Brown, 1990), so it is possible that many texts would not show the effect obtained by Whittlesea. Moreover, that effect was found using texts, whereas unrelated nouns and nonwords were used in Experiment 4. By design, it is highly unlikely that subjects in Experiment 4 could have formed even rudimentary messages capable of mediating an effect of consistent word order on rereading fluency.

Experiment 5

With evidence in hand for the contribution of comprehension processes to the fluent rereading of typographically transformed sentences, Experiment 5 was designed to demonstrate a similar function in the reading of normally printed sentences. A second objective of this experiment was to test the hypothesis advanced by Levy et al. (1991) that comprehension processes responsible for rereading fluency have a Stroop-like quality, in that they are applied to meaningful sentences even when this activity is counterproductive or contrary to prevailing instructions and task demands. Some evidence for this aspect of comprehension already is available. First, although Carlson et al. (1991) instructed a group of subjects to read aloud texts in a word-by-word manner, disregarding text meaning, subjects took less time on the first reading of texts presented in normal as compared to scrambled word order. Second, Masson and May (1985) found that searching for a predesignated target letter in sentences shown with the rapid serial presentation technique was more accurate when scrambled rather than normal word order was used. This *sentence-inferiority* effect was attributed to unitized processing of words when they appeared in meaningful sentences.

In Experiment 5 normal and scrambled sentences were read first under conditions that were intended to discourage meaningful processing of sentences. The rapid serial presentation method was used, in which a sentence's words were presented one at a time for a fixed, brief duration at the center of a computer monitor. The task was to determine whether the sentence contained an item that consisted exclusively of a string of consonants. To discourage post-presentation processing of sentences presented under these conditions (cf. Mitchell, 1984), on each trial a pair of sentences was presented in succession with no pause between them. This procedure has been shown to reduce text comprehension under rapid serial presentation (Masson, 1983). Two different presentation durations, 100 ms and 200 ms, were used. The longer duration is equivalent to a brisk reading rate of 300 words per minute. The shorter duration was used to determine whether proposition-construction processes believed to influence rereading fluency can be executed in much less time than that usually taken to read text.

In the test phase, normal and scrambled sentences were presented one at a time using rapid serial presentation, and the task was to report the words in the sentence. The critical question was whether comprehension processes would operate during the initial search task when normal sentences were presented and, if so, whether these processes could be reapplied to influence performance on the report task. If both of these conditions were to hold, subjects should more accurately report the content of normal test sentences that appeared in normal rather than scrambled word order during the training phase. This effect should not obtain for scrambled test sentences. Furthermore, if exposure to individual words contributes to fluent reading of sentences, reading scrambled sentences in the training phase should produce at least some advantage over new sentences.

METHOD
Subjects
A sample of 84 subjects were randomly divided into four groups of 21 subjects each, defined by a factorial combination of presentation duration in the training phase (100 ms, 200 ms) and sentence version during test (normal, scrambled).

Materials and design
A set of 60 critical and 120 filler sentences were created so that on each trial in the training phase a pair of sentences could be shown. The two sentences on a trial always consisted of a critical sentence followed by a filler, or two filler sentences. The two sentences shown on a given trial were of the same word order (normal or scrambled).

The 60 critical sentences, each 10-12 words in length, were constructed (e.g., We played a game of chess before our big exam) under the constraint that no word was longer than nine characters. The sentences were divided into three sets of 20 sentences each, and a scrambled version of each sentence was constructed by randomly reordering the words within the sentence. For each subject, one set of 20 sentences was assigned to each of the three training conditions: normal version, scrambled version, and new (not presented during training). This assignment was counterbalanced across subjects so that each set of 20 sentences was used equally often in each condition.

The 120 filler sentences consisted of 60 normal and 60 scrambled sentences. Twenty of the normal filler sentences were reserved for presentation with the 20 normal critical sentences in the training phase, and 20 of the scrambled filler sentences were set aside for presentation with the 20 scrambled critical sentences during training. The remaining 40 normal filler sentences were paired to form 20 pairs of normal fillers, and the remaining 40 scrambled filler sentences were paired to create 20 scrambled pairs. One sentence in each of these 40 pairs of filler sentences was selected to have one of its words replaced by a string of consonants. The consonant string was created by replacing each vowel, and occasionally some of the consonants, in a selected word with consonants (e.g., The salmon travels many difficult miles to sptbn in fresh water). The consonant string appeared in the first sentence for half of the pairs and in the second sentence for the other half. The lengths of the consonant strings varied as did their positions in the sentences. The filler sentences paired with critical sentences, and the critical sentences themselves, did not contain consonant strings.

Procedure

Subjects were tested individually in a single session. In the training phase subjects were presented 20 pairs of normal and 20 pairs of scrambled sentences that did not contain a consonant string (each pair consisting of one critical sentence followed by a filler sentence), and 20 pairs of normal and 20 pairs of scrambled sentences (all filler sentences) that contained one consonant string. Subjects were instructed to search through each rapidly presented series of words to determine whether a string of consonants was present. The fact that meaningful sentences would be presented on half of the trials was not mentioned. The sentences were presented one word at a time, with each word appearing in the center of the monitor for a fixed duration. The duration for each word was 100 ms for half of the subjects and 200 ms for the other half. There was no pause between the two sentences, although the first word of each sentence was capitalized and the last word included a period.

Each trial began with a row of nine + symbols presented for the same duration as the words that would follow and this display was immediately followed by the sequence of words. The last word was immediately followed by a row of nine ? symbols to indicate that the subject was to make a response. The subject pressed an appropriate key on a key pad to indicate whether a consonant string was present in the sequence of words. One key was labeled YES and the other was labeled NO. In the case of trials containing a critical sentence, no consonant string was present so subjects had to attend to the material until the end of the trial. For filler pairs, however, subjects knew what the response would be as soon as the consonant string was detected, although they had to withhold their response until the display ended. After the subject made a response, the monitor was cleared and 500 ms later the next trial began automatically. Subjects were allowed to take a brief rest after every 20 trials.

In the test phase, subjects read all 60 critical and four filler sentences presented one word at a time as in the training phase. Only one sentence was presented on each trial and the subject's task was to report as many words as possible, in their original order. Half of the subjects were presented the normal version of each sentence and they were told that they would be viewing sentences. The other subjects were shown the scrambled version of each sentence and they were told that they would see series of words. Each trial began with a display at the top of the monitor indicating the trial number and the word READY at the center of the monitor. The subject pressed a key on the key pad to begin the trial. The READY signal was erased and 500 ms later a row of nine + symbols appeared for 67 ms, followed by the words, each presented for 67 ms. After the last word, a row of nine ? symbols was presented for 67 ms, then the message WRITE DOWN WORDS appeared. The subject then recorded as many words as possible on a printed page containing lines numbered 1-64. The subject's response on a particular trial was written on the appropriately numbered line. When the subject finished recording the words, she or he pressed a key to erase the monitor and begin the next trial. The first two and last two trials were filler sentences, and the 60 critical sentences were presented in a random order.

Results and Discussion

Performance in the training phase was summarized by computing each subject's hit and false alarm rate for normal and scrambled sentences. Accuracy on this task logically should not and did not vary reliably as a function of the sentence version to be used in the test phase. Therefore, to simplify presentation of training phase data, the means were collapsed across the two test groups and the analyses reported here did not include test group as a factor. The mean hit and false alarm rates are shown in Table 3. The false alarm rates are based on trials involving the critical items. False alarms were not common, indicating that subjects only occasionally misperceived a word in a critical sentence as a consonant string. To test for differences in the two duration groups, an accuracy measure was derived by subtracting false alarm rate from hit rate. These accuracy scores were analyzed in an ANOVA with duration (100 ms, 200 ms) and sentence version (normal, scrambled) as factors. The analysis indicated that the effect of duration was significant (.86 for the 200-ms condition and .37 for the 100-ms condition), $F(1, 82) = 316.88$, $MS_e = 0.03$. The small accuracy advantage for the scrambled over the normal sentences (.63 vs .60) was reliable, $F(1, 82) = 4.98$, $MS_e = 0.01$, but the interaction effect did not reach significance ($p > .15$).

The effect of sentence version is consistent with the sentence-inferiority effect in letter search reported by Masson and May (1985). The filler sentences in Experiment 5, however, were not counterbalanced across the normal and scrambled conditions. A systematic difference in either the sentences or the consonant strings in these two sets of materials might have produced the difference in hit rates that was responsible for generating the present sentence-inferiority effect. The most important results of this analysis, however, are not compromised in this way and are that (a) performance on critical sentences, as measured by false alarm rates, was quite accurate, and (b) exposure duration had a large effect on detection accuracy.

Responses in the test phase were scored according to the following criteria. All critical sentences were included in the scoring, regardless of whether the subject made a response error on the trial containing that sentence in the training phase. Word order was not considered when scoring responses from

TABLE 3
Mean Hit and False Alarm Rates and Accuracy in the Training Phase of
Experiment 5

Duration and sentence version	Hit rate	FA rate	Accuracy
100 ms			
Normal	.44	.09	.35
Scrambled	.56	.16	.40
200 ms			
Normal	.89	.04	.85
Scrambled	.91	.05	.86

Note. Accuracy equals hit rate minus false alarm rate. The estimated standard deviations of subjects' accuracy scores, pooled across the two versions, were 0.17 and 0.11 for the 100-ms and 200-ms duration groups, respectively.

subjects in the scrambled test condition. For subjects tested with normal sentences, changes of word order that preserved the meaning of the sentence were allowed, otherwise a word reported in an incorrect location was counted as an intrusion. Words that contained spelling errors or changes in pluralization were counted as correct. For subjects in both the normal and scrambled groups, reported words that were not in the sentence (including synonym substitutions) were counted as intrusions. For each subject the proportion of correctly reported words and the proportion of intrusions (based on the total number of words presented in the sentences) were computed as a function of training version of the critical sentences (normal, scrambled, new). The mean proportion of correctly reported words in each condition is shown in Figure 3. The proportion of intrusions, averaged across all conditions, was .06. In an analysis of the intrusion data, none of the effects reached significance.

The proportion correct data were submitted to an ANOVA with test version (normal, scrambled), training version (normal, scrambled, new), and training duration (100 ms, 200 ms) as factors. The group tested with normal sentences reported reliably more words than subjects tested with scrambled sentences (.47 vs .28), $F(1, 80) = 23.27$, $MS_e = 0.080$, and there was a significant effect of training version (.41, .38, and .36 for normal, scrambled, and new, respectively), $F(2, 160) = 23.12$, $MS_e = 0.002$. The only other significant effect was the interaction between training and test form, $F(2, 160) = 5.20$, $MS_e = 0.002$.

The training version effect and its interaction with test version were explored by two further ANOVAs; one compared the normal and scrambled training versions and the other compared the scrambled and new versions. In

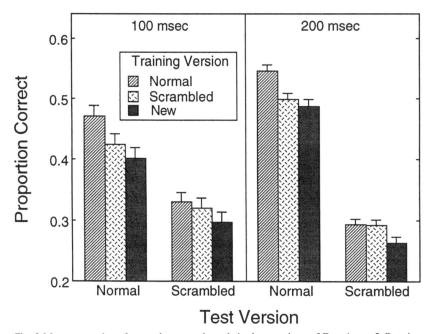

Fig. 3 Mean proportion of correctly reported words in the test phase of Experiment 5. Data in the left panel are from the 100-ms training duration group; data in the right panel are from the 200-ms training duration group. Error bars indicate one standard error of the difference between means, computed separately for each cluster of three training version conditions.

both analyses there was a reliable effect of test version, but the results of interest concern training version. The normal training version produced reliably more correctly reported words than the scrambled version, $F(1, 80) = 13.88$, $MS_e = 0.002$, but this effect interacted with test version, $F(1, 80) = 9.48$, $MS_e = 0.002$. From the means in Figure 3, it is clear that the advantage for normal training sentences appeared only when sentences were tested in their normal version, indicating that the advantage bestowed by initial reading was based on the reapplication of comprehension processes rather than enhanced processing of specific words. The scrambled training version, in turn, generated more correct reports than sentences that had not been presented in training, $F(1, 80) = 8.05$, $MS_e = 0.002$, and this effect did not interact with test version ($F < 1$). The undifferentiated influence of prior reading of scrambled sentences suggests that the benefit of initially reading these sentences derived from more efficient lexical processing, rather than construction of a meaningful message from the randomly ordered words.

The most striking feature of these results is the fact that comprehension processes executed under the highly constrained conditions of rapid serial presentation created a memory representation sufficiently robust to facilitate later comprehension and report of sentences. Despite a large effect of initial exposure duration on the target detection task, this factor did not influence the effectiveness of reapplying comprehension processes in the test phase. These processes apparently can be executed with as little as 100 ms of processing on each word (see also Masson, 1986a). The aspects of comprehension that contributed to rereading fluency in this study once again appear to be based on the construction of meaningful propositions. If improved identification of individual words were the primary basis for rereading fluency, normal and scrambled sentences ought to have produced equal amounts of improvement. Instead, training with normal sentences produced more enhancement than did scrambled sentences, but only when sentences were tested in normal form – an arena in which proposition-construction processes play a critical role. In keeping with the proposal made by Levy et al. (1991), the actuation of these comprehension processes seems to be impervious to task demands and goes forward even at the cost of reduced performance on the primary task, as indicated by reduced target detection when normal sentences were presented.

Experiment 6

In Experiments 1-5 evidence was obtained to support the conclusion that processing of meaningful propositions that comprise a sentence can be executed more fluently when that sentence is reread. This propositional processing may reflect construction of individual propositions, integration of propositions, or both. Experiment 6 was conducted to test the possibility that integration of causally related propositions contributes to fluent rereading. Integration of propositions can be seen as a conceptual activity of higher order than building the constituent propositions, inasmuch as integration requires inference making to link related propositions (e.g., Fletcher & Bloom, 1988; Singer, Halldorson, Lear, & Andrusiak, 1992; Trabasso & van den Broek, 1985).

Preliminary evidence that integration of propositions or clauses contributes to reprocessing efficiency was provided by Franks, Plybon, and Auble (1980) in a sentence listening task. Two-clause sentences presented against a background of white noise were more accurately reported if the pair of clauses had earlier been heard in the same sentence rather than as components of different sentences. The problem with this result, however, is that when clauses originally appeared in different sentences, those sentences were not comprehensible (e.g., The breakfast was excellent because the needle on the Christmas tree fell). The disadvantage for sentences in the recombined-clause condition could have been due to failed comprehension during training rather than the lack of reinstatement of integration operations.

In Experiment 6 each sentence consisted of a pair of meaningful, causally related clauses. These clauses were constructed so that recombining pairs of clauses would produce new, meaningful sentences. After reading a training set of sentences, subjects reread these sentences either in their original form or with clauses re-paired to create different sentences. As in Experiment 5, all materials were presented in normal typography. If comprehension procedures that integrate causally related clauses are reapplied during fluent rereading, re-pairing clauses should reduce rereading fluency. Some fluency still should be observed relative to completely new sentences, however, because of improved efficiency with respect to processing individual propositions. Two different sentence processing tasks were tested to determine whether the purported influence of interclause integration would depend on directing attention to the causal relation between clauses. One task required subjects to detect anomalous clause pairings, requiring close attention to causal relation, and the other task involved detection of anomalous words. If interclause integration contributes to fluent rereading only when subjects specifically attend to integration, the re-pairing effect should be obtained only in the anomalous-clause detection task.

METHOD
Subjects
A sample of 48 subjects was randomly assigned to two groups of 24 subjects each. One group was assigned the task of detecting an anomalous word and the other group was given the task of detecting anomalous clause pairings.

Materials and design
A set of 75 critical sentences, each containing two causally related clauses (each ranging in length from 4 to 12 words), was constructed. Sentence (1) is one of the critical sentences.

(1) The presidential candidate had to resign when he was accused of being involved in a scandal.

All 75 critical sentences were shown in the test phase, but for the training phase these items were assigned to three lists of 25 sentences each. For each subject, one list was assigned to each of three training conditions: same clause, different clause, and new (not presented). These assignments were counterbalanced across subjects so that each list was used equally often in each training condition. Sentences in the new condition did not appear in the training phase and sentences in the same-clause condition appeared in the same form in both the training and test phases. Sentences assigned to the different-clause condition did not appear intact in the training phase. Instead, each of the two clauses of a critical sentence was paired with a filler clause to form two different, meaningful sentences that were presented in the training phase. Two filler clauses were written for each critical sentence, to be used when the sentence was assigned to the different-clause condition. For example, the two clauses of sentence (1) were presented in sentences (2) and

Critical sentences

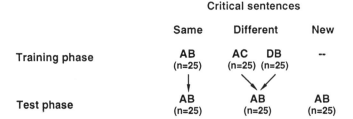

Filler sentences (anomalous-word task)

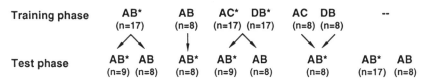

Filler sentences (anomalous-clause task)

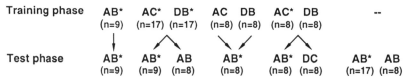

Fig. 4 Schematic summary of critical and filler sentences used in Experiment 6. A, B, C, and D indicate clauses; there were two clauses per sentence. Sentence pairs containing interchangeable clauses are indicated by AC DB. An asterisk indicates the presence of an anomaly.

(3) in the training phase when assigned to the different-clause condition (italics indicate the clauses from the critical sentence).

(2) *The presidential candidate had to resign* when it was found out he had bugged the office.

(3) The TV evangelist denied everything *when he was accused of being involved in a scandal.*

Continuing with this example of the different-clause condition, sentence (1) was presented in the test phase and its two clauses had appeared during training, but not jointly, so their integration was novel. The arrangement of the critical sentences is summarized in Figure 4.

Two versions of filler items were constructed, one for each anomaly detection task. The arrangement of the filler items for both tasks is summarized in Figure 4. For the anomalous-word detection task, three sets of filler sentences consisting of two causally related clauses were constructed. One set of 25 filler sentences appeared in both the training and test phases. These fillers contained an anomaly either during training or test, or on both occasions. In the training phase, 17 of the fillers contained an anomalous word that had been substituted for a content word in one of the clauses (e.g., The doctor ordered some new equipment as he was updating his milk), and the remaining eight contained no anomaly. When these sentences were presented during the test phase, nine of the sentences that contained an anomaly in the training phase contained a different anomaly (e.g., The doctor ordered some new equipment as he was floating his office), and the other eight previously anomalous sentences had the original word put back in place of the anomalous word to create a proper sentence. The eight sentences that were not anomalous in the training phase had an anomaly inserted for the test phase.

The second set of filler sentences used in the anomalous-word task was constructed as 25 pairs of sentences consisting of interchangeable clauses (similar to sentences (2) and (3)). Each pair of fillers appeared in the training phase and was used to construct one new sentence, consisting of one clause from each member of the pair, that was presented in the test phase. As with the first set of fillers, anomalies appeared in these fillers in the training or test phase, or in both phases. Seventeen of the pairs of fillers contained an anomalous word and the other eight pairs containing no anomaly in the training phase. In the test phase, nine of the sentences constructed from the 17 anomalous pairs contained a new anomaly and the other eight contained no anomaly. The eight test fillers constructed from the eight pairs of anomaly-free training sentences were altered to include an anomalous word.

The third set of 25 filler sentences used in the anomalous-word task appeared only in the test phase. In this set, 17 sentences contained an anomalous word and the remaining eight did not.

This arrangement of filler sentences meant that in the test phase, as in the training phase, 51 of the 150 sentences (75 filler and 75 critical) were anomalous. Moreover, considering filler and critical sentences together, there were 50 sentences that had not appeared in any form in the training phase, and 100 that had appeared in training in some form (same- or different-clause pairing). In each of these classes of sentences, 34% were anomalous; thus, the percentage of anomalous sentences was the same among new as among familiar sentences. Of the 34 anomalous test sentences that had appeared in some form in training (same- or different-clause pairing), 16 were not anomalous in training. Finally, of the 100 critical and filler test sentences that had appeared during training, 32 (all fillers) changed their anomalous status between phases. Therefore, familiarity with a sentence was no guarantee of how it should be classified or of whether the classification should be the same as on the initial encounter.

The filler sentences constructed for the anomalous-clause detection task contained an anomaly that was created by pairing two clauses that did not make sense together (e.g., The sleeping baby began to cry as he wanted to continue his corporate law practice). A set of nine anomalous filler sentences were presented unaltered in both the training and test phases. A set of 17 pairs of anomalous filler sentences were presented in the training phase and a new sentence was created from each of these pairs by combining one clause from each sentence. The resulting 17 new sentences, nine anomalous and eight meaningful, appeared in the test phase. For example, sentences (4) and (5) were presented during training, and sentence (6) was presented during test.

(4) The child's birthday gift arrived late as she did not have any appointments for the afternoon.

(5) The playground became a hive of activity because the mail was delayed.

(6) The child's birthday gift arrived late because the mail was delayed.

An additional eight pairs of meaningful sentences were shown in the training phase. A new anomalous sentence was created from each of these eight pairs by taking one clause from each sentence in the pair; these eight sentences were presented in the test phase. A further set of eight pairs of sentences, one anomalous and one meaningful sentence in each pair, were presented in the training phase. Clauses from these eight pairs were recombined to produce eight new anomalous and eight new meaningful sentences for use in the test phase. Finally, a set of 17 anomalous and eight meaningful fillers were presented only in the test phase.

The arrangement of filler sentences used in the anomalous-clause detection task ensured that, as in the anomalous-word task, across critical and filler test sentences 34% of completely new and 34% of familiar (clauses that had been read before but not necessarily in the same sentence) sentences were anomalous, and 32% of the familiar sentences changed their anomalous status across phases, rendering familiarity an unreliable cue to a sentence's classification.

Procedure

Sentences were presented using the same equipment as in the earlier experiments. All materials were shown in normal typography and read silently. Subjects participated in a training session and a test session that were separated by one day. They were instructed to read each sentence as quickly as possible and to classify it as sensible or nonsense. The appropriate characteristic of nonsense sentences (an anomalous word or clause) was explained to the subjects. In the training phase subjects read four practice sentences (two containing an anomaly), followed by 75 critical and 75 filler sentences in random order. On each trial the sentence was presented in normal typography, left-justified on the middle line of the monitor. The sentence remained in view until the subject pressed one of two response keys on a key pad, one labeled YES (to indicate a sensible sentence) and the other labeled NO. The sentence was then erased. If the response was correct, the next sentence was presented after a delay of 750 ms; if the response was incorrect, an error message (ERROR, INCORRECT RESPONSE) was presented for 1 s before the next trial started. Subjects were allowed to take a brief rest after every 50 trials. At the end of the training phase, subjects were reminded to return for the second session. They returned to the laboratory the next day and were given a review of the instructions from the training phase. Subjects were then given two practice trials, followed by 75 critical and 75 filler trials, all presented as in the training phase.

RESULTS

Any trial on which the response latency exceeded 10 s (0.5% of the critical trials) was excluded from computation of error rates and response latencies. The overall error rates (combining performance on critical and filler items) were analyzed in an ANOVA with task (anomalous-word, anomalous-clause) and phase (training, test) as factors. The only statistically significant effect was the difference between the two phases (8.9% and 6.9% for the training and test phases, respectively), $F(1, 46) = 6.57$, $MS_e = 15.27$. The error rates on the critical trials in the test phase, conditionalized on a correct response during the training phase, are shown in Table 4. An analysis of these error rates, with task and training version (same pairing, different pairing, new) as factors, revealed only a main effect of training version (0.6%, 2.3%, and 3.0%, respectively), $F(2, 92) = 9.76$, $MS_e = 7.24$. This effect was explored further by comparing the same- and different-pairing conditions. The error rate in the same-pairing condition was reliably lower, $F(1, 46) = 8.72$, $MS_e = 7.83$, and the effect held across both tasks as there was no interaction with group.

The mean response latency in the training phase, based on critical trials on which a correct response was made, was 2.98 s and 3.45 s for the anomalous-word and anomalous-clause groups, respectively. This difference was marginally reliable, $t(46) = 1.80$, $SE_{dm} = 0.26$, $p < .10$. The mean response latencies in the test phase for critical items that were classified correctly in both phases are shown in Table 4. These data were submitted to an ANOVA with task and training version as factors. The effect of task was marginally reliable with shorter latencies on the anomalous-word task (2.51 s vs 2.91 s), $F(1, 46) = 2.91$, $MS_e = 1.98$, $p < .10$, and the effect of training version was significant (2.57 s, 2.68 s, and 2.88 s for the same, different, and new conditions, respectively), $F(2, 92) = 27.95$, $MS_e = 0.04$. The interaction was not significant ($F < 1$).

TABLE 4
Mean Response Latency (in seconds) and Percentage Error in the Test
Phase of Experiment 6

Task	Training version		
	Same pairing	Different pairing	New
Anomalous word			
Response latency	2.39	2.45	2.69
% error	0.54	1.83	2.67
Anomalous clause			
Response latency	2.76	2.90	3.07
% error	0.67	2.29	2.96

Note. The estimated standard deviations of subjects' mean response
latencies, pooled across all three training versions, were 0.60 and 1.01, for
the word and clause tasks, respectively. The estimated standard deviations
of error percentages were 2.34 and 2.49.

Contrasts between same- and different-pairing conditions and between different-pairing and new conditions were done using two separate ANOVAs including task as a factor. There was a significant advantage of same- over different-pairing, $F(1, 46) = 5.47$, $MS_e = 0.05$, and an advantage of different-pairing over new sentences, $F(1, 46) = 29.88$, $MS_e = 0.03$. In both analyses there was a marginally reliable effect of task ($ps < .10$), and no interaction between training condition and task ($Fs < 1$), indicating that the training effects were consistent across tasks.

DISCUSSION

The results of Experiment 6 indicate that interclause integration was accomplished more efficiently when the two clauses comprising test sentences had been presented together in the training phase. The enhancement arose from experience with specific pairs of clauses during the training phase, and did not depend on task demands that required subjects to focus on the causal connection between clauses. Similar effects were found on response latency and error rate measures, ruling out speed-accuracy trade-off as a viable account of the response latency difference between same- and different-pairing conditions. Thus, comprehension processes devoted to integrating causally related clauses appear to be fluently reapplied when the same pair of clauses is encountered up to 24 hours after the initial reading experience. In addition to added fluency associated with integration of clauses, sentences in the different-pairing condition were classified in less time than completely new sentences. This result indicates that even when integration processes are novel, significant enhancement in fluency arises from prior experience with individual clauses or propositions.

General Discussion

The fluent rereading of sentences observed in the experiments reported here clearly reflects the influence of a specific episodic experience that involves comprehension processes. In Experiment 1 it was shown that fluent reading of typographically transformed, meaningful sentences is due to the processing of coherent propositions rather than to syntactic regularity or to the juxtaposition of semantically related words. Experiments 2 and 3 showed that the fluent rereading of a meaningful sentence printed in transformed typography depended in large part upon having processed the sentence's propositions on an earlier reading. Reading a randomly ordered list of words that was later rearranged to form a meaningful sentence did little (Experiment 2) or nothing (Experiment 3) to increase the fluency with which that sentence was read. In Experiment 4 lists of unrelated nouns or nonwords were read twice. It was found that altering the order of items within the lists across the two readings had no measurable effect on rereading fluency. This result indicated that the benefits of earlier reading episodes observed in Experiments 2 and 3 did not stem from a simple repetition of word order. The crucial effect of scrambling word order in Experiments 2 and 3 was to destroy propositional coherence.

These conclusions regarding the role of coherent propositions in fluent rereading were extended to normally printed sentences in the last two experiments. In Experiment 5, meaningful sentences presented using rapid serial presentation were reported more accurately if they earlier had been read in the same form than if the earlier reading involved scrambled versions of the sentences. Integration of propositions was shown in Experiment 6 to contribute to rereading fluency. When test sentences consisted of two causally related propositions that had been read earlier in separate sentences, subjects took longer to comprehend them in comparison to sentences that were held constant across both readings.

PROCEDURAL MEMORY FOR READING EPISODES

A promising way of framing this episodic influence of prior reading is in terms of the fluent reapplication of comprehension processes (Craik, 1991; Kolers & Roediger, 1984; Levy, Di Persio, & Hollingshead, 1992; Levy & Kirsner, 1989; Masson, 1989). In this view, specific reading experiences are encoded in memory as procedures that represent perceptual and conceptual processing operations. The present experiments, in conjunction with earlier work, reveal a number of attributes that this procedural representation must have.

First, the procedural memory is specific to the message conveyed in a sentence. Varying the message by randomly reordering the words results in a representation that is of limited or no value when the sentence is reread in normal word order (Experiments 2, 3, and 5). Thus, comprehension processes that are enhanced by specific prior reading episodes include procedures that operate at least at the level of phrases or clauses, not individual words. Nor do these effects arise simply from sensitivity to the visual pattern created by a particular ordering of words (Experiment 4). Additional support for this conclusion is provided by the Craik and Gemar study (cited in Craik, 1991) in which sensitivity to changes in the typographical transformation used on first and second readings of a sentence was found. This result was apparent even among words that appeared in different sentences and therefore were read in both typographies during the training phase. Sensitivity to typography, therefore, is entwined with comprehension of multiple word units such as phrases. This view is consistent with the proposal that encoding episodes are represented and ideally recruited in a wholistic manner (Jacoby et al., 1992; Levy, 1993; Levy & Kirsner, 1989).

Second, memory for comprehension processes applied during specific reading episodes is robust over retention intervals as long as four months (Experiment 3) or even a year, if Kolers' (1976) result is to be interpreted as advocated here. Moreover, there was no evidence for a reduction in the enhancement due to specific prior experience with a meaningful sentence when test intervals of zero and seven days were compared (Experiment 2 and its replication). The durability of these fluency effects stands in sharp contrast to the reliable decrease in recognition memory for previously read sentences (in either normal or transformed typography) over intervals as brief as one or two days (Kolers & Ostry, 1974; Masson, 1984).

Third, at least a subset of the comprehension processes that contribute to rereading fluency have a Stroop-like quality in the sense that these processes operate even when proscribed by instructions (Carlson et al., 1991) or when task performance suffers as a consequence of their implementation (Experiment 5; Levy et al., 1991; Masson & May, 1985). These comprehension processes are assumed to include those proposed by McKoon and Ratcliff (1992) as responsible for generating the minimal set of inferences encoded automatically during reading. This feature of the comprehension processes that contribute to fluent rereading is consistent with a crucial assumption regarding the reapplication of comprehension processes when a sentence is reread. In line with other proposals regarding an episodic basis for repetition effects (e.g., Jacoby & Brooks, 1984; Jacoby et al., 1992; Levy et al., 1992; Levy & Kirsner, 1989; Logan, 1988; Masson, 1986b; Masson & Freedman, 1990), I assume that episodic memory for relevant prior experiences is recruited automatically, under context-specific constraints. Support for this assumption comes from an aspect of Experiment 3. Episodic memory for normal sentences read in the training phase was of no significant value in rereading those sentences in scrambled word order four months later, yet a significant benefit was derived if those sentences were once again read in normal order. The opposite pattern of results was obtained for scrambled sentences from the training phase.

AN EPISODIC BASIS FOR FLUENCY

The characterization outlined here and by others (e.g., Jacoby et al., 1992; Levy, 1993; Levy & Kirsner, 1989; Levy et al., 1992) of the episodic basis for comprehension fluency shares a number of fundamental attributes with the episodic view of repetition effects that has been developed primarily in the arenas of word and object identification (e.g., Jacoby & Brooks, 1984; Roediger et al., 1989). These features include the long-lasting nature of the effects of experience when revealed through fluent reprocessing (e.g., Tulving, Schacter, & Stark, 1982) and robustness across a variety of task demands (e.g., Jacoby & Dallas, 1981). A particularly interesting characteristic is the dissociation between fluent rereading and conscious recollection of text content that has been demonstrated with amnesics (Musen et al., 1990), which parallels the dissociation obtained in word identification tasks (e.g., Graf, Squire, & Mandler, 1984). In both cases, amnesics perform as well as control subjects on tests involving fluent reprocessing or word identification, but are impaired on tests that require intentional remembering. A dissociation of this form involving a linguistic message does not conform to the view that indirect measures of memory reflect the operation of specialized perceptual representation systems (e.g., Tulving & Schacter, 1990). A more accommodating perspective is one that emphasizes memory for procedures that operate on a range of information types, including perceptual and conceptual data carried by a message.

The most fundamental aspect of fluent rereading that also is observed in studies of repetition effects on word and object identification is its basis in memory for a specific encoding episode (Jacoby & Brooks, 1984). Fluent rereading arises in part from a general improvement in reading skill that may reflect accommodation to the particular demands of an experimental procedure or to an unusual typography, but this contribution is clearly separable from the effects of experience with specific sentences. Just as the episodic view of word repetition effects has been placed in contrast to the claim that these effects arise from activation of stable lexical representations (e.g., Jacoby & Dallas, 1981), the characterization of comprehension processes involved in rereading fluency as episodically inspired contrasts with the traditional notion of comprehension processes as constituting a stable, generic rule system (e.g., Miller & Isard, 1963). An interesting question that emerges from this observation is whether skilled comprehension is based on memory for a collection of specific prior experiences. This possibility is also under consideration in the related domain of artificial grammar learning (e.g., Vokey & Brooks, 1992). It is now possible to conceptualize a wide variety of skilled comprehension processes as grounded in a form of episodic memory for specific experiences, and this view may provide a valuable framework for guiding future exploration of language comprehension.

The research reported here was supported by a grant from the Natural Sciences and
Engineering Research Council of Canada. A preliminary report of Experiment 3
was described by Masson (1989). I am grateful to John Henderson, Betty Ann
Levy, and Murray Singer for helpful comments on an earlier version of this article.

Correspondence regarding this article should be sent to Michael Masson,
Department of Psychology, University of Victoria, P.O. Box 3050, Victoria, British
Columbia, Canada V8W 3P5. Electronic mail address: mmasson@sol.uvic.ca.

References

Carlson, L.A., Alejano, A.R., & Carr, T.H. (1991). The level-of-focal-attention
hypothesis in oral reading: Influence of strategies on the context specificity of
lexical repetition effects. *Journal of Experimental Psychology: Learning,
Memory, and Cognition, 17*, 924-931.

Carr, T.H., & Brown, J.S. (1990). Perceptual abstraction and interactivity in
repeated oral reading: Where do things stand? *Journal of Experimental Psychology: Learning, Memory, and Cognition, 16*, 731-738.

Carr, T.H., Brown, J.S., & Charalambous, A. (1989). Repetition and reading:
Perceptual encoding mechanisms are very abstract but not very interactive. *Journal
of Experimental Psychology: Learning, Memory, and Cognition, 15*, 763-778.

Cohen, N.J., & Squire, L.R. (1980). Preserved learning and retention of
pattern-analyzing skill in amnesia: Dissociation of "knowing how" and "knowing
that." *Science, 210*, 207-209.

Craik, F.I.M. (1991). On the specificity of procedural memory. In W. Kessen, A.
Ortony, & F.I.M. Craik (Eds.), *Memories, thoughts, and emotions: Essays in
honor of George Mandler* (pp. 183-197). Hillsdale, NJ: Erlbaum.

Fletcher, C.R., & Bloom, C.P. (1988). Causal reasoning in the comprehension of
simple narrative texts. *Journal of Memory and Language, 27*, 235-244.

Franks, J.J., Plybon, C.J., & Auble, P.M. (1982). Units of episodic memory in
perceptual recognition. *Memory & Cognition, 10*, 62-68.

Graf, P., & Levy, B.A. (1984). Reading and remembering: Conceptual and
perceptual processing involved in reading rotated passages. *Journal of Verbal
Learning and Verbal Behavior, 23*, 405-424.

Graf, P., Squire, L.R., & Mandler, G. (1984). The information that amnesic patients
do not forget. *Journal of Experimental Psychology: Learning, Memory, and
Cognition, 10*, 164-178.

Horton, K.D. (1985). The role of semantic information in reading spatially transformed text. *Cognitive Psychology, 17*, 66-88.

Jacoby, L.L., & Brooks, L.R. (1984). Nonanalytic cognition: Memory, perception,
and concept learning. In G. H. Bower (Ed.), *The psychology of learning and
motivation* (Vol. 18, pp. 1-47). New York: Academic Press.

Jacoby, L.L., & Dallas, M. (1981). On the relationship between autobiographical
memory and perceptual learning. *Journal of Experimental Psychology: General,
110*, 306-340.

Jacoby, L.L., Levy, B.A., & Steinbach, K. (1992). Episodic transfer and automaticity: Integration of data-driven and conceptually-driven processing in reading. *Journal of Experimental Psychology: Learning, Memory, and Cognition, 18*, 15-24.

Kintsch, W. (1974). *The representation of meaning in memory.* Hillsdale, NJ: Erlbaum.

Kolers, P.A. (1975). Specificity of operations in sentence recognition. *Cognitive Psychology, 7*, 289-306.

Kolers, P.A. (1976). Reading a year later. *Journal of Experimental Psychology: Human Learning and Memory, 2*, 554-565.

Kolers, P.A., & Ostry, D.J. (1974). Time course of loss of information regarding pattern analyzing operations. *Journal of Verbal Learning and Verbal Behavior, 13*, 599-612.

Kolers, P.A., & Roediger, H.L. (1984). Procedures of mind. *Journal of Verbal Learning and Verbal Behavior, 23*, 425-449.

Levy, B.A., Barnes L., & Martin. L. (1993). Transfer of Fluency Across Repetitions and Across Texts. *Canadian Journal of Experimental Psychology, 47*, 401-427.

Levy, B.A., & Begin, J. (1984). Proofreading familiar text: Allocating resources to perceptual and conceptual processes. *Memory & Cognition, 11*, 1-12.

Levy, B.A., & Burns, K.I. (1990). Reprocessing text: Contributions from conceptually driven processes. *Canadian Journal of Psychology, 44*, 465-482.

Levy, B.A., Di Persio, R., & Hollingshead, A. (1992). Fluent rereading: Repetition, automaticity, and discrepancy. *Journal of Experimental Psychology: Learning, Memory, and Cognition, 18*, 957-971.

Levy, B.A., & Kirsner, K. (1989). Reprocessing text: Indirect measures of word and message level processes. *Journal of Experimental Psychology: Learning, Memory, and Cognition, 15*, 407-417.

Levy, B.A., Masson, M.E.J., & Zoubek, M.A. (1991). Rereading text: Words and their context. *Canadian Journal of Psychology, 45*, 492-506.

Levy, B.A., Newell, S., Snyder, J., & Timmins, K. (1986). Processing changes across reading encounters. *Journal of Experimental Psychology: Learning, Memory, and Cognition, 12*, 467-478.

Logan, G.D. (1988). Toward an instance theory of automatization. *Psychological Review, 95*, 492-527.

MacLeod, C.M. (1989). Word context during initial exposure influences degree of priming in word fragment completion. *Journal of Experimental Psychology: Learning, Memory, and Cognition, 15*, 398-406.

Marks, L.E., & Miller, G.A. (1964). The role of semantic and syntactic constraints in the memorization of English sentences. *Journal of Verbal Learning and Verbal Behavior, 3*, 1-5.

Masson, M.E.J. (1983). Conceptual processing of text during skimming and rapid sequential reading. *Memory & Cognition, 11*, 262-274.

Masson, M.E.J. (1984). Memory for the surface structure of sentences: Remembering with and without awareness. *Journal of Verbal Learning and Verbal Behavior, 23,* 579-592.

Masson, M.E.J. (1986a). Comprehension of rapidly presented sentences: The mind is quicker than the eye. *Journal of Memory and Language, 25,* 588-604.

Masson, M.E.J. (1986b). Identification of typographically transformed words: Instance-based skill acquisition. *Journal of Experimental Psychology: Learning, Memory, and Cognition, 12,* 479-488.

Masson, M.E.J. (1989). Fluent reprocessing as an implicit expression of memory for experience. In S. Lewandowsky, J. C. Dunn, & K. Kirsner (Eds.), *Implicit memory: Theoretical issues* (pp. 123-138). Hillsdale, NJ: Erlbaum.

Masson, M.E.J., & Freedman, L. (1990). Fluent identification of repeated words. *Journal of Experimental Psychology: Learning, Memory, and Cognition, 16,* 355-373.

Masson, M.E.J., & May, R.B. (1985). Identification of words and letters during reading: A sentence inferiority effect for letter detection. *Canadian Journal of Psychology, 39,* 449-459.

Masson, M.E.J., & Sala, L.S. (1978). Interactive processes in sentence comprehension and recognition. *Cognitive Psychology, 10,* 244-270.

McKoon, G., & Ratcliff, R. (1992). Inference during reading. *Psychological Review, 99,* 440-466.

Miller, G.A., & Isard, S. (1963). Some perceptual consequences of linguistic rules. *Journal of Verbal Learning and Verbal Behavior, 2,* 217-228.

Mitchell, D.C. (1984). An evaluation of subject-paced reading tasks and other methods for investigating immediate processes in reading. In D. E. Kieras & M. A. Just (Eds.), *New methods in reading comprehension research* (pp. 69-89). Hillsdale, NJ: Erlbaum.

Moravcsik, J.E. & Kintsch, W. (1993). Writing Quality, Reading Skills, and Domain Knowledge as Factors in Text Comprehension. *Canadian Journal of Experimental Psychology, 47,* 360-374.

Morris, C.D., Bransford, J.D., & Franks, J.J. (1977). Levels of processing versus transfer appropriate processing. *Journal of Verbal Learning and Verbal Behavior, 16,* 519-533.

Moscovitch, M., Winocur, G., & McLachlan, D. (1986). Memory as assessed by recognition and reading time in normal and memory-impaired people with Alzheimer's disease and other neurological disorders. *Journal of Experimental Psychology: General, 115,* 331-347.

Musen, G., Shimamura, A.P., & Squire, L.R. (1990). Intact text-specific reading skill in amnesia. *Journal of Experimental Psychology: Learning, Memory, and Cognition, 16,* 1068-1076.

Musen, G., & Squire, L.R. (1991). Normal acquisition of novel verbal information in amnesia. *Journal of Experimental Psychology: Learning, Memory, and Cognition, 17,* 1095-1104.

Roediger, H.L., Weldon, M.S., & Challis, B.H. (1989). Explaining dissociations between implicit and explicit measures of retention: A processing account. In H.L. Roediger & F. I. M. Craik (Eds.), *Varieties of memory and consciousness: Essays in honor of Endel Tulving* (pp. 3-41). Hillsdale, NJ: Erlbaum.

Singer, M., Halldorson, M., Lear, J.C., & Andrusiak, P. (1992). Validation of causal bridging inferences in discourse understanding. *Journal of Memory and Language, 31*, 507-524.

Tardif, T., & Craik, F.I.M. (1989). Reading a week later: Perceptual and conceptual factors. *Journal of Memory and Language, 28*, 107-125.

Trabasso, T., & van den Broek, P. (1985). Causal thinking and the representation of narrative events. *Journal of Memory and Language, 24*, 612-630.

Tulving, E., & Schacter, D.L. (1990). Priming and human memory systems. *Science, 247*, 301-306.

Tulving, E., Schacter, D.L., & Stark, H.A. (1982). Priming effects in word-fragment completion are independent of recognition memory. *Journal of Experimental Psychology: Learning, Memory, and Cognition, 8*, 352-373.

Vokey, J.R., & Brooks, L.R. (1992). Salience of item knowledge in learning artificial grammars. *Journal of Experimental Psychology: Learning, Memory, and Cognition, 18*, 328-344.

Whittlesea, B.W.A. (1990). Perceptual encoding mechanisms are tricky but may be very interactive. *Journal of Experimental Psychology: Learning, Memory, and Cognition, 16*, 727-730.

15 Reading and Language Processing: Similarities and Differences

FERNANDA FERREIRA   Michigan State University
JOHN M. HENDERSON   Michigan State University
MURRAY SINGER   University of Manitoba

We organized this volume around the theme of reading and language processing, and accordingly, we invited contributors who were renowned for their work in these fields. We were fortunate not only to receive articles describing the state of the art in each group of researchers' own field, but also somewhat unintentionally, the articles now allow us to evaluate the conjoined phrase "reading and language processing" itself. For many researchers in cognitive psychology, the study of reading and the study of language processing are almost interchangeable. According to this view, it makes little difference whether linguistic materials are presented visually or auditorily; comprehension processes are generally agnostic about the mode in which linguistic information is presented. The contributions made to this volume indicate that this view is probably correct for just one specific area of research, namely text comprehension. Quite strikingly, a large number of papers in this volume indirectly make the point that the form in which linguistic information is presented is an important consideration in any study of language processing, and an important area of research in its own right. Auditory language processing may differ from reading on a variety of important dimensions—for example, in the temporal unfolding of information. Conversely, reading is not merely language comprehension made visual. Instead, the reading system to some extent operates according to its own mechanisms and principles (as the articles by Buchanan and Besner, by Daneman and Reingold, by Pollatsek, Raney, Lagasse, and Rayner, and by Henderson and Ferreira make clear), and in addition, the way in which linguistic information is visually laid out affects (at least to some extent) the way the information is processed.

The first four articles in this volume make the point explicitly. The researchers who contributed these papers are concerned with perceptual and attentional processes involved in extracting linguistic information using the eyes. Buchanan and Besner explore whether the writing system used by a language—the format that is used for translating that particular language to print—influences visual word identification. Daneman and Reingold investigated whether phonological codes are obtained obligatorily during reading and found that they appear not to be. Pollatsek, Raney, Lagasse, and Rayner determined that the perceptual span for the reading of English text spans only the line being fixated. Henderson and Ferreira found that eye movement measures associated with a given word are not affected by characteristics of the subsequent word. Thus, in one way or another, each of these teams of researchers has shed light on basic processes that are particular to reading.

The next grouping of articles—the contributions by Clifton, by Ferreira and Henderson, and by Spivey-Knowlton, Trueswell, and Tanenhaus—concern syntactic processing. In this subarea of the language processing field, researchers generally tend to present materials visually, and assume that the processes that appear to operate during reading operate during language processing more generally. To a large extent, this assumption is correct. Clifton, for instance, uses eye movement data to argue that the initial analysis of temporarily ambiguous structures is consistent with principles of parsing he and his coworkers have formulated in previous work, principles that presumably are general to reading and listening. However, the Ferreira and Henderson study as well as the study by Spivey-Knowlton et al. suggest that conclusions concerning the operation of the syntactic processor based on data obtained in reading studies must be made cautiously. Ferreira and Henderson found that the process of reading seems to have its own "rhythm," so that readers speed up as they proceed through a sentence. Therefore, it is difficult to compare reading times for words in different sentences when those words are also preceded by different amounts of material. (Note that this is not a concern in the Clifton study, because sentences in different conditions did not differ in length.) Similarly, Spivey-Knowlton et al. found that different patterns of results are observed when readers are able to view only one word at a time in the moving window paradigm compared to a condition in which they may view two. They found that when subjects could view just one word, they obtained evidence supporting what has been termed a "modular position" (see Introduction to this volume); but when subjects could view two words at a time, they obtained evidence more consistent with an interactive position. The Ferreira and Henderson and the Spivey-Knowlton et al. studies both seem to indicate that basic processes involved in reading may affect some aspects of syntactic parsing. It is possible, then, that some aspects of syntactic parsing are not entirely agnostic about the way in which information is presented to the language processing system.

The studies of rereading fluency presented by Levy, Barnes, & Martin and by Masson make this point further. Their work as well as the work of many of their colleagues who have examined transfer effects during language processing show what are termed "data-driven" effects. The modality in which information is presented affects amount of transfer, and even within a modality, transfer is reduced when (for example) visually presented materials are presented in different fonts on successive presentations. The Masson study is particularly striking in showing that transfer effects can be extremely long-lasting, although his particular study did not examine transfer associated with "data-driven" features, and so the question remains whether transfer effects would be as long-lasting with variations in the physical features of the linguistic material. Nevertheless, this research area again indicates that language comprehension processes are affected by the way information is presented to the system.

The paper by Just and Carpenter makes a different and quite interesting contribution to these issues. Just and Carpenter provide an intriguing new technique for measuring intensity of processing, in contrast to existing techniques which measure duration of processing. As Just and Carpenter point out, the difference between intensity and duration is obvious when one considers physical work: One could lift a five-pound weight and a ten-pound weight in the same amount of time, but the intensity of effort required to the lift the heavier weight would be greater. Thus, our existing measures could very well be missing an important aspect of processing difficulty. Just and Carpenter present promising evidence that pupillometry may provide a useful measure of intensity. Furthermore, this technique may allow for further study of auditory language processing as well as reading, and perhaps even for direct comparison between the two, because pupil size can be measured during both visual and auditory presentation of linguistic stimuli. Thus, this technique might provide a powerful tool for examining the similarities and differences between reading and spoken language comprehension.

The papers by Singer, by Moravcsik and Kintsch, and by Dixon, Harrison, and Taylor are least vulnerable to the issues that we have raised in this concluding chapter, perhaps because the measures used by these researchers are the most "off-line," and the corresponding processes the researchers wish to tap into with those measures are the most high-level. Using visual presentation of his stimuli, Singer obtained a rather striking result: Not only does a pair of statements like "Dorothy poured water on the fire / The fire went out" invoke the knowledge that water extinguishes fire, but so does the pair "Dorothy poured water on the fire / The fire grew hotter." The latter pair is inconsistent with the knowledge that water puts out fires, but nevertheless, the comprehension system requires that knowledge in order to link the sentences in the pair together. Moravcsik and Kintsch depart from standard practice in the text processing literature and presented their stimuli auditorily. Moravcsik and Kintsch found that high quality writing facilitates construction of a solid textbase, and access to domain knowledge facilitates construction of the appropriate situation model. These two processes seem to operate independently of one another. Interestingly, Moravcsik and Kintsch also measured the level of comprehension skill in their subjects using a common measure of *reading* comprehension, the Nelson-Denny test. The use of a measure of reading comprehension for an experiment in which materials were presented auditorily implies that the processes involved in reading and in auditory language comprehension are so similar that skill in one can be taken as a good predictor of skill in the other. Of course, the results obtained by Moravcsik and Kintsch indicate that this assumption is justified (indeed, Dixon et al. obtained similar results to Moravcsik and Kintsch but with visual presentation of materials). Nevertheless, it is important to note that the assumption may be valid only for the types of high-level processes examined in the studies by Singer, Moravcsik and Kintsch, and Dixon et al.

We will end this volume by expressing our hope that the research described in this volume will not only inform researchers working in the particular areas covered here, and will not only showcase the quality of work currently being conducted on reading and language processing, but will also serve to interest at least some individuals in the issues we have raised in this concluding chapter. An examination of these issues, we believe, would not only lead to a better understanding of how the perceptual features of the input affect language processing, but would also permit a better understanding of the relationship between language processing generally and reading more specifically, a topic we know little about at present.

Author Index

343

Subject Index